D0528891

Research Skills
for Psychology

Research Skills for Psychology

Rebecca Wheeler
Stacey Bedwell

Los Angeles | London | New Delhi
Singapore | Washington DC | Melbourne

Los Angeles | London | New Delhi
Singapore | Washington DC | Melbourne

SAGE Publications Ltd
1 Oliver's Yard
55 City Road
London EC1Y 1SP

SAGE Publications Inc.
2455 Teller Road
Thousand Oaks, California 91320

SAGE Publications India Pvt Ltd
B 1/I 1 Mohan Cooperative Industrial Area
Mathura Road
New Delhi 110 044

SAGE Publications Asia-Pacific Pte Ltd
3 Church Street
#10-04 Samsung Hub
Singapore 049483

Editorial arrangement © Birmingham City University 2018

Chapter 1 © Birmingham City University 2018
Chapter 2 © SAGE Publications, Inc. 2016
Chapter 3 © Simon Watts and Philip Banyard 2015
Chapter 4 © Tim Burns and Sandra Sinfield 2016
Chapter 5 © Tim Burns and Sandra Sinfield 2016
Chapter 6 © Pete Greasley 2016
Chapter 7 © Tim Burns and Sandra Sinfield 2016
Chapter 8 © Tim Burns and Sandra Sinfield 2016
Chapter 9 © Gary Thomas 2017
Chapter 10 © Pete Greasley 2016
Chapter 11 © Zina O'Leary 2017
Chapter 12 © Pete Greasley 2016
Chapter 13 © Pete Greasley 2016
Chapter 14 © S. Alexander Haslam and Craig McGarty 2014*
Chapter 15 © SAGE Publications, Inc. 2016
Chapter 16 © Andy Field and Graham Hole 2003
Chapter 17 © Zina O'Leary 2017
Chapter 18 © Tim Burns and Sandra Sinfield 2016
Chapter 19 © Birmingham City University 2018
Chapter 20 © Andy Field 2018*

*IBM® grants permission to SAGE Publications to reproduce SPSS® screen images in the publication, Discovering Statistics Using IBM SPSS Statistics. Reprint here courtesy of International Business Machines Corporation, © International Business Machines Corporation. SPSS Inc was acquired by IBM in October, 2009.

Apart from any fair dealing for the purposes of research or private study, or criticism or review, as permitted under the Copyright, Designs and Patents Act, 1988, this publication may be reproduced, stored or transmitted in any form, or by any means, only with the prior permission in writing of the publishers, or in the case of reprographic reproduction, in accordance with the terms of licences issued by the Copyright Licensing Agency. Enquiries concerning reproduction outside those terms should be sent to the publishers.

British Library Cataloguing in Publication data

A catalogue record for this book is available from the British Library

ISBN 978-1-5264-6801-7 (pbk)

Typeset by: C&M Digitals (P) Ltd, Chennai, India
Printed and bound in the UK

At SAGE we take sustainability seriously. Most of our products are printed in the UK using responsibly sourced papers and boards. When we print overseas we ensure sustainable papers are used as measured by the PREPS grading system. We undertake an annual audit to monitor our sustainability.

Contents

Contents   **vii**

WELCOME TO PSYCHOLOGY AND RESEARCH SKILLS!

Editors' Note

Wheeler-Mundy, R. & Bedwell, S.

We are very excited to bring you our unique edited collection, designed exclusively for the level 4 Psychology and Research Skills module at Birmingham City University. The following chapters have been compiled by your module leaders specifically to aid your journey in becoming a scientific researcher.

Throughout the module you will be working your way through the book, covering topics such as *psychology as a science, study skills for academic success, developing a scientific argument* and *writing a research proposal*. Each chapter is linked to your assessment in Psychology and Research Skills and will provide an important basis for your development as a psychologist.

As you progress through the module we will be working on a range of research skills and activities designed to complement lecture materials and your reading. Together these will set you on the path towards becoming a successful researcher.

We look forward to getting to know each of you throughout the module and supporting you to take the first steps in your research career.

Your module leaders,
Stacey Bedwell & Rebecca Wheeler-Mundy

PART 1

PSYCHOLOGY AS A SCIENCE

Psychological Research: The Whys and Hows of the Scientific Method

McBride, D.

Consider the following questions as you read Chapter 1

- Why do psychologists use the scientific method?
- How do psychologists use the scientific method?
- What are the canons of the scientific method?
- What is the difference between basic and applied research?
- How do basic and applied research interact to increase our knowledge about behavior?

As an instructor of an introductory psychology course for psychology majors, I ask my first-semester freshman students the question, "What is a psychologist?" At the beginning of the semester, students typically say that a psychologist listens to other people's problems to help them live happier lives. By the end of the semester and their first college course in psychology, these same students will respond that a psychologist studies behavior through research. These students have learned that psychology is a science that investigates behaviors, mental processes, and their causes. That is what this book is about: how psychologists use the scientific method to observe and understand behaviors and mental processes.

The goal of this text is to give you a step-by-step approach to designing research in psychology, from the purpose of research (discussed in this chapter) and the types of questions psychologists ask about behavior, to the methods used by psychologists to observe and understand behavior and, finally, how psychologists describe their findings to others in the field.

WHY PSYCHOLOGISTS CONDUCT RESEARCH

Think about how you know the things you know. How do you know the earth is round? How do you know it is September? How do you know that terrorist threats are increasing around the world? There are probably many ways that you know these things. In some cases, you may know things because you used your intuition or previous knowledge to deduce these facts. For example, you may know from past experience that where you live, in the month of September, days tend to be warm but start to get cooler, especially at night. Therefore, remembering the characteristics of the weather you are experiencing, and knowing you are still living in the same location as past years, you can deduce that the month is September from your knowledge base. You may have first learned that the earth is round from an authority figure

❧

Intuition: relying on common sense as a means of knowing about the world

Deduction: using logical reasoning and current knowledge as a means of knowing about the world

Authority: relying on a knowledgeable person or group as a means of knowing about the world

Observation: relying on what one observes as a means of knowing about the world

like your parents, teachers, or text authors. You may have also observed that the earth is round by viewing photographs of the earth taken from space. You may know that terrorist threats are increasing from authority figures as well (e.g., magazine and newspaper reporters, your country's leaders' statements). These are the primary ways that we learn new facts: intuition, deduction, authority, and observation.

Suppose something occurred that caused you to suspect that the authority figures you have learned these facts from are not reliable sources of information. Perhaps they have been caught lying about other facts. You might also consider a situation where you do not have enough previous experience with a topic to use your intuition to determine the information for yourself. In these situations, what is the best way for you to find the facts? The answer is observation. If you had reason to believe, for example, that an increase in terrorist threat is not being represented accurately, you could examine the incidence of terrorist attacks (e.g., from public records) over a period of time to find out if people are representing the true conditions.

This is why psychologists conduct behavioral research; it is the best way to make certain that the information they have about behavior is accurate. By conducting careful and systematic observations, they can be certain that they are getting the most accurate knowledge they can about behavior. This does not mean that every study conducted will yield accurate results. There are many cases where the observations collected by different researchers conflict, but this is an important part of the process. Different ways of observing a behavior may yield different observations and these different observations help us to better understand how behaviors occur. See Table 1.1 for some examples of the different ways of knowing information.

Using Science to Understand and Explain Behavior

Observation is really what sets scientific fields apart from other fields of study. Someone who wants to know about the political situation during the Civil War may read historical documents and use his or her intuition to describe the situation based on these documents. He or she might also read books by experts (authority figures) on the Civil War period or books on important figures who lived during that time. However, historians typically cannot observe the historical event they are studying. Psychologists have an advantage in that the behavior they want to learn about is happening in humans and other animals in the world around them. The best way to learn about it is to just observe it.

Table 1.1   Examples of Ways of Knowing Information

Way of Knowing	Example
Intuition	I want to know if my phone is on. I decide that it is because my phone is always on.
Deduction	I want to know which direction I am facing. The sun is setting to my right, and I know the sun sets in the west so I know that west is the direction where the sun is setting.
Authority	I want to know what my pancreas does. I know that my pancreas produces hormones important for digestion because that is what my high school biology teacher told me.
Observation	I want to know how much sleep on average Americans get per night. I determine this by conducting a survey of Americans to learn that most Americans get an average of 6 to 8 hours of sleep per night (e.g., Moore, 2004).

Some behaviors, such as mental processes, cannot be directly observed (e.g., thoughts or memories). Thus, psychologists have developed techniques for inferring information about mental processes through observation of specific behaviors that are affected by the mental processes. Psychologists then attempt to understand mental processes through observation of these behaviors and the investigation of the factors that influence those behaviors. That is what this book (and the course you are taking) is all about—understanding the methods psychologists use to observe, measure, and study behavior and mental processes (Figure 1.1).

Research is the foundation of the field of psychology. Many people think of the *helping* professions when they think about what psychologists do. This is because most people with a graduate degree in psychology work in these helping (or related) professions (American Psychological Association, 2003). However, to do their jobs well, helping professionals, such as clinicians and counselors, need to understand the findings from research about behavior so that they know what types of treatments and therapies can best help their clients. The research studies conducted in psychology also help clinicians and counselors understand what constitutes "normal" behavior and what behaviors might be considered "abnormal."

Thinking about the field of biology may help you understand how influential research is in the field of psychology. In the biological field, there are researchers who investigate the way our bodies react physically to the world around us (e.g., after being exposed to a virus). This knowledge helps other researchers determine which drugs may be effective in helping us improve these physical reactions (e.g., reduce our symptoms as we fight the virus). Finally, the knowledge gained in biological research helps doctors correctly diagnose and treat their patients (e.g., what symptoms indicate the presence of a particular virus and which drugs are most effective in treating these symptoms). The field of psychology works a lot like the field of biology (although the term *psychologist* applies to both scientists and practitioners in psychology, sometimes causing confusion). Some researchers investigate what causes certain types of behaviors (e.g., distraction in people with attention-deficit/hyperactivity disorder, or ADHD). Other researchers investigate what treatments are effective in reducing these behaviors (e.g., rewarding someone for staying on task). Finally, some psychologists work with clients to help them deal with problem behaviors. For example, school psychologists work with teachers and parents to develop a reward system for students with ADHD who have difficulty complet-ing work in class because they become easily distracted. The research that investigated the behaviors associated with ADHD and the factors that can reduce those behaviors was necessary for the school psychologist to be able to develop an effective treatment plan for the student.

Stop and Think

(1.1) Think about some things you know are true about the world. For each of these facts, try to determine the way you know that information (intuition, deduction, authority, or observation).

(1.2) Suppose you wanted to know about the factors that cause college students to become anxious. Describe how you might learn about these factors using the observation way of knowing.

(1.3) Explain how the fields of psychology and biology are similar.

HOW PSYCHOLOGISTS USE THE SCIENTIFIC METHOD

Our starting place for conducting research studies in psychology is an understanding of the assumptions that come along with the methods of science. We need to keep some concepts in mind when we use the scientific method to understand behavior. As discussed earlier, scientific study requires observations. It is the primary aspect of the scientific method. However, there are actually four primary facets or *canons* (i.e., rules or principles that guide a field of study) that define the scientific method. They are empiricism, determinism, parsimony, and testability.

Empiricism

The first canon is empiricism and this is just what we discussed above—that the scientific method relies on observations. We have several important people to thank for the empirical nature of science. Galileo, for example, was an influential scientist who used observations to understand the world (Sharratt, 1996). Much of the learning up to Galileo's time (1564–1642) had relied on authority figures, such as Aristotle and Plato, and their ideas about the world to understand how the world worked. However, Galileo (Figure 1.2) and his contemporaries (e.g., Copernicus, Newton) claimed that to learn how the world works, one should observe it. When Galileo wanted to understand how our solar system worked, he *observed* the movement of the planets around the sun through a telescope, instead of simply accepting the authoritative position held by Aristotle that the earth was the center of the solar system and everything revolved around it. He made careful, systematic observations of the phenomena of interest to better understand those phenomena. What we do in psychology is not very different from what Galileo did. If developmental psychologists want to know about bullying behaviors in elementary school children, they go out and carefully observe specific playground behaviors among these children or systematically observe the behaviors of children who have been identified as bullies.

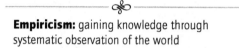

Empiricism: gaining knowledge through systematic observation of the world

Why do psychologists observe behavior? Observing behavior gives researchers a more accurate understanding of the causes of behaviors than other methods of gaining knowledge. Relying on an authority to learn about behavior, for example, greatly limits our understanding of behaviors across large groups of individuals, because not all authority figures are equally reliable and some may have faulty information.

How do we use empiricism to learn about behavior? There are many different ways to do this. We can simply observe people in their normal environment (e.g., children on a playground at recess). We can ask them to complete a survey (e.g., have the subjects respond to items that help us measure their mood). We can ask them to come into a lab and complete a task on a computer (e.g., test their memory for different types of information). Each of these methods allows us to gather empirical measurements of behavior (observation techniques are discussed further in Chapter 4).

One thing to keep in mind is that one observation (either from one individual or from one study) is never enough for us to be sure that the knowledge we are gaining is real. Chance factors can cause us to observe a particular behavior when we observe it only once. Therefore, it is important to replicate our observations, both across multiple individuals within a study and/or across multiple studies using different sets of subjects and, oftentimes, different procedures.

This replication of results assures researchers that the behaviors they observe are not just due to chance and can be used to make more confident conclusions about how behavior works. We will discuss the importance of replication across individuals further in our discussion of sampling in Chapter 6.

Determinism

Another important aspect of the scientific method is the adherence to determinism. This is the concept that phenomena in the world (and human behaviors) occur naturally and have identifiable causes (in extreme cases, determinism can indicate a denial of free will). In other words, by conducting studies to observe behavior, we can understand the factors that *cause* those behaviors to occur. One goal of psychological research is to be able to explain behavior by understanding the causes of different types of behavior. For example, why do people get depressed? What causes false memories? Does sleeplessness cause anxiety? Does anxiety cause sleeplessness? The assumption of determinism in psychological research is that each of these behaviors (depression, false memories, anxiety, and insomnia) has a specific cause or set of causes and we can understand these causes through observation of behavior in different circumstances. For many behaviors studied by psychologists, multiple causes may affect the behaviors. However, not all research is conducted to directly test causes of behavior. In some cases, the behavior first must be described and related factors identified. Although these types of studies do not directly test a cause of behavior, they do contribute to our knowledge of the behavior, which is one step in the scientific process of understanding its causes. We will discuss the different ways we conduct psychological studies and the different goals researchers may have in their studies in Chapter 4.

Figure 1.2   Galileo

SOURCE: https://geolocation.ws/v/W/File:Galilée%20 Offices.jpg/-/en (public domain).

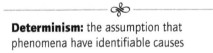

Determinism: the assumption that phenomena have identifiable causes

How is determinism used in psychological research? Because the overall goal of research is typically to gain a better understanding of behavior and its causes, researchers design their studies to contribute to this goal through the description of behaviors (e.g., How common is anxiety among college freshmen?), through the identification of factors related to the behaviors (e.g., Are students who are younger in age more anxious their freshmen year in college than older students?), and through the testing of specific causes of the behaviors (e.g., Does technology use in coursework reduce anxiety in college freshmen?).

Parsimony

In the 1997 film *Contact,* Jodie Foster's character, Dr. Ellie Arroway, attempts to explain her beliefs as a scientist to Matthew McConaughey's character, Palmer Joss. She tells him that simpler explanations of the world are preferred over more complex explanations, particularly if there is no scientific evidence that a complex explanation is correct. She calls this concept "Occam's Razor" (after the Franciscan friar who suggested it as an important part of the scientific method). Parsimony is what Arroway is speaking of when she talks about the preference for more simple explanations. In psychological research, we develop explanations of behavior starting with the simplest descriptions and expanding those descriptions only when it becomes clear that the behavior is more complex than our original description of it. In other words, simple explanations are preferred. It is assumed that the simpler explanation is more likely to be correct. More complex explanations should be developed only after simpler explanations have failed to be supported by research studies.

Why is parsimony useful in psychological research? Parsimony helps scientists test their ideas because it is easier to develop a study that might falsify a simple explanation than to develop a study that might falsify a more complex explanation. Falsification is an important part of the research process. This idea is relevant to the concept of testability as well and will be discussed further in the next section.

Testability

The fourth canon of science is testability. The scientific method can only be used to examine ideas that can be tested through observation. The only explanations of behavior that can be tested with the scientific method are those that can be contradicted with observations of behavior. *Why* is falsifiability important? It is important because a test of an explanation of a behavior that allows that explanation to be falsified provides a stronger test of that explanation. If we look only for evidence to support our explanations of behavior, we are likely to find that evidence and hold on to those explanations longer even if they are wrong. Seeking only confirmatory evidence and ignoring contradictory evidence is known as the confirmation bias. If, instead, we design research studies that can show us behaviors inconsistent with our explanations, we are more likely to find evidence against them, if such evidence exists. It takes only a few studies with results inconsistent with an explanation of behavior to falsify it. However, it takes many studies conducted in many different contexts to produce results consistent with an explanation of behavior to support it.

Parsimony: the assumption that the simplest explanation of a phenomenon is most likely to be correct

Testability: the assumption that explanations of behavior can be tested and falsified through observation

Confirmation Bias: seeking only evidence that supports our beliefs and ignoring evidence that contradicts those beliefs

---

Testability is one of the reasons that many of Sigmund Freud's ideas have not had more influence in current clinical and personality psychology theories—they are difficult to test using the scientific method. For example, Freud proposed that many of our personality traits are a product of a struggle between constructs of our minds (id, ego, and superego) that we do not have full conscious access to (Nairne, 2009). It is difficult to test this theory, because the constructs Freud proposed are difficult to connect to observable behaviors. Thus, it is difficult to systematically observe behaviors in a research study that would contradict the theory. We can, however, answer questions about other types of mental processes that are indicated by observable behaviors. For example, we can test the idea that anxiety causes sleeplessness. We can observe behaviors of sleeplessness in situations where people are placed in anxiety-provoking situations with anxiety verified by self-report. If anxious people are sleeping well, this contradicts our explanation of sleeplessness (i.e., anxiety) and provides us with a good test of our explanation (although this particular result is unlikely to be found). As psychologists using the scientific method, it is important that we ask questions and test explanations about behavior that can be falsified by observations of those behaviors.

How is falsifiability used in psychological science? As indicated above, falsification of explanations of behavior advances psychological science much more than supporting explanations (Platt, 1964). Whenever researchers can show that an accepted explanation is not supported, it changes the direction of investigation in an area of research and moves psychological science forward in gaining new knowledge about behavior. Making predictions about the results they will find in their studies helps researchers contribute to the testability of their observations. With clear predictions made before a study is conducted, researchers can design good tests of their ideas about behavior and help them avoid falling prey to the confirmation bias in believing the results are consistent with their ideas regardless of how they turn out.

The canons of science provide a general "how to" guide for psychologists designing research studies, because they help us conduct good tests of our explanations of the causes of behaviors and further our understanding of why certain behaviors occur. The rest of this text describes more of the details of how psychologists apply these canons in designing and conducting research and walks you through the process of developing research studies of your own.

Stop and Think

(1.4) Which assumption of the scientific method suggests that simple explanations are most likely to be correct? Which assumption of the scientific method suggests that observation is the best means of learning about the world?

(1.5) Explain how confirmation bias could affect your decision making.

(1.6) Explain why replication of results is an important part of the scientific process.

BASIC AND APPLIED RESEARCH

As you begin to consider the types of questions that can be answered in psychological research studies (a topic that will be covered more in Chapter 2), it is important to keep in mind the goals of two major categories of research: basic research and applied research.

The goal of basic research is to understand the most fundamental processes of behavior and how they operate. Research questions in basic research are typically about how a behavior works. How much information can we store in short-term memory? Who exhibits more symptoms of depression: men or women? Do we have implicit stereotypes that affect our social behavior?

Basic Research: research conducted with the goal of understanding fundamental processes of phenomena

Applied Research: research conducted with the goal of solving everyday problems

Applied research is generally focused on answering questions related to solving real-world problems. What type of automated teller machine (ATM) is the easiest to use? Which treatments are best in helping people who are depressed? What type of work environment increases productivity of employees?

Typically, basic research provides fundamental knowledge of how behaviors operate that is useful to researchers conducting applied studies. For example, suppose that a researcher finds that people who report having insomnia also report symptoms of anxiety (a similar result was reported by Morphy, Dunn, Lewis, Boardman, & Croft, 2007). A conclusion from this study might be that anxiety and sleeplessness are related in some way (note that this does not mean that anxiety *causes* sleeplessness, only that they are related). This conclusion represents basic knowledge about the connection between emotional state and sleeplessness or insomnia. Researchers interested in the more applied question of how we help people with sleep problems may use this basic knowledge to test treatments for sleeplessness that focus on reducing anxiety to determine whether the relationship found in the above study is causal or not. The basic research in this case is vital for the development of applied studies that address a real-world problem (i.e., insomnia). Table 1.2 provides some additional examples of basic and applied research studies.

It is also important to remember that the applications of basic research may not be obvious when it is initially conducted. The utility of such research to real-world problems may not be revealed until much later when enough is known about an issue to apply the knowledge gained in the basic research studies. For example, early neuroscientists (e.g., Santiago Ramón y Cajal, as cited in Meyers, 2007) conducted basic research studies to understand how neurons function. The applications of this knowledge were not clear until much later when neuroscientists better understood how this neural functioning affected behavior. For example, we now know that some types of disorders (e.g., depression) are linked to neuron functioning that is abnormal (e.g., higher levels of serotonin than are typical; Barlow & Durand, 2008), and drugs have been developed to alter neuron functioning to help individuals with such disorders. The understanding

Table 1.2   Examples of Basic and Applied Research Studies

Basic research

- Researchers investigated participants' awareness of the effects of handheld objects on their ability to pass through an opening (such as a doorway). Participants held objects while viewing an opening and reported whether they could pass through the opening holding the objects (Wagman & Taylor, 2005).
- To investigate possible spatial-ability differences in male and female infants, a group of 5-month-olds completed a task to determine if they recognized objects that had been rotated from their original orientation (Moore & Johnson, 2008).
- Participants were randomly assigned to mixed-race groups, while their brain activity was recorded to investigate brain areas involved in in-group biases (Van Bavel, Packer, & Cunningham, 2008).

Applied research

- Researchers investigated how to increase volunteers for charitable organizations by presenting participants with information about the organizations to determine what type of information affects whether someone will volunteer (Boezeman & Ellemers, 2008).
- Two experiments were conducted to determine which emotional states contribute to people being willing to accept advice from others (Gino & Schweitzer, 2008).
- From self, peer, and supervisor ratings, researchers determined whether managers with better work-life balances were less likely to advance in their careers (Lyness & Judiesch, 2008).

of the basic knowledge of neural functioning became useful in helping individuals with disorders long after this research had been completed. Thus, basic research is important to conduct, even if an application is not immediately clear.

Because applied research investigates realistic problems, applied researchers are often concerned with the external validity of their studies. This means that they attempt to observe behaviors that can be applied to real-life situations. This is important because these researchers want to be able to apply their results to a problem that generalizes to individuals who are not participants in their study

External Validity: the degree to which the results of a study apply to individuals and realistic behaviors outside the study

(as well as to those individuals who were observed in the study). External validity is also a consideration in basic research but in some cases can be less important than it is in applied research.

In turn, knowledge gained in applied studies can also help basic researchers refine their theories about how behavior works. Suppose in the above example regarding anxiety and insomnia, the applied studies showed that treatments reducing anxiety did not reduce the symptoms of insomnia (similar results were reported by Morin, Belanger, & Fortier-Brochu, 2006). In this case, the basic researchers may use this knowledge to hypothesize that the link between anxiety and insomnia may not be a simple causal relationship and conduct further studies to better understand the causes of insomnia and how it is related to anxiety. In this way, the two types of research, basic and applied, interact with each other, showing that both types of research are critical to the field of psychology.

As you encounter descriptions of psychological research, you may find that not all research fits neatly into basic or applied categories. Some research can both answer fundamental questions about behavior and help solve a realistic problem. It may be better to think about research as primarily basic or applied. In other words, basic and applied descriptors may be end points in a continuum of types of research studies with each research study falling somewhere between these end points.

WHY SHOULD I CARE ABOUT RESEARCH IF I DON'T WANT TO DO RESEARCH IN MY CAREER?

Through my years of teaching psychology methods courses, this question is often asked by students taking courses who don't think they want to conduct research in their careers. Many students majoring in psychology are interested in working as a practitioner of psychology or may be completing a psychology minor that is related to another career they want to pursue (e.g., education, social work, etc.) and do not understand why research methods courses are part of their curriculum. In fact, the majority of individuals who hold a degree in psychology do not conduct research in their jobs. As mentioned earlier, the majority of individuals working in psychological areas are in the helping professions. However, much of what we know about effective treatments and counseling techniques comes from research in these areas. When a new treatment technique is tested, its effectiveness is determined by the research conducted on it. Thus, just as medical doctors do, clinicians and counselors must evaluate the latest research in psychology to determine whether a new treatment is one they should adopt. Knowledge of how research is conducted can help them evaluate this research more effectively to aid their practice. In addition, it is important that we as individuals understand how to interpret the vast amounts of information we take in each day through media sources.

To give you a recent example, in debates about global warming and the seriousness of the problem, many opponents of global warming solutions point out that there is disagreement among scientists about the subject. As voters and consumers, it is important that we understand how research is conducted and that there will almost always be disagreement among researchers in an area, because no single study can fully answer a research question. In order to fully understand what answers the research provides on a question, we must consider the accumulation of data in many research studies. We must also understand that new knowledge is always gained and we must be flexible in our conclusions about an issue when new data suggest a different answer. Remember, there was a time when most humans believed the sun revolved around the earth. Scientific study revealed this idea to be false and over time humans adapted their beliefs to the new knowledge.

Understanding research methods can also help you better interpret research study results that are reported in the media. In almost all cases, media sources present concise and simplified reports of a research study and its results, leaving many questions about the quality of the study still to be answered. When one encounters reports of research in the media, some important questions should come to mind. Who were the research subjects? Was an appropriate sample tested? Was an appropriate method used to investigate the question? Were the results published in a high-quality source where other researchers were able to critique the work? How do the results correspond to past studies on this topic? The topics covered in this text and in your methods course will help you ask and answer these questions as you evaluate the reports you receive in the media to make decisions about your life.

Finally, the new knowledge you gain from your study of research methods may help you decide how to evaluate claims made by others in general. When you see an ad on television for a new miracle diet pill that the ad claims has helped people lose weight in studies, should you buy the pill? When your friends tell you that drinking energy drinks helps you study better and do better on exams, should you follow their advice? Hopefully, one of the things you will consider as you learn about research is to be skeptical about claims that seem too good to be true. As described earlier, a good researcher uses the data to decide what the best thing to do is rather than using unsubstantiated advice from others who just sound knowledgeable about a topic. Examples of how to evaluate claims and research reported in the media are given in the *Using Research* sections found at the end of some of the chapters in the text.

Stop and Think

(1.7)   Explain how external validity differs for basic and applied research studies.

(1.8)   In what way(s) can knowledge of the scientific process help you in your daily life?

CHAPTER SUMMARY

Reconsider the questions from the beginning of the chapter:

- Why do psychologists use the scientific method? Psychologists use the scientific method because it provides the best way to gain new knowledge about behavior.
- How do psychologists use the scientific method? Psychologists use the scientific method to observe behaviors as they occur in everyday life and in situations researchers are interested in learning about.
- What are the canons of the scientific method? The canons are empiricism, determinism, parsimony, and testability.
- What is the difference between basic and applied research? Basic research is designed to answer fundamental questions about behavior. Applied research is designed to gain solutions to everyday problems.
- How do basic and applied research interact to increase our knowledge about behavior? Basic research advances our understanding of the causes of behavior. In applied research, these explanations are tested in everyday situations to inform researchers about the best solutions for everyday problems. Knowledge gained about these problems in applied research can then inform basic researchers about how explanations of behavior may need to be revised to explain behaviors that occur in everyday life.

THINKING ABOUT RESEARCH

A summary of a research study in psychology is given below. As you read the summary, think about the following questions:

1. What behaviors are the researchers observing?

2. How are the observations being recorded by the researchers?

3. Were the researchers able to identify a cause of behavior from this study?

4. Were the researchers able to answer their research questions with the observations they collected? How?

5. What results would have falsified the explanation of behavior the authors were testing?

6. Do you think this study qualifies as primarily basic or applied research? Why?

7. What are some examples of real-world behaviors that the results of this study might apply to?

Research Study. Strayer, D. L., & Johnston, W. A. (2001). Driven to distraction: Dual-task studies of simulated driving and conversing on a cellular phone. *Psychological Science, 12,* 462–466. [Note: Only Experiment 1 of this study is described.]

Purpose of the Study. The researchers were interested in how use of a cell phone while driving influences driving performance. They describe previous studies that have shown that devices that require one's hands while driving (e.g., the radio, temperature controls, etc.) can reduce driving performance. In this study, they predicted that cell phone use would reduce driving performance. They tested two ideas about how cell phone use could decrease driving: (1) that the hand use of the phone would interfere with driving and (2) that the attention requirements of a phone conversation would interfere with driving.

Method of the Study. Forty-eight undergraduates (half male, half female) participated in the experiment. Each of the students was randomly assigned to one of three cell phone conditions: hand-held phone, hands-free phone, and no phone (radio control only). The participants performed a computer-simulated driving task where they moved the cursor on the screen to match a moving target as closely as possible, using a joystick. Red and green lights flashed periodically during the task and subjects were instructed to press the "brake" button as quickly as possible when the red light flashed. They performed this task on its own in a practice segment and two test segments, with a dual-task segment placed between the two test segments. In the dual-task segment, they were given an additional task that included one of the following to match the conditions listed above: hand-held phone conversation with another person (who was part of the research team) about a current news story, hands-free phone conversation with another person about a current news story, or controlling a radio to listen to a broadcast of their choice. The frequency of missing red lights and the reaction time to hit the "brake" button when a red light appeared were measured and compared for the three phone conditions.

Results of the Study. The two cell phone use conditions did not differ in their results, suggesting that driving performance in response to red lights is similar for hand-held and hands-free phone use. Figure 1.4 shows a graph for each of the measures according to the phone (combined for hand-held and hands-free conditions) and no-phone conditions. The data are shown in each graph separately for driving performance in the driving only segments (single task) and for the phone/radio task while driving (dual task) segment. The graphs show that more red lights were missed and time to press the "brake" button was longer when subjects were talking on the phone (compared with when only driving), but there was no difference in driving performance when subjects listened to the radio while driving and when they just performed the driving task on its own.

Conclusions of the Study. The authors concluded that phone use, regardless of whether it requires one's hands, interferes with driving performance more than just listening to the radio. This suggests that the attention component of phone use is the key factor in the driving performance interference.

Figure 1.4 Driving Performance as Measured by Responses to Red Lights in the Driving Task While Performing the Driving Task on Its Own (Single Task) or While Also Performing the Phone or Radio Task (Dual Task)

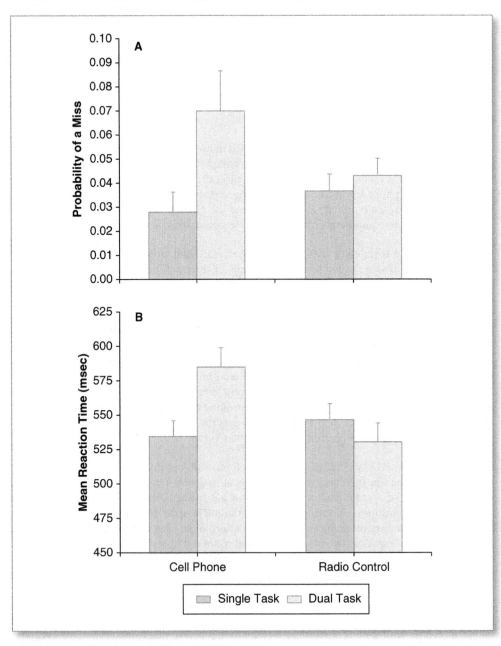

SOURCE: Figure 1 from Strayer and Johnston (2001).

COMMON PITFALLS AND HOW TO AVOID THEM

Problem: Assuming that psychology equals practice in a *helping* profession, ignoring or dismissing the scientific aspect of psychology.

Solution: Understand that science and practice are both important aspects of the field of psychology. In addition, although there is debate about this issue, many psychologists find it important that practitioners of psychology stay abreast of current research findings to ensure that they are using the most effective treatments.

Problem: Positive test bias—designing studies that provide supportive evidence of an explanation of behavior without including the possibility for contradictory evidence.

Solution: Carefully design studies to allow collection of data that can support or contradict explanations of behavior.

Problem: Misinterpretation of causation—study of cause and effect relationships requires manipulation (e.g., randomly assigning participants to different situations), but many people confuse reports of relationships with evidence of causation. In other words, correlation does not equal causation, but many people assume a link between two things means one caused the other.

Solution: Do not assume a reported relationship between factors is evidence that one factor causes another unless the study has been designed in such a way that other noncausal relationships can be ruled out.

Problem: Dismissing basic research—some people dismiss basic research as unimportant because it is not designed to solve a real-world problem.

Solution: View the "big picture" of knowledge in psychology to see how basic research informs applied research by providing fundamental knowledge of behavior that guides research questions and interpretation of results in applied studies. In addition, for a basic research study do not assume that because an application is not immediately evident the study is not valuable. Applications of basic research findings are often not clear until long after the basic research has been conducted.

USING RESEARCH

The number one cause of death in Americans today is heart disease, which can be caused by high cholesterol (Centers for Disease Control and Prevention, 2011). Many ads for fish oil supplements suggest that taking the supplements can reduce the risk of heart disease. Should you start taking fish oil supplements to prevent heart disease? Consider the following as you decide:

- The ads also indicate that the U.S. Food and Drug Administration (FDA) has not evaluated those claims. That means that there may not be research showing benefits for the supplements or the research may have been conducted only by the companies selling the supplements. Why should we be skeptical of research conducted only by the company selling the product?
- A recent study indicated that for men who had suffered a heart attack, taking fish oil supplements was associated with their chance of having another heart attack and/or dying suddenly. Should this result affect your decision to take fish oil supplements? Why or why not?

• The National Institutes for Health (2011) suggest that fish oil is effective for lowering triglycerides, an element of maintaining good cholesterol. What other questions are important to ask before using this information to decide about taking fish oil supplements?

TEST YOURSELF

Match each canon of science below with its correct definition.

1. Determinism   (a)   The scientific method can be used to test descriptions and explanations of the world that can be contradicted by observations.

2. Empiricism   (b)   The scientific method is used to examine phenomena that have an identifiable cause.

3. Testability   (c)   An assumption of science is that simpler explanations are more likely than complex explanations to be correct.

4. Parsimony   (d)   Knowledge is gained in science by systematically observing the phenomenon being studied.

5. Freud hypothesized that many of our personality traits are controlled by an unconscious conflict between aspects of ourselves—the id, ego, and superego—that we are not consciously aware of (Nairne, 2009). Using what you know about the scientific method, explain why this hypothesis is difficult to support with observations of behavior.

6. Explain how parsimony is helpful in psychological studies.

7. For each reference listed below, decide whether the study is primarily basic or applied.

(a) Drews, F., Pasupathu, M., & Strayer, D. (2008). Passenger and cell phone conversations in simulated driving. *Journal of Experimental Psychology: Applied, 14,* 392–400.

(b) Roediger, H. L., III, & Geraci, L. (2007). Aging and the misinformation effect: A neuropsychological analysis. *Journal of Experimental Psychology: Learning, Memory, and Cognition, 33,* 321–334.

(c) Bratcher, N. A., Farmer-Dougan, V., Dougan, J. D., Heidenreich, B. A., & Garris, P. A. (2005). The role of dopamine in reinforcement: Changes in reinforcement sensitivity induced by D-sub-1-type, D-sub-2-type, and nonselective dopamine receptor agonists. *Journal of the Experimental Analysis of Behavior, 84,* 371–399.

(d) Declercq, F., Vanheule, S., Markey, S., & Willemsen, J. (2007). Posttraumatic distress in security guards and the various effects of social support. *Journal of Clinical Psychology, 63,* 1239–1246.

(e) West, R. (2007). The influence of strategic monitoring on the neural correlates of prospective memory. *Memory & Cognition, 35,* 1034–1046.

(f) McClernon, C. K., McCauley, M. E., O'Connor, P. E., & Warm, J. S. (2011). Stress training improves performance during a stressful flight. *Human Factors, 53,* 207–218.

(g)   Weaver, J. R., & Bosson, J. K. (2011). I feel like I know you: Sharing negative attitudes of others promotes feelings of familiarity. *Personality and Social Psychology Bulletin, 37,* 481–491.

(h)   Blanchette, I., & Leese, J. (2011). The effect of negative emotion on deductive reasoning: Examining the contribution of physiological arousal. *Experimental Psychology, 58,* 235–246.

8. I believe that the best way to study for exams is to reread my notes three times from start to finish, because last semester I did that and I got an A on my psychology exam. I believe this despite the fact that I have tried this method before and did not receive an A on an exam. I am falling prey to the _____.

9. The scientific method relies on which way of knowing information about the world?

10. If I am concerned about whether the behavior exhibited in my research study maps on to the everyday behaviors of individuals, I am considering the _____ of my study.

Answers can be found at edge.sagepub/mcbride3e.

STOP AND THINK ANSWERS

(1.1)   Answers will vary—should use some of the ways of knowing: intuition, deduction, authority, and observation.

(1.2)   Answers will vary, but should include a measure that will indicate anxiety based on some type of observation.

(1.3)   Psychology and biology both have research and practice areas, where the two areas inform each other.

(1.4)   Parsimony, empiricism

(1.5)   Confirmation bias can hinder decision making in keeping you from considering all evidence for something because you are focused on finding evidence to support your own beliefs.

(1.6)   Replication is important because each individual study is based on just a small subset of subjects, and chance factors could be causing the results obtained.

(1.7)   External validity is typically higher in applied studies than basic studies, because applied studies are designed to solve a real-world problem, whereas basic studies are designed to understand a fundamental process of behavior with control over extraneous factors.

(1.8)   Answers will vary, but will be focused on considering evidence for something before deciding on things relevant for your life.

ⓈSAGE edge™

Visit edge.sagepub.com/mcbride3e for the tools you need to sharpen your study skills:

- Web Quizzes
- eFlashcards
- Thinking About Research

- SAGE Journal Articles
- Web and Multimedia Resources

How Psychology Became a Science

Science

Lead authors: Watts, S. & Banyard, P.

CHAPTER OUTLINE

2.1 INTRODUCTION

The history of psychology is not a straightforward tale. In fact, history is by no means an exact science: this means that the important stuff is inevitably a matter for interpretation and debate. What follows, therefore, is not *the* history of psychology, but *a* history. It's a history of psychology designed especially to introduce you to the main issues, concepts, people and debates that have helped to shape and define a fascinating and multifaceted discipline. Chapter 1 was about how we came to be human and we now move this on to look at how we came to develop theories of ourselves and our behaviour. It's a work in progress because there is so much to understand. Psychology has become an important part of the story of science and we will concentrate on that in this chapter.

FRAMING QUESTIONS

- How has the discipline of psychology developed? What have been the main stages in its development?
- To what extent has psychology developed as a natural science and to what extent as a social science?
- How have questions about what *type* of discipline psychology is affected what type of behaviour of experience we choose to study?

2.2 KEY MOMENTS IN THE EMERGENCE OF MODERN PSYCHOLOGY

The beginnings of modern psychology are usually traced to the year 1879. That's when **Wilhelm Wundt** (1832–1920) established the first dedicated psychological laboratory at Leipzig. The selection of this date is somewhat arbitrary. Wundt himself had, for example, highlighted the possibility of a distinct psychological discipline as early as 1862 (in his book *Contributions to the theory of sensory perception*). Yet the key events which led Wundt and others to this distinct discipline occurred even earlier.

Such events lie at the very heart of modern science, in the work of such great scientists as **Isaac Newton** (1642–1727) and **Charles Darwin** (1809–1882). Newton's work in physics had a profound influence on psychology. First, he developed a scientific 'method' consisting of observation, the formulation of hypotheses designed to predict events and outcomes, and the subsequent testing of these hypotheses through further observation. In this way, the scientific method worked towards the revelation of ever more general explanatory laws (Cushing, 1998). Such principles remain central to the scientific method that is used in psychology.

Second, and crucially, Newton had great success in applying these methods. He was able to offer an explanation of the entire physical universe based upon a limited number of basic laws (describing a limited number of basic 'forces'), each of which was expressed in a purely mathematical or quantitative form. In principle, it was thought that if you knew where all the physical bodies in the universe were at time *A*, Newton's laws would allow you to predict their future movements and hence to know (in advance) their respective locations at time *B*. Though this is a simplification, the basic point is that the behaviour of all physical bodies was shown to be lawful and knowledge of the laws appeared to make the subsequent trajectories and relative positions of these bodies entirely predictable. According to this theory, everything behaved in a mechanistic or machine-like fashion because the behaviour of everything was determined by the impact of the same set of basic forces.

2.2.1 DETERMINISM

This theory of mechanical determinism has been a strong influence on psychology. Newton's ideas also impacted on people in general. The pre-Newtonian worldview was characterised by its anthropocentrism. That is, people considered themselves to have a central and fundamental place in the universe. Newton's work brought this anthropocentrism into question. The universe was mechanical and its behaviour predetermined: it was 'as it was', regardless of our existence. Far from being central, people and their opinions and viewpoints appeared superfluous. The sense of alienation that resulted from this view was the key that opened the door to psychology. Alexandre Koyré captures this nicely:

> modern science . . . united and unified the universe. . . . But . . . it did this by substituting for our world of quality and sense perception, the world in which we live, and love, and die, another world . . . the world of quantity . . . a world in which though there is a place for everything, there is no place for man. Thus the world of science – the real world – became estranged and utterly divorced from the world of life. (Cited in Prigogine & Stengers, 1984: 35–36)

> **DETERMINISM** The idea that every event, including human thought and behaviour, is causally determined by an unbroken chain of prior events. According to this idea, there are no mysterious miracles and no random events.

> **ANTHROPOCENTRISM** OR **ANTHROCENTRISM** The belief that people (*anthro*) are the most important thing in the universe rather than the very small, here-today-gone-tomorrow little creatures that we are.

The point here is that Newton and his scientific methods – the modern mind at its best – solved the riddle of the universe, but in so doing produced a dramatic (and tragic) side-effect. They appeared to separate us from the universe. Serious questions followed about 'mind' itself, about where humans, and the qualities and perceptions of the everyday human world, fitted in. Our place in the bigger scheme of things was under threat. And, vitally for psychology, this threat made 'us' the next scientific riddle to be solved.

2.2.2 THE RIDDLE OF OUR SELVES

The 'riddle of our selves' became even more pressing following the publication of Darwin's *On the origin of species* in 1859. As we have seen, Newton had 'decentred' us and lessened our apparent importance. However, at least the principles of mechanical determinism remained and these were widely held to be 'consonant with the generally accepted theological belief in an omnipresent, omniscient God' (Cushing, 1998: 168). Newton himself stayed true to the belief that 'the mechanical universe required the active intervention of God, not just to create and order it, but also to maintain it' (1998: 168).

Darwin's theory of evolution by natural selection (see Chapter 1), on the other hand, sat far less comfortably with conventional religious ideas. In fact, it directly challenged them. Human beings, which Christian religion saw as the 'closest thing to God', became the 'nearest thing to apes' in the blink of a scientific eye (Figure 2.1). This was a bitter pill to swallow and one which **Sigmund Freud** (1856–1939) called 'the second great blow to the human ego' (following the Newtonian blow described earlier). Darwin's theory reignited debates about humans' fundamental nature. It was in the midst of this debate that Wundt's psychological laboratory was founded, just eight years after Darwin's publication of *The descent of man, and selection in relation to sex* (in 1871). It was a good time to be a psychologist.

FIGURE 2.1 AND FIGURE 2.2   The riddle of our selves. On the ceiling of the Sistine Chapel in Rome is a picture that shows one view of where people come from: God reaches out and creates the first man – Adam. Darwin's version would have Adam reaching back to touch his past – a monkey.

© Jim Zuckerman/Corbis and Frans Lanting/Corbis

2.2.3 AN IMPORTANT DECISION FOR PSYCHOLOGY

The previous section suggests that psychology emerged in order to solve the 'riddle of our selves'. Thanks to Newton, the discipline also appeared at a time when its most immediate subject matter (the human world of life, quality and sense perception) had been 'estranged and utterly divorced' from the *real* world that Newtonian science had begun to reveal. Our scientific approach has given us answers to many questions about how things work. We know something about how the planets move (the theory of gravity) and we know something about how our senses work (see Chapter 6). What is much more puzzling, however, is our own existence on this world and how we make sense of it. The contrasts in what we know and what we are still puzzling over is shown in Table 2.1.

The word *psychology* means 'a science of mind or soul', and the psychological world (psychology's most immediate subject matter) appears on the right of Table 2.1. It is worth remembering both these points as we proceed. For the moment, however, psychologists had to decide how best to study this subject matter. Two basic models presented themselves. On the one hand, there was Newton's natural science model, which employed quantitative research methods and pursued nomothetic knowledge as a priority (i.e. objective and lawful knowledge which is considered to be generally applicable). This system had triumphed in the physical world.

QUANTITATIVE DATA Focus on numbers and frequencies rather than on meaning or experience.

QUALITATIVE DATA Describe meaning and experience rather than providing numerical values for behaviour, such as frequency counts.

On the other hand, a social science model was also a possibility. This approach predominated in the humanities and was embodied by the German word *Geisteswissenschaft* (which means 'science of the spirit'). Under this model, the aim was to study humans, human life and human events by re-creating their meaning for the actors involved, in order to find out their *reasons* for doing what they were doing. To achieve this goal, qualitative research methods were generally employed and idiographic knowledge was pursued as a priority (i.e. subjective and specific knowledge of a person, event or situation which reveals that person, event or situation in its uniqueness).

This distinction (between the social and natural sciences) was popularised by the historian **Wilhelm Dilthey** (1833–1911). Dilthey offered clear advice to psychology. First, he acknowledged that humans and human events both possess important physical properties. As an example, your brain is a physical object and its physical properties are going to be pretty important if you want to think. I'm sure you'd realised that (see 'Aside'). This simple observation nonetheless creates a serious complication for psychology, because it means that our status as physical and material 'objects' has a massive effect on our capacity to be psychological. In other words, in order to fully grasp the psychological world (captured on the right of Table 2.1), the discipline of psychology must also engage with aspects of the physical world (captured on the left of Table 2.1). This latter task demands a natural scientific

TABLE 2.1   The big riddles. The universe that Newtonian science dealt with is on the left. The universe it missed out is on the right. Consider the opposing categories carefully. The dualism they represent has been fundamental to psychology and to Western thought and culture more generally

THE RIDDLE OF THE UNIVERSE	THE RIDDLE OF OUR SELVES
The world of *science*	The world of *life*
The *real* world	The *perceived* world
The *objective* world	The *subjective* world
The world of *quantity*	The world of *quality*
The *physical* world	The *psychological* world
The *somatic* world	The *semantic* world
The world *as it is*	The world *as it is experienced!*
A science of *matter*	A science of *mind [and of things that matter!]*

ASIDE

Thinking about thinking

Had you realised that 'thinking' (biologically speaking) involves the passage of electrical impulses through the nerve cells of the brain and the chemical transmission of those impulses across lots of tiny 'gaps' between the nerve cells called **synapses**? If you were to start counting the synapses now, at a rate of one per second, you would finish in approximately *30 million* years time. The brain is extraordinary. The number of possible pathways available to the brain's electrical impulses (and hence the possibilities for thought) are *greater than the number of atoms in the known universe*.

And to go a step further, when we describe these electrical impulses we are using an entirely different language from the language we use to describe thinking. Will it ever be possible to match up these two descriptions of the same event and connect the internal experience with the external observation?

approach. But while psychology cannot avoid our physical or somatic properties (the latter means 'of the body'), Dilthey also warned that:

> explaining human actions is fundamentally different from explaining physical events. A woman shooting a man is a physical event. However, understanding the event in human terms involves more than tracing the path of the bullet and showing how the bullet caused the man's death. We need to know *why* she shot the man, not just *how* she did so. (Leahey, 2004: 248)

'Why' questions are central to psychology. The brain, for example, is a good way of explaining *how* we think but not *why* we do it. It doesn't cause us to think, any more than having legs causes us to run. In the same way, any rigorous psychological explanation of running would require that we understand *why* the running is taking place and not just *how* it is taking place (the latter presumably involving a series of neuronal signals leading to a more or less rapid movement of the legs).

Dilthey wanted psychology to remember that its primary subject matter was the subjective or psychological world itself, not just the physical properties that made this world possible. Dilthey suggested that if we want to find out 'why', priority must be given to the psychological world – the ways that people make sense of their experience and the meanings they attach to them. In other words, to understand why I am running, you will first need to understand my experience of the current situation and the meanings I assign to it, because only in this way can you find out my motives and reasons for acting. This task demands a social scientific approach.

So what should psychology do? If the psychological world was its proper subject matter, then surely psychology was a humanitarian discipline? For this reason, Dilthey felt a social scientific approach was preferable. But the psychological world can only exist through the physical world. If I don't have a physical body I can't see or hear, for example. Psychology couldn't ignore this either. It needed to study the physical world as well and the natural scientific model dominated in this domain.

This double-edged nature of psychology was (and remains) both a challenge and an opportunity. Psychology had the chance to bridge the divide between the natural and social sciences and it could do so by retaining a foot in both camps (Danziger, 1990). Nomothetic and idiographic knowledge, quantitative and qualitative methods, could all be embraced. It needed to study its subject matter from both perspectives. Wilhelm Wundt tried to support this vision (as did other early psychologists), but it was not a vision that psychology would ultimately sustain. As we're about to see, psychology was intent on becoming a natural science.

NOMOTHETIC AND IDIOGRAPHIC MEASURES Nomothetic approaches look for laws of behaviour and collect measures that can be observed and verified and quantified. They are concerned with averages and norms. By contrast, idiographic approaches look for unique and individual experiences.

'NOMOTHETIC FALLACY' The common belief that if you can name a problem then you have solved it. For example, if you feel very upset and someone says you have post-traumatic stress, you still feel upset.

2.3 PSYCHOLOGY AS A STUDY OF THE CONSCIOUS MIND: HELMHOLTZ, FECHNER, WUNDT AND A 'NATURAL SCIENCE OF THE MENTAL'

All things being equal, psychology in the late nineteenth century is probably best categorised as one of the humanities (Windelband, 1894/1998). And the subject matter left to it by the natural sciences – the psychological and inherently subjective world of perception, quality and experience – probably required the application of methods traditionally associated with the social sciences. But all things were not equal. The unprecedented success of the natural science model had a big influence on the emergence of psychology. It also established the view that natural scientific methods were 'the only reliable methods for securing useful and reliable knowledge about anything' (Danziger, 1990: 41). In order to flourish, psychology *had* to align itself with the methods of the natural sciences.

This conclusion was nonetheless complicated by a long-standing philosophical belief that subjective, mental phenomena were not amenable to natural scientific analysis. **Immanuel Kant** (1724–1804), for example, had rejected the possibility of a 'science of mind' on the grounds that mental phenomena (1) had no spatial dimension, (2) were too transient to observe, and (3) could not be experimentally manipulated in a controlled fashion. Overall, Kant concluded that mental phenomena couldn't be mathematically analysed or described (Fancher, 1996). Such phenomena, he felt, could only ever support a qualitative and philosophical analysis.

REDUCTIONISM Curt describes reductionism as 'the attempt to reduce or "boil down" any complex phenomenon into the simple elements which are thought to constitute it or cause it' (1994: 241).

MATERIALISM Philosophically speaking, materialism encapsulates the view that the world/universe is entirely constituted of matter. This view leaves little room for the psychological world. Materialism is sometimes also known as 'physicalism'.

To overcome this barrier, psychology exploited the fact that our psychological world is connected to our physical properties. Earlier, we suggested (as a means of explaining Dilthey's arguments) that the brain does not cause us to think. But if the brain doesn't cause us to think, then what does? So psychology went along with the idea that all mental phenomena could, in fact, be explained in terms of physiological causes. This double whammy of reductionism and materialism reduced the psychological world to a by-product of the physiological properties which produced it. It also neatly sidestepped Kant's objections. As a by-product, subjective mental phenomena were no longer psychology's primary subject matter; physiology was. And natural scientific methods operated very comfortably in this physical domain. As Leahey puts it:

> by insisting that the nervous system is the basis of all mentality, and by defining psychology as the investigation of the physiological conditions of conscious events, the new field . . . could establish itself as a [natural] science. (Leahey, 2004: 235)

But defining psychology in this way was not enough. Establishing psychology as a natural science also demanded that psychological experimentation be carried out in the same way as the natural sciences, and this in turn demanded that psychological phenomena be mathematically measured and described. This was now to involve the 'investigation of the physiological conditions of conscious events' (rather than the events themselves), yet those conditions would still have to be counted and measured.

2.3.1 QUANTIFICATION

The first attempts at counting and measuring in psychology, otherwise known as quantification, were developed by a number of people in a number of different ways. In 1850 **Hermann von Helmholtz** (1821–1894), an eminent natural scientist, demonstrated that nerve impulses travelled at finite speeds which could be measured in terms of *reaction times*. He did this by passing electric currents through the severed leg of a frog. He also established the psychological principle that human perception (by which he implied the psychological reality we experience) was not a simple replication of the physical reality captured by our senses. Helmholtz proposed instead that sensations were *transformed* into perceptions in a mechanical and lawful fashion by the physiological machinery of our minds.

F.C. Donders (1818–1889) built upon Helmholtz's reaction-time work. Donders realised that the time between the presentation of a stimulus and a person's response to it could be used as a quantifiable measure of the speed of physiological and mental processes (processes which could not otherwise be observed). It was even possible, by making a person choose between two stimuli, to ascertain the exact duration of a mental judgement. This act of quantification (which became known as *mental chronometry*) was exactly what psychology needed if it was to distinguish itself as a natural science.

Gustav Fechner (1801–1887) quantified psychological phenomena in a different way. Like Helmholtz, Fechner had noticed that the information gathered by our senses was processed and transformed *before* it reached conscious awareness. In particular, he observed that the *perceived* intensity of a physical stimulus did not perfectly reflect its *physical* intensity. A lighted match would, for example, appear to be brighter when it was placed against a dark background. If, Fechner surmised, we could somehow measure the physical *and* the perceived intensity of the stimulus, it might become possible to mathematically determine their relationship (and hence to mathematically connect the psychological and physical worlds).

But how could we measure the perceived intensity? Fechner realised that you couldn't quantify it directly or as an absolute value. What you could do, however, was quantify the smallest *perceptual discrimination* people are capable of making, and you could do this as a function of changes in the physical intensity itself. Let's say, for example, that I put a weight in your right hand and its physical intensity is 100 grams. What is its perceived intensity? There is of course no pure mathematical answer. So suppose I start putting weights into your left hand, one by one – 101 grams, 102, 103, and so on. The question becomes, 'At what weight can you perceive a difference (or discriminate) between the two weights?'. And, thanks to Fechner, we know the answer. On average it's when the weight in your left hand is 1/30th (or 3.33%) heavier or lighter than the weight in your right (or, in our example, when the weight in your left hand is 103.33 grams or more). Fechner called this perceived change in intensity a 'just noticeable difference' (or JND) and it constituted a quantitative measure of perceived intensity.

Fechner was able to measure the JND across a range of sensory functions and to graphically represent the relationship between physical and perceived stimulus intensities in each case. He also demonstrated that the relationship between physical and perceived intensity could *always* be expressed via a single mathematical formula. In truth, this law was anything but perfect. Nonetheless, Fechner's psychophysical experiments had clearly shown that: (1) the content of the psychological world could be manipulated by controlling the stimuli presented to it; (2) while such content might actually represent a subjective 'distortion' of the physical world, such distortion was nevertheless carried out (by our physiology) in a mechanical and lawful fashion; and (3) as a result, the content of the psychological world could be shown to have a lawful and quantifiable relationship with the content of the physical world.

Other important work on counting and measuring psychological qualities was occurring at roughly the same time. Perhaps the most notable was the development of mental and intelligence testing procedures, via the work of **Francis Galton** (1822–1911) in Britain (see key researcher box and also Chapter 22), **Alfred Binet** (1857–1911) in France (see Chapter 22) and America, and latterly **William Stern** (1871–1938) in Germany. The truth is, then, that the new discipline's desire to become a 'natural science of the mental' was already well established before Wundt's laboratory ever appeared.

Wundt had indeed called his first taught course in psychology 'Psychology as a natural science' (in 1862), and both mental chronometry and Fechner-like experiments quickly characterised the work of Wundt's laboratory at Leipzig. Yet, in common with most German academics, Wundt remained a strong advocate of the distinction between the *Natur-* and *Geisteswissenschaften* (natural and social sciences), and his general approach recognised that psychology stood at the point of transition between the two. This is not surprising because Wundt had been employed at Leipzig to teach philosophy and to teach psychology as a part of that humanitarian discipline (Leahey, 2004). His methodological

EXERCISE: SENSATION AND PERCEPTION

Take a box of matches. Light one of the matches and hold it up in front of a light background. How bright does it look? Try to put a number on your judgement of brightness (your perception). Now light another match in front of a different coloured background. How bright does that look?

The amount of light from the two matches will be the same (sensation) but your judgement might well be different. Try this out with a number of backgrounds and explore the factors that change your perception. By the way, try not to burn down your house during this exercise.

KEY RESEARCHER Francis Galton (1822–1911)

FIGURE 2.3   **Francis Galton**

© Bettmann/CORBIS

Elsewhere in this text we have highlighted the work of contemporary psychologists, but in this chapter about the history of the subject we have chosen to look at an historical figure. Galton was a cousin of Charles Darwin and shared his interest in science. He contributed to a wide range of scientific areas and we mention him here because of the range of techniques and concepts that he developed (see Fancher, 1996), including:

- *Self-report questionnaires*: in 1873 Galton wrote to all the Fellows of the Royal Society (eminent scientists) with a lengthy questionnaire to discover the common features of people who are successful in science.
- *Twin studies*: he devised the first of these, as well as carrying out the first comparison of the resemblance of natural and adopted children to their parents.
- *Eugenics*: the term describing the attempt to breed a superior group of people was also invented by Galton.
- *Scatterplots*: Galton wanted to find ways to present his data on family resemblances and he devised the scatterplot.
- *Statistics*: Galton developed his scatterplots and also developed regression lines and the correlation co-efficient.

The above is a phenomenal list, but it is only a selection of his output and you can add *word association* to it. Galton devised a word association technique and the paper he wrote on this was read by Freud and contributed to the development of one of the major techniques of psychoanalysis. Oh, and he also produced the first weather map. We'll consider more of Galton's influence when we look at the heritability of intelligence in Chapter 22.

In 1884 Galton created a mental testing laboratory in the Natural History Museum (in Kensington) where he collected anthropometric measures such as visual acuity, strength of grip, colour vision, hearing acuity, hand preference etc., from the visitors to the exhibition who, incidentally, paid Galton for the privilege. He hoped to use these measures to estimate people's hereditary intelligence. Before Galton, psychology had been looking for general principles of experience. By contrast, Galton's anthropometric laboratory looked for individual differences. Although we would not recognise Galton's tests and measures of mental abilities today, they do mark the beginning of mental testing.

approach duly combined the new methods of quantification described above with a more traditional method called *introspection*, which had been employed by the 'old-fashioned philosophical psychology … to reveal the contents and workings of the mind' (2004: 237).

2.3.2 THE INTROSPECTIVE METHOD

In 1873, Wundt's *Principles of physiological psychology* described the emerging discipline of psychology. It combined physiology, which 'informs us about those life phenomena that we perceive by our external senses', with a psychological and introspective approach in which 'the person looks upon himself from within' (1873: 157). The introspective method, which relied on a process of self-report about the 'goings-on' in one's psychological world, had previously been dismissed by scientists and philosophers alike because of its unreliability and inherent subjectivity. Wundt himself doubted its effectiveness. He had responded, however, by trying to transform this unreliable act of internal perception into something akin to scientific observation (Danziger, 1990).

To do this, Wundt restricted his so-called physiological psychology to the study of processes that were simultaneously accessible to both internal and external acts of observation. In practice, a stimulus was presented to a participant and quantified response measures were gathered at the same time as subjective reports of the conscious content elicited by the stimulus (Figure 2.4). In this way, the introspective data always appeared alongside the more important objective measures. In order to control the style of the introspective reports they were only collected from trained researchers. This move was clever in as much as it gave introspection a new status as a special skill. Only a trained scientist could carry out these scientific observations with sufficient reliability. Despite this, the qualitative data introspection produced were still not accepted as a basis for knowledge claims. Only quantitative data could do that.

These many restrictions limited Wundt to the study of psychological processes on the edge of conscious experience: basically, sensation, perception and motor responses. But this did not concern Wundt, for he considered these to be the only processes properly accessible to natural scientific analysis and the only ones directly and mechanistically caused by physiological processes. Higher-order mental processes (complex thought, memory, voluntary effort, creativity, etc.) were, for Wundt, part of a distinct psychic causality, and they were caused not by physiology, but by an underlying layer of unconscious psychological mechanisms. These mechanisms were said to be qualitative in nature and for this reason Wundt

FIGURE 2.4   Wundt (right) in his laboratory in Leipzig: the team are shown taking part in a joke-telling experiment

felt they would always resist experimental or natural scientific analysis. Non-experimental approaches would also be required.

Wundt spent the last 20 years of his life developing his *Völkerpsychologie*, that is a kind of historical and comparative psychology which looked at people as part of a collective and which tried to understand them within their social, cultural and communal context. Wundt believed these historical, qualitative and distinctly social scientific analyses were a very necessary addition to experimental studies of individual people in the laboratory. He felt strongly that the 'experimental method plus *Völkerpsychologie* would furnish a complete, albeit not completely natural-scientific, psychology' (Leahey, 2004: 239).

Few agreed: Wundt's desire for psychology to retain links with the humanities was at odds with the prevailing vision. Psychology wanted to be a natural science completely. **Hermann Ebbinghaus** (1850–1909) had already demonstrated (in 1879) that the higher-order mental process of memory could potentially be made accessible to experiment (Fancher, 1996) and Wundt's influence was waning. He died in 1920 along with many of his ideas.

Introspection, meanwhile, was to flourish in the work of two of Wundt's students, **Oswald Külpe** (1862–1915) and **Edward Titchener** (1867–1927). Both the Würzburg School of systematic introspection established by Külpe and Titchener's 'structural psychology' relieved introspection of its restrictions. Memory, thinking and complex feelings became legitimate topics for introspective analysis and the resulting qualitative data took centre stage. Titchener described these changes in 1912:

> The experimenter of the early nineties trusted, first of all, in his instruments . . . [which were] of more importance than the observer. . . . There were still vast reaches of mental life which experiment had not touched. . . . Now . . . we have changed all that. The movement towards qualitative analysis has culminated in what is called . . . the method of 'systematic experimental introspection'. (Cited in Danziger, 1990: 43)

Yet this was ultimately a backward step. Simply calling introspection 'systematic' and 'experimental' could not hide the fact that psychology's subject matter had once again drawn the discipline away from the natural sciences and back towards the humanities. As Titchener's experimental psychology explored the 'vast reaches of mental life', so a qualitative analysis along the lines of the old philosophical psychology had reappeared. The first attempts to establish a natural science of the mental had reached a dead end. Alternatives were required.

2.4 TWO ALTERNATIVE WAYS OF FOUNDING PSYCHOLOGY: SIGMUND FREUD AND THE UNCONSCIOUS, WILLIAM JAMES AND FUNCTIONALISM

In truth, the work of Sigmund Freud is something of a distraction in a chapter about psychological science. Had Freud's work developed differently, this might not have been the case: when in 1894/1895 Freud was writing his *Project for a*

ASIDE

Hysteria

Hysteria is a condition in which physical symptoms appear in the absence of any obvious physical cause.

Today, hysteria might well be called a dissociative disorder. In Freud's time, only women were thought to be hysterical. Nice. This is a prime example of the masculine bias which has long afflicted psychology.

In fact, Freud initially proposed (*very* controversially) that all hysterics had suffered sexual abuse in childhood. He later retracted this 'seduction theory' of hysteria. He nonetheless retained the belief that many of the hysteric's 'potentially damaging' ideas and desires were of a sexual nature and that much of *everybody's* behaviour was driven by the repression of such sexual desires.

scientific psychology he 'defined his Newtonian "intention ... to furnish a psychology that shall be a natural science: that is, to represent psychical processes as quantitatively determinate states of specifiable material particles"' (cited in Leahey, 2004: 267). This statement, early in Freud's work, was reminiscent of Wundt's view. Yet Freud was to depart dramatically from these intentions.

Freud's work in psychology began with an interest in **hysteria**, a complaint in which physical symptoms appeared in the absence of any obvious physical cause, and his psychoanalytic approach emerged as a therapy to deal with this problem. He believed the physical symptoms were caused by unconscious (and potentially damaging) psychological memories, needs or desires, as they made themselves manifest in the hysteric's behaviour. Psychoanalysis itself was a 'talking cure' in which patients voiced their problems and feelings under the guidance of a therapist, with the aim of bringing the hitherto unconscious desires into conscious awareness.

On the basis of just six case studies of psychoanalytic therapy (of which only two were claimed as successes) and a process of self-analysis, Freud came to the conclusion that all human behaviour was caused by psychological drives and events occurring in the unconscious mind (and were of a primarily sexual and pleasure-seeking nature). In non-hysterics, Freud saw dreams as the primary means of uncovering and interpreting this unconscious content (and he regarded his 1900 publication *The interpretation of dreams* as his master work).

Freud undoubtedly wanted psychoanalysis to be a science. Yet most of his claims about the nature and influence of the unconscious mind have never been substantiated by scientific evidence. He did not try 'to create an experimental psychology of the unconscious, nor did he welcome attempts to scientifically verify his ideas' (Leahey, 2004: 265). As a result, Freud's ideas have generally been vilified by a psychological discipline intent on emulating the natural sciences (Eysenck, 2004).

It is nonetheless important to acknowledge the huge popularity of psychoanalysis. Freud's ideas and concepts have also greatly influenced 'contemporary ways of thinking about human feelings and conduct' (Gay, 1989: xii). It may not be science, but Freud's conceptual scheme clearly remains a compelling means of reading and interpreting human behaviour. Psychology was also affected by Freud in two further ways. First, his ideas led the way into abnormal psychology (and studies of mental health); and second, they showed that psychology was not just an academic discipline, but also an *applied* and therapeutic one. The psychologist could be a scientist and/or the practitioner.

2.4.1 AND IN THE USA . . .

This tension between academic and applied psychology was first noted by **William James** (1842–1910). James was to American psychology what Wundt had been in Europe: a founding father for the new discipline. He was initially impressed by the work of Wundt and the German physiological psychologists. The mechanical, causal explanations they offered and the idea that psychology might be based upon natural scientific principles excited him intellectually. On the other hand, he found its implications quite distressing from a spiritual perspective. And you can see his point. Are we really so mechanical and predictable? Are we really so controlled by our physiology? For James, such explanations left little room for the expression of human choice, creativity and free will.

EXERCISE: DO YOU HAVE FREE WILL?

The free will versus determinism debate remains a key argument for psychologists. Is our behaviour determined by physiology, unconscious forces or even environmental influences? Or are we free to act according to our own free will? It's a tricky one, but in everyday life we tend to fall down on the free will side of the debate.

Try this one out on family and friends. Try using determinist arguments to get yourself out of tricky situations like crashing your mum's car. For example, try saying 'I couldn't help myself, I was born that way', or 'I was just responding to the flux of neurochemicals washing around my brain'. If you get a response that is anything other than a two-word sentence where the second word is 'off', then let us know. That's how much people don't believe in determinism.

James's resolution of this personal conflict is ultimately central to understanding his later work. He decided that it was useful to accept mechanistic explanations in a scientific context. He even accepted that psychology had little choice but to progress in this direction. But this didn't mean he had to think and behave in a predictable and determined fashion. In this personal context, he would live creatively and with free will. This course of action, which rested on the principle that an idea may be true or have utility only in a specific context, was to become a central feature of James's later career in philosophy.

This personal accent on free will and his ultimate preference for philosophy also hint at James's subsequent attitude to psychology. In his much acclaimed *Principles of psychology* (1890), James strongly criticised the experimental and structural approach to psychology he associated with Wundt and Titchener. This approach was, for James, both very reductive and a bore! Its pursuit of basic mental structures or elements involved a wholly artificial and barbaric dissection of mental life. In contrast, James emphasised the continuous, indivisible and ever-changing nature of mental life via his concept of the stream of consciousness. He saw consciousness as both selective and functional. It was selective in so far as it evolved in order to help people choose (between various courses of action) and it was functional in as much as these choices were vital in helping the individual adapt to their environment.

European psychology had founded itself on the principles of Newtonian science and this allegiance created a focus on mental structures and underlying explanatory mechanisms. James's emphasis on the functional and adaptive significance of consciousness demonstrates the alternative but 'powerful influence of Darwin on early U.S. scientific psychology' (Hergenhahn, 2005: 313). From around 1900, American psychology steadily moved away 'from the traditional psychology of conscious content ... toward a psychology of mental adjustment inspired by evolutionary theory' (Leahey, 2004: 341–342).

This movement inspired important changes in the view of psychology and its subject matter. First, the conscious mind came to be understood as just another biological adaptation. It existed because it served an evolutionary function, and that function was to enable people to adapt their behaviour in relation to their current circumstances. Given this association of mind with biology, it is not surprising to find that mind and body, and particularly mind and behaviour, were increasingly viewed as inseparable and synonymous entities. Mind was an 'outgrowth of conduct, a superior and more direct means of adjusting the organism to the environment' (Bolton, 1902, cited in Leahey, 2004: 343). In a very real sense, mind *became* action.

This theoretical shift initially showed itself in renewed attempts by psychologists to make psychology useful in an applied and therapeutic way. Psychology, it was felt, had to have a practical *function*. And it could achieve this by bringing about improvements in education and learning, by intervening in matters of abnormal psychology (now increasingly defined as maladaptive behaviour), and by bringing about human and societal betterment through these interventions. If mind involved mental adjustment, psychology could help us adjust more profitably. The Great War (1914–1918), so damaging in so many ways, actually gave applied psychology a tremendous boost. The mental testing procedures of Galton and Binet, exploited most famously in America by **James McKeen Cattell** (1860–1944), thrived in this sort of applied environment. And they have done so ever since. These methods have formed the basis of an individual differences tradition in psychology. Section F in this text will tell you all you need to know.

But this applied success, while welcome, still failed to satisfy the natural scientific and experimental ideal that the academic discipline held so dear. This needed to be remedied. If mind *is* action, the argument went, then a person's psychological world was freely observable and accessible in the physical world by simple reference to what they do. Experimental psychology was about to start a new life, most 'satisfactorily defined as the science of human behaviour' (Pillsbury, 1911: 1).

2.5 CONDITIONING: WATSON, PAVLOV, SKINNER AND THE STUDY OF BEHAVIOUR

In 1913, **John B. Watson** (1878–1958) laid out an aggressive manifesto for this science of human behaviour in a paper entitled 'Psychology as the behaviorist views it':

> Psychology as the behaviorist views it is a purely objective branch of natural science. Its . . . goal is the prediction and control of behavior. Introspection forms no essential part of its methods, nor is the scientific value of its data dependent on the readiness with which they lend themselves to interpretation in terms of consciousness. The behaviorist . . . recognizes no dividing line between man and brute. (Watson, 1913: 158)

FUNCTIONALISM In the philosophy of mind, functionalism refers to the idea that mental states can be defined by their causes and effects.

BEHAVIOURISM A school of thought which holds that the observation and description of overt behaviour is all that is needed to comprehend the human being, and that manipulation of stimulus–response contingencies is all that is needed to change human behaviour.

This all seems quite straightforward. Introspection had reached a scientific impasse and the functionalists had begun to see mind as synonymous with behaviour. As one might predict, therefore, Watson's rejection of introspection caused little argument. Watson's technology of behaviour also set out to ignore the facts of consciousness, and for this reason even Titchener (the undisputed champion of introspection) did not see it as competition. It just wasn't psychology. Yet most psychologists trained in the ways of functionalism were quite happy to accept a form of methodological behaviourism which allowed them to acknowledge the presence of conscious experience, but also to ignore it as something hopelessly unsuited to scientific analyses.

The use of mentalistic terminology such as 'the mind' or 'consciousness' did indeed become more and more problematic for psychologists over the next decade or so. For the strict behaviourist, consciousness had no place in the discipline or in human life more generally. Behavioural adaptation was not a function of consciousness; it was instead a function of our capacity to learn.

This principle had already been demonstrated by **Edward Thorndike** (1874–1949) and perhaps more famously by **Ivan Pavlov** (1849–1936). Pavlov received a Nobel Prize for work which exploited the (delightful) fact that dogs salivate at the merest expectation of food. Pavlov demonstrated, by repeatedly pairing a particular stimulus (the food) with a sound (famously a bell, but more probably a metronome), that his dogs would eventually salivate in response to the sound alone. They had, in other words, learned to connect the food (known as the unconditioned stimulus) with the sound (or conditioned stimulus). This form of learning, in which new stimulus–response connections were created, became known as classical conditioning. Thorndike, on the other hand, showed through a series of clever 'puzzle box' experiments that animals could be trained to produce a specific behavioural response more frequently if that response elicited a tangible reward. This form of learning, which could be used to strengthen (or weaken) pre-existing response tendencies, became known as operant conditioning.

2.5.1 MAN AND BRUTE

These animal studies nonetheless became directly applicable to psychology only when Watson, in true Darwinian style, forcefully pointed out that 'man and brute' were no longer seen as divided. Watson argued that, because we are animals, so the study of other, simpler, animals could shed light on the way humans function. Following this emphasis on learning, Watson was also able to argue that 'instinct' was another concept that psychology could do without. We began life as a blank slate (with no personality, no intelligence – just a mental blank canvas) and everything we subsequently did, all our knowledge and skills, was the result of processes of learning or deliberate training. And the latter, the training and ultimate control of behaviour, was now the central aim of the psychologist. As Watson (1930) put it, we 'can build any man, starting at birth, into any kind of social or a-social being upon order' (cited in Leahey, 2004: 377).

KEY STUDY

Watson, J., & Rayner, R. (1920). Conditioned emotional reactions. *Journal of Experimental Psychology, 3*, 1–14.

Given the historical nature of this chapter we have gone for a historical classic as a key study. It appears in many introductory texts, and despite the controversial nature of the study is still very well known.

Watson and Rayner wanted to demonstrate that behaviourist theory could be applied to humans and set out to show that fear can be learnt. The sole participant in the study was an infant referred to in the text as Albert B (more popularly known as Little Albert). Using the principles of classical conditioning Watson and Rayner made a loud noise near to the baby by banging a hammer on metal at the same time that they showed him a white rat. They did this just nine times over a three-week period and this was enough to create an aversion in the child to the white rat and also to other things that had rat-like features, such as rabbits, fluffy toys and a man in a Santa Claus mask.

Albert's behaviour, as recorded by Watson and Rayner, suggested that emotional responses to stimuli can be learnt. Before conditioning, Albert demonstrated no fear of the white rat; after conditioning he did appear to be afraid of it.

The study is cited very widely in psychological literature despite it being based on the evidence from one case. Interestingly, it is often incorrectly reported in many textbooks with some adding a happy ending by suggesting that Albert's fear was deconditioned by Watson and Rayner. Harris (1979) reviewed the various descriptions of this study that appear in the psychological literature and suggested that the story of Little Albert has developed like a myth, with each generation of psychologists retelling the story to illustrate their own position.

Behaviourism reached its height between 1930 and 1950 and is now most prominently associated with the work of **B.F. Skinner** (1904–1990). Skinner developed Thorndike's ideas into a fuller theory of operant aka instrumental conditioning. Using similar apparatus, he focused on *contingencies of reinforcement*: in other words, the nature and specific patterns of reward-giving through which spontaneously emitted and random behaviours (or operants) could best be 'shaped' into direct, learned (or conditioned) responses. Theoretically, Skinner shared Watson's radical behaviourism: he stressed the determining influence of environmental influences on behaviour, while excluding all reference to mental states (Hergenhahn, 2005).

In two philosophical publications (*Walden two*, published in 1948, and *Beyond freedom and dignity*, in 1971), Skinner also explored the ultimate behaviourist vision of a utopian society in which people 'were conditioned into socially admirable ways of acting' (Harré, 2006: 18). In this brave new world, people would be rewarded for good behaviour and the society would be ordered, productive and calm. Crime would be low and happiness would be everywhere. It's easy to mock this ambition, but if we could create a better and happier world by engineering the rewards that people got for their behaviour, then at first glance this might appear to be a good idea. Further reflection, however, reveals a serious flaw with this ambition in that someone has to decide what constitutes a 'better' or 'happier' world and also what behaviours are worthy of reward. We could end up with a Ministry of Happiness run by psychologists in a world with no dissent and no challenge to authority.

Skinner and behaviourism were both enormously important. Skinner was voted the most influential psychologist of the twentieth century by other psychologists (Dittman, 2002). The methodological approach associated with behaviourism, which promoted 'a causal metaphysics, an experimental methodology based upon independent and dependent

FIGURE 2.5   The human Skinner box. Skinner applied his science to designing a living box for babies. Called the 'air crib', it provided a temperature- and humidity-controlled environment that was relatively dust free. It captured the public imagination because it looked like an attempt to mechanise child care but nothing could have been further from the truth, as confirmed by his daughter Deborah as an adult (see her article in *The Guardian*, Skinner-Buzan, 2004)

© Bettmann/CORBIS

GESTALT PSYCHOLOGY A school of psychology that began in Germany in the first half of the twentieth century. It proposed that an experience or behaviour can only be understood as a whole, not by understanding the individual constituent parts.

variables applied to a population and the use of statistics as the main analytical tool', is still used by the discipline as *the* benchmark for 'what a scientific psychology should be' (Harré, 2006: 8). The classes in research methods that you attend will no doubt confirm that this methodology is still very much alive and well in psychology.

Eventually, however, the influence of behaviourism itself began to give way. In Europe in particular, work in a more traditional psychological vein (with a focus on active mental processes) had continued throughout the period of behaviourist domination. **Frederic Bartlett's** (1886–1969) work on *Remembering* (1932) and **Jean Piaget's** (1896–1980) approach to cognitive development are good examples, as is the work of the Gestalt psychologists. Even in the midst of American behaviourism, influential theorists like **Edward Chace Tolman** (1886–1959) and **Clark Leonard Hull** (1884–1952) also promoted the idea that mental processes played a fundamental role in the determination of behaviour. Both acknowledged these processes as 'intervening variables' (so called because they intervened between the stimulus and response) in their respective behaviourist theories.

In the end, the demise of behaviourism was almost inevitable. It had always been problematic to draw conclusions about humans on the basis of animal studies. Animals often behaved in an apparently mindless fashion, but this needn't mean that humans were similarly without minds. The image of humans as pawns in the environment also seemed unnecessarily negative. It is a depressing view of humanity if we think of ourselves as being puppets that are manipulated by changes in our environment.

The most damning indictment of behaviourism was nonetheless painfully straightforward: it wasn't psychology. Psychology, after all, means the study of mind, so abandoning that concept really did create a problem and limit the areas that psychology could investigate. We have seen throughout this chapter that psychology has tended (for mainly methodological reasons) to sidestep what may be its key subject matter: the subjective world of mental phenomena. But behaviourism took this avoidance to its logical conclusion. In the final section we will briefly consider modern attempts to put this right.

2.6 MODERN PSYCHOLOGY: COGNITIVE SCIENCE, HUMANISM AND THE RETURN OF THE SOCIAL SCIENCES

In the middle of the last century behaviourism ran out of steam, and it became obvious that we needed to look at the thought processes that intervene between stimulus and response. It was no longer enough to see us as puppets just responding to whatever stimulus came our way. Cognitive science (the study of mental processes) took over from behaviourism as the dominant paradigm in psychology around 1960 and it remains dominant to this day. A benefit of this is that cognitive science's tendency to exploit the behaviourist experimental model, combined with a focus on information processing, has made psychology look like a 'natural science of the mental' once again. It has made a significant contribution to the discipline's progress in recent years (the cognitive approach is dealt with in Section B).

On the downside, many psychologists would argue that cognitive science has again avoided the psychological world of subjective, mental phenomena in order to study a whole host of supposedly more permanent mental and causal structures which are said to lie beneath. These structures have various names – traits, attitudes, schemas, personalities, and so on: the list is very long. And unlike the subjective, mental phenomena themselves, these entities are hypothesised to have an enduring existence, to be experimentally manipulable in a controlled fashion, and hence to possess a substance which allows mathematical analysis and description. The problem is that nobody has ever proved their existence. Harré launches a critique along precisely these lines:

> People, for the purposes of psychology, are not internally complex. They have no parts. . . . There are no mental states other than the private thoughts and feelings people are aware of from time to time. There are no mental mechanisms by which a person's powers and skills are implemented, except the occasional private rehearsals for action in which we sometimes engage. The whole top heavy apparatus of . . . cognitive psychology is at worst a fantasy and at best a metaphor. (Harré, 1998: 15)

A related critique focuses on methods. Clearly, natural science has progressed a long way since Newton; yet despite its long-held desire to emulate these disciplines, psychology has not moved with it (Harré, 1999). The experimental methodology based upon independent and dependent variables we described earlier is, in truth, an invention of psychology (Harré, 2006) which is not properly reflective of any natural science model.

Psychologists are nonetheless resourceful creatures and two distinct responses to this situation are now discernible. The experimental and quantitative tradition in psychology has, for example, developed a number of statistics and techniques which are closely related to modern developments in physics and chemistry (Gelman & Hill, 2007). Huge advances in both structural and functional brain scanning technology have also allowed *cognitive neuroscience* to link subjective mental phenomena to brain function (and physiology) in ways that would have amazed Wundt and James (Frith, 2007).

A second response has involved the re-emergence of more 'humanitarian' values and methods within psychology. This began with the humanist movement in the 1960s, which offered itself as a 'third force' in psychology. It aimed to provide an antidote to the negativity which seemed to characterise behaviourism and Freudian psychoanalysis. Most associated with **Abraham Maslow** (1908–1970) and **Carl Rogers** (1902–1987), humanism suggested that the subjective mental phenomena (or 'reality') which psychology had so often ignored were actually the primary guide for human behaviour. Behaviour was not *caused*; rather, it was motivated by each individual's desire to *self-actualise* and reach their full potential. Humanism stalled, however, primarily because it failed to come up with a method of collecting data about people and ultimately because its uncritical and positive assessment of humans felt more like a form of wishful thinking than a serious scientific endeavour.

In the last 30 years, the social scientific model has nonetheless returned to psychology in a more rigorous fashion. To a large extent, this movement continues to be inspired by suspicions that natural science may be inappropriate as a model for psychology. There is a renewed belief that the subjective world of meaningful human experience (look at Table 2.1 again!) really *is* psychology's rightful subject matter. A proliferation of qualitative research methods has duly emerged to interrogate particular aspects of this extraordinarily diverse, and very human, world of life (see Willig & Stainton Rogers, 2007).

2.7 CONCLUSION

This is an exciting time to be studying psychology. As we've just discussed, the natural and social scientific models are showing marked signs of convergence. Psychologists are connecting human meaning-making and creativity to brain function in ever greater detail (Edelman, 2006). Psychology is now armed with a range of quantitative and qualitative methods, as well as some very advanced technologies, which all satisfy the scientific ideal (in a range of different ways). Research which deliberately 'mixes' methods traditionally associated with the natural and social sciences has also become very fashionable (Creswell & Plano Clark, 2007). Psychology finally seems to be accepting its position at the divide between the natural and social sciences, and acknowledging that to take full advantage of this position it really *has to* retain a foot in both these (increasingly connected) camps. Now comes your chance to contribute …

2.8 CHAPTER SUMMARY

Modern psychology traces its immediate origins to the late nineteenth century, when Wilhelm Wundt created his laboratory in Leipzig. Since that time, the discipline has moved to and fro between conceptions of psychology as (1) a natural science and (2) a social science. Much has hinged on the question of focus: to what extent should psychology study the mind and our experiences of the world, and to what extent should it focus on what is externally observable and measurable? Over the past 150 years psychology has developed a range of methods, approaches and measures, yet the central questions remain.

(?) DISCUSSION QUESTIONS

As we have seen, psychology has developed through debate between those who believe the discipline should be modelled on natural science and those who believe it should be modelled on social science. What arguments can you see for and against each of these positions? Where do you stand yourself on this debate?

What are the implications of the two views above for (1) what topics or phenomena should be studied, and (2) the methods that should be used?

SUGGESTIONS FOR FURTHER READING

Benjamin, L.T. (1996). *A history of psychology*. New York: McGraw-Hill. If you want a comprehensive account, there are a number of large texts designed for US courses on the history of psychology of which this is one.

Fancher, R.E. (1996). *Pioneers of psychology* (3rd edn). New York: W.W. Norton. One of the best texts to pick up to explore the beginnings of psychology. This book looks at key ideas and key people chapter by chapter, and provides very useful background to several other chapters in this text.

Miller, G. (1966). *Psychology: the science of mental life*. London: Penguin. Another text that has stood the test of time, this also covers the pioneers of psychology with some interesting insights into their lives and ideas.

Richards, G. (2010). *Putting psychology in its place: critical historical perspectives* (3rd edn). Hove: Routledge.

Tyson, P., Jones, D., & Elcock, J. (2011). *Psychology in social context: issues and debates*. London: BPS Blackwell. A readable text written for the UK market.

Still want more? For links to online resources relevant to this chapter and a quiz to test your understanding, visit the companion website at edge.sagepub.com/banyard2e

PART 2

PSYCHOLOGY STUDY SKILLS

How to Learn, How to Study

Burns, T. & Sinfield, S.

We're not born knowing how to study – these learning and studying strategies will help you make the most of the study aspects of university.

Introduction

In this chapter we bring together arguments about learning with an exploration of how to study – and how to study at university. We begin by asking you to examine your past learning experiences – and consider a multi-sensory approach to learning and how to harness this. We explore when, where and how to study – with a focus on how universities organise their teaching and learning; assessment is tackled in Chapters 11 and 12. As always – think: what do I know? What do I need? How will I harness this information to promote my active learning and study success?

Past learning experiences

Before moving on, we'd like you to think back to your own past learning experiences. In particular, think about the conditions that helped you to learn – and the things that got in the way of your learning. Make brief notes to answer the questions below – then read what another student has said.

- Think back to a previous successful learning experience. It does not have to have been at school – it could be learning to drive or sky dive. Why was it successful – why did you learn?
- Now think back to an unsuccessful learning experience. What was it? Why did little or no learning take place?
- Looking over these good and bad experiences of yours – can you sum up: 'Things that help learning to happen' and 'Things that prevent learning'?
- If you wish, use your notes to free write quickly on 'Things that help me learn – and things that stop me from learning'.
- Once you have completed your own thoughts, compare your thoughts with those written by another student, below.

> Things that helped me to learn were an interesting course with a good teacher – you know, one that has enthusiasm for the subject and lots of energy. I seem to work better if I feel that the tutor likes me. It also helps when I actually *want* to do the course; where I have chosen it for myself and I actually want to learn. When I'm committed, I turn up and do the work – because I want to. The last course I did, there was a really supportive atmosphere – I felt challenged and stretched – but it was also safe to make mistakes, there were people around to help. Nobody laughed at you or made you feel a fool.
>
> The worst learning experience I had was at school. I had to be there – it was compulsory – but I never really saw the point of it. I just felt so powerless all the time. I never knew what we were doing or why or when or how. It was a nightmare and one of the reasons that I left school the minute I could!

Do you recognise some of yourself in the responses? What might this tell you? One thing we can see is that if we are going to be successful when learning, then we must want to learn: we must be interested and motivated.

On the other hand, what seems to stop people from learning is feeling unmotivated, confused, unhappy, fearful and powerless. These are some of the reasons that compulsory education does not work for some people.

TIP

Whenever you start to study, sit down and write your own personal goals for that course. Put them on Post-its and display them over your desk. Cut out pictures that represent your success to you and stick these up also. Use these to keep you motivated and interested.

What is learning?

Learning is not about the empty student coming to university to be filled with knowledge and wisdom – though some people might wish that it was! Learning is active and interactive; it is a process. Learning involves engaging with ideas – and engaging with other people as they engage with ideas (Wenger-Trayner, 2014). An early author on study skills, Devine (1987), describes learning as a series of processes:

- gathering new ideas and information
- recording them
- organising them
- making sense of and understanding them
- remembering them
- using them.

Learning is about gathering new ideas and information – engaging with and acquiring information from classes, lectures, seminars, tutorials, discussions, practical activities, reading (textbooks, journals, newspapers and more). It is notemaking – recording what is important. We encounter information in many forms, in many places and at different times – we have to reorganise the information to make sense of it for ourselves and remember it. Finally we have to be able to use the information – we have to be able to discuss it with other people and use it in our assignments. Learning also changes us, once truly learned something cannot be unlearned – we have crossed a threshold and become someone slightly different (Land, 2010).

—TIPS—

- Before you can forget your lecture or class, don't rush home, go to the canteen and talk about it.
- Get a study partner or form a study group: discuss lectures and seminars. Discuss your reading.
- Write before you know or understand it all.
- Discuss your writing.

Harness a multi-sensory approach to learning

So learning is active and social and it also involves all the senses. If you went to a Montessori primary school, you would already have been encouraged to see, hear, say and do in order to learn effectively; for we learn some of what we see, we learn some of what we hear, we learn when we speak or discuss (when we say) and we learn when we do (when we make something or engage in an activity) – but it is argued that we can learn most when we see, hear, say *and* do. Here we explore visual (sight based), auditory (sound based) and kinaesthetic (touch, feel or movement based) learning.

- *Sight*: to learn by seeing, enjoy learning by reading and by watching television, film or video. Enjoy watching your lecturer and seeing how they convey information – how they show you what is important. Use pictures in your learning and revision activities: draw cartoons and pictures to illustrate your points, draw pattern notes, put in colour, and put in memory-jogging cartoon images or visuals. (See also Chapters 5 and 6.)
- *Sound*: to learn by hearing and speaking, enjoy learning through listening and joining in discussions. You will learn as you explain things to other people. Make audiotapes to support your learning using songs, rhymes and jingles that you write yourself as learning and revision aids. Tape yourself and sing along. Talk yourself through your assignment.
- *Feel*: to harness the kinaesthetic, enjoy practical learning activities, from making something, to performing a science experiment to role-playing. Make charts and patterns of the things you want to remember – role-play ideas or act them out in some way. Care about your subject – find meaning and value in your course.

Activity

Watch, listen, learn: Barbara Oakley has given an interesting TED Talk on 'How to learn' (https://youtu.be/O96fE1E-rf8). Watch the video and make notes whilst thinking, 'How will I use this information to become a better student?' Reflect: How much of the information did I hear? How much did I see? How much of it did I feel was right?

Studying: when, where and how

> I'm a mum, I work, I've got my parents to look after … I guess I'm organised!

Studying is more formalised learning – and it tends to be hard work. We are going to explore when, where and how to study and provide you with very practical advice and tips.

When should I study?

> I know we are supposed to start work weeks before the deadline, but I usually start two or three days before.

Many students do not start work until a deadline really frightens them – they need the hit of adrenalin to get them over their study fears and into working. The trouble is that whilst adrenalin is great for getting you out of a burning building – it does not help you develop the depth and breadth you need for university level thinking and writing.

> The best tip I ever got was to do at least half an hour's work each day. This has put me on top of all my studies … And usually once I start I get a little bit more done and I feel so much better.
>
> I know what I should do, I really know … but I just can't face it.

Studying can feel unbearable, un-do-able, like climbing a mountain. But there is more than one way to face a mountain. For some a mountain is so large and danger-ous that they are afraid of it. For some a mountain is an exciting challenge. For some a mountain is just a thing to be tackled sensibly one step at a time. If you normally fear or dread your assignments – change the way you see them. Adopt a 'one step at a time' approach. Look at assignment questions at the beginning of a course. Think about the question before lectures and classes and before you start reading. Break the question down into manageable chunks. Read about one 'chunk' at a time. Write one paragraph at a time – then revise and improve as you do more reading.

> I never seem to feel like studying.

Nobody leaps out of bed in the morning going, 'Wheee – this is the day that I tackle that huge assignment!' So do not rely on feeling like studying. You have to make the time to study – you need a system. Every university student has to work out for themselves just how much time they are prepared to give to their studies – but it should be 35 hours or more each week. You have to decide how much work you are prepared to put in, to get the results – the grades – that you want. Study five days a week – plan and use your time – even when you don't feel like it.

When planning out your time think about:

- *Best time of day?* Are you a morning, afternoon or evening person? Try to fit your study times around your maximum performance times. Work with your strengths.
- *Travel time*: reading on the bus or train is a really effective use of time.
- *Friends and family time*: your studies are important – but most of us would like to have friends and family still talking to us when our studies are over. Help them to help you be a successful student.
- *Housework time*: we need to keep our homes at least sanitary. Watch out though – housework and all chores can become excellent excuses for not working. They become displacement activities – sometimes it feels as though it is easier to completely re-build the house rather than write an essay!
- *Paid work time*: these days we need to earn money whilst we study – we have to work – and still fit in 35 hours of study each week. Sometimes universities help by fitting lectures and other classes into one or two days a week. Beware – this does not mean that all your studying can fit into two days a week! Remember you have to give 12 to 16 hours to classes – and another 20 or so hours to independent study – *each week*. If you cannot do this, you will be in trouble.
- *Rest and relaxation time*: studying is hard work – it can also be very stressful. It is important to get sufficient rest whilst you study and it is useful to build stress relief activities – dancing, exercise, gym, meditation, massage, yoga – into your timetables right at the beginning of your studies.

—TIPS—

- **Find paid work at your university – this helps you be there more.**
- **Join your university gym – use it at least once a week.**

- *Prioritise time*: make lists and prioritise tasks. Keep a diary – note when you are going to read; note which assignment you are writing – when.

- *Study timetables*: timetables give you a strong guide to your work – if you keep to them. But more than that, without timetables you may feel that every time you are not working you ought to be studying. You may not do that studying, but you worry – and this exhausts you. Eventually it may feel that your whole life is work, work, work. Something will have to go – and it could be your studies! Use the timetables at the end of this chapter – plan when you will study – and when you will not study.

Where to study

Everyone deserves a nice place to study, but real life is not always like that; sometimes we just have to adapt to what we have and make it work. Here are some tips about making a study space work for you.

- Negotiate a space with family or flatmates. Creating a study space helps everyone in your life – including you – realise just how important your studies are.
- A good place to study needs light and air – you need to see and breathe – but does not necessarily have to be a completely quiet place. Work out what works for you.
- You will need space to lay out your work, pin up your timetables, deadlines and notes. Have your textbooks out and open.
- Pin up all the new words that you are learning, immerse yourself in your learning.
- Do not tidy your work away. Having your work visible keeps it alive in your mind whereas putting it all away can give the impression that you're finished.
- Have pens and pencils, also highlighters, a stapler and staples, paper clips, correction fluid, Post-its, coloured pens – and all sorts of different sizes of paper. Play around with materials and colour, get an injection of energy and enthusiasm.

Practise being positive: 'Now I am working', 'I enjoy being a student'. Avoid those old negative thoughts: 'I don't want to be here', 'This is too hard'. Negative thoughts have a negative effect – positive thoughts have a positive effect. Give 100% whenever you sit down to study. Act as if you and your studies are important – they are – so are you.

What other students have said:

> It felt really good having my own study space. It made me feel like a real student.
>
> I felt that at last I could settle down to some real work.
>
> I felt a bit frightened at first – you know? Like now I couldn't put it off any longer! I'd have to take it seriously.

> Sometimes I use my space to sort of trick myself into working. I think, I'll just sit there for a minute … Next thing I know I've been working away for an hour and I feel really good.
>
> I felt guilty at having to cut myself off from the kids. It just felt so selfish. I have to work really hard at still giving them some time.
>
> I used to get so frustrated; it was like every time I sat down to work they would start demanding things from me. Now we all sit down to work at the same time – even if they are just crayoning or reading a storybook. This has helped us all feel better.
>
> I still like going to the library to work – but it's great having a proper place for my stuff at home. It really does help.

Experiment with working at home, in the library and when you travel – being a commuter adds hours of study time to your week, if you use it. But whether you want to work in a library or on a bus, you will also need a study space at home.

TIP

If you have children, try to make a family study time – so you all work together.

How to study

University is supposed to be a full-time occupation – using up to 35–40 hours of your time per week. You are supposed to be studying and learning full time, through lectures, seminars, tutorials, the virtual learning environment (VLE) and through your independent study. Here's how:

The lecture

One lecturer plus a large group of students – can be 150 or more. The lecturer is an expert, a researcher at the cutting edge of the subject. The lecturer gives a short-cut to key information – and successful students make notes – and use those notes to seed further reading, thought and writing. Always prepare before you attend a lecture. Always think – what is it about? What do I know already? Why this topic? How will it help me with my assignment?

The seminar

A seminar usually consists of a lecturer plus 10–30 students. A seminar is supposed to seed your thinking and develop your ideas through discussion – it is active learning. Join in the discussions. Prepare beforehand: read, watch or write what you are supposed to.

Learn seminar survival strategies: know how to present your opinions assertively, not aggressively; learn how to interrupt the person who never stops talking; and learn how to draw out quiet people who may actually have much to offer. Don't worry whether people are making friends with you – you make friends with other people.

The tutorial

A tutorial is like the seminar but with one tutor to four or five students. There is definitely no hiding place in a tutorial. You will have to be prepared and you will have to join in.

The VLE

Universities include virtual, blended or e-learning experiences as part of their teaching and learning practices. Find out how your course is going to be delivered – and how to make the most of it. Even though the information is 'virtual' – the work is still real – and the learning is still social and interactive.

Be prepared to join in with online conversations about the work. If you are expected to post comments or blogs in the VLE – do so; and remember to read and 'like' the comments left by your peers – be supportive, encouraging and friendly. See also Chapter 10.

Independent learning

In the UK we 'read for' our degrees – that is, our thinking and learning is seeded by lectures and seminars – and then we are expected to read and read and read. There is much emphasis on independent learning. That is, you will be expected to follow up ideas in various ways, including reading around a subject, on your own and on your own initiative. For more on academic reading, see also Chapter 4.

TIP

Be an interdependent learner: have a study partner or group.

A beginner's guide to taking control of your studies

This whole book is designed to get you studying in more successful ways, but here are some very practical things to do right now.

Want it: you will not learn anything unless you want to. Know what you want from each course that you are studying. Know how your life will be changed when you reach your goals.

TIP

Write your goals on Post-its and stick them up in your study space. Write your learning contract (below) for each course, module or unit that you do.

Get the overview (Chapter 11.1): read and understand the aims and the learning outcomes. Know what you have to do and learn to pass your course – and how you will be assessed.

Epistemology: every course has its own theory of knowledge – what counts as argument and evidence – its epistemology. Make sure you know the what, why and how of all your subjects. Read the journals to get a model of how to argue and write in your subject.

Be positive: just as an athlete will perform better if they think they can win – so a student will learn more if they can adopt positive attitudes; if your motivation runs low, act like a successful student, believe that you can succeed.

Pace yourself: work for an hour – take a break. We concentrate best in 15-minute bursts. When we study we have to get into the habit of regularly recharging our mental batteries to wake up our brains. We can do this by:

- taking a short rest
- changing what we do
- making the task very important
- making the task interesting, stimulating or more difficult.

Prioritise time: be strategic – do first the assignments that carry the most marks or whose deadlines are coming first.

Use time: we know students who sit down to study – out come the pens and paper – they get rearranged. Out come the books and the highlighters – they get rearranged. They go for a coffee. They go for a glass of water. They put one lot of books away and get out another set. They look at the clock – oh good! An hour has passed – they put their materials away. But they have done no work. Before you study – set goals. Afterwards – reflect. Make the learning conscious.

Worry about one assignment at a time: put up a set of shelves in your brain. Put all your different worries on the shelves. Learn to take down one thing at a time and give it your total concentration. When you have finished with that, put it back on the shelf and take down something else.

Be active: listen/read actively, asking questions as you go. What does it mean? Do I understand it? If not, what am I going to do about that? How does it connect with what I already know? How will I use it in my assignment?

Review actively: at the end of each study session — reflect on what you have read or heard.

TIP

Write a blog post at the end of every day.

Study partners and groups: for many, study is best when undertaken actively, interactively and socially; this is where a friend, study partner or a study group can be invaluable.

Don't end on a sour note: try not to end a study session on a problem — it is demotivating and it can make it that little bit harder to start studying again. Use a study partner, friend or online discussion space to talk it over.

Relaxation and dealing with stress: make time to rest, relax and let go of stress. When we are stressed our body releases cortisol — a hormone that has a direct impact on the brain causing the cortex to shrink — and adrenalin — the flight or fight hormone. The combination of these hormones eliminates short-term memory and produces the narrow, tunnel vision necessary for fight or flight. This might save our lives when escaping from a burning building, but works against us when studying where we need breadth and depth of vision.

TIPS

- Make a note of the problem and sleep on it — sometimes the solution comes to you when you wake up. But don't lie awake fretting all night; this does not solve the problem and you have made everything worse by losing sleep and gaining stress.
- Join the gym. Take up yoga. Practise meditation.

Organisation and time management: if you are now feeling overwhelmed by all your responsibilities as a student, try this five-step plan to tackling those worries — and getting things done:

1. List everything that you need to do: this may feel like a really bad idea and that you'll be even more frightened; but the opposite is true. Once you write the list, and you can see the reality of the 'problem', it becomes more manageable and less overwhelming.
2. Divide each big task that you have to do into smaller steps. So do not just put down: 'write essay'. Break it down: 'brainstorm question', 'read up on ...', 'write a paragraph on ...', etc.

3. Organise your big list into things that must be done now; soon; later.
4. Do one of the *now* tasks immediately and cross it off. You will instantly feel more calm and in control.
5. Prioritise your list and put it into a 'to do' order.
   (With thanks to our colleagues at Reading University.)

Still procrastinating? You have to be organised – you have to be methodical – do not procrastinate – just do it! Try this activity suggested by Michelle Reid of Reading University. Work with a group of friends, especially if they are fellow students. You will need Post-it notes and pens.

Activity

The time sponge

Everybody takes one large Post-it and writes their biggest time sponge at the top (a time sponge is anything you find yourself doing instead of working – checking your phone, messaging friends, etc.).

Everybody passes their Post-it to the person on their left. You all read someone else's time sponge problem and write a possible solution.

Pass to the left again and write another solution to another problem.

Keep going until you have run out of space on the Post-its.

Everybody takes a turn to read out the problem on the Post-it they have been left with – and the various solutions offered.

Everybody says one thing they will now do differently after listening to all the sponges and solutions.

When planning your time – think about these:

- *Study timetable*: this is a 24/7 timetable (24 hours a day, seven days a week) that covers how many hours per day go to non-study and how many go to your studies. It is where you can plan which subjects to study and for how long. It takes some trial and error and experiment to get this right – so do give it that time.
- *Assignment timetable*: this is a record of all the assignment deadlines that are coming up either in a term, a semester or across a whole year. Fill in deadlines and pin it up on your wall and place a copy in your folder and diary. Never let a deadline take you by surprise.
- *Exam timetable*: similar to the assignment timetable, this is a record of all the exams you will be taking. Note dates, times and locations. It is all too easy to turn up at the wrong time, on the wrong day and in the wrong place!

- *Revision timetable*: at the appropriate time, each student should devise their own revision timetable where they work out when they are going to test their knowledge and practise for the exams that they are going to sit

Photocopy the timetables below: experiment with using them to help you focus on your work and get the most from your time.

Summary

We have looked at learning and considered when, where and how to study; some authors call this SHAPE: style, habit, attitude, preference and experience. The trouble is that we may stay with unsuccessful study habits even when they do not work, just because they are that – a habit or a preference. None of the good practice in this chapter will mean anything unless and until you put the ideas into practice. Until you push through your discomfort and learn new, successful practices.

Further reading

BBC Scotland's Brain Smart website: www.bbc.co.uk/scotland/brainsmart/.
Devine, T.G. (1987) *Teaching Study Skills*. Newton, MA: Allyn and Bacon.
Wenger-Trayner, E. (2014) Key note at ALDinHE Conference, Huddersfield University, 2014.

Activity

Two key things to do right now: learning contract and timetables

1 Write a learning contract
Reflect on what you have read so far and write a brief learning contract saying what you want from your course: what you're prepared to do to achieve your goals, what might stop you, and what's in it for you (what will change about your life when you achieve your own goals).

- What I want from this course is …
- What I'm prepared to do to make this happen is … (Use the six steps to success like this … Build on my visual strategies like this … Visit the library … Write for half an hour every day …)
- What might stop me is … (Note the issues in your life: work, family, friends … How might these affect your studies? What are you going to do about that?)
- What's in it for me (WiiFM) is … (Knowing WiiFM can help motivate you on those cold, wet days when it feels too hard to get out of bed …).

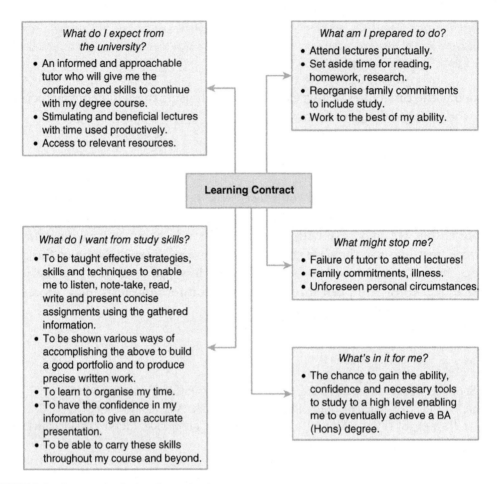

What do I expect from the university?
- An informed and approachable tutor who will give me the confidence and skills to continue with my degree course.
- Stimulating and beneficial lectures with time used productively.
- Access to relevant resources.

What am I prepared to do?
- Attend lectures punctually.
- Set aside time for reading, homework, research.
- Reorganise family commitments to include study.
- Work to the best of my ability.

Learning Contract

What do I want from study skills?
- To be taught effective strategies, skills and techniques to enable me to listen, note-take, read, write and present concise assignments using the gathered information.
- To be shown various ways of accomplishing the above to build a good portfolio and to produce precise written work.
- To learn to organise my time.
- To have the confidence in my information to give an accurate presentation.
- To be able to carry these skills throughout my course and beyond.

What might stop me?
- Failure of tutor to attend lectures!
- Family commitments, illness.
- Unforeseen personal circumstances.

What's in it for me?
- The chance to gain the ability, confidence and necessary tools to study to a high level enabling me to eventually achieve a BA (Hons) degree.

FIGURE 2.1   An example of a learning contract

2 Fill in your timetables

Take some time to complete the following timetables – and experiment with them – see how to use them to organise and motivate yourself.

─TIP─

We have put in *two* blank 24/7 timetables – complete one as a *plan*; complete the other as a *review*. Then decide how you will need to adjust your plans to be more successful.

Filling in the 24-hour timetable:

- Fill in the first one, indicating when you expect to work, sleep, do chores and so forth. Think about the time that you have left. Put in times for study and relaxation. Think about it – are you being realistic? Make sure that you are not under- or over-working yourself. Run that programme for a few weeks.

- After a couple of weeks, review your success in keeping to the study times that you set and in achieving the goals that you had in mind.
- Change your timetable to fit in with reality. Use the second blank timetable for this.
- Remember to do this every term, semester, year.

Time	Monday	Tuesday	Wednesday	Thursday	Friday	Saturday	Sunday
1.00							
2.00							
3.00							
4.00							
5.00							
6.00							
7.00							
8.00							
9.00							
10.00							
11.00							
12.00							
13.00							
14.00							
15.00							
16.00							
17.00							
18.00							
19.00							
20.00							
21.00							
22.00							
23.00							
24.00							

FIGURE 2.2   Blank 24-hour timetable – plan

Time	Monday	Tuesday	Wednesday	Thursday	Friday	Saturday	Sunday
1.00							
2.00							
3.00							
4.00							
5.00							
6.00							
7.00							
8.00							
9.00							
10.00							
11.00							
12.00							
13.00							
14.00							
15.00							
16.00							
17.00							
18.00							
19.00							
20.00							
21.00							
22.00							
23.00							
24.00							

FIGURE 2.3 Blank 24-hour timetable – review and improve

Events and deadlines				
Write down the dates of the following events each term:				
	Course 1	Course 2	Course 3	Course 4
Course title				
Exam(s)				
Essay deadline(s)				
Laboratory report deadline(s)				
Seminar presentations				
Field trips/visits				
Project report or exhibition deadlines				
Bank holidays or other 'days off'				
Other events (specify)				

FIGURE 2.4   Course events and deadlines timetable

	Term plan – what is happening over your terms/semester?						
	Monday	Tuesday	Wednesday	Thursday	Friday	Saturday	Sunday
Week 1							
Week 2							
Week 3							
Week 4							
Week 5							
Week 6							
Week 7							
Week 8							
Week 9							
Week 10							
Week 11							
Week 12							
Longer term deadlines:							

FIGURE 2.5   Term plan timetable

Keep a weekly plan: key events and activities each week							
Week Number:	Monday	Tuesday	Wednesday	Thursday	Friday	Saturday	Sunday
8am							
9am							
10am							
11am							
12 noon							
1pm							
2pm							
3pm							
4pm							
5pm							
6pm							
7pm							
8pm							
9pm							
10pm							
11pm							
12 midnight							
1am							

FIGURE 2.6   Weekly plan timetable

PART
3

REFLECTION

How to be Reflective

Burns, T. & Sinfield, S.

Without reflection there is no learning – it is as simple as that. Reflect and make your learning conscious – self-test to check that you have remembered – or you forget everything you have heard or read or seen.

Introduction

Welcome to this reflective learning section where we focus on the learning log and blog. As you have gathered by now – this is not the only section on reflection in this book. We ask you to revise after every study session – to revise your notes in order to remember them, and to revise your own progress in your PDP and CV files. This form of reflection and self-testing is essential if we are to learn anything at all. Learning is not random. We need to take control of our learning by active goal setting – active learning – and active reflection.

This chapter looks particularly at the learning log and blog – you may also want to re-visit Chapter 2: How to learn, how to study; Chapter 5: How to make the best notes and especially Chapter 13.1: PDP and HEAR. Whilst these chapters are separate, their message is uniform: in terms of successful academic practice, reflection is something that you should be actively engaged in, for without review, there is no learning. In this chapter we are going to suggest that you keep a reflective learning diary or blog to make your learning more effective and successful.

What is reflective learning?

Reflective learning involves a process of thinking over what you have done – of making your learning conscious – of actively revisiting and testing what you have learned. It is part of the active learning that we practise throughout this book. With each chapter we ask you to think about what you need from the chapter itself – to set your own goals. Within each chapter we present information – supported by activities, questions and discussion that are all designed to get you to engage actively with the information. After the chapter we want you to actively review the learning that has taken place for you: *What did I want from this? What have I gained? Where and how will I use what I have learned?* And right here in this chapter we suggest that you blog about your learning, because telling others what you have done is the best way to revise and learn yourself. All the evidence on learning emphasises that no matter how active all your other learning practices are, without this active reflection, there will be no learning. In this chapter we are going to explore how to formalise this active reflective learning in a learning log or blog.

─TIP─

Check out this blog post on how to learn – make notes of the new information there, and on how you will use it to develop your study practices – then blog about it: http://bigthink.com/neurobonkers/assessing-the-evidence-for-the-one-thing-you-never-get-taught-in-school-how-to-learn.

Beyond the revision cycle

Active revision equals successful study – it is as simple as that. We hear students complain about being asked to reflect on their learning – it feels like doing it all again – it feels like hard work. But if this is not done, then no learning has taken place. All those hours sitting in lecture theatres – all those hours reading – and wasted. Now that is what we call hard work – hard work is wasted work – because without revision, nothing was learned in the first place:

- Without a revision cycle we forget 98% in three weeks.
- Revision starts from day one – and should be ongoing. We need to actively choose what to learn from every lecture, seminar or piece of reading.
- This is different from exam revision – which means revising to pass an exam; this is learning for life (though if you do want to know how to revise for and pass exams, see Chapter 12.6).
- A reflective learning log or blog is a form of reflective writing that will help you to understand, learn and write about your course material.

Why be reflective?

Ongoing review of what you are learning – and why – puts you in control of your own development. This is essential for your learning and pragmatically it will enable you to produce your assignments. This is why more universities are encouraging students to produce learning logs or blogs – or to engage in PDP (Chapter 13.1). It is not some exquisite form of torture devised to make your life miserable – they are hoping to demonstrate in practice that when you actively reflect – you do learn more … but this only works if you engage with some level of enthusiasm. Don't just go through the motions. Reflective learning is for you – not the university. Set your own goals, reflect on what you have learned and take control of your own learning.

How: Keep a reflective learning diary

Your reflective learning diary, log, journal, sketchbook or blog is your own analytical, detailed and yet concise record of your studies. The process of completing this diary allows you to test your own learning as you make it active and conscious; this improves the quantity and quality of your learning.

Writing your diary should follow swiftly upon a study session – and the writing itself should be purposeful and concise. As said, we have had students complain that it feels like doing all the work again. But in many ways – that is the point.

By reflecting on a study session, you are quickly doing all the work again – and thus you are learning it. Without doing this activity – you will forget it. So, although it may feel frustrating – it is learning. and without it you might as well not have bothered going to that lecture or that class.

Most recently we have asked our students to do this active reflection in a blog – using an online writing space like WordPress (https://wordpress.com/) where you can create your own website for free. We want students to make their learning conscious in words and pictures – and we hope that they will also read each other's blogs and comment upon them. This encourages deep reflection. It also encourages dialogue between learners so that the learning becomes social and interactive. Our experience is that when students do this, not only do they learn more – they also develop their ability to write about what they learn – and therefore their assignment grades radically improve.

The structure outlined in the beginner's guide to reflective learning below works with our students; once you have tried it, re-shape it so that it takes the form or shape that works best for you.

TIPS

- Keep a diary or a blog for each module that you do.
- Spend a few minutes after each study period – a class, lecture or independent study – completing your journal.
- When completing your learning diaries – make conscious what you remember – follow up what you didn't understand.

A beginner's guide to reflective learning

This reflection has ten parts: what, why, learned, illustrations, reaction, successes and problems, link to assignment, reading, writing, and goal setting. It does not have to be a rigid thing – experiment until you find a structure that best meets your needs and suits your learning approach.

Write your diaries in beautiful notebooks that inspire you to use them – on blog spaces that you have customised to reflect who you are (see also the section on blogging to learn in Chapter 10) – use notebooks for some modules and blogs for others.

Write briefly in short paragraphs – or use a pattern note format. The important thing is to be concise and focused. Use key words and phrases – and colour and cartoons to make them memorable.

- *What*: make *brief notes* of what you did – the lecture or seminar that you attended, the reading that you have done.
- *Why*: make brief analytical notes. Why did you do it? If a book, why did you read it? If a lecture or seminar, what was the lecturer trying to achieve? Why did they run that session? What did you want from it? How was it useful? What learning outcomes did it cover? What part of the assignment question is it helping you with? Know why you are doing something and you move from being a passive to an active learner.
- *Learned*: make brief notes on all that you think that you learned from the lecture, class or reading. These notes are where you make your learning conscious, it is an instant form of self-testing, which improves both the quantity and quality of your learning. When we do not do this we are in danger of leaving the learning behind as we walk away from that lecture or close that book. Make this section of your review detailed, but concise.

TIPS

- Think – what part of my assignment will this help me with?
- Write to make it interesting for your reader – this helps you take control of the material for yourself.
- Diaries and blogs get easier with practice – and develop your academic writing.

- *Illustrations*: think about what you have learned and try to draw it in diagrams or simple cartoons. This extra engagement with the ideas will help you understand what you are learning. Make your drawing unusual, funny, bizarre – and this will make it memorable. With blogs, you can upload photographs of your drawings or you can find images online that bring the ideas to life.
- *Reaction*: make brief notes on your emotional response to the activity – notice the affective dimension to your learning. This allows you to build a picture of yourself as a learner and as a student. This reflection allows you to notice what and how you like to learn, the subjects and topics that you enjoy – and the ones that you do not like so much. This means that you can choose modules and teaching and learning strategies that suit you. It might also help you choose the right sort of job for you (see also Chapter 13.2).

TIPS

- Be honest. You will not get a true picture of your own likes, dislikes and preferences if you paint a rosy picture of yourself.
- Use the discoveries that you make here to inform your subject choices – and your job choices.
- Use the information to help you refine your own learning style.

Burns, T. & Sinfield, S.

- *Successes and problems*: it is all too easy just to focus on our failings – so note your successes, too. What did you do well? What preparation had you done that made the session more successful or easier for you? What bits didn't you understand? Which bits were confusing or difficult? What did you do about that? How did you solve the problems that you encountered as you studied?
- *Link to assignment*: consciously think – how will I use this in the assignments? Make notes. Again – this is vital – without this sort of active reflection, you might forget why you were making those notes in the first place – you will not use the information in your assignments.
- *Reading*: what will you now read? Why? When? You are supposed to read about the theories and concepts that you hear about in lectures and classes. Evidence suggests that if you do the active reflection suggested here – you will see the point of the reading and actually do it. If you do not – you will not.
- *Writing*: what will you now write – a sample paragraph for one of your assignments? Get into the habit of writing briefly after every class. Obviously the log and blog are part of that writing. But it can also be good to draft rough paragraphs for the module assignments – gaps in the paragraphs show you what else you need to find out – they show you what to read.
- *Goal setting*: make brief notes about anything else that you will do next … nothing will ever give you 'all you need to know' on a subject. Therefore, you should always be thinking: what next?

---TIPS---

- Make this reflective process a habit – just do it – do not waste time moaning and resisting!
- Make it creative and fun – enjoy writing for a reader – illustrate your online blog with photographs of your notes and other pictures.
- Produce a sketchbook of ideas, thoughts and learning – use a real sketchbook that you draw in and illustrate in many different wondrous ways.
- See the Visual Directions website for advice on reflective learning, sketchbooks and podcasts from staff and students – and beautiful images of what a journal could look like: http://cltad-web2.arts.ac.uk/cetl/visual-directions/
- We practise what we preach and write our own blogs: *Becomingeducational* on WordPress and *Lastrefugelmu* on Blogger – you are welcome to search them out and see how we do it!!

‘ Without doing my review, I wouldn't even have understood the class, let alone remembered it! ’

Case study: Chloe's blog

Chloe Noble was one of our students this year. She initially really hated the idea of blogging her learning – in fact one of her first blog posts was called: Why I really hate blogging! However, as time went on, Chloe not only used her blog to reflect on her learning – she developed her blog into something wonderful and inspiring.

Chloe developed 'challenges' to issue to other students – we really liked her 30 day drawing challenge in which several students in our class took part – and which was used by students from around the world. Chloe started to put together video diaries for her future self – and she developed short tutorials teaching people how to draw: You don't have to be able to draw to make visual notes (https://noblechloe.wordpress.com/first-year-learning-logs/visual-notes/who-says-you-need-to-be-able-to-draw-to-make-visual-notes/).

Chloe has produced one of the most inspiring blogs that we have seen – and it demonstrates some key things about being a successful student – you don't need to like the idea of something to be able to do it. You don't need to be automatically good at something to be able to do it … You do need to overcome your own resistance. You need to get past seeing things only as a problem. Once you do that – you can do anything.

No matter how much you dislike the idea of blogging to learn – try to see the opportunities for you in it – and make it work for you. Here's a link to Chloe's blog: https://noblechloe.wordpress.com/.

Summary

An ongoing review system will allow you to make your learning conscious such that you revise and remember. Reinforce your active learning by using reflective learning diaries and blogs – where you enjoy writing about and illustrating your learning. This improves both the quantity and the quality of your learning and it will improve your academic writing and other assignments. This process should help you to notice any problems that you are having understanding or learning the material – so that you do something about that. You should also start to notice the subjects, situations and learning strategies that suit you best – which may help you choose a job that will actually suit you. Finally – if you really want to check whether it works – why not write a brief reflection on your engagement with every chapter in this book?

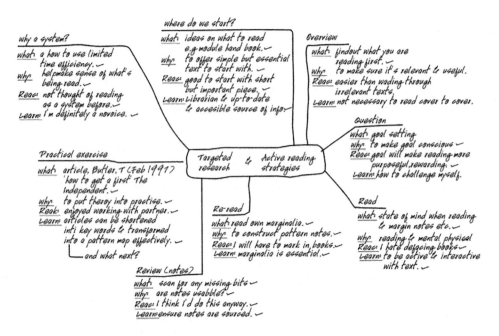

FIGURE 8.1   Example of a student's learning log on 'How to survive academic reading'

Activity

Get blogging

Use this reflective learning template to help you structure your own reflective learning logs or blogs. As you get used to writing and illustrating these, you will find that you start to adapt the template to your own style – but remember to always think about how a study session will be used in your assignments – and always illustrate your logs and blogs – this makes them memorable – and appealing.

Reflective learning diary or blog – template	
What	Make brief notes of what you did: the lecture or seminar that you attended, the reading that you have done.
Why	Make brief analytical notes: why did you do it? How was it useful? What learning outcomes did it cover? What part of the assignment question is it helping you with? Knowing why you are doing something helps you move from being a passive to an active learner.
Learned	Make brief notes on all that you think that you learned from the lecture, class or reading. Make it interesting for your reader. Be engaging.

Illustrations	Draw pictures or diagrams that illustrate what you have learned. Sketch funny cartoons to make the learning memorable. Remember – you don't need to be able to draw to make visual notes: https://noblechloe.wordpress.com/first-year-learning-logs/visual-notes/who-says-you-need-to-be-able-to-draw-to-make-visual-notes/
Reaction	Make brief notes on your emotional response to the activity: notice the affective dimension to your learning. It allows you to build a picture of yourself as a learner and as a student. It may help you choose the sort of job that suits who you are.
Problems/ solutions	If you encounter any problems understanding or learning the material – make a note – and make a note of how you solved the problem.
Link to assignment	How you will use the key information in that study session in your assignment? This is probably the most important thing you can do to promote active learning and study success!
Reading	What will you now read? Why? How will you use that in your assignment?
Writing	What will you now write? When? Tip: Start drafting rough paragraphs for your assignments way before the deadline.
Goal setting	Make brief notes about anything else that you will do next … nothing will ever give you 'all you need to know' on a subject. Therefore, you should always be thinking: what next?

FIGURE 8.2   Reflective learning template – use for logs or blogs

PART 4

WORKING EFFECTIVELY IN GROUPS

6

Group Project Work, or 'Hell is other People'

Greasley, P.

It was the existentialist philosopher Jean-Paul Sartre who coined the phrase 'hell is other people' in his play *No Exit*. Three people are sent to Hell expecting to be tortured for their sins, but are surprised to find themselves simply left in a room together. As they begin to get on each other's nerves, one of the characters realises that *they* are the instruments of torture – that hell is other people! Group work can feel like this, particularly when your degree classification depends on the performance of others. I can still recall as an undergraduate witnessing a classmate scrambling over chairs and desks in a desperate bid get as much distance between himself and a particularly vociferous student who happened to be sat next to him. If group work is on the agenda, choose where you sit wisely.

On a more positive note, working with others provides the opportunity to share ideas, skills and expertise and learn from each other. Collaboration and teamwork are essential for many tasks in the real world; it would have taken one person a very long time to achieve President Kennedy's aim of 'landing a man on the moon and returning him safely to the earth'. As an old African proverb puts it: 'If you want to go fast, go alone; if you want to go further, go together.'

The key stages of project work are:

1. Define and plan

2. Assign roles and tasks

3. Monitor progress and completion of tasks

4. Review, evaluate and reflect on the project

But it is people who implement projects; so, above all, it is crucial to maintain good relationships within the group.

Tip 128: **Projects fail at the start not at the end – have clear aims and objectives**

The importance of a clear aim and objectives has already been discussed in Chapter 15 (Tips 108 and 109). Just to recap, the aim should be a general statement outlining the ultimate purpose of the project (e.g. the aim of this project is to produce an information leaflet for people with diabetes); and the objectives are the means used to achieve this aim. Try to make them as SMART as possible:

- **S**pecific: clearly defined with completion criteria
- **M**easureable: clear targets so you can measure progress
- **A**chievable: attainable (and agreed – so people can own them)
- **R**ealistic: given resources – time, money, equipment
- **T**ime-bound: clear timeframes

It sounds simple, doesn't it? But it isn't. Consider the project outline in Figure 18.1, where the brief is to produce a stall for a health promotion event. Are you clear from this what the aim and objectives of the project are? I wasn't. This is because the students have not spelled out a clear and simple aim. Indeed, the objectives are more like broad, vague aims; they certainly don't specify how the project will achieve them. For example, *how* will they 'educate people about obesity'? Will they be producing leaflets, doing a play, providing a video with some information about what constitutes obesity and some statistics about the associated risks? If you don't start with clear aims and objectives, your project will be like setting out on a journey without a clear destination or map.

But let's assume you have identified an aim and the relevant objectives for achieving this. What happens next? You should then be asking whether

---

Project specification

Obesity

Brief description of project

According to NHS UK obesity is the accumulation of excess fat in the body and this arises as a result of an imbalance between energy expenditure and energy intake. Obesity has a serious implication on health, such as cancer, type 2 diabetes, high blood pressure, depression, short life, mental illness. Obesity is mostly dictated by measuring body mass index (BMI). The Obese BMI is between 30 and 39.9.

Project objectives

- Educate people about obesity causes and its cost. BBC, 2012 stated that obesity cost NHS at least 500 million a year and it's growing rapidly.
- To empower people on how to eat healthy
- Motivate students on healthy lifestyle
- Keep them informed, alert, and aware of the risks associated with obesity.

Figure 18.1 A project outline with unclear aims and objectives

the aim is worthwhile. In other words, is the project worth doing? As the 'management guru' Peter Drucker (1909–2005) once remarked: 'There is nothing so useless as doing efficiently that which should not be done at all.'

Tip 129: **Plan to avoid the known unknowns and the unknown unknowns**

When the then US Defence Secretary Donald Rumsfeld was asked in 2002 about the lack of evidence linking the government of Iraq with the supply of weapons of mass destruction to terrorist groups, he famously replied:

> Reports that say that something hasn't happened are always interesting to me, because as we know, there are known knowns; there are things we know we know. We also know there are known unknowns; that is to say we know there are some things we do not know. But there are also unknown unknowns – the ones we don't know we don't know. And if one looks throughout the history of our country and other free countries, it is the latter category that tend to be the difficult ones.

Projects rarely go to plan, so it's important to build in time to deal with 'known unknowns' and 'unknown unknowns'.

There are various techniques to help you plan a project, but the Gantt chart is the most commonly used visual device, providing a list of the tasks that need to be completed, and by when. There is a simple example of a Gantt chart for completing an assignment in Chapter 4 (Figure 4.2), but for more complicated projects you will need to be more specific about the sub-tasks as well as identifying the people responsible for completing the tasks. For example, Figure 18.2 details the tasks involved in planning a charity event attempting to break the Guinness world record for the most people you can fit in a Mini (adapted from Maylor, 2010).

Comments from survey of tutors

- Ensure that the group has key objectives/targets to meet, clear deadlines, and particular people responsible for achieving particular tasks
- Set out ground rules and agree responsibilities and allocate tasks at the outset
- Ensure that the workload is divided fairly
- Share out the work and agree/assign clear roles
- Keep a record of meetings - who attended and what was said - and, most importantly who is going to do what

	Weeks											
Activities	1	2	3	4	5	6	7	8	9	10	11	12
Obtain car												
Contact local dealers												
Visit dealers to negotiate borrowing car												
Collect car day of event												
Arrange insurance												
Meet with university department												
Arrange insurance for driving car to site												
Continued...												

Activities	**Person responsible**
Obtain car	John
Contact local dealers	
Visit dealers to negotiate borrowing car	
Collect car on day of event	
Arrange insurance	Paul
Meet with university department	
Arrange insurance for driving car to site	
Organise barbeque	George
Contact university catering	
Obtain barbeque	
Ask supermarkets for free food	
Collect/purchase food day of event	
Collect BBQ day of event	
Satisfy health & safety	Ringo
Meet with health & safety	
Carry out risk assessment	
Promote event	John/Paul
Design and produce posters	
Alert local radio and newspaper	
Set up university stall on walkway	
Arrange venue	George/Ringo
Look for suitable venues	
Select venue and back-up venue	

Figure 18.2 Gantt chart and task allocation for charity event attempting to break the Guinness world record for most people you can fit in a Mini (adapted from Maylor, 2010)

Tip 130: **Assigning roles and tasks: people are better at some things than others**

When allocating tasks try to take into account the preferences and abilities of each member of the group. In this respect Meredith Belbin's nine team roles, summarised in Table 18.1, are a popular management tool for identifying the strengths and weaknesses of people working in teams. Which one are you?

Table 18.1 Belbin's nine team roles

Team Role	Contribution	Allowable Weaknesses
Plant	Creative, imaginative, free-thinking. Generates ideas and solves difficult problems	Ignores incidentals. Too preoccupied to communicate effectively
Resource Investigator	Outgoing, enthusiastic, communicative. Explores opportunities and develops contacts	Over-optimistic. Loses interest once initial enthusiasm has passed
Co-ordinator	Mature, confident, identifies talent. Clarifies goals. Delegates effectively	Can be seen as manipulative. Offloads own share of work
Shaper	Challenging, dynamic, thrives on pressure. Has the drive and courage to overcome obstacles	Prone to provocation. Offends people's feelings
Monitor Evaluator	Sober, strategic and discerning. Sees all options and judges accurately	Lacks drive and ability to inspire others. Can be overly critical
Teamworker	Co-operative, perceptive and diplomatic. Listens and averts friction	Indecisive in crunch situations. Avoids confrontation
Implementer	Practical, reliable, efficient. Turns ideas into actions and organizes work that needs to be done	Somewhat inflexible. Slow to respond to new possibilities
Completer Finisher	Painstaking, conscientious, anxious. Searches out errors. Polishes and perfects	Inclined to worry unduly. Reluctant to delegate
Specialist	Single-minded, self-starting, dedicated. Provides knowledge and skills in rare supply	Contributes only on a narrow front. Dwells on technicalities

Source: www.belbin.com

Belbin defines these team roles as: 'a tendency to behave, contribute and inter-relate with others in a particular way' (www.belbin.com). He found that teams with a good balance of these roles worked best:

> For example ... a team with no Plants struggled to come up with the initial spark of an idea with which to push forward. However, once too many Plants were in the team, bad ideas concealed good ones and non-starters were given

too much airtime. Similarly, with no Shaper, the team ambled along without drive and direction, missing deadlines. With too many Shapers, in-fighting began and morale was lowered. (www.belbin.com)

Now obviously, you may not have the luxury of picking the members of your team according to the criteria proposed by Belbin (which requires completing an assessment), but it is important to think about who does what according to their strengths and weaknesses as group members.

Comments from the survey of tutors

- Different people have different strengths and styles with respect to group working so, where possible, work with them rather than against them

- Teamwork is the key. Make sure you consult with all members of your team regularly

Tip 131: Beware of 'social loafers'

The most common complaint about group work is directed at certain members who don't contribute and leave others to do most of the work. There is a term for these people – 'social loafers' – because they tend to put in less effort when part of a group and they can produce a great deal of resentment amongst team members.

So what should you do if certain members of the group are shirking the work? Well, after complaining first to the student and then to the tutor, you could suggest some kind of peer evaluation for the project – where each member of the group awards marks to all the other members of the group reflecting their contribution to the project, in terms of attending group meetings, contributing to discussions, and completing tasks well and on time. There are various ways to do this. If it's not already in place, ask your tutor about it.

Tip 132: Be nice – be polite

Imagine that you want someone to open a door. How are you going to ask them? Which option would you select from the following:

1. Open the door.

2. I would like you to open the door.

3. Can you open the door?

4.   Would you mind opening the door?

5.   May I ask you whether or not you would mind opening the door?

Personally I would probably go for option 3, but it would depend on the context. If I were asking a stranger to let me into a building because I am holding a large heavy object I might opt for 4, but if I were being chased by an angry student wielding a machete I would more likely go for 1.

The issue is one of politeness, which sometimes has to be balanced against directness: option 1 is the most direct; option 5 is the most polite. No matter how many Gantt charts and task allocation tables you produce to make sure your project is well planned, the most common issue that can scupper a project is poor relationships with other people. Successful group project work depends on fostering good relationships, so consider setting some team values at the outset – for example, to show respect and consideration; to listen to what others have to say; to contribute equally; to avoid negativity. I'm sure there are others you would like to add.

Tip 133: **Keep tabs on progress: monitor and control**

Try to plan your project in stages with tasks and sub-tasks, like those in Figure 18.2, so that you can monitor progress at key junctures. Keeping tabs on progress may be done by email or phone, but it is also important to schedule meetings in your plan (Gantt chart) so that you can review progress at key stages (milestones). This is a very important control mechanism for ensuring the project is still on track to achieving its objectives and ultimately fulfilling the overall aim.

Comments from the survey of tutors

- Plan your meetings, deadlines and targets in advance
- Arrange a clear schedule for the project with small achievable targets to aim for
- Illustrate tangible outputs
- Set targets for the group and individuals
- Keep evidence of plans and schedules
- Hold regular group meetings to review progress
- Check in regularly with each other and reassign tasks if key tasks haven't been completed
- Don't assume anything

Tip 134: **Know how to work out the overall module mark**

Feelings can run high when your mark depends on the performance of others. I recall one group of students continually bickering about the direction of their project and allocation of tasks, and when I heard one say to another 'It's no wonder you're bald, with the amount of stressing you're doing', I knew it wouldn't be long before I'd be called in to mediate.

Working out how much damage might be done by the group project to your degree classification (and hence your choice of career, and therefore your life generally) is important: you need to know how much the group project work actually accounts for the overall module mark, which often consists of an individual assignment and a group work assignment. There are various ways to allocate marks, but below I've provided a simple example.

Imagine that the group assignment is going to account for 20% of the module marks, and your own individually written assignment will account for 80%. In order to work out the mark you simply need to multiply your mark by the percentage allocated to it. Here are two illustrations.

Scenario 1. The group task is going to bring down your individual mark: you've done worse in the group task than the individual assignment:

$$\text{Assignment} \quad = 70\% \times 0.8 = 56\%$$

$$\text{Group Project} = 50\% \times 0.2 = 10\%$$

$$\text{Total} \qquad\qquad\quad = 66\%$$

In this case, you got 70% for your individual assignment (well done) but only 50% for your group assignment (those b******s have ruined your life!). So the group task has reduced your individual assignment mark by 4%.

Scenario 2. You've done better in the group task than the individual assignment:

$$\text{Assignment} \quad = 58\% \times 0.8 = 46\%$$

$$\text{Group Project} = 70\% \times 0.2 = 14\%$$

$$\text{Total} \qquad\qquad\quad = 60\%$$

In this case, you've improved your mark by 2% (well done for aligning yourself with a good group!).

Tip 135: **Remain optimistic**

Projects rarely go to plan and regularly overrun in terms of time and cost, so try to keep the following advice in mind:

- When things are going well, something will go wrong. When things cannot get any worse, they will. When things appear to be going better, you have over-looked something.

- A carelessly planned project will take three times the time expected to complete. A well-planned one will take twice as long.

Finally:

- Whatever you did, that's what you planned.

summary

The tips in this chapter outline the key ingredients for successful group projects. These require clear aims and objectives, appropriate allocation of tasks, and milestones for monitoring progress towards objectives. Most crucially though, group projects require good communication skills to promote, rather than hinder, collaboration.

PART 5

WRITING STYLES AND ASSIGNMENT TYPES

The Ten Step Approach to Better Assignments

Burns, T. & Sinfield, S.

Introduction

Nobody really enjoys being assessed, being judged, it means that we can fail; we can make mistakes – mistakes that reveal us to be foolish or inadequate. Funnily enough, that is not really the point of assessment. Assessment is designed to be *of*, *for* and *about* learning. That is, a good assessment is designed to provoke active learning as we produce an assignment that 'shows what we know'. University assignments contribute to our final qualification – the final tally of your grades is used to award the level of your degree. Essays, reports, presentations, seminars … are some of the major forms of assessment used in universities; they each have their own structure and function. We look at these common assessment forms – and then offer a ten step approach to succeeding in any assignment that you are set. We conclude by discussing feedback and how to use it.

University assessments

As you read these, work out how knowing the information might help you to be a more successful student.

The essay

An essay (Chapter 12.1) is a discursive tool – you are supposed to argue for and against a topic and come to a reasoned conclusion using mainly theoretical evidence (what you have read). The essay demonstrates your analytical and critical thinking. One of the most formal academic forms, essays are typically written in the third person, past tense with extensive accurate references to supporting arguments and evidence taken from the key players in your discipline.

The report

A report (Chapter 12.2) is a practical document where you write up the findings of your investigation into real-world problems – think scientific experiment or business report. Reports are written for specific readers, in the third person, past tense and are signposted with headings and sub-headings.

The dissertation

A dissertation (Chapter 12.5) is an extended piece of writing associated with Honours level projects or postgraduate study – Masters or PhD. The dissertation records the findings and conclusions of independent research into specific phenomena. The typical dissertation structure is like that of a formal report, but it has an extended literature review and is written discursively like the essay.

The literature review

The literature review (Chapter 12.5) can be part of a dissertation – though some courses set a literature review as an assignment in its own right. The literature review demonstrates your exploration and understanding of the most up-to-date literature and research in the area that you are studying. The process of reading for and writing a literature review is designed to enable you to gain deep knowledge of the key issues and debates. Your literature review becomes your analysis of the most up-to-date and relevant knowledge-claims in your area and becomes a measuring stick against which you can compare your research findings.

The presentation

A presentation (Chapter 12.3) is a talk of a set length, on a set topic – to a known audience. It is similar in structure to the essay – but is supported by audiovisual aids. The purpose of the presentation is usually to demonstrate the student's subject knowledge and their oral communication skills.

The seminar

The seminar combines written and oral elements. The seminar giver has to present their research, normally to a group of fellow students. The research is discussed and new ideas generated. The workshop is becoming more popular than the seminar – here you teach something to a group of your peers and in a very inter-active and creative way. (For both see Chapter 12.4.)

The exam

The exam (Chapter 12.6) is designed to test learning. Students use information learned on a course in new situations. Exams can be open or closed book, time or word length limited, or other variations. Always know what sort of exam you are preparing for.

The reading record

A reading record is not an essay or a literature review. It is designed to be an annotated account of the reading a student has undertaken on a particular course. The annotations are not supposed to be descriptive: 'This book was about …' but analytical: 'This text is key for this topic outlining the major theoretical perspectives of …' or 'This text could be used to support the arguments of …' or 'However, Y and Z would take issue with the following aspects of the major arguments …'. A tutor might set a reading record to test that students are reading in an active and analytical way (Chapters 4 and 7) – thus your annotations should demonstrate your understanding of the text and its relationship to the key debates in your subject.

The annotated bibliography

An annotated bibliography is a condensed version of the reading record. A conventional bibliography records author (date) *title*, place of publication: publisher, in alphabetical order, by author's surname. In an annotated bibliography, you also note down information on a text's strengths or weaknesses; on how useful it was and why – in relation to the aims and learning outcomes of the module and the key theoretical debates of the discipline.

The digital artefact

A digital artefact (Chapter 10): as universities enter the digital age, some tutors are setting digital rather than written assignments. The most typical one that we have encountered is where students are asked to produce an artefact that could be used to teach or revise some part of the course. If set a task such as this, discover whether there are certain tools that you have to use – investigate just how creative you are allowed to be.

A beginner's guide to better assignments: ten steps …

We have looked at the *why* and the *what* of assessment, so let's now move on to *how* to prepare and write your assignments. We have broken this down into ten key stages.

1 Preparation

> The Americans talk about the five paragraph essay. This is where a typical 1,500 word essay has an introduction; three paragraphs and a conclusion. You are looking for one big idea per paragraph.

Start to work on an assignment as soon as possible: week one or two of your course would be good. Open a folder or an A4 envelope for every module that you do – and every question that you have to answer. Open the folder early and put information in there. Start collecting information from week one. Allow several weeks for reading and writing – and several more weeks to re-draft and refine your work. Work on it for half an hour a day and your academic life will be turned around.

PLANNING TIPS

- Write the whole question out exactly as it is.
- Put the question in your own words and say it back to another student or a tutor.
- Free write before you read.
- Underline every important word in the question – each is a research opportunity.
- Be creative: brainstorm and question matrix the key words (Chapters 6 and 7).
- Make sure that you do something about every word – don't leave any out.
- Add key words from the aims and learning outcomes module – research these as well (Chapter 11.1).
- Action plan: what will you now read? If working with a study partner or group – who will read what, when?

2 Targeted research and active reading

Once you understand the question and know what you are doing, read actively and interactively, using your active reading technique (Chapter 4) and asking questions as you go. Remember to get physical with the texts – mark them up, annotate, make comments and cross-reference. You will get much more from your reading when you do this.

Don't look for the whole answer to the question in any one piece of reading. When reading, look for references to plug the gaps in your free writing – or the answers to the questions generated by your brainstorm or question matrix (Chapters 6 and 7). Be generally alert and make notes of useful things you see, read and hear, and put the notes in your research folder. Record the source on the outside of the envelope – write: author (date) *title*, place of publication: publisher ... and you will build up your bibliography as you go.

3 Make paragraph patterns

Gather information by topic – rather than by source. That is, as you read, do keep an index card record of everything that you read (Chapter 4) – but also put ideas and information straight into paragraph patterns. Paragraph patterns save time. Use the flowing steps to make paragraph patterns:

- Use really large sheets of paper – A1 rather than A4.
- Write on one side of the paper only – this way you can see all of your notes.
- Remember to put author (date) *title*, place of publication: publisher, and page numbers for quotes.
- Put a key word or phrase from the question in the centre of each sheet: your *paragraph pages*.
- Collect notes from different sources onto each paragraph page – once you have a few ideas or references – you can turn each paragraph pattern into a paragraph.

4 Write – read – write

As you are reading and making notes (and building your paragraph patterns) – take the time to draft possible paragraphs for your assignment. Do not wait until you have finished reading to start the writing.

TIPS

- You are not looking for the one right answer that already exists – there are usually several ways of tackling a question.
- Write your 'favourite' paragraph first to get you started.
- Free write a conclusion to get an idea of where you want your answer to go – change the conclusion later.
- Write ideas on separate pieces of paper. Move these around to discover the best structure for the answer.
- Remember a reader who keeps saying, 'What if ...?' Your reader will be thinking of the opposite arguments and evidence: do not just ignore inconvenient or contradictory evidence – know what it is and argue against it.
- Remember a reader who keeps saying, 'So what?' Make points – remember the question (see Chapter 12.1).

5 Settle on a first draft

After you have struggled to write, read and write – settle on a first draft. Then and only then write a draft introduction and a draft conclusion to this first draft.

An introduction should acknowledge what an interesting or useful question it was – and should give the agenda of your essay – you should indicate how you are going to answer the question.

A conclusion has to prove that you have answered the whole question. Use the words from the question in your conclusion. Remember – do re-state main points; do not introduce new evidence.

6 Leave it!

Once you have achieved a first draft you feel great, your answer is great, your friends are great and life is great. Do not believe this! Put the work to one side and leave it for a while. This will give you some distance and objectivity, but more than this: your unconscious mind will seek to close the gaps that you left. The brain likes closure and will not be happy with all the gaps in your assignment. Thus your brain will struggle to close the gaps that you have left. If you allow a break in your writing process you are allowing the brain to close the gaps – you are working with your brain.

7 Review, revise and edit: struggle to write

This is the stage where you go back over your work and struggle to make it the very best it can be. Here you have to re-read what you have written – and change it. Sometimes we have to change everything – and nothing of our first draft gets left. This does not matter. We are writing to learn, so our thoughts *should* change as we write. Also, we would never get to a good version if we did not go through our rough versions.

Be prepared to draft and re-draft your work. Don't even try for perfection on a first draft – it is bad technique and it can actually stop you writing anything. On your first review, you might read from the beginning of your essay and improve, polish, as you go. After that, try to concentrate on one paragraph at a time – and not always in the order it is written but in any order.

TIPS

- Allow plenty of time for revising.
- Revising is where you go back and put in the 'best' word. This is where you put in the verbs. This is where you shorten long sentences so that you make clear, effective points.

- Index surf to brush up your paragraphs. That is, once you have completed your major research, and you are happy with it, you can index surf to get little extra bits and pieces to take your work that little bit further.
- When you have finished polishing paragraphs, check the 'links' between paragraphs – make sure that they still connect with each other.

8 Proof read

Once you are happy with your assignment, you are ready to stop revising it and to say: 'This is the best I can do'. Sometimes we are never really 'happy' with our work, but there still comes a time to stop and move on to the next task. At this point you have to proof read the final version.

Proof reading is not editing: you are not looking to make huge changes to what you have written, you are going through looking for mistakes, grammatical errors, tense problems, spelling mistakes or typographical errors.

You know that the brain likes closure – it will work to fill the gaps. This works against us when we are proof reading, it can mean that our eyes will 'see' what *should* be there rather than *what is there*. To get over this we have to make our proof reading 'strange'.

---TIPS---

- Read your assignment aloud (if it is a presentation, rehearse before a critical friend).
- Swap assignments with a friend – proof read each other's work.
- Cover the assignment with paper and proof read one sentence at a time.
- Proof read from back to front.
- Proof read from the bottom of the page to the top.
- Proof read for one of 'your' mistakes at a time.
- Like everything else we do, proof reading gets better with practice.

9 Hand it in – celebrate

You should now be ready to hand your work in on or before the deadline. And remember that deadline. On most university programmes a late submission is awarded an automatic fail – at best many marks are deducted. This is serious.

So once your assignment is done – congratulations! But before you rush off and celebrate remember to always keep copies of your work. Never hand in the only copy.

Obviously if you are writing on a computer, save your work to the hard drive and to a memory stick and email it to yourself and save in a 'cloud' – you can't be too careful!

If writing or producing something by hand – photocopy. And if the assessment unit loses your assignment, do not hand in your last copy – photocopy that. A student of ours came back and told us that the assessment unit lost her essay – the same one – three times!

10 Getting it back

When we get work back, we look at the grade, feel really happy or really unhappy, throw the work to one side and forget all about it. This is not a good idea.

What is a good idea is to review what you have written, and see if you still think it is good. As an active learner, you should try to take control of your own work and you have to learn how to judge it for yourself and not just rely on the tutor's opinions.

At the same time, you should also utilise the feedback that you get from the tutor. Be prepared to use that feedback to write a better essay next time. So a good thing to do is to perform a SWOT analysis of our own work, that is, look for the:

- Strengths
- Weaknesses
- Opportunities
- Threats.

When you SWOT your work look for the things that you think you did well or not so well. Then look for the things that the tutor appears to be telling you that you did well or not so well. Resolve to do something about your strengths and your weaknesses.

It's a struggle – and then there's the feedback

So assignments provide evidence of your achievement, but most importantly, the *process* of preparing an assignment is heuristic – it brings about powerful active learning. That is, as you wrestle with a question and struggle to read and write about it, you learn your subject. The learning cycle is completed when we receive and act upon feedback on our assignments.

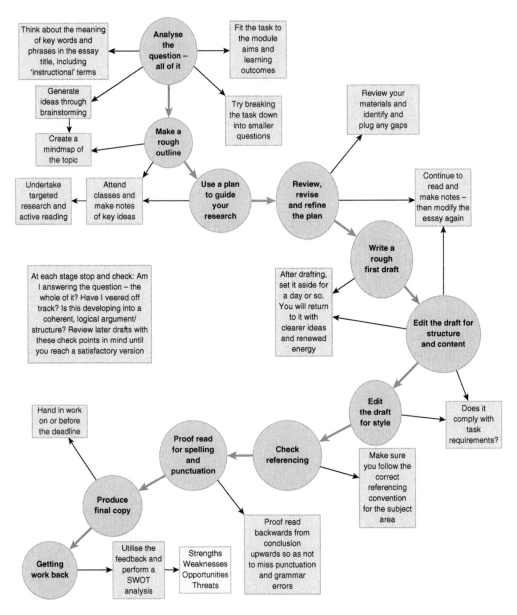

FIGURE 11.3.1   The assignment journey

Assessment and feedback

- Formative assessment is developmental. Designed to measure a student's progress at a particular moment in a subject, there should be an emphasis on tutor feedback where that feedback is designed to help you do better in the summative assessment.

- Summative assessment is final. Usually at the end of a programme of study, it is designed to measure the student's overall achievement in the unit, course or programme.
- Feedback. The best forms of assessment bring about learning in the student – especially when you can use the feedback that your tutors provide. Whether the assessment itself is formative or summative, most tutors will give you feedback on what you have written. This is a critical commentary designed to show you what you have done well (look for the ticks) – and what not so well (look for the advice about what you should have read – or referenced ...). Most students look at the grade – but forget to look at or use the feedback.

TIPS

Always try to find three things that you did well in an assignment – and three things that you could have done better.

It helps if you view assessment in a positive light. Try to see assessment as a chance to:

- **be dynamic and creative and show what you know**
- **write to learn your material**
- **write often – for 30 minutes a day**
- **use the feedback (see below).**

Dealing with feedback

It's hard to take feedback – it can feel like a personal attack or rejection. We have to learn how to use the feedback that we get. Here is how one student responded to some short sharp feedback. (Examples taken with permission from 'An Essay Evolves': http://evolvingessay.pbworks.com/w/page/19387227/FrontPage.)

The assessor's feedback on the assignment:

> ... could be improved by having a clearer focus and a stronger take-home message, which could perhaps be achieved by interpreting the title in a narrower way.

The student's response:

> I feel that in this case (and in some others!) I slipped away from my main task which is usually identified by a thorough question analysis. Looking back, instead of presenting the strengths and weaknesses of Freud's theory of personality as measured against the yardstick of evidential science I decided at too early a point to become an advocate for it. I tried also to question the appropriateness of the

> paradigm often used to assess Freud when it might have profited me (in terms of more marks) to stick with it. It may have helped me achieve the stronger take-home message counselled by the assessor. And interestingly, in this case I carried out my question analysis belatedly.

That's a brilliant way to respond to what must have felt like really negative feedback. She had worked long and hard on that task – and then it must have felt like it was being attacked. Would you have been able to do that? It is something we all have to learn – how to listen to feedback whilst not taking offence – not taking it personally – but thinking of what to do differently next time.

For more of this student's essay, search online for 'An Essay Evolves' – and read the essay as it developed – and the student's blog about her thoughts and feelings when writing the essay.

Summary: becoming a successful writer

We have considered the what, why and how of assessment – arguing that the assessment *process* is part of becoming a graduate whilst the *products* provide tangible evidence of your work. We stressed the active learning aspects of assessment: all the reading, thinking, discussing and struggling that you do to produce an assignment. We divided the assignment process into ten manageable stages – and considered how to approach feedback. You should now feel in a better position to approach your assignments.

Activity

Use the paragraph questions to prompt your writing

For each paragraph that you write – answer the following questions:

- What is this paragraph about?
  - introduce topic (and claim)
- What exactly is that?
  - define/clarify/explain
- What is your argument?
  - give argument in relation to question

- What is the evidence? What does it mean?

  - offer evidence and discuss it

- What is the opposing evidence? What does that mean?

  - Therefore …?

- What is your final point (in relation to the question)?

  - tie what you have written to the question. It is not down to your reader to guess what you are try-ing to say – or to think 'I wonder how this relates to the question?' If your reader has to do that then something is missing from your answer.

Access the companion website to this book and find helpful resources for this chapter topic:
https://study.sagepub.com/burnsandsinfield4e

PART
6

PRESENTATION SKILLS

How to Deliver Excellent Presentations

Burns, T. & Sinfield, S.

Okay – we're all terrified of public speaking! This chapter is designed to crack the code of the academic presentation. This chapter is supported by a Presentations Pack downloadable from the Sage website (https://study.sagepub.com/burnsandsinfield4e/).

Introduction

> I really hated the thought of presentations, but once they were over I felt so good about myself. In the end I wanted more of them.

Presentations are meant to exploit the fact that most of us are much better at speaking than we are at writing. Of course, what this glosses over is that students, like every other normal human being on the planet, tend to be terrified of public speaking, of presentations. In this chapter we are going to explore the what, why and how of presentations. We cannot make all the fear go away, but we can help you to realise that you can get really good at presentations – you might even get to enjoy them.

What is a presentation?

There are several 'whats' to a presentation that we are going to cover here – they are all true. The trick for you, as always, is to think, 'How will knowing this help me to give better presentations?'

It's a talk

> I remember this presentation, it was on breast cancer, a really frightening topic, and the students had left all the funny noises on their PowerPoint. So there they were giving life and death statistics and scaring everyone silly, and all the while there are explosions, whistles, flying noises and breaking glass!

A presentation is a formal talk of a set length on a set topic given to a set audience. When preparing your presentation you have to think about all these factors: time, topic, audience. That is, you have to fit the topic into the time you have been given – and no longer. Check with the tutor if there are penalties for going over time.

You also have to pitch the topic at your actual audience. Again, as with the report, think about real people with real knowledge, thoughts and feelings. You have to make sure that your language, style and tone are just right for the real people that you are going to address. Finally, you have to make sure that any audiovisual aids (AVA) – your supporting material, handouts, PowerPoint, websites, photographs, posters – are appropriate and will connect with your actual audience. There are two main purposes of using AVAs:

- to help the audience follow and make sense of your presentation, e.g. an outline of the whole presentation, a poster or pattern note of the whole presentation
- to illustrate, emphasise or underline key points, e.g. a quote, a picture, an example, a physical object.

TIP

Use posters to support your presentation – even if not asked to – they help your audience follow and understand your talk. Prepare a creative visual collage – or go for the more formal academic poster: www.fobit.biz/?p=1605.

It's an act

No matter what anyone else tells you, remember that a presentation is a *performance*. You are standing in front of people and talking to them: they are looking at and listening to you – this is a performance. Therefore you are a performer. Use this knowledge – and *act*. To make presentations work for you, act happy, confident and interested – even if you are bored silly or scared witless. If you are happy, your audience can be happy, if you are not, they cannot. If you are bored – your audience will be too … So act your socks off.

TIPS

Positive body language

- Do face the audience.
- Do not only look at the wall or whiteboard behind you.
- Do stand or sit straight.
- Do not hold anything in front of your face.
- Do smile.
- Do not tap your foot or make chopping motions with your hands.
- Do draw people calmly into your presentation with brief welcoming gestures.
- Do not hold your arms defensively in front of your body.
- Do stand in a relaxed manner.
- Do not stand there with clenched fists or looking as if you want to be somewhere else.
- Do dress for success.
- (In a group presentation) do not act as if you hate everybody else on the team.
- Do *act* calm, confident and in control.

It's interactive

As a performer, you will have to build a rapport with your audience and create a relationship with them: you *interact* with them. This means that you will need to *look at them.* You will have to make eye contact with your audience.

So ignore those who advise you to look at the ceiling at the back of the room. That may be okay if you have an audience of 1,000 or more people, but in a small group it looks weird, and not in a good way. You will need to look at people to draw them into your talk and take them with you. You will need to check that they are following and understanding what you say – to check if you need to repeat or explain something. You will never discover this if you do not look at your audience.

Finally, for it to be a successful interactive performance, just like an actor on the stage, *you must never, ever speak from a script.* You must not read a presentation. You must learn your presentation and then deliver it fresh, as though for the first time. Reading a presentation is the quickest way to lose your audience and lose marks.

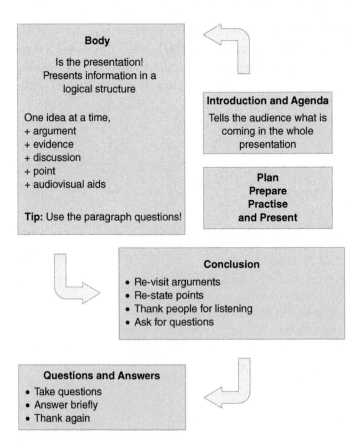

FIGURE 12.3.1 Structure of a presentation

It's a formal convention

The presentation has the same shape as the essay – and it has the same need to address real audiences as the report. Therefore, you should have a sense of the presentation already from what you now know about essays and reports.

A beginner's guide to presentations

Introduction

The introduction should include a clear agenda:

- Introduce yourself.
- Give the topic title.
- Hook your audience.
- Give the agenda.

The introduction is where you acknowledge the question and help the audience understand how you are going to tackle it. Think hook and agenda: the *hook* tells them *why* they should be listening to you: are you going to be interesting, useful or funny? Will it help them pass an exam or get better grades? Will it save them time or effort? Think of something. The *agenda* is where you tell the audience exactly *what* is coming in your presentation. Without an agenda the audience does not know where the talk is going. This is unsettling – and confusing. A confused audience is not a happy audience. Tell them what is coming … and this simple technique will dramatically improve the presentation itself – and your marks.

Presentation body

This is the presentation. This is where you answer the question that you were set, making a logical case. As with the five paragraph essay, think: three big ideas – introduction – conclusion. For each idea, think: argument – evidence – AVA.

TIPS

Use the paragraph questions to structure *each section* of your presentation:

- **What is this section about?**
- **What exactly is that?**

- Tell me more?
- What is your evidence? What does it mean?
- How does this relate back to the question as a whole?

Conclusion

As with the essay conclusion, this is where you draw the whole presentation together. Re-visit your main arguments, re-emphasise your main points – and use all the words from the question to prove that you have answered the whole question.

TIPS

- Write introductions and conclusions last.
- Accept this is a repetitive structure: tell them what is coming; tell them; tell them what you told them. This can feel silly, obvious or uncomfortable, especially in a short presentation. But this is what is required, so bite the bullet and do it!

The question and answer session

It's over – you want to rush out screaming! Don't. You now have to thank the audience for listening and ask them for questions.

TIPS

- Do re-phrase difficult questions – check that you have understood.
- Do keep answers short.
- Do keep answers good-natured.
- Do notice when people put their hands up – take questions in order.
- Do not fight with your audience.
- Do not try to make everyone agree with you.
- Do not think that you have to know everything (unless it is a job interview or an oral exam).
- If you cannot answer why not try: 'That is a very good question – what does everyone else think?' If no one else knows, 'Well, that has given us all something to think about. Thank you again for listening!'
- Do bring the question and answer session to a firm end. The audience likes to know when it is all over safely.

Why do we set presentations?

As with planning and preparing any assignment, the process of preparing a presentation is designed to be an active learning process. As you plan, prepare, practise and perform your presentation you are really getting to grips with and learning the material. As you think about how to *communicate* a topic effectively to your audience you are synthesising and using information.

It's an opportunity

> I did everything you said and practised again and again. The tutor said I was a natural – if only she knew.

And, yes, presentations really are an opportunity to shine. Before you have successfully delivered and survived your first presentation you may find this hard to believe, but once you have done this, you may find that given the choice between an essay and a presentation, you would choose the presentation every time. Once you have cracked how to do presentations well, you will realise that it is easier to get good grades for a presentation than for a piece of writing.

It's a job skill

Further, good oral communication skills are definitely required by employers – some even require a formal presentation as part of the interview. Developing good presentation skills whilst at university can make the difference between getting that job you want – or not.

TIP
───

Make notes on what you did well in all your presentations and put these in your CV folder (see Chapter 13.1).

It's self-confidence

Finally, once you can do presentations, your self-esteem really improves. From the very first one that you plan, prepare, practise and present, you start to feel better about yourself as a student and this enhances all your studies. This is not just something that we are telling you here to make you feel better – this is something that all our students have told us: succeeding in presentations is the best confidence booster they have ever had.

Think positive thoughts to drown out your negative ones: *I can do this; This is a great presentation.* Check out Chapter 3.

How to succeed in presentations: the four Ps

Here we will be looking at the four presentation Ps: plan, prepare, practise and present.

Plan

Think about your time limit, your topic and your audience:

- *Time limit:* how can you fit the topic in the time you have been allowed? What will you have to put in – what will you have to leave out?

---TIP---

Be interesting!

- *Topic and audience:* remember – an audience is made up of real people with real knowledge and expectations of their own. They will not want to be patronised – they will want to learn something.

---PLANNING TIPS---

> I knew a postgraduate student who went all the way to Japan to deliver a presentation based on a video. The technologies were incompatible, they couldn't show the video. The whole thing was a huge and expensive disaster!

When you start planning your presentation, consider the following:

- What can I expect my audience to know about this topic before I start?
- What will I want them to know when I have finished (= the aim of your presentation)?

- How will I get them from where they are to where I want them to be (= a logical structure to your presentation)?
- What language, tone and style will be right for this audience?
- What arguments and evidence will they understand – and relate to?
- What audiovisual aids will help – and will work with this audience?

  - think of visual aids to *illustrate the topic* – photographs, charts, diagrams, key quotes, posters
  - think of visual aids that will help people *follow your presentation* – have the agenda on a handout or write it on the board, make a large pattern note of your presentation, and display it, make a poster.

- How will my audience react to this topic? Will they be resistant, happy, frightened, interested? What will I have to do to get them to respond positively?
- What questions might they ask me? What answers will I give?

Action plan: now that you have considered all these things: what will you do, read, find and make to get your presentation ready?

Prepare

> I must stress the research and preparation!! When I've participated in presentations, either on my own or in groups, confidence came from how well we had worked together and how much research we had done.

Preparing a presentation requires the same research and hard work that an essay does, and then you have to make audiovisual aids as well.

Some preparation guidelines

- *Remember the ten steps* (Chapter 11.3): brainstorm the topic, link to the learning outcomes …
- *Read actively and interactively*: gather all the information you need to answer the question.
- *Plan the presentation*: give it the shape that will take your audience from where they are to where you want them to be.
- *Be interesting!* Never tell the audience everything from A to B to C. This is boring. Choose an interesting aspect of the topic – focus on, elaborate and illustrate that.
- *Remember to make your AVA*: with backups (e.g. handouts of PowerPoint slides).
- *Convince yourself first*: if you can act as though you believe it, it will help the audience to believe you.
- *Prepare a script*: once you have collected all your data and understood and shaped it, you may wish to prepare a script for the presentation. A script can give you a sense that you have

taken control of your presentation and organised your material to your satisfaction. That is okay – if you remember that you must not read from your script. So at some point you *should destroy your script*. ·

- *Prepare your prompts*: make cue cards or prompt sheets to guide you through the presentation itself. This could include:

  ○ key words or pictures instead of words
  ○ key examples and quotes
  ○ key names and dates.

- *Number your cue cards and your points.*
- *You must destroy your script* – no really!

TIPS

- **You must not read from a script – you will be boring and dull and you will lose your audience.**
- **Re-create your presentation from the key words on your cue cards.**
- **It does not matter if you forget something – the audience won't know. Better to be lively and miss a bit – than say everything and be dull and boring.**

Practise, practise, practise

> The success of the group presentation relied very heavily on how well we had got on before the day and the solo presentation relied very heavily on how much effort I had put into the preparation and research. There were very few students who could 'wing' it and often those that tried fell short when questions were put to them.

Once you have a shape to your presentation, with your prompts prepared, you are now ready to review, revise, edit and learn your presentation – and this comes through practising or rehearsing your presentation. You must not say the presentation for the first time in front of an audience – the words will sound extremely strange to you. You will confuse and upset yourself. This is not a good thing. You must learn and be comfortable with your presentation.

There are several key stages to your rehearsal:

- *Tidy it*: your first rehearsal allows you to review, refine and finish your presentation – and turn it from a written thing to an oral thing. When speaking we have to get to the point – quickly.
- *Learn it*: rehearse your actual presentation – in front of a critical friend. Keep making it shorter – more direct – more effective. Walk around your home delivering the presentation to your cat or a chair. Make yourself feel comfortable speaking those words out loud.

Do not rehearse in front of your children. Our mature students always say that their children tend to say 'it's boring, it's silly'.

- *Refresh it*: once you are comfortable with speaking out loud and you know your presentation by heart, then you need to practise until you can say it every time as though you are saying it for the first time. This will keep your presentation fresh and alive and it will appeal to and grip your audience.

Perform: tips and tricks

> I think one of the pitfalls of doing the presentation is not approaching it in the same way as any other assessment ... and forgetting the extra element of practising beforehand.

Okay – you are going to be nervous. Do not focus on that. Think positive thoughts and get on with it. Here are some positive things to do.

Before your presentation

- *Be positive*: read 'Believe in yourself' in Chapter 3. Practise your positive thinking. Keep saying: 'I am prepared', 'This is a great presentation'.
- *Be mindful*: when travelling to your presentation, run through your main points with and without your cue cards. Reassure yourself that you do know it.
- *Be early*: get to the room early so you will be as cool, calm and collected as you can be. Rushing in late will increase your stress levels.
- *Be organised*: take control of the environment. Organise the seating. Where will you want people to sit so that you feel good and they can all hear you? Do you want them in rows, in a semi-circle, sitting on the floor?

TIP

Arrange to stand behind a desk or a lectern. This small barrier between you and your audience will help you feel safe and in control.

- *Be in control*: check that the equipment is working.

-TIP-

Have a back-up system in place – have print-outs of your PowerPoint slides to circulate as handouts if the computer does not work.

- *Be alert*: use your adrenalin – it will help you think on your feet.
- *Be positive again*: say, 'I am prepared' and, 'I can handle this'.
- *Be physiological*: stress has a biofeedback effect where the things our bodies do when we are stressed actually increases our stress. We have to learn to de-stress our bodies. If too stressed before or during your presentation:
  - stop
  - sigh
  - drop your shoulders (we hold our shoulders up when tense and this increases tension)
  - wriggle your toes (we clench our feet when stressed and this increases our blood pressure and hence our stress levels)
  - unclench your fists – this is a typical anger/fear reaction – let it go
  - take a few deep, slow breaths (deep quick ones and you will pass out)
  - start again more slowly (stopping and refocusing never counts against you, it can even impress your tutor).
- *Be on the ball*: write your agenda on the board, on a handout, on an overhead transparency (OHT) or on the flip chart.

During your presentation
- Introduce yourself and your topic.
- Give a brief introduction and say your agenda even if it is written up.
- Speak slowly and clearly. Let people hear and follow you.
- If you get lost – don't panic! Pause, look at your prompts, and carry on.
- Remember to use linguistic markers: 'We have looked at …', 'Now we are going to cover …', 'Moving on to …'
- Make good eye contact – look at everyone in the room.
- Do stand so that you can see everyone and everyone can see you. Don't stare fixedly at one person so that they want to get up and leave.
- Use your AVA with confidence. Make sure everyone can see your AVA. Allow people to notice what is there – then take it away.

-TIP-

Do not write an essay on your slides: key words or pictures only.

- Remember your conclusion – re-visit and re-state your main points ... no matter how silly it seems. Your audience does not know the topic as well as you do – they will need to be reminded of what you have talked about and what it means.
- Thank people for listening – ask for questions.
- Chair the Q&A session fairly – keep those answers short and sweet. Bring the Q&A to a firm conclusion. Thank people again.
- After your presentation, review your performance.

After your presentation – be a SWOT

As with the essay and the report, it is useful for you to be able to review and evaluate your own presentations. However, because of the especially emotional dimension of presentations, we recommend that you undertake this in two stages:

1. Immediately after your presentation, tell yourself what a wonderful presentation it was and how brave you were for giving it. Do not dwell on anything that went wrong; this just makes it harder to do a presentation next time. So make this first review a very positive one.
2. After some time has elapsed undertake a more detailed SWOT analysis of your presentation.

- What were your strengths? What did you do very well? What sections of the presentation were you particularly pleased with? Why? Sometimes we are so busy correcting our faults that we forget to repeat our strengths. Make notes so that you remember.
- What were your weaknesses? What did not go so well? Why was this? Was it *form* – perhaps it was not structured or presented properly? Was it *content* – was it a poor argument unsupported by evidence? Did you forget to discuss your evidence? Did you forget to refer back to the question? Make notes.
- Opportunities: now, go on, try to think of just how good you can become at presentations and of all the opportunities this gives you, both as a student and in future employment. Make notes.
- Threats: if you are still feeling threatened by presentations, what are you going to do next? Will you practise more? Do you need more support with your positive thinking? Do you need to find a study partner? Do you need to seek out Learning Development or Academic Support and get some more help? Make notes.

TIPS

- Make notes of your strengths – repeat them.
- Make notes of your weaknesses – repair them.
- Use your tutor feedback.
- Use video play-back to refine your performance.

Get creative

> One presentation that really impressed me was one on Fibonacci numbers in maths. The group used sunflowers and pineapples to illustrate the numbers in nature. One played the flute to illustrate the link between maths and music. There were wonderful drawings illustrating numbers and rabbits (don't ask!) ... I thought it was excellent.

The presentation can be more flexible than the essay. Whilst it is not usually a good idea to write a poem when you have been asked to write an essay, it can be a good idea to be creative with a presentation. If your tutor is the sort of person who will appreciate a little creativity, then play with how you will communicate with and involve your audience. We have seen tutors really impressed when students have performed a mini-play instead of giving a straight presentation. So when thinking about your presentation – do all the good planning and preparation discussed above – but also think whether a different sort of performance would actually get you a higher mark – and go for it.

Presentations: essential things to do

> I feel that you need to really emphasise group presentations, as they can differ greatly and rely heavily on the success or failure of the group. My group presentations worked because we got on – we worked together well – and we rehearsed together.

- *The three-minute presentation*: before delivering an assessed presentation for your coursework, practise by preparing and delivering a three-minute presentation to a friend, study partner or study group. Choose a simple topic like a hobby or a holiday – but something that really interests and engages you. Use your energy and enthusiasm for the topic. With this presentation get the form right: introduction, agenda; body = logical structure + AVA; conclusion; Q&A. This will build your confidence for your assignment.
- *Rehearse, rehearse, rehearse*: for an assessed presentation, practise with a critical friend. Use their feedback.

TIP

Use the presentation checklist to evaluate yourself and ask your friend to complete one for you, too.

- *Team work*: if asked to prepare and deliver a group presentation – plan together, get together, make the AVA together, rehearse together:
  - Have a *team leader* and a *note taker* – help people play to their strengths. Encourage everybody – hate no one!
  - Do *look like a group* – have badges, dress in similar colours.
  - Do *act* as though you were a good group that worked really well together – even if you all now dislike each other!
  - Do *listen to each other* when presenting – do not chat whilst someone is speaking – look fascinated.
  - Do *learn each other's sections* – be ready to carry on if someone disappears.
- *Role-play*: build some element of dramatic performance into your presentation, especially with a group. When students act out a scenario or role-play a point to illustrate it, tutors are usually really impressed and give higher marks.
- *Poster presentations*: even if not asked to prepare a poster for your presentation, make one anyway. Research indicates that audiences find it easier to follow, understand and enjoy a presentation that has been backed up by a well-designed and beautifully illustrated poster.

Summary

We have looked in some detail at the academic presentation, emphasising the opportunity for developing your communications skills, your self-confidence and your employability. As with all assignments, presentations are heuristic, they bring about active learning – and the presence of an audience is an excellent incentive to ensure that you communicate well what you have learned. Try to enjoy your presentations – and use the four Ps of the presentation: plan, prepare, practise and present – and the 'fifth P' – positive thinking.

Activity

Use the presentation checklist

Photocopy this checklist and use it to review your own presentations.

- ☐ My introduction: tells the audience what I am talking about and why.
- ☐ It has a 'hook' telling the audience why they should listen – it is …
- ☐ I have a clear agenda telling people the 'order' of my talk.
- ☐ I will write my agenda – and speak it.
- ☐ I have a logical structure – it does answer the question set.
- ☐ I have thought about my audience – in terms of language, tone, style and interesting AVA.
- ☐ I prepared a script – made my cue cards – then destroyed my script.

☐ I have illustrated my main points in my AVA.

☐ I have made a poster to support my presentation – and will display that as I speak.

☐ I have made a PowerPoint or Prezi presentation and embedded all my resources on that.

☐ I will not pass anything around because that disrupts a presentation.

☐ My slides and handouts are simple and clear – I have used mainly pictures – and few words.

☐ Each part of my presentation follows the paragraph questions.

☐ I discuss my evidence.

☐ When I want people to make notes, I will pause and let them do so.

☐ I have concluded each section by making a point that relates back to the overall question.

☐ I have remembered my signposts and my discourse markers.

☐ I have a conclusion that revisits my main arguments and re-states my main points.

☐ I am prepared for the question and answer session.

☐ I have checked my mannerisms or gestures (I won't fiddle with a pen or scratch my nose).

☐ I have practised my positive thinking.

Access the companion website to this book and find helpful resources for this chapter topic:
https://study.sagepub.com/burnsandsinfield4e

PART 7

LITERATURE SEARCHING AND IDENTIFYING A GAP IN THE LITERATURE

The Literature Review

Thomas, G.

Once you have outlined the problem or issue that you wish to examine and you are happy with the expression of this in the form of an initial question or questions, you will need to find out about what other people have accomplished in researching this topic. Assuming that you have done your work properly in making sure that your research question is precise and doable, this review of the literature should lead you down some paths that will help you to define more exactly what you wish to do. Ultimately, you will be able to refine your research questions.

In thinking about a literature review, you first need to establish what's meant by 'literature'. Literature can be almost anything that represents the results of research or scholarship on a subject. It is written material that may appear in books, articles, conference proceedings, dissertations, websites, and so on. The shorthand for these kinds of information is *sources*.

Just running through these sources, you will see, even at first glance, that they are of different kinds, and they will be viewed differently by your tutors. Some have more credibility than others, and you must be careful not to be taken in by something just because it is in print. Just because it is in written form doesn't mean that it is of unimpeachable quality as a piece of information. You will need to be clear about the status of the evidence that you are drawing on when you cite literature. You should ask yourself what kind of literature it is. Let's look at a few sources as shown in Table 3.1.

Primary and secondary sources

In Table 3.1, you'll notice that mention is made of primary and secondary sources, and I note that secondary sources are not usually as highly thought of as primary sources. It is worth spending some time looking at this distinction between primary and secondary, since tutors may place stress on using one

(usually primary) rather than the other. Most of the sources mentioned in Table 3.1 will usually be primary (though textbooks are always secondary). Let's look at some others.

Examples of primary sources:

- autobiographies
- diaries
- government documents and statistics
- letters and correspondence (including electronic kinds such as email)
- original documents (such as birth certificates)
- photographs and audio or video recordings
- reports from commercially produced surveys or other research (e.g. using focus groups)
- speeches
- technical reports.

Examples of secondary sources:

- biographies
- dictionaries and encyclopaedias
- review articles
- textbooks.

A primary source is 'straight from the horse's mouth' – in other words, no other person has subsequently analysed or summarised it. A secondary source is a reworking of usually many primary sources, either in analysis or summary. Textbooks are the most common form of secondary source.

The main difference between a primary source and a secondary source is in the directness of the data or evidence being presented. Think of the primary source representing a first presentation or first analysis of the data, and the secondary source representing a second look, usually by someone other than the author of the primary source. In practice, it is difficult sometimes to distinguish between a primary and a secondary source, so you should not get too worried about strict demarcations between them. And one thing that Table 3.1 highlights is that there is no automatic **correlation** between the quality of a source and its 'primary-ness' or 'secondary-ness'.

Some primary sources may be very suspect, while some secondary sources may be excellent.

You'll notice that I include *review articles* in secondary sources, and these are worth a special mention since they are taken to be rather more authoritative reviews of the literature than those that exist in encyclopaedias and textbooks. There are two kinds of review article: the *systematic* review and the *narrative* review. The systematic review uses particular methods to search for research on a topic in a wide range of **peer review** sources. Only studies of a predetermined type and/or quality are included in the ultimate review. A narrative review, by contrast, discusses and summarises the literature on a particular topic without conforming to a particular search formula. Narrative reviews often do not report on how they searched for literature or how they decided which studies were relevant to include. There are also **meta-analyses**. These are studies which use particular techniques for selecting and summarising the findings of many pieces of research.

Review articles and meta-analyses can be very valuable as sources, if you can find up-to-date ones which are relevant to your topic. While they appear in general academic journals, you can look especially for journal titles that contain 'Review' such as the *Review of Educational Research* or *Educational Review*.

A relatively new and increasingly important resource is the 'collaboration' that brings together high-quality evidence and then synthesises and summarises it for the reader. The most important of these for the social sciences is the Campbell Collaboration (www.campbell collaboration.org/). This gives as its general purpose 'Improving decision-making through systematic reviews on the effects of interventions within the areas of education, crime and justice, and social welfare'. This is an example of one of its summaries on the impact of street lighting in the reduction of crime:

This review of 13 studies of street lighting interventions in the United Kingdom and United States, spanning four decades, finds that crime decreased by 21% in areas that experienced street lighting improvements compared to similar areas that did not. The review also notes that street lighting appears more effective at reducing crime

Table 3.1 Sources of written information

Kind of source	What is it?	☺ Good things about this source	☹ Not-so-good things about this source
Article in a peer review journal (usually primary)	This has been offered by the author to the journal to be judged. The peer reviewers (i.e. other academics in the same field) will ask themselves if it is good enough for publication. Only the best articles will be accepted, and for this reason the peer review journal is seen as the 'gold standard' for quality.	Only the best articles get published. You can therefore be sure of quality (in theory).	This material is published for the author's peers in the academic community, and may be difficult for anyone else to understand. Also, it will usually be on esoteric or cutting-edge matters and not necessarily straightforward issues. It may give little attention to explaining the wider context, or explaining in simple terms.
Article in a professional journal (usually primary)	A professional journal is similar to a peer review journal, and may be reviewed by peers. However, criteria for judgement will be rather different. It will be judged principally on its practical usefulness to the professional, rather than on the satisfactoriness of the design of the study or the methods used.	Likely to be of practical relevance.	May be simply the view of the author. The work will not have been subject to such stringent scrutiny of research design, method, analysis, etc. It is difficult to assess the difference between a professional journal and a peer review journal, since both have elements of peer review. If in doubt, try to make an assessment of the article itself. Does it just seem to be a personal view? Is it well referenced? How thoroughly does it seem to have been done?
Authored book (usually primary)	Books vary in their 'scholarliness'. They will usually have been written as a major presentation of the author's work – research work or academic study – but they may be explanations of other people's work (see 'Textbook').	Books written by a single author represent an extended academic treatment of a particular topic. Because they are by one person they have integrity: they tend to 'hang together'.	Tend to be personal representations of a topic, unmoderated by the comments or views of others. So be cautious: this may be a very particular 'take' on a subject, or a personal view.
Chapter in an edited book (primary or secondary)	Edited compilations are books all on one theme brought together by an editor. These are like journals, but without the same degree of peer review.	Edited books are a good way of gathering related material on a topic. The editor will be an expert in the field, often taking an interesting slant.	Can be 'bitty', with some very weak chapters interspersed with good ones. The multiple authorial 'voice' may be confusing.

Kind of source	What is it?	☺ Good things about this source	☹ Not-so-good things about this source
Textbook (secondary)	A textbook is a bringing-together of much work on one theme. This is not original work by the author, but work that she or he has summarised for the particular purpose of meeting students' course needs.	Saves a lot of time searching sources. It may, if the textbook is good, provide a very effective summary.	Because an author is reporting on others' work it is susceptible to distortion or misunderstanding (think of 'Chinese whispers'). It is referred to as a 'secondary source' for this reason. When other people's work is brought together in this way by a textbook author it is summarised, perhaps not very well. It can become out of date quickly. For all these reasons a textbook is not valued highly as a source.
Conference paper (usually primary)	A paper that has been presented at an academic conference and that has then been printed in a collection of papers (called the 'proceedings' of the conference).	Usually right up to date, and often reporting on work that is still in progress.	Conferences vary in their status, and papers are often subject to only a minor form of peer review, if they are peer reviewed at all. Conference proceedings are therefore of very variable quality.
Thesis or dissertation (usually primary)	The theses and dissertations that you will be able to gain access to are written by students who have written master's degrees or PhDs.	May be on a topic very similar to your own. May be very good (but may not – see the next column).	May be very weak. Do not use one as a model for your own. It may only have scraped a pass.
Research or technical report (usually primary)	A report written by researchers and addressed directly to the people who funded the research.	Direct, to the point and well focused on the issue being researched.	Not peer reviewed, so no quality control. Also, since paid for by the funder ('contract research'), conclusions may have been influenced by those funders.
Magazine or newspaper article (usually secondary)	Like other forms of publication, newspapers and magazines (periodicals) take various forms, though the differences are more marked. Some periodicals and newspapers are as 'respectable' as some journals. Others are not.	Right up to date, and can be used as a starting point which leads you to a more reliable source.	Most of these publications depend on good sales and may be willing, even the 'high-quality' ones, to distort material to make it more interesting. Reporters are subject to none of the peer review checking used in academic journals. It is not unheard of for reporters simply to make up stories.
Website (usually secondary)	These are as varied as the sources of information above. A website is really just a medium for carrying a range of sources and has no inherent strengths or weaknesses. It's up to you to judge.	Most websites carry reliable information, some for example taking you directly to a publisher's site, where you can download peer-reviewed articles.	Some websites, even quite well-known ones, carry misleading information. Be particularly wary of those offering off-the-shelf answers to essay questions. Wikipedia can be helpful for giving you an impression of the breadth of the area, but is unreliable. Always verify from another source.

in the United Kingdom compared to the United States – a 38% reduction compared to 7%. In general, the American studies were older and several reported just nighttime crime, rather than both nighttime and daytime crime.

A similar resource is the Evidence for Policy and Practice Information and Co-ordinating Centre (EPPI-Centre) at http://eppi.ioe.ac.uk/cms/.

Another of these banks of summaries is at the Cochrane Collaboration (www.cochrane.org/). This is a library of systematic reviews in healthcare. Also see the Educational Evidence Portal (www.eep.ac.uk/DNN2) and digests such as the Social Policy Digest Online (http://journals.cambridge.org/spd/action/home). This provides an easily accessible listing of new developments across the whole social policy field.

I'll finish this section on the quality of sources with a warning story. In 2007 BBC News, the *Guardian*, the *Independent*, *The Times* and Reuters all wrote obituaries of the composer Ronnie Hazlehurst. Unfortunately, they all contained an error that revealed that the obituary writers had simply cut and pasted a phoney fact from Wikipedia. A joker had maliciously edited the Wikipedia entry for Hazlehurst to say that the composer had emerged from retirement to write a song called 'Reach' for the pop group S Club 7, and this strange and interesting 'fact' was duplicated by the journalists without bothering to check its veracity. Result: red faces all round.

However, the moral is about more than just Wikipedia, which can be (and usually is) an excellent resource. It's about all published material. Try to avoid using only one source, and wherever possible corroborate and verify from others. Use primary sources if you can. It's not just facts that can be wrong. Perhaps more of a problem is the impression that you can get from one source where matters of opinion are involved and varied interests at play. If interpretations of data or analysis are involved, be aware that these can take many shapes and hues. By reading from a variety of sources you will get an overview and a more rounded picture of the topic.

Quality of sources

Aside from your judgement about the source that is being used, make a more general assessment of the work that you are referencing. Ask the following questions of it:

- Is this literature written following a piece of research? If so, what kind of research was being undertaken? Was it a large-scale or small-scale study? What was being claimed of the research? Usually research authors are 'up-front' about the limitations and weaknesses of their research, and work that is published in a good journal should not have been accepted if it makes unrealistic claims. This is not to say that small-scale research is in any way inferior to large-scale research: each has its strengths and weaknesses. The main thing is to be aware of these and to show that you understand the limitations of any kind of research – to show that you are critically aware (see 'Critical awareness' below).

- Or, if it is not a piece of research appearing in a journal, is it, by contrast, someone's opinion? Who is the person? What authority do they have? Do they have any vested interests that may have caused them to give the opinion or advice that they have given?

Not all sources are equal. Think about the quality of the source. Is it primary or secondary? Is it based on research evidence? Has there been a peer review process?

Your literature review should tell a story – it should not be a list

Your aim is to examine the literature for material that is relevant to your research topic. What have other people done that is relevant to your research question? You don't, after all, want to be reinventing the wheel. Your search will take you up against some disparate ideas and some interesting information, but your principal aim here isn't simply to make a list of everything that has been written on a topic. Such *summarising* and listing is necessary but is by no means enough. To conduct a good literature review, you also need to *synthesise* and *analyse*.

Summary is not too difficult, and this is perhaps why it tends to dominate student literature reviews. Analysis and synthesis are more difficult.

When you *analyse*, you see what is going on; you see how one part relates to another; you see the wood for the trees. For example, political journalists don't simply write down everything that is said in Parliament: they analyse how one statement relates to another; they remember what was said last month and note whether it is consistent with this; they look for the vested interests that might be held by those making a statement.

> Your literature review should be a story with a beginning, a middle and an end. It is a synthesis that links ideas or finds differences. It is not a list.

When you *synthesise*, you bring things together, relating one to another to form something new. When chemists synthesise a new molecule from two existing molecules, they don't simply glue one molecule to the next one. Rather, they put the molecules through some process that creates something entirely new and different, with different qualities from the two original molecules. This is what happens in the best literature reviews: there is an intelligent appraisal of a range of sources that in some way extracts the key messages and accounts for them in the context of an overarching statement or idea.

In the end, your literature review should make sense as a story with a beginning, a middle and an end, with lots of connections between one part and another. You outline the issues at the beginning; you provide the analysis and synthesis in the middle (always linking one bit with another: 'Sikes found more fluff in men's trouser pockets, while Cratchett discovered more in women's. The reasons for this may be found in ...'); and you tie it up at the end by summarising the issues, differences, paradoxes, dilemmas and questions yet to be resolved.

Making it a story

I have stressed that your literature review should be more like a story than a list. The aim is to find themes – or, by contrast, discontinuities, breaks, disagreements – that run through the literature. When you have done a reasonable amount of searching you will be able to see these emerging, and it is useful at this stage to draw a storyboard – a plan that sums up and brings together the ideas that are emerging from your literature review.

Let's look at the storyboard in Figure 3.1. The original question that has been posed is 'How do head teachers cope with difficult people?' This might be the sort of question posed by a head teacher or deputy head teacher undertaking a master's degree in education. To draw your storyboard you will need to have done some reading already, and it will help if you have thought about or brainstormed on this reading.

Think of this process of combining summary, analysis and synthesis as telling a story or a series of stories. A story makes sense: it is not simply a list. A story has a beginning, a middle and an end, and you can make your literature review take this structure.

Try to build an interest in the area, rather like a novelist does. Start by establishing what the great educator Jerome Bruner (1997: 142) calls the 'trouble' in the story – not literally 'trouble', of course, but rather the issue, question or uncertainty. A good novelist begins a story by capturing the reader's interest with this 'trouble', and this is what you should do when you begin your literature review. You could begin by saying, for example, that although your area of interest is clearly a matter of national concern, researchers have tended not to focus on it, or have focused on an aspect of it that is not relevant to the practising professional. Or you could establish some 'trouble' by pointing out a major area of controversy, which still exists even after decades of research. You then need the 'middle' of the story – the establishment of what people are actually saying, and how they are disagreeing or agreeing. The end will come with a summing-up and a moving-on to the reasons for doing your own thesis.

Do authors concentrate on a particular theme? Do they disagree? Are there areas of controversy? Are there surprising areas of agreement or similar findings? Are there gaps that no one seems to be looking at?

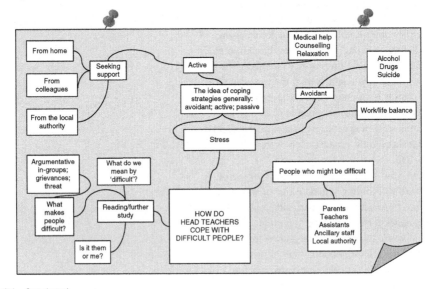

Figure 3.1 Storyboard

Use your words cleverly to tell the story

When writing your literature review, try to make links between different areas of work and make those links explicit with the words that you use at the beginning of sentences or paragraphs. For example, if Smith has found something different from Brown, don't simply list one after the other. Instead, show that you recognise the difference in their opinions by simply inserting a 'however', and relating one with the other: 'Smith (2006) found that boys in Year 9 were significantly below the level of girls in reading ability. However, Brown (2007) found no such difference.' Useful linking words are given in Table 3.2.

Figure 3.2 shows a few paragraphs from the literature review of my own PhD thesis, which was about additional adults in the classroom – people such as classroom assistants and parents. In this particular bit, I was looking at how difficult it seems to be for adults to work together there and I was making connections with similar kinds of situations that had occurred earlier, during the 1960s and 1970s, in team teaching. This excerpt is useful, I think, since it shows how different ideas can be linked.

In this excerpt you can see that I was trying to do two things as far as telling a story is concerned. I was trying to *link* the work of the researchers (Geen and Cohen) that I had located, and I did this by using words and phrases such as 'similar' and 'like Geen'. I was also linking the ideas that seemed to be coming through from the literature – ideas that were linked with the kinds of observations I had made myself and which had made this an area I wanted to research. I had noticed that working together in classrooms seemed to be difficult, and here were researchers saying exactly the same, and proffering reasons for the difficulties. So those difficulties were a thread I could pull out of the review. It wasn't simply a question of summarising what was found by the researchers, but rather a question of finding a theme or themes. For me, the theme was about teams being much more difficult to operate in classrooms than anybody seemed to be assuming.

Table 3.2 Useful linking words

When there is a difference	When there is agreement	When one idea leads to another
however; but; notwithstanding this; although; yet; conversely; in spite of this; nevertheless; on the other hand; despite; then again; besides	moreover; indeed; further; furthermore; additionally; likewise; also; similarly; equally; and; what is more; again	hence; because of this; thus; for example; as a result; consequently; therefore; accordingly; so; for this reason; this is why; otherwise; then; finally

And this is where your own research fits into the review. Would you be aiming to add some weight to one view or another? It is here that your research will begin to take shape, since you may now see the original research question you posed in a different light as you start to uncover what other people have already discovered.

Joining the pieces

Being in a research area is a bit like being told to go into a room in which pieces of a jigsaw puzzle have been scattered around the furniture, with half of the pieces missing: not only do you have to find the pieces you have been given and how they fit together; you also have to understand what is missing. Doing the literature review is like being at that first stage; doing your own research is the second – filling in the bits that are missing. In the first stage you have to discover what is already there and how one bit of the puzzle relates (or doesn't relate) to another. But when you embark on a literature review you are not only

looking for pieces, you are also seeing how they fit together and interrelate. Does this piece go here, or there? What can we tell from these several pieces that seem to fit together? What do they tell us about the gaps that are in the area that is missing?

Speed reading and taking notes

You will not find a stock of books and articles that cover the precise subject of your project. You will, however, find literature that is related and you must do what you can to see the relevance of this.

When you are reading, try to develop the skill of speed reading – 'gutting' an article or book for the material that you need. Keep an eye out for key words or phrases and ignore what is irrelevant. You cannot read an academic book in the same way that you read a novel or even a newspaper. Academics write in strange prose that is sometimes meaningful only to the limited group of people who work professionally in that area, and if you spend your time trying to decipher it all you will go mad. For a particularly important book or article that you need to study in detail (maybe it is a key reference for your research), you may wish to try the SQ2R method. (Francis Pleasant Robinson developed what is called the SQ3R method – see the 'Further reading' section at the end of this chapter – but I suggest a variant which deletes the last 'R', so it becomes SQ2R.) It's a good method, because it avoids the feeling that you have to plod through, interpreting or remembering every word. It reminds you that you are reading for a

...

In team teaching, relationships are found which raise many of the issues already outlined: there may be clashes in educational ideology among participants, and/or interpersonal tensions. However, there will also be managerial issues in determining where sets of responsibilities begin and end, and who defines them, as well as practical issues concerning time for negotiation and planning.

Synthesis, analysis and the drawing of a narrative

Geen (1985), in tracing the history of team teaching in England and Wales, found that there are serious difficulties encountered when teachers are expected to work together in one class. He found, from sending letters to Chief Education Officers in the 104 LEAs of England and Wales, that despite the enthusiasm for team teaching in the sixties and seventies, 'it has failed to establish itself as a permanent strategy in many schools'. Out of 49 schools who pioneered team teaching in the 1960s only 7 retained it by 1984.

Reporting directly on specific findings from the literature and relating these to other findings.

Among the reasons Geen identifies for schools abandoning team teaching are: the time and energy consumed in planning; the reluctance of some teachers to teach before colleagues; and differences between team members. These relate to the constructs already identified: time and energy in planning is a practical issue; reluctance before colleagues an interpersonal one; differences between team members may be due to clashes in ideology or personality.

The opening of this sentence links the previous and present paragraphs.

Interestingly, very similar results are found in the US. Cohen (1976) longitudinally analysed questionnaire data from 469 teachers. The data are taken at two points: in 1968 and 1975. She notes, like Geen, that the amount of teaming has dropped substantially over the period; in 1968, teams of five or six teachers were common but by 1975 the most common team size was only two (45% of all teamed teachers were in teams of two; 35% were in teams of three and only 8.5% were in teams of 5 or more). Suggested reasons for the decline were to do with the amount of coordination and communication needed for the effective functioning of the larger group; teachers do not have the time for it. Associated with successful teaming are attention to team dynamics and the support of school management; teaming was 'not unconditionally associated with teacher satisfaction'. Satisfaction rested in part on the balance achieved in the teaming process with balance in turn being determined by the enabling of participation in all team members. Analysis of respondents' replies led to a growing understanding of the fact that when team participation was good it was very good, and when it was bad it was awful (p 58). Cohen concludes that team arrangements are extremely fragile: 'Teaming appears to be an organisational innovation trying to survive without effective preparation or support' (p 61).

These two words, 'like Geen', link the ideas of Cohen and Geen.

Drawing links between two particular findings and drawing out themes.

Figure 3.2   Telling a story

purpose, summarised by the questions that you set yourself as part of the process.

- *Survey* or skim the whole piece, remembering that key nuggets of information occur at the beginning and end of a chapter or article, and at the beginning and end of paragraphs.
- *Q* – now ask yourself *questions*, related especially to what you intend to find out. Don't worry too much about stuff that is irrelevant: stick to questions that are important to you.
- *Read* the whole piece, again fairly quickly, don't get hung up on difficult bits – and, if the book is yours, mark it with a highlighter or a pencil for key words or phrases, especially those that are relevant to your questions.
- *Recall* what was in the piece (having shut the book first). Jot down notes. If you aren't able to remember anything, start again with *survey*.

Whether or not you are using the SQ2R method for your speed reading, keep a Word file of notes from your reading. Call it 'My project notes' (or something more imaginative). To this file you can add downloaded material from online copy or from websites. Internet material is easy to copy by cutting and pasting, so paste straight into your file. Then create a new folder into which you can put this file. If you don't know how to create a folder, click on 'Start' (at the bottom left of your screen), then 'My Documents', 'File', 'New, Folder' and a new box will appear in your Documents called 'New Folder'. You can now type in your name in the place of 'New Folder'. So type in 'Lucy's project folder' (only if your name is Lucy, obviously), and your folder is made – and it didn't cost you a penny. Now drag 'My project notes' into 'Lucy's project folder'. Now, into this folder you can add all of the files that you download. Your main file in this folder will be 'My project notes', but it will also comprise all of the files of articles and webpages that you have downloaded. It's worth noting that when you download a file from the internet, it will be directed straight to 'My Documents' (or possibly 'Downloads'), so drag all of these downloads from 'My Documents' (or 'Downloads') into 'Lucy's project folder'. A quick tip: if, like me, you tend to lose files on your computer (and, like me, you find the new Windows search facility incomprehensible) download a free program called Agent Ransack, which ferrets around wonderfully to find all your lost stuff.

Critical awareness: be your own Jeremy Paxman

Critical awareness is a key phrase that will come up again and again in your university work, and despite the efforts of tutors to instil it in their students, it remains a rare commodity. You will get good marks for having it, and you will be marked down for not demonstrating it.

What, then, is critical awareness? The key thing about study in higher education is your *attitude* to knowledge rather than the *amount* of knowledge that you can show you possess. While at school the key thing seems to be to learn as many facts as possible and then reproduce them in a more or less logical form for an assignment, the attitude at university is rather different. Certainly there may be issues and knowledge with which you will be expected to be familiar, but it is your attitude to such knowledge that is more important than your familiarity: your approach should always be of scepticism – of suspicion and doubt. You will be expected to be aware that there will always be different ways of interpreting some observation, different ways of arguing a case, different interests at play in any argument. In short, you'll be expected to recognise, and to demonstrate that you recognise, that truth is hard to come by.

Why is this lying bastard lying to me?

You will usually be marked more for your *approach* to facts than for your knowledge of them. You should understand how someone comes to a decision, judgement or conclusion, and understand that there will always be other kinds of decision, judgement or conclusion that could have been drawn from data that have been gathered. As the great biologist J.B.S. Haldane put it, this is really about 'the duty of doubt'. Or as René Descartes (1647/1996) said: 'Doubt is the origin of wisdom.'

Or as Jeremy Paxman put it, less elegantly though perhaps more straightforwardly: 'Why is this lying bastard lying to me?' Actually, Jeremy Paxman claims that he never said this. He says of his reported use of this phrase:

Do I think that everybody you talk to is lying? No I do not. Only a moron would think that. But do I think you should approach any spokesman for a vested interest with a degree of scepticism, asking 'why are they saying this' and 'is it likely to be true'? Yes of course I do. (Wells, 2005)

What Jeremy Paxman says is just about the best way of summing up critical awareness, and it applies not just to politicians and spokespersons. It applies to anyone who reports a finding or expresses an opinion, because everyone reports those findings and expresses those opinions in the context of their own experience. And this experience may be more or less valid, more or less loaded, more or less interested (where 'interested' means 'having a stake in'). You have to put out of your mind the idea that all researchers, indeed all people who write anything anywhere, are fair-minded, neutral observers. There may be any one of a thousand reasons why someone takes a particular slant on a research question, so they will go out and look for data in a particular way or analyse those data in particular ways to suit their purposes and end up with the sort of findings that they expect. They may simply start off with an involvement or personal investment in a particular area, or they could be sponsored by a particular company or government department which may have an interest in a particular finding being made. So, start with Paxman's question (paraphrased), 'Why are they saying this?'

Critical awareness, however, is not just about spotting bias or personal involvement of this kind. It is about an awareness that knowledge is frail, not fixed, and that you should approach everything you read and hear with a questioning mind, always asking yourself whether something could have been done differently.

So, however respectable the source, be questioning, be critical. Also, be tentative about any conclusions that you yourself feel you are able to make: avoid phrases such as 'this proves' and 'this shows' and instead use words such as 'this indicates' or 'the evidence suggests' or 'points towards' or 'implies'. Try to use moderating phrases such as 'tends to' or 'one might conclude that' instead of bolder ones. Academic writing is an area where it pays to be tentative: no one will give you high marks for making unwarranted claims about your own research, or for gullibly believing the reports of others. Doubt everyone's findings, even your own. Remember again 'the duty of doubt'.

That duty of doubt, of *critical thinking*, has a long and illustrious intellectual tradition. Socrates started the ball rolling 2,500 years ago. He emphasised that you cannot rely on the views and declarations of those in authority. Authorities – that is to say, people in positions of power and influence – may sound impressive but may in fact be irrational and confused. He said that we should always subject any claim to knowledge to rigorous questioning as to its validity. His system of questioning has become known as the 'Socratic method'. All our beliefs, all our knowledge, should be subjected to such questioning, so that we can separate reasonable beliefs from those which lack rational grounding or adequate evidence.

> Demonstrating critical awareness, critical thinking and reflective thought is as important as anything else in your work. It's about being instinctively sceptical about claims to knowledge and truth.

You can employ critical thinking about sources that you encounter – any piece of research or any scholarly argument – in your literature review by asking yourself these questions:

- Are there any vested interests at play?
- Might the writers' objectives in undertaking the research sway their reasoning in some way?
- Would different methods have yielded different findings?
- What sources of information are being drawn upon – is there evidence of balance, or are sources being 'cherry picked'?
- What is the quality of the data being drawn upon – are they from good primary sources?
- Is the writer's reasoning sound? So, if you were arguing with them, what would you say? (But ask yourself also how much validity your own criticisms would have, and whether you yourself are likely to be swayed by tradition, sentiment or vested interest.)

Click on 'Search': finding information

Finding information is one of the areas that has changed most dramatically over the past few years. Before the mid-1990s, researchers had to rely on printed articles in paper journals and on abstracts and indexes catalogued on paper, microfiches and cards. They had to go to the library to find these resources. Then at the end of the 1990s came the widespread use of the internet, and researchers came to depend on big library databases, using key words to search them.

But then came Google. I'll say this very quietly so not too many of my colleagues hear (and I'm hoping you won't tell them), but when I am doing my own research I rarely use any other means of starting my searches. There is no point in being snobbish about Google. It works. Not only does it work, but it works better than all of the posh library databases. Somehow (and it remains a total mystery to me how it does it) it seems to know what I am thinking and what I am wanting. It is free, reliable and quick. Not only is there Google, but there are also Google Scholar and Google Books. If you don't already know how they work, here's how ...

Google

Unless you have been residing on Mars for the last 20 years you will know how to use Google. Just a few hints:

- Type as much or as little as you wish into Google's search box. For example, if you are interested in whether the Head Start programme produces beneficial consequences for primary school children, you could either type in the whole sentence (that is to say, just like this: *Does the Head Start programme produce beneficial consequences for primary school children?*) and click on 'Search', or you can pick out the key words (*primary Head Start benefits*). Try it in different ways and see what emerges.

- Google searches for the words in your query in any order; it doesn't keep the words you type in as phrases. If you want to keep the words in the same order – as phrases – then put them in double quotation marks. So, for example, if you wanted Google to search for the phrase 'Head Start' among the other words, you would type in *primary "Head Start" benefits*. It will then search just for the phrase 'head start', leaving out all other occurrences of 'head' and 'start'.
- If you want to search for something and you want the search to become narrower, so that it leaves out references to certain subjects or areas, you can put in a minus sign before a word or term that you wish to omit. So, if I wanted to find out about primary Head Start benefits, but I wanted only to look at children above reception age, I could type in *primary "Head Start" benefits -reception*. It's good to practise with many different ways of phrasing a Google query.

Google Scholar

Google Scholar works in much the same way as Google, but it is more targeted at the kinds of reading material you will be looking for in university life. You can access it from http://scholar.google.com/. Once you have accessed the Google Scholar main page you use it in the same way that you would have used Google. That is to say, you can type in a question or a more targeted inquiry based on a particular article that you have already identified.

For example, try typing in the same question that I used above for testing Google: *Does the Head Start programme produce beneficial consequences for primary school children?* When you do this and click on 'Search' you will get many thousands of responses, as you do on ordinary Google. However, these responses, rather than being general, will only be to books and articles. The 'best' ones will usually be at the beginning, but you will also find good ones lower down (though they will become progressively less relevant as you proceed downwards).

Figure 3.3 shows the first 'answer' I got when I typed that question into Google Scholar. The figure shows the various elements of the Google Scholar 'answer' page. As with all forms of electronic resource, the key is to keep playing with it: click on links to see what happens.

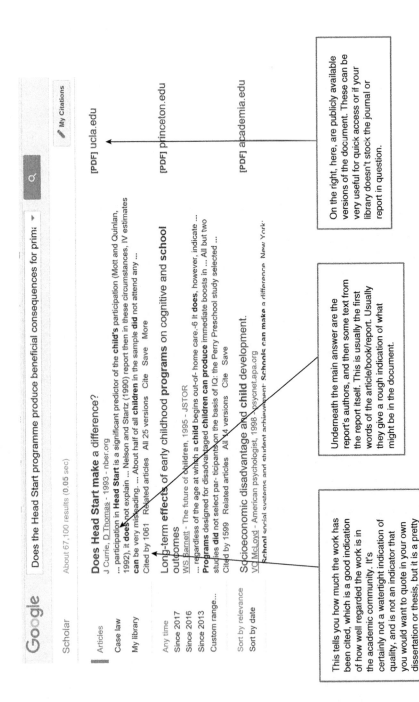

Figure 3.3   Google Scholar – the important bits

I am reliably informed by librarians that Google Scholar will not pick up all relevant references because the information released to it is sometimes restricted by publishers. Although this may change with time, do be aware that you will also need to use the subject-specific databases I mention later in this chapter. You can start off with a Google Scholar search and then supplement it with the targeted databases.

Google Books

As if Google Scholar weren't miraculous enough, there is also Google Books, which will find relevant books, point you to the page(s) relevant to your search inquiry, and even show you the page(s) themselves. From the Google main page, just type 'Google books' directly into the search box.

Typing a general inquiry is less likely to be successful with Google Books than with a general Google search. So you may have to begin your search by using fewer words and making a more general enquiry. Remember that when you are asking Google just to look for books it is searching a far narrower range of resources, so keep your options open by reducing the number of words in your search.

Getting access to journals via your library

Some of the sources that you access using Google will be journal articles. You will emerge from the Google Scholar page with a publisher's journal page which provides an abstract and an invitation to buy a full download of the article. Don't be tempted to buy it, because you will probably have access to the journal through your university library. Most, if not all, university libraries nowadays enable you to access, without paying, a huge array of journals via a central jumping-off point. That jumping-off point at my university is called FindIt@ Bham; the one at yours will be called something similar, such as iDiscover or SOLO. When you click on the right page, you'll come up with a screen something like the one in Figure 3.4.

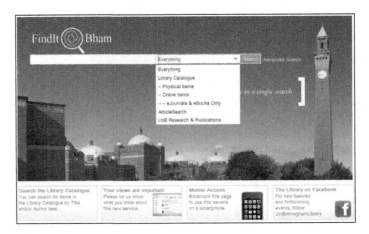

Figure 3.4   Finding resources in your university library

In the empty box near the top left, you type the name of the resource that you want (e.g. *Harvard Educational Review*), and from the drop-down menu to the right of it you click on the appropriate option. I advise avoiding the 'Everything' choice since it seems to check everything in the world, which – maybe it's just a personal thing – leaves me confused by the sheer multiplicity of offerings; if you want the online version of the journal, click on 'Online Items' but remember that while most *journals* are online, not many *books* are.

University libraries get access to packages of journals (for which they pay large amounts of money) via something called 'Shibboleth', which should take you automatically to a set of resources. (You don't actually need to know about Shibboleth, since your search should take you robotically through the system; I'm only mentioning it in case 'Shibboleth' flashes up momentarily on the screen, as it sometimes does, and you think 'What the plonking hell is Shibboleth?') If, on your introductory tour of the library, you haven't been told about how to get access to journals in this way, go along to one of the librarians and ask about it. Don't be frightened to do this: in an information age this is what librarians are expected to do – to help you gain access to all kinds of information sources. It's what they get paid for.

Figure 3.5   Searching for an e-journal

Remind them of this. (That's a joke, by the way.)
Actually, most librarians I know don't conform to the
frosty stereotype at all; they are friendly and helpful.
And the new information finding systems are easy to
use: just be prepared to invest an hour or two playing
with whichever system your library uses and seeing
what it can do for you.

You will be given a username and a password for your
library system. Usually these will be the same ones as for
your university. Once you have entered your username
and password details you will have access to an array of
databases that carry the journal. Figure 3.5 shows the sort
of page that emerges when you have done this. It is from
my own university library, and yours will be similar.

Type in the name of the journal that came up from
your Google inquiry and press 'Go' (or the equivalent in
your library's system) and you will come up with a page
like the one in Figure 3.6. My library's system gives
information about which databases have access to the
journal, and when I press 'Find It!' at the bottom of the
page it gives me the choice of locating the article I want
in one of several databases. It doesn't matter which one
you use, but just check that the particular database
(such as SwetsWise) carries the journal for the *year* that
you want.

Figure 3.6 Selecting from the databases

Because every university's system is different, giving you more exact information from this point on in the process will not be of much use to you. So the next step is to make that library visit. Before you start asking librarians lots of questions, though, ask for the library's various leaflets and sheets on electronic access and try to make sense of them. Play around for a while on the computer, and find what you can and can't do – what you can and can't access. Make a list of what will hopefully be more targeted questions and then go and see the librarian.

The Web of Science

The Web of Science provides the fullest and most authoritative resource on citation information. In other words, it gives you 'leads' to all of the articles published on a particular subject (or by a particular author) in reputable peer review journals over a certain timespan; and, like Google Scholar, it will also tell you lots of other information about those articles, such as the other articles that have referenced it.

You will be able to log in to the Web of Science only if your university subscribes (and nearly all do), so you will need to log in via your university library system. Type 'Web of Science' into the library search box and look for the answer that comes up with 'Thomson Scientific'. Once you are at the Web of Science home page and you are asked which databases you want to search (under the dropdown box labelled 'All Databases'), click the option labelled 'Web of Science™ Core Collection'. You'll be able to search for a range of years, by topic and/or by author.

It's big. Because of its size it has a bit of a reputation for being clunky to use. However, it has recently been

Citation: A reference to a particular piece of work, usually by using the Harvard system (e.g. 'Smith, 2002').

redesigned and is now much more user-friendly. Because of its size, though, it's easy to miss out on many of its features, and I would recommend taking a look at the official Thomson Scientific tutorial on how to use it. To find this, type 'Web of Science quick tour' into your search engine.

Zetoc

Your university library will provide a way for you to use Zetoc, which gives access to the British Library's 30,000 journals and 16,000 conference proceedings, published every year. Type http://zetoc.jisc.ac.uk/ and fill in your university's details. Zetoc is particularly useful as it includes an email alerting service to help you keep up to date with relevant new articles and papers – in other words, Zetoc will automatically send you an email when a new article appears that 'hits the spot' as far as certain criteria that you specify are concerned. You could, for example, tell it to send you all articles by a certain author, or all articles with certain key words in the title, or all articles in each new issue of a certain journal.

Zetoc will give you:

- a *search* facility, for citations of journal articles and conference proceedings – a bit like Google Scholar.
- the *alert* facility, to send you email alerts of new articles that may be of interest to you.
- *facilitated access* to full texts of articles and papers. Zetoc itself provides access to the table of contents rather than the full text. However, once you have found an article of interest, the full record page provides links to help you access the full text.
- *feeds* (also called RSS feeds – RSS stands for Really Simple Syndication), which help you to keep automatically up to date with what is happening in a journal. Click on 'Zetoc RSS – Access' in Zetoc, and then click on the feed you want to see. In the example in Figure 3.7, I've clicked on the feed for the *American Educational Research Journal*. When you subscribe to the feed, it will be added to your 'Favorites Center' in your browser, which will automatically check the website and download new content so you can see what is new since you last visited the feed.

Finding books

As with journals, your first port of call in finding books will be your university library site. Here, the usual course of action is to use your university's library catalogue, which will normally have some kind of search box. You can then use key words (any combination

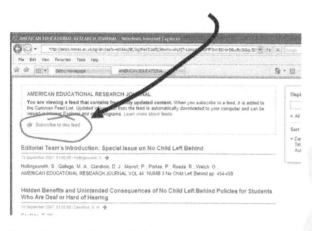

Figure 3.7   Subscribing to a feed

of subject key words, words in the title or authors' surnames) to find what you are looking for.

There are other resources for hunting down books which may not be in your university library's stock:

- *WorldCat* is a catalogue of major libraries throughout the world which can show the location of specific titles in the libraries nearest to you.
- *The Library of Congress* catalogue is a major catalogue which is often used to check bibliographic details of hard-to-find books.
- *Bookdata Online* is a database of books in print available from UK and some US publishers. It can search for chapters or sections within books as well as by title, author and publisher, and it also keeps details of books which have gone out of print.
- *Amazon* is also a good resource for finding books (but not articles). Type www.amazon.co.uk (or www.amazon.com for the US version). It's not as good as Google Book Search but it does have some useful features such as 'Look Inside!' which allows you to look at the contents pages and to read the first chapter, the index and some other information about the book. Also, it gives you information about what other customers who have bought the book have also bought – surprisingly useful, since many will, inexplicably, seem to be on much the same train of thought as you. There will be a publisher's synopsis of the book too and, if you are lucky, some reasonably informative reviews (but often also some spectacularly uninformative ones). Clearly, this is not information disinterestedly given by Amazon out of the love of knowledge – they want to sell you books, so be wary.

Something that the Amazon website is particularly useful for is when you are compiling your reference list. Unless you are absolutely perfect, you will have lost certain references, or you will have somehow missed off a key bit of the reference when making your notes. The Amazon website has co-authors, the publisher, the date of publication and dates of various editions, and this is often all you need to enable you to plug the holes.

EThOS

EThOS is the British Library's digital repository of all doctoral theses completed at UK institutions. Such work can provide invaluable help on precisely targeted subjects, though I should re-state the point I made earlier – don't use other people's theses as a model for your own, since they are of highly variable quality.

EThOS is part of the British Library's programme of digitisation of research theses in the UK. A lot of theses are already digitised, in which case you can download them straight away as PDFs, but those that are not you can ask to have digitised (amazing!).

To search further afield for relevant theses, you can try:

- Networked Digital Library of Theses and Dissertations: Electronic open-access theses, available at http://search.ndltd.org/
- DART-Europe e-Theses Portal: Electronic open-access theses from Europe, available at www.dart-europe.eu.

Find these via your favourite search engine if they are not immediately available via your library.

Inter-library loan

I've been at pains to point out that you should be very wary about clicking on any link that asks you to part with money for an article download. This is partly because there is an excellent chance that you will be able to access the article or book completely free through your university library account. Or you will be able to see enough of it to gain a sufficient impression of what it is about. If the worst comes to

the worst, though, and you decide that you simply must have a copy of the article and you are not able to access it by one of the means already explained here, you can get the article via inter-library loan, either electronically or as a photocopy. Ask your librarian about this. There will probably be a charge, but it won't be nearly as much as it would be from a publisher's website.

Specific subject databases

Aside from the generic databases I have just mentioned, there are also specific databases for particular subjects.

ERIC

ERIC stands for the *Education Resources Information Center*, which is an online digital library of education research and other information. (I'm not actually sure how an 'online digital library' is different from a database, but never mind, I'll give it its Sunday-best name since that's what its publishers call it.) ERIC is paid for by the United States Department of Education, and, as you would guess given these credentials, it is a pretty hefty piece of kit. It provides access to over one million records, including the 'grey literature' of, for example, fact sheets, information briefs, research syntheses, conference papers and policy reports. The latter are difficult to get hold of from any other source, and ERIC is worth consulting for this alone. It is updated continuously. With a move to open-access publishing of scientific findings now, many of the records are available in full text.

To search on ERIC, Google 'ERIC basic search', and try their Thesaurus for key terms that will take you to the area in which you are interested. Also try 'My ERIC', which enables you to join a community of people interested in the same subject as you, and lets you save searches, get alerts and even submit your own material for inclusion in the database.

BEI

The BEI is the British Education Index, which is the British equivalent of ERIC. It is rather smaller than ERIC, with, at the time of writing, 175,000 references to journal articles. The database grows by over 8,000 records per year. One particularly interesting feature of the BEI is the access it gives to Education-*line*, which offers a collection of over 6,000 full-length texts, most of them conference papers.

PubMed

If you work in healthcare, including medicine, you will almost certainly want access to PubMed, which is the repository for biomedical literature. It is truly enormous, containing 26 million citations for biomedical literature from life science journals and online books.

CINAHL

For students of nursing, CINAHL offers, as the producers put it, 'the definitive research tool for nursing and allied health professionals'. It indexes more than 5,400 journals, with full text for more than 1,400. The topics included cover nursing, biomedicine, health-sciences librarianship, alternative/complementary medicine, consumer health and 17 allied health disciplines. It also gives access to healthcare books, nursing dissertations, conference proceedings, educational software, audiovisuals and book chapters.

PsycINFO

Primarily for psychologists, PsycINFO is run by the American Psychological Association and contains 4.2 million records in the behavioural sciences and mental health. It ranges over the literature in psychology and allied disciplines such as education, linguistics, medicine, nursing, pharmacology, physiology, psychiatry and sociology.

Other databases

There are dozens of other subject-specific databases. To review these to see which would be useful for you, go to your appropriate library webpage. As I have already noted, most university libraries nowadays will provide a page that is a bit like Google, which lets you search the vast expanse of the whole library. My library's (open to everyone) is at http://findit.bham.ac.uk/. From here, you go to the top right of the page and click on 'Find Databases', then click on 'Search by Subject', then choose a category such as 'Healthcare', and then a subcategory (if you wish) such as nursing, and the webpage will list all relevant subject-specific databases.

It's worth finishing this section on the world of subject-specific databases and other online resources by saying that some of them offer remarkable resources, while others don't seem to last very long. In fact, I wonder how some of them last even as long as they do, given the power of the competition in big search engines such as Google Scholar. How should you judge which to look into? I think that you should look to see if these resources offer some added value over Google, such as the ability to connect with other like-minded people or the facility to export citations or help you to organise and format those that you export. These latter features can be really useful.

Reference managers

One of the advantages of using databases such as ERIC, PubMed and Web of Science is that they enable you to export citations directly into reference management programs such as *EndNote, Reference Manager* or *ProCite*. Your university library will have a webpage which explains how to use these. The reference management software will organise all of your references for you and even format them appropriately. For undergraduates, I think that probably the easiest to use is a web-based system called *RefWorks*, to which you will have free access if your university subscribes. (If it doesn't, you have to pay, but 1,200 universities across the world do subscribe so there's a fair chance yours will.) It enables you to gather, manage, store and share all types of information, as well

as generate citations and bibliographies. Once you have been a member, you stay a member, even when you leave your university.

Similar to RefWorks are WorldCat, which finds books and articles in the collections of 10,000 libraries worldwide and lets you export the citations that you find into your own **bibliography** or **references** list, and CiteULike, which offers reference to 8.4 million articles and enables you to receive automated article recommendations and to share references with your fellow students.

Think Digital **working with other students and researchers** Research can be isolating. It's surprising how often I feel that I know all I think it is possible to know about a subject, having done a thorough literature search, and then I talk to a colleague or to one of my students and I'm off on an entirely new line of inquiry that I hadn't even considered before I spoke to them. It might be a tangential topic that turns out to be not so tangential, or the name of a researcher who happens to be at the centre of the field of inquiry, but for some reason had eluded my gaze. For this reason, it's good always to try to connect with others, and there are now some easy ways of doing this via special social networking services:

- MethodSpace (www.methodspace.com) is a social networking service for social scientists run by the publisher SAGE. As well as networking, it offers video clips and advice.
- ResearchGate (www.researchgate.net) offers networking with other researchers (mostly professional researchers) and a search engine that browses academic databases.
- Graduate Junction (www.graduatejunction.net) is a social networking service aimed at postgraduates and postdoctoral researchers.
- Academia.edu enables you to connect with professional researchers and to keep updated with their latest publications.

Hints on searching – separating the wheat from the chaff

When you begin to search the literature, it's a good idea, first of all, to draw up a *search strategy* in which you assemble key words and phrases, together with

NOTES

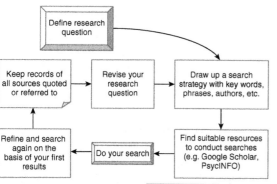

Figure 3.8   Developing a search strategy (with thanks to Zbig Gas of Birmingham University Library Services)

key authors. Then, think about the search engines and databases that may be helpful, such as Google Scholar, ERIC and PsycINFO. When you have completed your searches, refine the first search by perhaps adding a new key name that you have found in your first search, or making one of your research terms more tightly defined. And don't forget: keep records of where sources have emerged from (particularly page numbers, if you quote), together with the internet reference (the URL) if the material is only available from an internet source. If you record all of this information at this stage, you'll save yourself a lot of time later on. The process is summarised in Figure 3.8. Note that the process is cyclical: it may be the case that you need to redefine your research question after you have done your first search, for you may discover that there is already a lot of research on the topic you wanted to address, or you may find that there is a particular area that is clearly crying out for further research.

Two common problems that students come up with on doing a literature review are (1) that they can find no information, and (2) that there is just too much information.

Let's look at the first one: you can find absolutely no information at all on your topic of interest. The thing is, it is most unlikely to be the case in reality that there is no information to find on your topic, so if you are finding nothing in your various searches you should examine where you may be going wrong. It may be the case that you are not using enough search facilities, or, more likely, that you are making your search too narrow. You are pinpointing your search terms too finely, or throwing away related information that is not on the precise subject of your interest, but is connected and therefore useful. Remember that your literature review ultimately will not be on the exact topic of your research, but rather it will be on the more general subject *surrounding* your research. So, if you wanted to look, for example, at how head teachers cope with difficult people and you are coming up with nothing, it may be that you are searching too specifically. Your searches may need to concentrate on something broader, such as teacher stress, and you may wish to think about what 'difficult people' means. This will in turn suggest that you think about the 'people' with whom head teachers come into contact: there are the other teachers in the school, other head teachers in the area, parents, pupils, teaching assistants, administrators, support staff, etc. Were you thinking of all of these when you posed your question, or just certain categories? So, think about the broader ways that your question may be framed. Think about alternative search terms.

Think like a search engine. Find alternative ways of formulating ideas connected to your research question.

You'll see in Figure 3.9 that the original question about how head teachers cope with difficult people has been reformulated into a range of terms that you might not have thought of originally; you might, for example, ask why 'drugs' and 'suicide' are included as alternatives to 'coping'. The key is to try to think like a search engine. The search engine is sorting through words and phrases in an unimaginably large set of websites, a tiny fraction of which will contain, in some sense or other, 'stories' about head teachers and difficult people. But these 'stories' are hardly likely to be framed in these exact terms. They are more likely to contain words that are associated with the words you have identified. What are difficult people likely to do to a head teacher? To cause stress. What does stress lead to? Possibly drinking excess alcohol, taking drugs or even suicide. These may not be the coping strategies you were thinking of, but they will lead into stories that address the topic, perhaps comparing these routes out of stress with more positive ones. So the key is – if you don't at first succeed, try thinking like the search engine and formulating your question in a number of different ways using a range of related words.

Remember also that your literature review is a general contextualisation. So stress in *teachers* as a *general* group is likely to be of relevance when you are thinking about stress in *head* teachers. Don't limit your search by a very precise word when you may find some very interesting information that relates to broader issues.

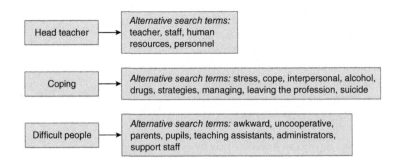

Figure 3.9 Turning your question into alternative search terms

Now the second common problem: you are swamped with information on the topic. Suppose you are interested in the attainment of black boys and you enter *black boys attainment*. The search emerges with nearly four million 'answers'. If you now put in a term that is related to your interests (say *14–19*) it will reduce the number dramatically. Or you can put in the name of a key academic or a key commentator to delimit the search. Ask your tutor for key names. For example, if I put in the name of someone who I know is an expert here – *'Gus John'* (in double quote marks because I want Google to find *only* references to Gus John, not to all the Johns and all the Guses in the world) – it reduces the four million to 3,280.

So, the key is to imagine that in your literature review the process is like sieving: with too coarse a mesh you let through too much; with too fine a mesh you don't get enough. Or imagine that you are trying to separate the wheat from the chaff. If you blow too hard you get rid of the wheat as well as the chaff. If you don't blow hard enough you don't get rid of the chaff.

Understanding how sources are cited – the Harvard referencing system

You need to understand the Harvard referencing system for two reasons. First, when you are reading, you need to understand the way that sources are referenced by authors in books and journal articles. Second, when you are writing, you need to know how to provide references yourself when you write up your literature review – in other words, how to give the full details of books and articles you refer to so that others can find them. There are various ways in which referencing can be done, but the overwhelmingly preferred method in the social sciences is the Harvard system. (It has several variants, and you will find that the Harvard system may be called one of these variants, notably 'APA', which stands for American Psychological Association. Don't worry too much about the variations unless you want to submit something for publication: just go for bog-standard Harvard.)

This is how it works. You find a source – let's say an article written by Jane Brown. If you then want to refer to the article in the literature review of your project you do so by using the author's surname, followed by the year of the publication in brackets – for example, by saying 'In a large study, Brown (2004) discovered that little bits of fluff accumulate in people's pockets.' You will then give the full details of Brown's publication in a list headed 'References' at the end of your report (not 'Bibliography', incidentally, which has the meaning of 'here are some interesting books that are related to my thesis' – by contrast, 'References' applies only to the works you have actually referred to in your text). We'll come on to how to compile the list in a moment, but first let's look at how you make reference to various kinds of sources in the text, since these will take a variety of forms.

How you make reference *in the text*:

- For a single author of a book or a journal article, use the author's surname (without first name or initial) followed by the date of the publication in brackets, e.g. 'Sweedlepipe (2005) found that the fluff referred to by Brown (2004) is composed mainly of cotton fibre and dead skin.'
- Where a work is by two authors, use both authors' names followed by the date in brackets: 'Sweedlepipe and Sikes (2007), in later work, showed that the ratio of cotton fibre to dead skin (by weight) is between 3:1 and 5:1.'
- For more authors, use the first author's name, followed just by 'et al.' (which means 'and others'), e.g. 'Sweedlepipe et al. (2008) illustrated the mechanism by which cotton fibre bonds to dead skin.'
- If you actually quote from the author, you must give the page number from which the quotation comes, putting the page number after a colon after the publication date: 'Sweedlepipe (2005: 134) sums up the importance of the topic this way: "The precise mechanism involved in the accumulation of fluff in the pockets is one of the greatest mysteries remaining for science to solve."'
- In the unlikely case of an author having two outputs in 2005 that you are referencing in the text, this is indicated by 'a', 'b', 'c', etc. after the date: 'Sikes (2005a) found that trouser pockets of male students contained significantly more fluff than those of female students, and in later work (2005b) hypothesised that the lower amounts of fluff in

female pockets were due to a higher frequency of personal hygiene measures (principally by washing and clothes laundering) among females.'
- A book that has been republished long after the original publication may be cited with the author's name as usual, but followed by both the first publication and republication dates, e.g. Ryle (1949/1990).

Then, at the end of your dissertation, you will have a *reference section*, headed 'References', which contains the full details of all the material to which you have referred. This is how you set out your 'References' section:

- For a book: name(s) and initial(s) of author(s) followed by year in brackets, followed by book title in italics, followed by place of publication and publisher. For example:

  Sweedlepipe, P. (2005) *The Fluff in People's Pockets*. London: Sage.

- For a journal article: name and initial(s) of author(s) followed by year in brackets, followed by article title, followed by name of journal in italics, followed by volume number, issue number and page numbers. For example:

  Sweedlepipe, P. and Sikes, B. (2007) Ratios of cotton fibres to exfoliated skin in trouser pockets of US males. *International Journal of Fluff and Allied Detritus*, 31 (1), 252–7.

- For a downloadable internet source: name and initial(s) of author(s) followed by year in brackets, followed by article title, followed by the words 'Available at' and the internet source, followed by the date you accessed it in brackets. For example:

  Wells, M. (2005) Paxman answers the questions. *Guardian Unlimited*. Available at: https://www.theguardian.com/media/2005/jan/31/mondaymediasection.politicsandthemedia (accessed 15 January 2017).

When formatting the reference list, it looks good if each reference has a hanging indent – in other words, the first line is formatted to the left, as normal, and the subsequent lines are indented. You can produce the hanging indent in Word by putting the cursor anywhere in the reference and pressing Ctrl+T. Or do the whole lot together by selecting all the references (with your mouse, left-click at the beginning and drag down to the end) and then pressing Ctrl+T.

The list should be in alphabetical order. To alphabetise a list automatically in Word (pre-2007),

select the whole list with your mouse, then click on
'Table', then click on 'Sort', and click on 'OK'. In Word
2007 (and after) look for the 'Sort' button. You will find
this under the 'Home' tab, in the 'Paragraph' group:
there's a little box that looks like this: ⊞. Click on it.
The list will miraculously appear in order. (If it doesn't,
the settings on your copy of Word may have been
changed and you will need to look at the particular
instructions under 'Sort' more carefully.)

As I mentioned in relation to subject-specific
databases, there are now several software systems for
organising your references automatically, such as
EndNote, Reference Manager and RefWorks, and your
library will almost certainly offer support in using
these through leaflets, courses and email query and
will provide a web link on this and related issues. My
own library's (open to everybody), which also offers
detailed advice on the use of the Harvard method, is at
www.i-cite.bham.ac.uk/. This excellent website
provides all you need to know and more. Click on
'How to reference correctly' and on the next page click
'Harvard (author-date)'. It's most likely that you will
be asked by your tutors to use Harvard referencing, but
it may be the case in some subjects that you will be
asked to use Numbering (Vancouver) or Footnotes or
OSCOLA (for law students). The website also gives
guidance on all of these.

Taking notes and quotes

There used to be a time when people had to take careful
notes on small cards of every source they consulted,
which would be filed alphabetically. (For people like me,
who suffer from a mild variant of Asperger's syndrome,
this was enormously satisfying.) Researchers had to be
meticulous about everything they did, punctiliously
keeping records of references – because if you lost one or
forgot to record it, it would take hours or even days to
track it down again. Things aren't like that any more:
you can now find a lost reference on the internet in
seconds. And note-taking is different too: you can now
be a lot more creative and idiosyncratic in the way that
you keep notes on your word-processor. The problem

with the old card index file systems was that they almost encouraged you to think of the literature review as a collection of names and notes. Now, though, if you take notes more fluidly – as I suggest in the next section – you can add observations, make connections and link one source with another through the notes that you take as you are reading.

A notes file in Word

The software packages I have just mentioned (End-Note, etc.) seem to work for some people. However, I find a simpler system is just to paste everything that would conceivably be of interest into a Word file which I can then search for the key words that I want. When I say 'key words' I don't mean anything very technical. I just mean that I use Word's search facility (Ctrl+F) to look for a word or part of a word that will find the topic I am looking for. So, for example, if I were interested in finding anything mentioning *science* or *scientists* I would ask the program to find 'scie'.

As I am reading, I copy quotations (and, importantly, the references from which they come) willy-nilly into the file. I always make a point of recording the reference as exactly as possible, and then the notes as I see fit at the time. I make it clear with the use of quotation marks which are my own words and which are the author's. This may not have the satisfying tidiness of the old card index, but the question arises how far that alphabetical imperative is still necessary. When you can now simply find what you need to find in a file, why does it need to be in alphabetical order? You simply need to type a search word or phrase into the 'Find' box and the machine will do the rest. When you can easily fillet and sort a list alphabetically (see pp. 84–5), why bother putting them in alphabetical order at the outset?

Many of the notes I take are copied directly from the internet by cutting and pasting. This is particularly useful in copying reference details. However, you should always be very clear in your recording which are the author's words and which are your

own. Whenever you quote someone else's words you must always *make full and clear attribution to the author in question.*

Plagiarism

Occasionally students are tempted to try to pass off the work and the words of others as their own. Your university will almost certainly have a policy on plagiarism, how it is defined, why you should not do it, how you can avoid it and the penalties for doing it. My own university defines plagiarism as:

the submission for formal assessment of an assignment that incorporates, without proper citation or acknowledgement by means of an accepted referencing standard, the intellectual property or work of a third party.

Its policy, which is fairly typical of all, is given at https://intranet.birmingham.ac.uk/as/studentservices/conduct/misconduct/plagiarism/index.aspx.

> *What your supervisor wants* **for your literature review** You'll probably have to produce a draft of your literature review, which your supervisor will usually comment on and edit, probably using 'Track Changes' in Word. (Find out how to use 'Track Changes' in Chapter 2.)

Having had the sense to read my book, you are not of course the sort of person who plagiarises. However, just speaking generally for a moment, plagiarism is a pity for a number of reasons.

- First, it is against the spirit of the thing: the aim is to learn, develop and improve – not just to get a certificate. So why pretend?
- Second, there is a real risk of being caught, as the likelihood of being found out is increasing as plagiarism software improves, and the penalties at any university are serious for those who are found plagiarising. Indeed, most universities are now demanding that all work must pass through plagiarism software such as Turnitin at submission, and students may be deducted marks, made to resubmit or even failed if they are deemed to have plagiarised.

- Third, there is no penalty for drawing from others or using their ideas and words, as long as these are acknowledged. In fact, your marker will be pleased to see evidence of wide reading and the intelligent synthesis of this.

Although, having said this, you should avoid overdoing quotations. Generally, one short quotation per page would be the maximum I would want to see, with perhaps the occasional extended quotation. The aim in a literature review is to outline and demonstrate interconnections, not to present a list of other people's verbatim words. The key is analysis and synthesis, and quotations do not really play a role in either, unless you are using them to provide an excellent illustration of a point that an authority is making.

Overview

Your literature review is not an add-on: it should be a major contributor to the development of your project. It should help you to shape your questions by enabling you to find out what has already been done. The literature exists in many shapes and forms and you should be discriminating in what you choose to include – even seemingly unimpeachable sources can be wrong. This is where critical awareness begins: show that you understand that there is always room for interpretation in the reading of any piece of work. Interpret and understand what others have done, and weave their contributions into a narrative. The literature review should be a narrative – a story – not a list.

Further reading

Arksey, H. and O'Malley, L. (2005) Scoping studies: towards a methodological framework. *International Journal of Social Research Methodology*, 8 (1), 19–32. Available at: http://eprints. whiterose.ac.uk/1618/1/Scopingstudies.pdf. **Defines, describes and discusses the use of detailed literature reviews, which are sometimes called 'scoping studies'.**

Campbell Collaboration. Available at: http://www.campbellcollaboration.org/. **This contains systematic reviews in education, crime and justice, and social welfare. Useful not just for the analysis and synthesis of studies, but also for examples of the way that evidence is balanced.**

Cochrane Collaboration. Available at: http://www.cochrane.org/. **This is a library of systematic reviews in healthcare.**

Evidence for Policy and Practice Information and Co-ordinating Centre (EPPI-Centre). Available at: http://eppi.ioe.ac.uk/cms/. **This is similar to Campbell, but tends to focus more on education.**

Fink, A. (2013) *Conducting Research Literature Reviews: From the Internet to Paper* (4th edn.). London: Sage. **Systematic, with good examples on searching in health, education and business domains. Not just the process, but also good on evaluating the articles you select to review.**

Hart, C. (2018) *Doing a Literature Review: Releasing the Social Science Research Imagination* (2nd edn.). London: Sage. **This detailed book goes far beyond the mechanics of the literature review to discuss the organisation of ideas, the development of argument and the liberation of what the author calls 'the research imagination'. Oriented towards the postgraduate rather than the undergraduate.**

Pears, R. and Shields, G. (2016) *Cite them Right: The Essential Referencing Guide* (10th edn). Basingstoke: Palgrave Macmillan. **Very helpful on the intricacies of sorting out your Harvard from your APA, and especially good on the problems of referencing internet sources.**

Research Information Network (2011) *Social Media: A Guide for Researchers*. Leicester: RIN. Available at: http://www.rin.ac.uk/system/files/attachments/social_media_guide_for_screen_0.pdf (accessed 14 October 2016). **This is an excellent guide on the value of social networking and social media generally, with some good advice on how to connect with others.**

Ridley, D. (2012) *The Literature Review: A Step-by-Step Guide for Students* (2nd edn.). London: Sage. **Practical and easy to read with lots of examples, and a good section on 'voice'.**

Robinson, F.P. (1970) *Effective Study* (4th edn). New York: Harper & Row. **Good for advice on speed reading.**

Williams, K. and Carroll, J. (2009) *Referencing and Understanding Plagiarism*. London: Palgrave. **A useful little book that tells you all you need to know about the subjects of the title.**

 Still have questions? Check out my supporting website for more advice and activities at: https://study.sagepub.com/thomasrp3e

CHAPTER 3 CHECKLIST

You may find it helpful to copy this table and write down the answers to the questions. Have you …

	Notes	
1 … used the main databases in your field of applied social science to locate relevant literature?		☐
2 … secured some relevant and high-quality sources from which to draw?	What are the main themes, agreements and disagreements? Write them down here.	☐
3 … mapped out the main issues?		☐
4 … drawn a storyboard?	What are the 'stories' that emerge? Which will you follow?	☐
5 … understood how the Harvard referencing system works?		☐

10 Reading and Researching the Literature

Greasley, P.

Most of the learning that happens at university is achieved by you – the student. We're just there to facilitate learning – and provide some feedback. Unfortunately, for some students at least, this means researching and reading the literature. And that doesn't mean a quick look at Wikipedia.

In this chapter we'll look at the importance of exploring the literature and taking account of different perspectives (being aware that just because something is in print doesn't necessarily mean it's true), along with some advice about the kinds of references you should be citing in your assignment.

Tip 14: One thing leads to another

This is not a tip about amorous liaisons; rather it's about the process of reading and researching for an assignment. If you're doing it right, one thing should lead to another. That is, you might start with (heaven forbid) Wikipedia, or perhaps a general textbook, and then follow the references to other sources of literature. It's called research and it's like conducting an investigation, digging deeper and deeper into the literature.

When I used to write assignments I would often spend the day on a tangent: having read one article, the references would lead me to another, and then that would lead me to another, and so on, until I found myself in another place completely. As the following comments from the survey (see Chapter 2) show, this is a good thing (if you have the time). It shows that you're adopting the role of the explorer (Chapter 1), venturing beyond the set texts (and in doing so you may be able to impress the tutor by telling them something they didn't know – Tip 21).

What tutors like

- Reading widely and using the literature to develop a critical argument

- A good, broad range of quality references that are appropriately employed and correctly cited

- Demonstrating wide, detailed reading around the subject

- Evidence of a good range of reading (including texts taking a different perspective)

- Reading over and above the set texts

- Use and critique of appropriate reference resources that demonstrate a thorough literature search

- Well-referenced points

- Good use of references to support discussion such as when students cite several authors for one 'statement', showing they have read around and integrated what they have read

What tutors dislike

- Failing to engage with literature

- Not reading widely enough to give a basis for the arguments (or assertions)

- Reliance on only one or two reference sources

- Poor reading round the subject and not using up-to-date references

Tip 15: **Use up-to-date references**

Obtaining up-to-date references can be crucial for a good mark. I recall marking one assignment discussing the evidence for homeopathy (an 'alternative therapy') and it failed to discuss or reference the most recent review of the evidence, which I had, incidentally, highlighted in the lectures. This oversight significantly reduced my impression of the assignment, and the mark, which was largely justified: here was a key reference that had been ignored. This also highlights the importance of conducting a literature search (see Tip 22).

The most up-to-date articles will be in journals, and it's worth checking whether such articles are available in a preprint electronic version, since journal articles can actually take a while before they become available in print. For example, it took over two years to publish the results of the survey upon which this book is based (Greasley and Cassidy, 2010). Now obviously, this depends on the article and the journal. If the title is 'A cheap and simple cure for all known diseases' or 'Cold fusion repeatedly demonstrated', it may only take a few months for it to appear in print. But if it's 'Injuries due to falling coconuts', or 'Pigeons' discrimination of paintings by Monet and Picasso', you could be waiting a while. (These are actual articles – the former appeared in the *Journal of Trauma* and the latter appeared in the *Journal of the Experimental Analysis of Behavior*.)

Tip 16: Avoid dodgy sources

The source of your references may be crucial to the reliability of the information you are providing in your assignment. For example, I remember reading an essay evaluating the evidence for acupuncture in which the main reference was from *Acupuncture Today* (a 'trade' magazine) – which is not necessarily the most objective and unbiased source of information. It's a bit like citing *Flying Saucer Review* for evidence of UFOs.

It's not surprising, then, that 'poor-quality references' was an issue raised in the survey of tutors.

What tutors dislike

- Using weak references, e.g. Reader's Digest, 9 o'clock news
- Not using original sources, e.g. Doctor on the video shown in the lecture talking about his research [rather than a published source of information]
- Citing the *Sun* newspaper as the main source of evidence for whether a therapy works!

Imagine if the assignment preceding yours has been citing original articles from the *Lancet*, the *British Medical Journal*, the *Quarterly Journal of Experimental Psychology* and the *Harvard Law Review*, and all you've got to offer is the *Sun*, *Wikipedia* and 'the video shown in the lecture'. It's not going to look good, is it?

Tip 17: www.usesparingly.com

The increasing use and reliance on references from the Web was another source of marker distress. Here are a few comments.

What tutors dislike

- Using too many internet references

- Internet reference sources - a small number may be OK, particularly when they come from reputable sources, however copious unrecognised sources will not do

- Non-existent web addresses on the references list [markers do sometimes check the web references - especially if they look dodgy]

Perhaps the key word in the above comments is 'reputable': synonyms include 'of good reputation', 'highly regarded', 'trustworthy'; antonyms might include 'dubious', 'biased' or 'dodgy'. The problem is one of quality assurance. Unlike articles in journals, there is no peer-review process (where other academics review the quality of the article prior to acceptance).

There is no doubt that the internet is a wonderful tool – information at your finger tips – but you need to be selective. Aside from dubious websites promoting their own agendas (e.g. alternative remedies that will cure all ills), some people purposely enter false information, on Wikipedia, for example.

Tip 18: **Wikipedia: cite it at your peril?**

Wikipedia, the online encyclopaedia, is one of the most popular sites on the web – the seventh most visited site, according to web information service Alexa. And no wonder, it contains over 10 million articles, nearly 3 million in English, covering virtually everything you would ever need to know as a student. But you already know this. Surveys suggest that most students consult Wikipedia when writing assignments. For example, a survey of Cambridge University students reported that over 75% 'had used Wikipedia for researching essays'. But you are probably also aware that most tutors discourage the use of Wikipedia – especially citing it as a primary source.

So what's wrong with using Wikipedia? Why do tutors have such a problem with it? Well, aside from the fact that Wikipedia is a secondary source of information (a second-hand summary of original research reported elsewhere), the primary concern is the reliability of the information, since anyone with access to the internet can contribute and edit the contents. So there are justifiable concerns about the quality of the information contained on the site – its accuracy, validity and objectivity, all of which are key criteria in assignments.

It is for this reason that one academic department proposed a 'wiki ban' on students. In 2007, tutors in the history department at Middlebury College in the USA voted to bar students from citing Wikipedia in their assignments. While a ban was not enforced (or enforceable), the head of the department warned that Wikipedia is not an appropriate source for citations: 'The important point that we wish to communicate to all students taking courses and submitting work in our department in the future is that they cite Wikipedia at their peril' (Jaschik, 2007).

How unreliable is Wikipedia? In 2005 the highly respected British journal *Nature* asked expert reviewers to check the accuracy of information in a range of scientific articles on Wikipedia and compare this to articles in the *Encyclopaedia Britannica* (a more established source of information). They reviewed 42 entries and reported:

> Only eight serious errors, such as misinterpretations of important concepts, were detected in the pairs of articles reviewed, four from each encyclopedia. But reviewers also found many factual errors, omissions or misleading statements: 162 and 123 in Wikipedia and Britannica, respectively. (Giles, 2005: 901)

So, in terms of accuracy, it would appear that Wikipedia is nearly as reliable as the well established and generally respected *Encyclopaedia Britannica* (although the reviewers did report concerns about the 'readability' of some articles which were poorly structured and confusing). But that's still, on average, four errors per article (162 errors in 42 articles).

Perhaps the sensible advice would be to consult Wikipedia as a convenient initial source of information and use the links provided, but not to cite it. The same advice would be given for citing any encyclopaedia. Use it as an initial source of information but try to consult and reference original sources or reputable textbooks.

Tip 19: **Make the move to journals as soon as you can**

What should you be reading and what should you be citing in your assignment? Well, you might start with general textbooks in your first year and then begin to include more specialised sources like journals in your second and third years, but this does depend to some extent on the academic discipline. For more classical subjects in the arts and humanities, the relevant literature may be more book-based, but for scientific subjects where the evidence is constantly updated, you will need to consult the academic journals which contain the most up-to-date literature.

So while a good textbook is excellent for general information, providing an overview of the subject, as you progress through the years you should be consulting and referencing journal articles more and more, as the following reflection from a student illustrates:

> I think it was learning the research skills. I didn't know how to research really and you pick that up as you go along using the libraries and journals. In the

first year I tended to get a lot of the information from books and also searching other areas like the internet. I was getting Cs. In the second and third year
I started to go beyond that and started to use journals. [And then her grades
started to improve.] (Norton et al., 2009: 28)

We've already noted that the information from journals should be more up to
date than that found in books (which can take a few years to write). It may also
be more reliable due to the peer-review process.

When an article is submitted to a journal it will be sent out to (typically)
three academics with some expertise in the area to 'referee' or 'review' it, that
is, to appraise the design of the study, note any errors, suggest improvements,
etc. Once the article has been reviewed, the journal editor will write to the
author(s) with recommendations about what needs changing for the article to
be accepted in the journal (or not accepted, as the case may be). Most recommendations are along the following lines:

- Accept without changes (rare – especially if you've got three academics picking at every word)

- Accept with minor revisions (corrections, clarifications, etc.)

- Reject but invite resubmission with major revisions (e.g. rewrite, collect more
  data)

- Reject outright (fundamentally flawed, or it could be that the article is not
  appropriate for that particular journal)

So the peer-review process helps to ensure a level of 'quality control'.

Tip 20: **You can get any rubbish published**

Articles in journals may have been through the 'peer review' process, but you
should still remember that 'peer review' only means that the paper has been
critically evaluated by two or three other academics. The review process is
usually anonymous and quite a good means of quality control, but it certainly
doesn't mean that the content of the article is 'the truth'. It just means that the
article has been through a process to try to maintain standards.

You should also be aware that standards vary across journals. The 'top'
journals, such as *Nature* and the *British Medical Journal*, only publish about
5% of submitted articles. The acceptance rate for many other journals, however, can be much higher. So you need to be mindful of the hierarchy of
quality across different journals. As the former editor of the *British Medical
Journal* once commented: 'You can get any rubbish published, just go down
and down and down and down the food chain [of medical journals]' (Fister,
2004: 923).

Although this quote refers particularly to medical journals, the same principle applies in most academic subjects: the top journals in your subject area will
usually contain the most important and more rigorously conducted studies,

but there will be journals where the standards are less rigorous. As the deputy editor of the *Journal of the American Medical Association*, Drummond Rennie, once commented:

> There seems to be no study too fragmented, no hypothesis too trivial, no literature too biased or too egotistical, no design too warped, no methodology too bungled, no presentation of results too inaccurate, too obscure, and too contradictory, no analysis too self-serving, no argument too circular, no conclusions too trifling or too unjustified, and no grammar and syntax too offensive for a paper to end up in print. (Cited in Smith, 2009)

This is a very important message to remember: journals may be a good source of information, but that doesn't mean you should accept what they say without question, even if they are subject to peer-review:

> Editors and scientists alike insist on the pivotal importance of peer review. We portray peer review to the public as a quasi-sacred process that helps to make science our most objective truth teller. But we know that the system of peer review is biased, unjust, unaccountable, incomplete, easily fixed, often insulting, usually ignorant, occasionally foolish, and frequently wrong. (Richard Horton, editor of the *Lancet*, cited in Horton, 2000: 148)

Remember, no study is perfect, and the authors will usually be requested to present their own list of limitations at the end of the study, all of which reinforces the importance of appraisal skills when reading journal articles. (We will be discussing critical appraisal in Chapter 8.) As an interesting aside, Box 5.1 provides an example of 'the rubbish' that can actually appear in a journal.

box 5.1

Sokal's hoax journal article

In 1996, Alan Sokal, a professor of physics at New York University, sent an article to the American cultural studies journal *Social Text*. The article, entitled 'Transgressing the boundaries: toward a transformative hermeneutics of quantum gravity', was submitted as an 'experiment' to see if a leading North American journal of cultural studies would 'publish an article liberally salted with nonsense if (a) it sounded good and (b) it flattered the editors' ideological preconceptions' (Sokal, 1996b: 62).

When the article duly appeared in the spring/summer 1996 issue of *Social Text* (Sokal, 1996a), Sokal announced that it was intended as a hoax, full of meaningless sentences and nonsensical quotations about physics and mathematics produced by prominent French and American intellectuals. For example:

In the second paragraph I declare, without the slightest evidence or argument, that 'physical reality' [note the scare quotes] ... is at bottom a social and linguistic construct. Not our *theories* of physical reality, mind you, but the reality itself. Fair enough: anyone who believes that the laws of physics are mere social conventions is invited to try transgressing those conventions from the windows of my apartment. (I live on the twenty-first floor.) (Sokal, 1996b: 62)

For a detailed account of the hoax see Sokal and Bricmont (1998) or Sokal's webpage: http://www.physics.nyu.edu/sokal/ (accessed September 2010).

Tip 21: 'Tell me something I don't know'

Some students are not very adventurous – they don't stray beyond the confines of what is covered in the lectures. Perhaps this reflects lack of time, but an assignment which simply regurgitates what was covered in the lectures is not flattering, it's disappointing. The lectures should be seen as the start of your reading and investigation, not the end. Obviously you will need to do the essential reading that has been recommended for your assignment, but as the comments from the survey illustrate, if you really want to impress your tutor, try going beyond the set texts and 'thinking out of the box'.

How to impress tutors

- Telling me something I didn't know by going beyond the reading/lectures
- When I actually learn something from what I've read
- Students who tackle the question in a new/original way
- Thinking out of the box ... occasionally you do get a very well written, meticulously researched and highly polished piece of work that either subverts the question or deals with it in an unusual, but pertinent way. Nice when that happens. Especially if you've got a bunch of 150 scripts to mark!

So try to tell the tutor something they don't know and tackle the question in a different or original way (though make sure you follow the guidelines and meet the learning outcomes, of course).

Tip 22: **Do a literature search**

Although you should be provided with a list of essential and recommended reading, a further search of the literature identifying other good sources of information will usually impress tutors. As we've noted, students who receive the higher marks will usually delve further into the literature, exhibiting the 'deeper' approach to learning.

You might start with a search on the internet. Google Scholar, for example, will provide you with an indication of what's been published in academic journals, along with links to relevant citations, but if you want reliable academic sources use your library's online subject databases. In Table 5.1, I've listed some of the common databases in my own subject area, the social and health sciences.

Table 5.1 Some common literature review databases

Subject	Database
Health	**AMED** (Allied and Complementary Medicine Database)
	Includes: physiotherapy, occupational therapy, rehabilitation, palliative care and complementary medicine
	CINAHL (Cumulative Index to Nursing & Allied Health)
	Nursing and allied health
	Cochrane
	Database of systematic reviews for health interventions
	PubMed
	PubMed comprises more than 24 million citations for biomedical literature from MEDLINE, life science journals, and online books. Citations may include links to full-text content from PubMed Central and publisher websites
Social sciences	**ASSIA** (Applied Social Sciences Index and Abstracts)
	Health, social services, economics, politics, race relations and education
Psychology	**Psychinfo**
	Psychology (journals from 1887 to the present)
Business and Management	**Proquest**
	Business and management

Techniques for searching the literature within these databases vary, so you will need to consult the relevant guides provided by your university library (which may also offer training in the use of electronic resources), but they generally share the following principles:

1. **Select the appropriate database** for your search, e.g. Medline for medical topics, Psychinfo for psychological topics. (Note: it may be possible to search across several databases at the same time, avoiding the need to repeat your search strategy across individual databases.)

2. **Identify the key words/terms** for your search, e.g. 'acupuncture' and 'pain'.

3. **Use 'filters' to restrict and focus** the literature retrieved, e.g. dates, context. You can also ask it just to search for literature reviews on some databases. This can be a good start if you find one that's recent.

4. **Keep a record** of your literature search by saving the search. Aside from saving you repeating the search at another time, this might be useful to put in an appendix if your assignment warrants it (e.g. if it's a research proposal).

For example, a search of the literature on 'acupuncture' and 'pain' might proceed as shown in Table 5.2. The aim is to reduce the number of 'hits' to a manageable amount. At step 4, I could have filtered by a more recent year of publication to reduce the 'hits' to a manageable amount (publications since 2006), but instead I chose to have a look for any recent literature reviews – which is usually a good start.

Table 5.2   Narrowing down a literature search

Step	Search	Results
1	Search term: 'acupuncture'	= 2,000 hits
2	Search term: 'pain'	= 4,000 hits
3	Combine 'acupuncture' and 'pain'	= 400 hits
4	Filter by year of publication (studies published since 2000)	= 200 hits
5	Restrict to literature reviews only	= 10 hits

For larger assignments, like dissertations or postgraduate research projects, you may be required to conduct a more thorough review of the literature. Indeed, conducting a literature review may be the assignment itself. Chapter 16 provides more detailed guidelines about how to conduct a systematic literature review.

summary

In this chapter we've seen the importance of:

- using up-to-date references – especially for subjects where the knowledge base is updated regularly through new research (e.g. health interventions)
- citing reputable sources (e.g. peer-reviewed articles in good journals)
- being aware that just because something has been published in a book or a journal doesn't mean it's 'the truth' (reliable, beyond criticism, etc.)

(Continued)

(Continued)

- obtaining different perspectives from different sources
- going beyond the recommended reading and perhaps tackling the assignment in a different or original way (telling the marker something they don't already know)
- doing a literature search

So, you've read the relevant literature and identified some interesting information. Now you just need to start working backwards ...

PART 8

IDENTIFYING A RESEARCH QUESTION

Developing your Research Question

O'Leary, Z.

Learning objectives

- The importance of good questions

    o To understand why the articulation of a research question is so crucial
    o To be able to use a research question to define an investigation and provide direction

- The preliminaries: defining your topic

    o To understand the value of creativity and inspiration in defining a topic
    o To understand how literature can be used to narrow into topic
    o To be mindful of the practicalities that can set parameters for research

- From interesting topics to researchable questions

    o To be able to engage in a process that moves topics to researchable questions
    o To understand the iterative nature of question development
    o To understand how and when hypotheses are appropriate for research

- Characteristics of good questions

    o To be able to assess the efficacy and researchability of potential research questions

THE IMPORTANCE OF GOOD QUESTIONS

The scientific mind does not so much provide the right answers as ask the right questions.

Claude Lévi-Strauss

You're ready. You have got yourself set up and have a pretty good idea of what you are in for. You even have a few research ideas. Next step? To develop and articulate a clear research question.

Now you may be thinking, 'I have a pretty good idea about what I want to research. Is working on my actual question so important?' Well, the answer is an unequivocal 'yes'. There are a lot of students who want to jump right into their research project without taking the time to really think through and develop their research question. Some have ideas about their topic, but they are not clear on the aspects they want to explore. Others will have their ideas pretty much narrowed down, but have not clearly articulated this in a researchable question.

I have to say that I am a real stickler for good research questions. I believe they are absolutely fundamental to good research; and your ability to articulate one is essential. After all, how will you know when you have found the answer to your question, if you can't say what your question is?

Remember: research is a decision-making journey. The process, in fact, demands that you constantly engage in decision-making that is logical, consistent and coherent. And what do you think is the benchmark for logical, consistent and coherent decision-making? It's that the choices you make take you one step closer to being able to answer your research question credibly. So without clear articulation of your question you are really travelling blind.

Research questions are essential because they:

- *Define an investigation* – A well-articulated research question can provide both you and your eventual readers with information about your project. It can: define the topic – youth suicide, environmental degradation, secularization, etc.; define the nature of the research endeavour – to discover, explore, explain, describe or compare; define the questions you are interested in – what, where, how, when, why; define your constructs and variables – income, age, education, gender, self-esteem, pollution, etc.; and indicate whether you foresee a relationship between variables – impacts, increases, decreases, relationships, correlations, causes, etc.
- *Set boundaries* – Along your research journey you are likely to find yourself facing plenty of tangents, detours and diversions, and a well-defined question can help you set boundaries. When faced with an interesting tangent, ask yourself: 'What does this have to do with my question?' I would suggest that there are three potential answers: (1) actually very little – I will have to leave it and maybe pick it up in my next project; (2) actually it is quite relevant – if you think about it, it really does relate to ... (this can be exciting and add new dimensions to your work); and (3) well, nothing really, but I actually think this is at the heart of what I want to know – perhaps I need to rethink my question.
- *Provide direction* – A well-defined, well-articulated research question will act as a blueprint for your project. It will point you towards the theory you need to explore; the literature you need to review; the data you need to gather; and the methods you need to call on. In fact, I would suggest that it is nearly impossible to define a clear methodology for an ill-defined research question. If you do not know what you want to know, you will not be in a position to know how to find it out.
- *Act as a frame of reference for assessing your work* – Not only does your question provide continuity and set the agenda for your entire study, but it also acts as a benchmark for assessing decision-making. The criteria for all decisions related to your project will be whether or not choices lead you closer to credible answers to your research question.

Now I don't want to make it sound like research questions are reductionist devices that take all exploration, creativity and fluidity out of the research process. Not at all. Research questions themselves can be designed so that they are open and exploratory. As well, research questions can, and often do, change, shift and evolve during the early stages of a project. This is as it should be, since your engagement in the literature evolves both your knowledge and thinking. Yes, research questions define an investigation and provide direction, but it is up to the researcher to define and redefine questions so that they can most appropriately accomplish these tasks.

THE PRELIMINARIES: DEFINING YOUR TOPIC

All this talk about the importance of research questions is fine, but what if you're not even sure what interests to pursue? Well, you are not alone. Yes, there are plenty of students who are quite clear about what they want to research, but there are also a lot who really struggle with the idea of generating a research topic. In fact, many feel that coming up with something worthy of research is beyond them.

So how do you focus in on a topic? Well, as highlighted below and in Box 3.1, you work on generating ideas by homing in on your curiosity and creativity; looking for inspiration; and exploring your options with an eye towards practicalities. It is the first step in moving from real challenges and opportunities to research questions.

Curiosity and Creativity

Discovery consists in seeing what everyone else has seen, and thinking what no one else has thought.

Albert Szent-Györgyi

Ideas for research are generated any time curiosity or passion is aroused. Every day we are surrounded by events, situations and interactions that make us wonder, stop and think, or bring joy, frustration, relief or anger bubbling to the surface. This is the rich and fertile ground from which research ideas are born. Think about what stirs you, what you argue about with your friends, family and peers, and what issues are topical in the world, at home or in your workplace. You will soon find that research topics abound. If you can learn to catch yourself thinking, 'Gee, I wonder …', you will have an unending supply of ideas.

An option worth trying here is a concept map. Mapping allows you the freedom to think laterally as well as linearly. It uses free association to encourage the mind to jump from one idea to another, thereby enhancing creative processes. Concept mapping can facilitate brainstorming, drawing out connections and building themes; and can also be a great tool for overcoming writer's block. Figure 3.1 shows a simple concept map used to draw out potential research topics.

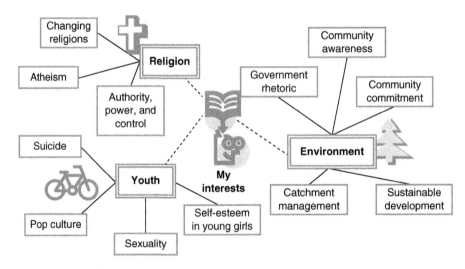

Figure 3.1   Concept map of potential research topics

Turning to Literature

The importance of reading for research cannot be overemphasized. Never do we know everything about our topic, and rarely do we know enough. Getting abreast of the background, context, controversies, academic debates and political agendas surrounding your area of interest is time well spent. It will certainly help you identify research interests and research needs. You may find yourself drawn to the exploration of an important aspect of a problem that has been ignored in the literature. You may want to question some of the assumptions that underpin common understandings. You may decide to add to a raging debate with an innovative approach. You may want to take up an opportunity to gather definitive data evidence for much needed evidence-based decision-making. You may want to take up the challenge of answering further questions posed at the end of a research paper.

In addition to topical literature, you might also develop questions through your engagement with theory. This happens when you are reading 'theory' and it suddenly resonates. You think 'aha', maybe that is why a particular situation is the way it is, or perhaps that is why they do what they do. A student of mine had such a moment when he read a work by Althusser highlighting the role that institutions such as the family, schools and the Church have in embedding government ideology into individual consciousness. The student began to view the role of the Church in a new light and decided to investigate if and how the Irish Catholic Church operates as an arm of the government in the socialization of its citizens.

An early literature task is the *preliminary literature review* (see Chapter 6). This is an attempt to become aware of scope of research that has been conducted in your area. By understanding what has been researched, what has not been researched, the methods employed and the efficacy of those methods/projects, you can begin to understand the need for and scope of potential projects in your space. An early literature review is an excellent way to begin to narrow into your research.

Looking for Inspiration

Another approach for narrowing in on your topic (see Box 3.1) is to be highly attuned to the world around you. Inspiration might be drawn from:

- *Personal insights and experiences* – Everyone has experience and insight they can draw on. Take the workplace, for example. Just about anyone who has ever had a job will tell you that workplaces are rife with problems: red tape, inefficiencies, ineptitude, incompetence, decision-makers not in touch with the coal-face, corruption, profit before service, morale and motivation. Your own frustrations are often tied to the frustrations of many – and if they can also be tied to the goals, aims, objectives and vision of the organization, community or institution in which they sit, then there is a good chance those very frustrations will have 'research' potential.
- *An observation* – It can be quite hard to see what surrounds us, so viewing the world through fresh eyes can provide powerful research insights. This happened to a student of mine who was on a train when he suddenly became fascinated by the unwritten rules of personal space. He found himself intrigued by the rules that governed who sat where, how close they sat, who moved away from whom and under what circumstances. He watched with fascination as people jockeyed for seats as the number of carriage occupants changed with each stop, and decided that he wanted to study the rules that govern such behaviour.
- *Contemporary/timely issues* – Sometimes an old topic can take on fresh life. A topic might suddenly become an agenda at the workplace, or may even become the focus of global attention. The Western world's interest in, fascination with and judgement of Islamic faith is a case in point. 'Angles' become easy to find and questions such as 'How are the media covering the topic?', 'What are the policy, practice and rhetoric of government?' and 'What impact is this having on schoolyard racism?' become quite easy to generate.
- *Identifying stakeholder needs* – Stakeholder needs can be extremely broad and can range from the need for an equitable health-care system, to a need for remediation of blue-green algae blooms in the local catchment, to a need to motivate students to stay in school. Identifying needs can come from following media coverage, reading letters to the editor or listening to stakeholders at various forums including town council meetings, workplace meetings or any other place where stakeholders may gather to express their concerns.

BOX 3.1

Selecting Issues Suitable for Research

Below is a list of research topics some of my students are working on and how/why these issues were selected.

- *The impact of the accessibility of pornography on the sexual expectation of teens* – Selected by a high school counsellor concerned over what he sees as a worrying trend.
- *The inclusion of climate change risk as a factor in fire management planning* – Selected by a manager in the New South Wales Rural Fire Service who recognized the need for currency in planning processes.
- *A large percentage of non-recyclable materials in household recycle bins* – Selected by a frustrated council officer in charge of waste management who was undertaking a higher degree.
- *Decision-making in a health promotion centre without any evidence base* – Selected by the new centre director who was unsure how to prioritize issues.
- *Violence towards nursing staff in emergency wards* – Selected by a former nurse undertaking an occupational health and safety postgraduate degree after being forced into a career change by a patient attack.
- *Bastardization and ritual hazing at university* – Selected by a student who went through such practices in her first year at university.
- *Subcontractors in the construction industry with poor safety records* – Selected by an occupational health and safety student because of current media coverage related to the topic.
- *Underutilization of experiential learning in the classroom* – Selected by an education student through the literature she came across in the course of her degree.
- *The motivations of individuals adopting strategies to mitigate climate change* – Selected by a student fascinated by apathy in spite of individuals' knowledge of a threat.
- *Disregard of fire alarms in Hong Kong high-rises* – Selected by a fire safety officer undertaking a higher degree, who was in charge of an investigation where seven people died because they ignored an alarm.

 **I have a question!**

Do I have unlimited scope in choosing my research topic?

In a word. No. As limiting as it may seem, all budding topics need to be checked against practicalities. No matter how interesting a topic appears, in the end your project must be 'doable'. At the stage of topic definition 'doability' includes: (1) Appropriateness – some ideas are simply not relevant to the degree you are undertaking. Even if a topic has potential, it may be at odds with your academic programme. If this is the case, it is a signal to sit down and really think about your research, academic and career goals … and seek alignment. (2) Supervision – not many students manage to negotiate a major research project without a great deal of supervisory support. Finding out whether appropriate supervision for your topic is available before you lock yourself into a project is well advised. (3) Funding body/employer requirements – if a funding body or employer has sponsored you to conduct research in a particular area, you may not be able to shift topics. Keep in mind, however, that even within a defined project, there can be scope to concentrate on particular aspects or bring a fresh perspective to an issue. Open negotiation and even a 'sales pitch' covering the relevance and possible benefits of your proposed research can give you more creative potential.

FROM INTERESTING TOPICS TO RESEARCHABLE QUESTIONS

Hopefully, you now recognize the importance of developing a clear research question and have an interesting topic in mind. It's time to begin narrowing in on your question.

Narrowing in

While expansive questions can be the focus of good research, ambiguity can arise when questions are broad and unwieldy. Being bounded and precise makes the research task easier to accomplish. If you are worried about being too limited, keep in mind that each question can be likened to a window that can be used to explore rich theory and depth in understanding. 'Focused' is not a synonym for 'superficial'. There are two strategies I recommend for narrowing in. The first is to revisit your concept map, while the second is to work through the four-step question generation process outlined below.

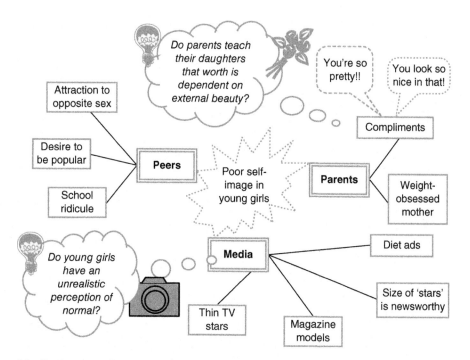

Figure 3.2 Mapping your questions

The Concept Map Revisited

Just as a concept map can be used to brainstorm research topics, it can also be used for question clarification. The map in Figure 3.2 explores 'Why young girls have poor self-image'. The student has mapped out some major influences – peers, parents and the media – and has begun to think about causes of the 'problem'. This leads to some interesting ideas that might all be researchable. The student then takes this further by asking two things: (1) what aspects am I most interested in; and (2) do I have any insights that I might be able to add? From this, the student has two 'aha' moments, and research questions begin to come into focus. The first looks at the role of the media as a whole and asks: 'What do young girls consider normal in terms of body image?' The second comes from an interesting reflection on the compliments parents give to daughters, and how often they relate to how 'pretty they are'. The student begins to wonder whether parents are subconsciously teaching their daughters that worth is determined by external beauty.

Four-step Question Generation Process

A more linear process than concept mapping is to work through the following four steps:

1   Using only one- or two-word responses, write down the answers to the following questions:

   (a)   *What is your topic?* For example, back pain, recycling, independent learning, social media bullying …
   (b)   *What is the context for your research?* For example, a school, local authority, hospital, community …
   (c)   *What do you want to achieve?* For example, to discover, to describe, to change, to explore, to explain, to develop, to understand …
   (d)   *What is the nature of your question?* Is it a what, who, where, how, when or why question?
   (e)   *Are there any potential relationships you want to explore?* For example, impacts, increases, decreases, relationships, correlations, causes …

2   Starting with the nature of the question – who, what, where, how, when – begin to piece together the answers generated in step 1 until you feel comfortable with the eventual question or questions. Suppose your problem was the large percentage of non-recyclable materials in household recycle bins (as discussed in Box 3.1). The answers from step 1 might lead to a number of questions:

   (a)   Topic: recycling. Context: domestic/community. Goal: to explore why there is a lack of efficiency. Nature of your question: who and why. Relationship: correlation between demographic characteristics and inefficient recycling.

Question: Is there a relationship between household recycling behaviours and demographic characteristics?

   (b)   Topic: recycling. Context: domestic/households. Goal: to understand how individuals go about the task of recycling. Nature of your question: how. Relationship: N/A.

Question: How do individuals engage in decision-making processes related to household domestic waste management?

   (c)   Topic: recycling. Context: domestic/community. Goal: to describe the nature of recycling inefficiencies so that an effective community awareness campaign can be developed. Nature of your question: what. Relationship: N/A.

Question: What are the most common non-recyclable items found in household recycle bins?

3   If you have developed more than one question (remember: any one problem can lead to a multitude of research questions), decide on your main question based on interest and practicalities as well as the advice of your supervisor.
4   Narrow and clarify until your question is as concise and well-articulated as possible. Remember: the first articulation of any research question is unlikely to be as clear, helpful and unambiguous as the third, fourth or even fifth attempt.

These two processes should go a long way in helping you define a solid research question – something essential for setting you on the right methodological path. But getting there can be a process. Box 3.2 gives you a few examples of research question evolution.

■■■■■■■■■■■ BOX 3.2 ■■■■■■■■■■■■■■■■■■■■■■■■

The Evolution of a 'Good' Research Question

Initial Question: How should schools deal with child abuse?

Problems: *High ambiguity* – need to define schools; need to define child abuse; need to define 'abusers'; need to define 'deal with'.

After several iterations that included consultation with literature, key stakeholders and supervisor …

Final Question: What is best practice for UK elementary schools in managing allegations of physical, emotional or sexual mistreatment of school children by school staff?

Initial Question: Does mandatory reporting decrease domestic violence?

Problems: *Ambiguity* – need to define mandatory reporting; need to define domestic violence; need to define stakeholders. Possibly wrong question – questions that start with 'Does' are yes/no questions; not generally what you want.

After several iterations that included consultation with literature, key stakeholders and supervisor …

Final Question: Have the Northern Territory Domestic and Family Violence Act amendments introducing mandatory reporting of domestic violence decreased incidents of violence, in spite of statistics that show an increase in reported events?

Initial Question: Should Facebook be open to exploration by researchers?

Problems: *Ambiguity* – need to define what aspects of Facebook; need to define researchers; need to define exploration. Possibly wrong question – another yes/no question; worth reconsidering what you really want to know that sits under this articulation.

After several iterations that included consultation with literature, key stakeholders and supervisor …

Final Question: Under what circumstances might an analysis of Facebook posts be warranted by professional researchers and how can this be managed in an ethical fashion?

The Need to Redefine

You now have the perfect research question. You are on track and ready to set that question in stone. Well, perhaps not – research questions can, and often do, change, shift and evolve during the early stages of a project; and not only is this fine, it is actually appropriate as your engagement in the research process evolves both your knowledge and thinking. Developing a clear question is essential for direction setting, but it is important to remember that the research journey is rarely linear. It is a process that generates as many questions as it answers, and is bound to take you in unexpected directions.

Consider the following. In order to do research, you need to:

1. Define your research question so that you can identify the body of literature you need to become conversant with and eventually review.
2. Read and review a body of literature so that you are in a position to form appropriate, researchable questions.

So what comes first, the chicken or the egg? In the case of reading and question setting, one does not necessarily precede the other. They should, in fact, be intertwined. Research generally starts with an idea, which might come from any number of sources. The idea should then lead to reading; this reading should lead to the development of a potentially researchable question; the potential question should lead to more specific reading; and the specific reading should modify the question. As shown in Figure 3.3, forming a question is an iterative process, one that needs to be informed by reading at all stages.

A similar situation can occur when you begin to explore your methodology. Delving into 'how' your research might unfold can pique your interest in aspects of your topic not reflected in your currently defined question. Yet without that defined question, you might not have gone as far in exploring potential methods.

In fact, as you get going with your research, you may come across any number of factors that can lead you to: query your aims and objectives; modify your question; add questions; or

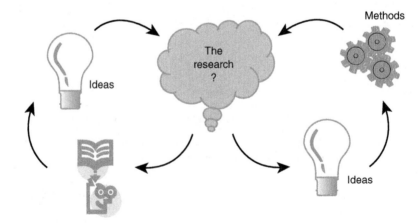

Figure 3.3 Cycles of research question development

even find new questions. The challenge is assessing whether these factors are sending you off the track, or whether they represent developments and refinements that are positive for your work. Discussing the issues with your supervisor can provide invaluable support in making such determinations.

The Hypothesis Dilemma

'Do I need a "hypothesis"?' This must be one of the most common questions asked by students, and there seem to be two clearly defined paradigmatic schools of thought driving the answers. Positivists (see Chapter 1) believe that the hypothesis is the cornerstone of scientific method and that it is an absolutely necessary component of the research process. Post-positivists, however, often view the hypothesis as a reductionist device designed to constrain social research.

Unfortunately, this tendency for dichotomization offers little assistance to students struggling to figure out if a hypothesis should drive their research. To answer this question, students need to know two things: what a hypothesis actually does; and whether a hypothesis is appropriate given their research question.

Hypothesis   Logical conjecture (hunch or educated guess) about the nature of relationships between two or more variables expressed in the form of a testable statement.

A hypothesis takes your research question a step further by offering a clear and concise statement of what you think you will find in relation to your variables, and what you are going to test. It is a tentative proposition that is subject to verification through subsequent investigation. And it can be *very* useful in the right context.

Suppose you are interested in research on divorce. Your research question is: 'What factors contribute to a couple's decision to divorce?' Your hunch is that it has a lot to do with money – financial problems lead to divorce. Here you have all the factors needed for a hypothesis: logical conjecture (your hunch); variables (divorce and financial problems); and a relationship that can be tested (leads to). It is therefore a perfect question for a hypothesis – maybe something like 'Financial problems increase the likelihood of divorce'.

A question like 'Is there a relationship between the hours teenagers spend on social media and their self-esteem?' is also a fairly good candidate for hypothesis development. Your hunch is that social media engagement has an impact on self-esteem. What is needed, however, is directionality in the relationship. Do you suspect that self-esteem is positively or negatively correlated with social media engagement? Once that is determined you have all the factors needed for a hypothesis: logical conjecture (your hunch); variables (social media engagement and self-esteem); and a relationship that can be tested (self-esteem increases or decreases in relation to media engagement). Your hypothesis might end up as 'Teens who spend a large amount of free time on social media have high levels of self-esteem'.

Basically, if you have (1) a clearly defined research question, (2) variables to explore and (3) a hunch about the relationship between those variables that (4) can be tested, a hypothesis is quite easy to formulate.

Now not all research questions will lend themselves to hypothesis development. Take the question 'How do high school students engage in decision-making processes related to career/further study options?' Remember: a hypothesis is designed to express 'relationships between variables'. This question, however, does not aim to look at variables and their relationships. The goal of this question is to uncover and describe a process, so a hypothesis would not be appropriate.

Generally, a hypothesis will not be appropriate if:

- *You do not have a hunch or educated guess about a particular situation* – For example, you may want to study alcoholism in the South Pacific, but you do not feel you are in a position to hypothesize because you are without an appropriate cultural context for educated guessing.
- *You do not have a set of defined variables* – Your research may be explorative in a bid to name the contributing factors to a particular situation. In the case of alcoholism in the Pacific Islands, your research aim may be to identify the factors or variables involved.
- *Your question centres on phenomenological description (see Chapter 8)* – For example, you may be interested in the question, 'What is the experience of drinking like for Pacific Islanders?' A relationship between variables does not come into play.
- *Your question centres on an ethnographic study of a cultural group (see Chapter 8)* – For example, you might want to ask 'What is the cultural response to a defined problem of alcoholism in a South Pacific village?' In this situation, force-fitting a hypothesis can limit the potential for rich description.
- *Your aim is to engage in, and research, the process of collaborative change (see Chapter 9)* – In 'action research', methodology is both collaborative and emergent, making predetermined hypotheses impractical to use.

In short, whether a hypothesis is appropriate for your question depends on the nature of your inquiry. If your question boils down to a 'relationship between variables', then a hypothesis can clarify your study to an extent even beyond a well-defined research question. If your question, however, does not explore such a relationship, then force-fitting a hypothesis simply won't work.

CHARACTERISTICS OF GOOD QUESTIONS

Once you come up with a research question, you need to assess if it is going to be researchable at a practical level. Try running through the following checklist (summarized in Box 3.3 and also available online). If you find yourself feeling uncomfortable with the answers, it may indicate a need to rethink your question.

Is the Question Right for Me?

Common wisdom suggests that setting a realistic research plan involves assessing (1) your level of commitment and (2) the hours you think you will need to dedicate to the task – then double both. You need to consider whether your question has the potential to hold your interest for the duration. As discussed in Chapter 2, it is very easy to lose motivation, and you are likely to need a genuine interest to stay on track.

There is, however, a flipside. Questions that can truly sustain your interest are usually the ones that best bring out your biases and subjectivities. As discussed in Chapter 3, these subjectivities need to be carefully explored and managed in ways that will ensure the integrity of the research process. You may want to give careful consideration to:

- Researching questions where you know you have an axe to grind. Deep-seated prejudices do not generally lend themselves to credible research.
- Researching issues that are too close to home, such as domestic violence or sexual abuse. While researching such issues can be healing and cathartic, mixing personal and professional motivations in an intense fashion can be potentially detrimental to both agendas.

Is the Question Right for the Field?

The role of research is to do one or more of the following: advance knowledge in a particular area/field; improve professional practice; impact on policy; or aid individuals. Research questions need to be significant – not only to you, but to a wider academic or professional audience as well.

I often ask my students to imagine they are applying for competitive funds that will cover the cost of their research. Before they can even begin to make arguments that will convince a funding body they are competent to do the research and that their approach is likely to give meaningful and credible results, they will need to convince the body that the topic itself is worth funding. They need to be able to articulate:

- Why the knowledge is important.
- What the societal significance is.
- How the findings will lead to societal advances.
- What improvements to professional practice and/or policy may come from their research.

An early task in the research process is to be able to clearly articulate a rationale for your study that outlines the significance of the project. Your question needs to be informed by the literature and be seen as significant.

Is the Question Well Articulated?

A research question not only indicates the theory and literature you need to explore and review, but also points to the data you will need to gather, and the methods you will need to adopt. This makes clear articulation of research questions particularly important. Terms need to be unambiguous and clearly defined.

Take the question 'Is health care a problem in the USA?' As a question for general debate, it is probably fine. As a research question, however, it needs a fair bit of clarification. How are you defining 'health care'? What boundaries are you putting on the term? How are you defining 'problem'? Social, moral, economic, legal or all of these? And who are you speaking for? A problem for whom? The more clarity in the question, the more work the question can do, making the direction of the study that much more defined.

Another point to consider is whether your question rests on unfounded assumptions. Take the question 'How can women in Fijian villages overthrow the patriarchal structures that oppress them?' There are a few assumptions here that need to be checked:

1   That there are patriarchal structures. This information might exist and be found in literature. Assuming this is true …
2   That these patriarchal structures are indeed oppressive to the women concerned.
3   That there is a desire on the part of Fijian women to change these patriarchal structures.
4   That 'overthrowing' is the only option mentioned for change. It is a loaded term that alludes to strong personal subjectivities.

Is the Question Doable?

Perhaps the main criterion of any good research question is that you will be able to undertake the research necessary to answer the question. Now that may sound incredibly obvious, but there are many questions that cannot be answered through the research process. Take, for example, the question 'Does a difficult labour impact on a newborn's ability to love its mother?' Not researchable. How do you define 'love'? And even if you could define it, you would need to find a way to measure a newborn's ability to love. And even if you could do that, you are left with the dilemma of correlating that ability to love to a difficult labour. Interesting question, but not researchable.

Other questions might be researchable in theory, but not in practice. Student research projects are often constrained by:

* a lack of time
* a lack of funds
* a lack of expertise
* a lack of access
* a lack of ethical clearance.

Making sure your question is feasible and that it can lead to a completed project is worth doing early. Nothing is worse than realizing your project is not doable after investing a large amount of time and energy.

Does the Question Get the Tick of Approval from Those in the Know?

When it comes to articulating the final question it makes sense to ask the advice of those who know and do research. Most supervisors have a wealth of research and supervisory experience, and generally know what questions are 'researchable' and what questions will leave you with a massive headache. Run your question past lecturers in the field, your supervisor and any 'experts' you may know.

━━━━━━━━━ BOX 3.3 ━━━━━━━━━━━━━━━━━━━━━━━━━━━━━━━━━

The Good Question Checklist

Is the question right for me?

- Will the question hold my interest?
- Can I manage any potential biases/subjectivities I may have?

Is the question right for the field?

- Will the findings be considered significant?
- Will it make a contribution to knowledge?
- Does it have the ability to effect change?

Is the question well articulated?

- Are the terms well defined?
- Are there any unchecked assumptions?

Is the question doable?

- Can information be collected in an attempt to answer the question?
- Do I have the skills and expertise necessary to access this information? If not, can the skills be developed?
- Will I be able to get it all done within my time constraints?
- Are costs likely to exceed my budget?
- Are there any potential ethical problems?

Does the question get the tick of approval from those in the know?

- Does my supervisor think I am on the right track?
- Do 'experts' in the field think my question is relevant/important/doable?

 **I have a question!** ━━━━━━━━━━━━━━━━━━━━━━━━━━━━━━━

I am having a hard time getting down to one single research question. In fact, I have about five questions. Do I really need to narrow down to one?

I would certainly advise it. Sub-questions are fine – but my suspicion is that one of your questions is the main game. Or that a main game question is still unspoken. Identifying/articulating this question is quite important. It is your way of centring into your research. Your thinking will become much clearer and more manageable once you can confidently articulate, *in one sentence*, what your research attempts to discover.

Chapter summary

- Developing a well-articulated research question is essential because it defines the project, sets boundaries, gives direction and acts as a frame of reference for assessing your work.
- The ability to generate topics for research can be a real challenge. Research inspiration can come from any number of areas, including literature; personal insights and experiences; observations; contemporary/timely issues; and stakeholder needs.
- Research directions are not always at the full discretion of the researcher. Practicalities you need to be mindful of include: appropriateness of the topic; your ability to get supervisory support; and funding opportunities and commitments.
- Moving from topics to researchable question can be daunting. Using a concept map or development process, as well as continued refining, will help you develop a researchable question as well as a strong hypothesis, as appropriate.
- Good research questions need to be: right for you; right for the field; well articulated; doable; and get the tick of approval from those in the know.

FURTHER READING

Most research methods texts give some coverage to developing research questions. Books with particularly good chapters on question development worth a look are:

Booth, W. C., Colomb, G. C. and Williams, J. M. (2008) *The Craft of Research*. Chicago: University of Chicago Press.
Bryman, A. (2012) *Social Research Methods*. Oxford: Oxford University Press.
Robson, C. (2011) *Real World Research*. Oxford: Blackwell.

There are, however, two excellent works that are solely dedicated to the challenge of research question development:

Alvesson, M. and Sandberg, J. (2013) *Constructing Research Questions: Doing Interesting Research*. London: Sage.
This book delves into the power of a well-conceived research question, not just to accept and expand on current theory, but to challenge existing theories and develop new ways of seeing.

White, P. (2009) *Developing Research Questions: A Guide for Social Scientists*. Basingstoke: Palgrave Macmillan.
This book takes students through common questions such as: what makes topics suitable for research; how you go from topics to questions; and how you refine to the point of 'researchability'. Lots of grounded tips here.

Companion website materials available at
https://study.sagepub.com/oleary3e

PART 9

DEVELOPING A RATIONALE AND WRITING PERSUASIVELY

Introductions, Conclusions and Structure

Greasley, P.

Introductions

As we all know, essays should have a beginning (introduction), a middle (main section) and an end (conclusion). Basically, you tell the reader what you are going to say, say it, and then tell the reader what you've said. In this chapter we'll look at each of these elements, along with more general issues about structuring assignments.

And that was the sum total of my original introduction to this chapter – the problem being that it's too short, which is a common problem in assignments. The trouble is that most people, me included, don't like wasting time (and words) going over what we are going to say; it's tedious – we'd rather just get on with it. But as we'll see in this chapter, a good introduction may be more important than you think when it comes to writing assignments. So let's have another go.

Introductions (second attempt) ...

As we all know, essays should have a beginning (introduction), a middle (main section) and an end (conclusion). Basically, you tell the reader what you are going to say, say it, and then tell the reader what you've said. What could be simpler? Well, if it is that simple, why did issues relating to structure, introductions and conclusions feature so highly on the list of things that frustrate and impress tutors? In this chapter we'll be discussing each of these elements: introductions, conclusions, and then more general issues about structuring assignments.

First, we'll see that a good introduction is crucial for an assignment – providing an outline and overview of the contents, and signposting the route you've taken to address the question (a planned itinerary rather than a mystery tour). We'll also look at *five key criteria* for an effective introduction, proposed by Townsend et al. (1993), which were shown to improve the grade of an assignment.

Next we'll look at three key criteria for a good conclusion, along with an interesting tip about when to write it (not at the end). And finally, we'll examine some tips for maintaining a clear, logical structure to your assignment, using headings and subheadings along with signposting throughout to help the marker on their journey.

It is concluded that paying attention to your introductions and conclusions may be especially important in assignments due to the psychological impact of first and last impressions – which may have a significant influence on markers.

There, so much better, don't you think? I've provided a clearer outline of the contents, added a couple of sentences in the first paragraph justifying the discussion of introductions, conclusions and structure (because they featured as common problems in the survey of tutors) and I've also added a few details about the conclusion.

Tip 23: **Use signposting**

When markers pick up an assignment they often have very little idea of what's in store for them. A good introduction can resolve this problem in a few lines by stating the aims of the assignment and providing a brief outline of the content and argument. It gives the reader a map of where they are going to be taken on the essay journey. In contrast, an essay without an introduction is a bit like a mystery tour – no one has a clue where they are going. So a good introduction shows that you've thought about the itinerary and planned the route.

Not surprisingly, then, the main source of marker distress in the survey of tutors was failing to provide a simple outline or overview of the essay.

What tutors dislike

- Failing to provide a simple introduction and outline of the subject (what is this essay about?)
- Poor introductions which give little overview of the assignment and what to expect
- Not introducing to the reader the content of the assignment or the context
- Not stating the aim of the essay

If you want to impress the marker you should provide a clear introduction that outlines the content, as the following comments illustrate:

What tutors like

- A clear introduction that presages a clear structure
- Good introduction summarising the assignment
- Identifying clearly in the introduction what issues the student is going to investigate

Clearly, it is a good strategy to summarise what you are going to say, with some signposting indicating the route and the directions you will be taking. This is what the introduction to this chapter did – at the second attempt.

Five key criteria for a good introduction: how to move up a grade

A study by Townsend et al. (1993), published in the *Journal of Educational Psychology*, examined a range of essay-writing guides and arrived at five key criteria for an effective introduction. A good introduction for an essay should:

1. Discuss the importance or timeliness of the topic
2. State the problem to be addressed
3. Indicate the scope of the essay
4. Define the terms to be used
5. Delineate the argument to be presented

What makes this study more interesting is that the researchers used these criteria to alter the introductions in some students' essays and found that the marks awarded rose by one grade (see Box 6.1).

box   6.1

An introduction proven to increase your grade

When Townsend et al. (1993) removed the original introductions from student essays, and substituted the following introduction constructed using the five key criteria, the grade increased on average from a B to a B+.

(Continued)

(Continued)

Essay Question: Discuss the role of genetic and environmental factors in IQ scores.

'Geniuses are born not made!' Is it really that simple? The 'nature vs nurture' dispute, in relation to intelligence, remains unresolved. In an attempt to separate the influence of genetic and environmental factors, two kinds of investigation have been important – twin studies and adoption studies. This research has shown that both genetic and environmental factors interact with each other to determine an individual's IQ score. The evidence presented in this essay indicates that IQ is shaped by many influences. In the context of current concerns about the validity of intelligence testing, an understanding of these influences is essential.

This is a good introduction because it:

1   Opens with a common belief about the subject which sets up the debate to be examined and questioned
2   Points out that this is an issue which remains unresolved (the problem to be addressed)
3   Delineates the scope/content to be discussed – evidence from twin and adoption studies
4   Indicates the outcomes of this research and the argument/conclusion in the essay (that IQ is shaped by an interaction between genetic and environmental factors)
5   Concludes by putting the debate into a context – concerns about the validity of intelligence testing (importance/timeliness of the topic)

Why might a good introduction like the one in Box 6.1 make such a positive impact on the grade? Because when you provide an overview of the assignment in this way it helps the marker to understand the relevance of what follows; it contextualises and frames the assignment, and facilitates comprehension.

Bearing this point in mind, try to work out what the following passage is about:

The procedure is actually quite simple. First, you arrange things into two different groups. Of course, one pile may be sufficient depending on how much there is to do. If you have to go somewhere else due to lack of facilities, that is the next step; otherwise you are pretty well set. It is important not to overdo things. That is, it is better to do fewer things at once than too many. In the short run this might not seem important, but complications can easily arise. A mistake can be expensive as well. At first the whole procedure will seem complicated. Soon, however, it will become just another facet of life. It is difficult to foresee an end to the necessity for this task in the immediate future, but then one can never tell. After the procedure is completed, one arranges the material into different groups again. Then they can be put into their appropriate places. Eventually they will be used once more, and the whole cycle will have to be repeated. However, that is part of life.

Did it make sense? Struggling? What about the next passage:

A newspaper is better than a magazine. A seashore is a better place than the street. At first it is better to run than to walk. You may have to try several times. It takes some skill, but it is easy to learn. Even young children can enjoy it. Once successful, complications are minimal. Birds seldom get too close. Rain, however, soaks in very fast. Too many people doing the same thing can also cause problems. One needs lots of room. If there are no complications, it can be very peaceful. A rock will serve as an anchor. If things break loose from it, however, you will not get a second chance.

Just as bad? Just as frustrating? Well, perhaps it would make sense if you knew that the first passage was about washing clothes and the second was about making a kite. And that was the point of John Bransford and Marcia Johnson's experiment from 1972 when they presented these passages to people with or without this contextual information: readers required some knowledge of the topic in order to facilitate comprehension.

While these are quite extreme examples, I think they illustrate the point quite well: you need to signpost and guide the reader/marker through the relevance of what you are saying. This will help them to read it and mark it.

The 'halo effect' and 'confirmation bias'

It is important to note, in this respect, the famous 'halo effect', where our judgements about a person are influenced by a favourable or unfavourable first impression (e.g. Nisbett and Wilson, 1977). A good first impression, at a job interview, for example (smart, friendly), might create a positive feeling towards the candidate, minimising the impact of any subsequent gaffes. A poor first impression, on the other hand, can have the opposite effect – finding fault, etc. – which is known as 'reverse halo effect' (or 'devil effect'). In terms of assignments, then, it may be that a well-written introduction creates a 'halo effect', favourably disposing the marker to the assignment; a poor introduction, on the other hand, may have the opposite effect. Although it could also be that the quality of the introduction simply reflects the quality of the rest of the assignment. In the words of an old Japanese saying, 'One instance shows the rest'.

Studies have also shown that we tend to seek out information that confirms our views and beliefs. This is known as 'confirmation bias' (Nickerson, 1998; Shermer, 2002). For example, if you believe in astrology, and you know the supposed personality traits associated with the different star signs, then you'll tend to look for confirmation in the people you know. Your Taurean friend actually is quite stubborn and bullish. But isn't everyone at times? Aren't they also quite indecisive at times, like Librans, or inquisitive, like Geminis? Confirmation bias means you'll tend to find what you're looking for.

One instance shows the rest...?

Illustration 6.1

How might this apply to the marking of an assignment? Well, if it starts with a good first impression from the opening introduction, then the marker might be predisposed towards focusing on those aspects that confirm this initial positive impression. Conversely, a poor first impression might bias them towards focusing on any errors and inadequacies. As the philosopher Francis Bacon (1561–1626) recognised many years ago:

> The human understanding when it has once adopted an opinion ... draws all things else to support and agree with it. And though there be a greater number and weight of instances to be found on the other side, yet these it either neglects and despises, or else by some distinction sets aside and rejects. (Cited in Shermer, 2002: 296)

A good introduction and a less good introduction: two examples

Bearing all this advice in mind, Box 6.2 provides an example of a very good introduction. It is taken from an assignment written by a second-year student, which received a very high mark. As the comments after each paragraph show, this introduction meets most of the criteria suggested for a good introduction:

1. **Importance and timeliness of the topic (criterion 1) along with the problem to be addressed (criterion 2).** National statistics are provided, stating the scale of the problem, and local statistics indicate relevance for the

local context – also justifying the need to consider new treatments (like acupuncture).

2. **The scope of the essay (criterion 3) and the argument to be presented (criterion 5).** The second paragraph outlines the aim of the report (looking at the possibility of introducing an alternative treatment) and refers to a systematic review that will (presumably) be discussed. Finally, there is an overview of the contents, reflecting the assignment brief: the report will discuss the history, rationale and evidence – leading to an informed decision about using acupuncture to treat chronic asthma.

---

box **6.2**

Example of a good introduction

The following introduction is taken from a student assignment, which asked students to evaluate a complementary therapy:

> Assignment question/brief: Having been employed in a local health clinic, your manager has asked you to write a 2,000 word report outlining your views and specific recommendations about using a complementary therapy. The report should discuss the history, underlying principles and research for the therapy. You should justify your choice of therapy as being relevant to the clinic where you are working.

> **Essay title: A review of acupuncture as an alternative treatment for chronic asthma**

> ### 1. Introduction

> According to the National Asthma Campaign, there are 5.4 million people in the UK currently receiving treatment for asthma and the cost to the NHS is over £996 million per year[1]. In 2007, Killingham's Primary Care Trust had the 4th highest hospital admissions rate for asthma[2] in the whole of the UK, which suggests that the management, treatment and education of asthma are not effective in the Killingham area. New strategies to help reduce strain on emergency departments, respiratory clinics and local GP surgeries need to be brought into play to ensure that asthma sufferers are receiving the treatment they require, when they need it.

> ✓

This introductory paragraph states the scale of the problem, providing general statistics *and* local statistics – making an interesting argument for looking at acupuncture, justifying and contextualising the issue for the assignment.

> This report will focus on the possibility of introducing a complementary and alternative medicine as a treatment option for chronic

(Continued)

(Continued)

asthma at the Killingham Royal Infirmary (KRI) Respiratory Clinic[3]. In 2003, McCarney et al. carried out a systematic review on investigating the effects of acupuncture[20] in treating chronic asthma. This review has recently been updated, sparking new interest in the treatment. The history, rationale and evidence of the alternative therapy will be critically reviewed in this report, leading to an informed consideration of whether acupuncture has a potential role in treating chronic asthma, and essentially in the health care system.

✓

This second paragraph focuses on a particular clinic addressing the assignment question, and provides an overview of contents - history, rationale and evidence 'critically reviewed', as requested in assignment brief.

It is worth noting that this introduction is 200 words in length – which is 10% of the assignment. Given the importance of a clear introduction which summarises the contents of an assignment, I would recommend that an introduction is at least this length. Indeed, my only slight criticism is that the introduction might also have given an indication of what the assignment concludes – is the recommendation in favour or against the use of acupuncture as a treatment for asthma? For example, the writer might have added:

It is concluded, based on this review of the evidence, that acupuncture may have a role to play in the treatment of asthma, but further research is needed in case of possible adverse effects.

Box 6.3 provides an example of a poor introduction – a second-rate version of the one provided in Box 6.2. In comparison, it is short, vague, cursory and tokenistic.

box   6.3

Example of a poor introduction

Essay title: Acupuncture as a treatment for pain

Introduction

This assignment will provide a discussion of the principles and practices of acupuncture. The assignment will provide a brief background to acupuncture, look at the practice, and discuss the evidence from research. Some types of health problems it might be used for, and risks, are also discussed. Finally, the conclusion will end with a discussion of my recommendations about using acupuncture.

× ☹

While this introduction does provide an overview of the contents, it's very tokenistic. Compared to the very good introduction in Box 6.2, this is just a vague regurgitation of the assignment brief. It needed to be longer, more specific and detailed.

Tip 24: Complete the writing of your introduction after you've written your assignment

If the introduction is going to provide an overview of what is in your assignment (the topics, issues and argument), it is better to write it up properly after you've completed the assignment. So it's pointless agonising over it too much before you start. A rough outline should suffice until the assignment is completed.

Tip 25: Write 'a lot about a little' rather than 'a little about a lot'

Chris Mounsey (2002: 30) makes an interesting observation about the transition from school to university:

> An important difference in essay writing between undergraduate level and school ... is that at the higher level you are graded more on your ability to make a coherent argument, and less on the amount of information presented. The way to think about it is to remember that in all the essays you have written so far, you have had to say a little about a lot of information. In an undergraduate essay, you need to say a lot about a little bit of information.

In other words, you need to focus. However, this does not mean, for example, providing every minute detail of a research study. Rather, it's about focusing on a few things in depth rather than many things superficially (depth rather than breadth).

Why is this relevant to introductions? Well, because the introduction needs to set the parameters, the scope and the focus of the assignment. In a typical 2,000-word assignment you can only cover so much about a topic, so you have to be selective. If you acknowledge this in your introduction, it shows that you are aware of the broader issues, but that you have set your parameters. As we shall see later, this strategy is also important to avoid covering too much ground (superficially) at the cost of more detailed argument and analysis.

Conclusions

Conclusions are *very* important. Remember, this is the last thing a marker will read before they turn to the marking sheet.

Tip 26: **Provide a good conclusion summarising your answer to the question**

What tutors like

- An ability to sum up

- A concise conclusion that reflects the introduction and the student's own conclusion

- A good conclusion, summarising the answer to the question

- A conclusion that really does conclude what has been presented

A good conclusion should be arrived at: if you've written your assignment well, your conclusion should be obvious, since it should summarise the arguments made throughout the body of the essay.

The study by Townsend et al. (1993), referred to earlier, examined a range of essay-writing guides and arrived at three criteria for an effective conclusion. A good conclusion should:

1. Summarise the main ideas of the essay

2. Provide an answer to the question posed

3. Discuss the broader implications of the topic

Using these criteria, they constructed a conclusion for the essay 'Discuss the role of genetic and environmental factors in IQ scores' and came up with the example provided in Box 6.4.

box 6.4

A model conclusion

This is the 'model' conclusion constructed by Townsend et al. (1993), using key criteria from essay writing guides, for the essay title 'Discuss the role of genetic and environmental factors in IQ scores':

In conclusion, statements such as 'Geniuses are born not made' are too simplistic. The evidence from studies of twins and adopted children demonstrates the importance of both genetic and environmental factors in the development of intelligence. While the genotype may set the upper and lower limits for development, a range of environmental factors determine the extent to which that potential will be realized. Rather than attempting to answer the 'nature vs nurture' question, researchers should investigate ways to enhance the cognitive potential of all individuals.

Notice how this conclusion:

- starts by referring back to the opening quote
- summarises the outcomes from the evidence discussed
- discusses broader implications by making recommendations about further research

In Box 6.5 I have also provided the conclusion from the student assignment discussed earlier, which does a fairly good job of meeting these criteria within the context of a 2,000-word assignment.

box   6.5

Example of a good conclusion

The conclusion below is taken from the student assignment discussed earlier, in which the student evaluated the use of acupuncture for chronic asthma.

Conclusion

In conclusion, the McCarney et al. systematic review has been critically analysed to allow consideration of whether acupuncture would be useful treating asthma at the KRI Respiratory Clinic. The background, rationale and efficacy of the alternative treatment have been reviewed and it has been suggested as a treatment option at the Clinic. Further research is needed into the area along with analysis of the treatment's adverse effects in relation to chronic asthma. Acupuncture may have a role in the health care system as there were some positive findings in the review. Whether these are purely placebo-based may have to be further researched, so more funding will be needed.

This provides a good conclusion to the assignment, with recommendations:

(Continued)

(Continued)

1   It provides a summary - the assignment has critically analysed the evidence (from a systematic review) as well as reviewing the background, rationale and efficacy of the treatment (all as requested in the assignment question and guidelines).

2   It provides an answer to the question posed - based on this review the conclusion says that acupuncture is recommended as a treatment option for the clinic.

3   It also refers to broader implications by identifying limitations of the report and further areas of research - the issue of possible adverse effects and placebo effects, which may require further research or monitoring if acupuncture is used as a treatment in the clinic.

Tip 27: Do not introduce new information in your conclusion

And remember, a conclusion should summarise what has been discussed – it should not introduce new information:

What tutors dislike

- New information in the conclusion

- Things talked about in conclusion that were not discussed in the body of the text leaving me to go back to see if I missed it!

Tip 28: Write your conclusion before you start and your introduction after you've finished (eh?)

We already know (Tip 24) that you should complete the writing of your introduction after you've finished your assignment, so you can provide an overview of the contents – what you've actually discussed. By the same token, you might like to formulate your conclusion before you start, remembering that 'clever people work backwards' (Tip 5). To use our analogy of a journey again, it's no good charting the route before the destination has been decided.

General structure and organisation

In the survey of tutors, issues relating to structure came seventh in the list of common problems and fourth on the list of things that impress markers.

Problems relating to structure

Problems included:

- hopping from one theme to another - and back again
- lack of signposting
- lack of headings
- use of appendices

The following tips address each of these issues.

Tip 29: Don't hop about: keep all the information on one issue / theme / topic in one place

One of the main causes of marker distress was essays that lack a logical development and seem to flit back and forth from one theme to the next:

What tutors dislike

- Essays that lack structure and seem to hop from one theme to the next at random; no sense of flow, very little (if any) signposting
- Poor structure, which means going back and forth through pages
- Poor structure, which means that you comment on the absence of detail when the relevant detail appears later on

These last two comments certainly hit a nerve, especially when you've made notes on the script about the need for further details only to find said details turning up later in the essay. The key point here, then, is to keep all the information on one issue, theme or topic together.

Tip 30: Use signposting to summarise and make your essay flow

What tutors like

- Clear signposting of ideas that enables the work to flow in a logical manner to a conclusion

- A clear structure, especially when signposted

- Logical structure so the marker is not required to keep going over parts that have already been read in order to keep a grasp of how the parts of the assignment/ essay interrelate

- That the points made clearly link into each other

We've already talked about signposting in the context of introductions, but signposting is also an important strategy throughout the assignment. At certain points/junctures it is useful to provide a brief reflective review of your argument and look towards the next section of the assignment. For example, you might make the transition from one section to another like this:

> Having critically appraised the underlying rationale for acupuncture, we will now examine the evidence from research studies.

> There have been hundreds of studies over the years, but I will be focusing on two recent systematic reviews as the best source of evidence ...

This helps you *and your tutor* to monitor your argument and the points you are making.

Tip 31: Use headings (and subheadings) to structure your work

Personally, I like headings. You know where you are with headings. Literally – as a writer or as a reader/marker – you can see what's where.

What tutors like

- Good use of headings and subheadings

- Use of subtitles – as long as the discussion then matches the subtitle!

Headings and subheadings are useful because they help to structure an assignment into manageable chunks. They can also help to show that you've addressed the relevant areas in the right proportions. In the complementary therapies assignment, for example, students often used the following headings:

- Introduction
- Historical Background
- Rationale of Therapy
- Principles of Practice
- Research Evidence
- Conclusion

These headings are useful to ensure that the relevant issues are covered in the assignment.

However, if you are using headings/subheadings to help structure and organise your assignment, don't overdo it. Too many headings may be disruptive; they should only be used to delineate major sections of a report. So if you end up with 40 headings in your 2,000-word assignment, something is not right.

Tip 32: **Check with your tutor about the use of headings**

The use of headings may depend on the type of assignment. Strictly speaking, using headings in an essay may not be recommended by some tutors, especially if it's a very short essay, but for research reports or projects they are extremely important and, indeed, essential to ensure that all relevant aspects of the project are clearly reported. Since these are a special case, I've provided a brief outline of the typical sections used in a research report in Chapter 15 (which also includes some common problems).

Note: if your tutor is an essay purist and does not want you to insert headings, you can always write it with headings to help you structure the assignment, and then remove them when you actually submit the assignment. But don't forget to check the flow after you've removed the headings; you may need to add some linking sentences.

Tip 33: **Don't use appendices as a dumping ground**

Problems with appendices were noted by quite a few tutors and, in fact, came eighth on the list of common problems.

What tutors dislike

- Appendices that are not referred to or discussed in an assignment or have little point for being there

- Putting lots of information in appendices and expecting me to sift through it for the relevant bits

- Poor use (almost any use) of appendices, usually an attempt to gain more words

Appendices are used to provide further information that is relevant but not essential to the main body of a report (if it is essential information, it should be included in the body of the assignment). They are more typically used in reports, such as research proposals, or portfolios of work, to include additional materials that would otherwise clutter up the main body of the text, for example a copy of a questionnaire referred to in the main text, or tables of raw data which, importantly, should have been summarised in the main text. They should not be used as an attempt to gain more words since they are not usually included in the word count of an assignment. If the information is important and necessary to address the assignment question/brief, it should be integrated into the body of the text. Appendices should be treated as additional information which may be consulted by the interested reader.

If you do need to include appendices make sure you refer to them in the text (they should be numbered of course) and also guide the reader through the information. Do not use it as a dumping ground and expect your tutor to sift through it for relevant information. On a practical note, it can sometimes be difficult for the marker to locate the relevant appendix in larger documents (such as dissertations, which may include quite a few appendices), so it's helpful if you can include the page number to help the marker locate it, for example '(see Appendix 10 on p. 79)'.

summary

In this chapter we've seen the crucial importance of:

- providing a good introduction which outlines the content of your assignment (along with five key criteria that could raise your grade)
- concluding your assignment with a summary of what you said and how you've answered the question
- using 'signposting' (in the introduction and throughout the assignment) to help the reader navigate through the assignment

- using headings to structure your assignment
- focusing the scope of your assignment (by writing a lot about a little, rather than a little about a lot)

We've also seen the importance of first impressions - how the 'halo effect' and 'confirmation bias' may influence the marker in subtle ways. There's an interesting phenomenon in psychology which shows that our memory is influenced by what are known as 'primacy' and 'recency' effects (Murdock, 1962; Jones et al., 1968). For example, we tend to remember the first words and the last words in a list more than those in the middle. You might like to think about this when writing your assignment. It would suggest that the introduction and the conclusion are disproportionately prevalent in a tutor's thoughts when it comes to completing the mark sheet. In other words, it's back to making a good first impression and a good last impression.

Critical Analysis, Perspective and Argument

Greasley, P.

If you can't say anything nice, don't say anything at all.

(Old English proverb)

Good advice for social occasions, perhaps, but potentially disastrous for your assignments.

In this chapter we'll be discussing the importance of adopting a critical perspective, developing an argument, and making a case for the position you have decided to adopt. To help you appreciate the significance of this when writing your assignments, we'll be looking at:

- a model of learning and teaching that probably forms the basis for how your course is taught and how your assignments are assessed
- some questions you might ask when presented with a theory, a model, or the findings from a research study
- a crucial difference between what you think is important when writing your assignments and what tutors think is important when marking your assignments
- the importance of adopting a perspective on the issues you are discussing (and making a case for your position)

You'll also learn that there are no 'right' answers, and that you should trust no one.

Tip 43: **Stop describing, start critiquing**

One of the most significant outcomes from the survey is that it highlights the importance of critical thinking and argument as the feature that tutors value highest when marking assignments. The message is that you need to step up a gear: from simply describing and reporting to being analytical, critical and evaluative. In this respect, there's something you should know about. It's called Bloom's taxonomy (Figure 8.1) and it probably forms the basis for how your course is taught and assessed.

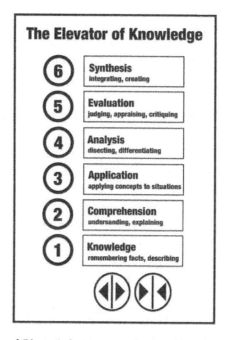

The Elevator of Knowledge

6 Synthesis
integrating, creating

5 Evaluation
judging, appraising, critiquing

4 Analysis
disecting, differentiating

3 Application
applying concepts to situations

2 Comprehension
undersanding, explaining

1 Knowledge
remembering facts, describing

Figure 8.1   Illustration of Bloom's taxonomy of educational objectives

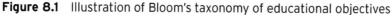

Bloom's taxonomy (Bloom et al., 1956) outlines six levels of thinking, from the simple to the complex. Pay particular attention to what lies at the bottom in Figure 8.1: description, recalling facts, and simply reporting what others have said. If you want high marks, particularly as you progress through the years at university, you will need to climb this ladder by applying, analysing and critically evaluating concepts.

So you start by building up your knowledge about a concept, theory, model, etc. until you are able to understand it, describe it, give examples and then apply it, but then you progress beyond this level of understanding (merely knowing about and accepting something because it's in a book or a manual) to a more critical, analytical perspective.

Generally speaking, then, description won't get you many marks; it certainly won't get you high marks. So, if the question asks you to 'analyse', 'critically appraise' or 'evaluate' and you spend most of the essay describing things, reporting lots of facts and figures and covering as much ground as possible, you're heading for disappointment. This emphasis on critical analysis rather than description is highlighted in the comments from the survey of tutors:

What tutors dislike

- Description rather than analysis (particularly from second year upwards)
- Presenting lots of bullet points instead of discussion
- Long bits of description which could be condensed into a sentence or two
- Not providing some sort of critique of, or reflection on, the work they've read (i.e. assuming because it's in print it must be 'right')

What tutors like

- Students who attempt to look critically at models/theories
- Analysis of reading rather than description
- Concise critical appraisal (with citations in support, where appropriate)
- Ability to see more than one side of an argument
- Being aware that just because something is in print it doesn't make it a for-all-time, concrete, unassailable fact!
- A good mixture of discussion and argument
- Comparison of sources and analysis
- Critical comment on the literature (author A takes this view in contrast to author B – what they both fail to account for fully is...; or an alternative interpretation can be offered by...; or this does not account for the problematic nature of [this concept], etc.)

Tip 44: When presented with a theory, a model, or the findings from a research study, there are certain questions you should ask

If you are going to adopt a more critical perspective, it's useful to have some questions at the ready to get you started (Neville, 2009a; G. Taylor, 2009). I've listed a few below along with some examples of how they might be applied.

Where does the theory/model/statistic come from? Who says? How do they know? What's the evidence? What's the sample?

Did you know, for example, that women talk more than men? Of course you did: an average 20,000 words per day compared to 7,000 for men. When these statistics were featured in *The Female Brain*, a bestselling book by Louann Brizendine

(2006),they were circulated throughout the media (e.g. 'Women talk three times as much as men, says study' was the headline in the *Daily Mail* newspaper; Macrae, 28 November 2006). However, on closer inspection it was discovered that these figures were derived from a self-help book and other second-hand sources – not research – and they were removed from a later edition of the book (Lilienfeld et al., 2010). A more reliable primary source based on a study by Mehl et al. (2007), reported in the journal *Science*, found that men and women both use around 16,000 words per day, though with 'very large individual differences'.

Does it make sense based on your own experience?

Your own experience may lead you to question the conclusions from the Mehl et al. (2007) study. There were, after all, 'very large individual differences', and the study was based on a particular sample: 396 university students (210 were female).

Does it apply across different contexts and cultures?

We should also question whether these results apply across different contexts and cultures since the study was limited to a sample of university students from the USA.

Does it apply in the real world?

When Newstead and Dennis (1994) asked 14 experienced examiners to mark six essays some of the marks were so inconsistent that they ranged from a 2:2 to a first – for the same essay. Does this mean that the mark you are awarded for your assignment depends to a large extent on the tutor who is marking it? Not necessarily, because this was an experiment rather than real-life marking with real consequences for the student. Furthermore, the marking was conducted by tutors not involved on the course, it was a 'rather abstract and obscure topic that examiners might have great difficulty in marking' (Newstead, 2002: 73), and they weren't using marking schemes with clear criteria. In research terms, this is known as lacking 'ecological validity', because the study didn't really reflect the real-life situation.

Is it plausible?

The problem with research is that it can be contradictory. Think about health advice: one minute we are advised to eat fewer eggs and the next minute we are told we can eat as many as we like (within reason of course). In my own area of interest, complementary and alternative therapies, there have been decades of research providing conflicting evidence on whether treatments like homeopathy or acupuncture work or not. While it's important to be selective about the evidence you choose to believe (the more robust studies), it's also important to look at the *plausibility* of the treatments: what's the rationale – the underlying mechanism of action? Is it plausible that acupuncture works because it claims to release a mysterious 'energy' called 'qi' through equally mysterious channels referred to as meridians? At this point you might want to consider carefully the underlying rationale for a particular therapy. We would apply the same criteria to pseudosciences like astrology.

Are there exceptions which challenge the theory/model?

Most students in the social sciences will at one time or another come across Abraham Maslow's (1987) famous model outlining the 'hierarchy of human

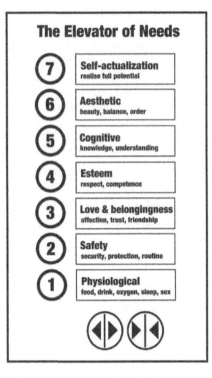

Figure 8.2   Illustration of Maslow's hierarchy of human needs

needs'. I've represented it as an 'elevator of needs' in Figure 8.2. The model has been used to account for why most people are never satisfied: having satisfied one set of needs, our priorities move on to the next. For example, once you've achieved safety and security (job, house, etc.), you might then start to focus on 'love and belongingness' (personal and social relationships); and once that's sorted out, you might start to think about your esteem needs (e.g. promotion at work); and so on. The problem is, of course, that there are many exceptions. For example, many people in affluent countries are satisfied with a house, car, family, etc., and don't crave a higher level of 'self-actualisation' epitomised by the famous few upon which Maslow's concept of 'self-actualisation' was based (e.g. Albert Einstein, Abraham Lincoln). They may be happy with their lot. Another problem is the idea that we have to satisfy needs at one level before moving on to the next. For example, must we satisfy the more basic physiological needs before dealing with the higher needs? (Dear Tutor, I won't be attending your lecture today because I have some needs lower down the hierarchy that I have to satisfy...).

There is an important issue to be aware of here: beware of simplified secondary accounts of a theory. For example, in many textbooks Maslow's hierarchy is criticised for stating that we must satisfy the lower needs before moving up to the higher needs. But Maslow didn't actually say this in such simplistic terms. He took a more realistic approach, pointing out that we move up the hierarchy when lower levels are partially satisfied. New motivations *emerge* as lower needs are becoming fulfilled. He was also well aware of exceptions (e.g. the starving artist who forgoes the more basic needs in favour of aesthetic needs).

This illustrates an important point: be careful that you don't simplify or mis-interpret the theory/model. This highlights the importance of comparing a few sources of information and, preferably, going back to the original source.

Tip 45: **Appreciate the good as well as the bad**

It's important to remember that being critical is not just about being negative. Rather, it's about demonstrating that you appreciate the *pros and cons* – discerning the good and the bad – of something. In academic studies this usually means evaluating a theory, model, research study, etc., but in real life we do it all the time when we make judgements about the quality of a movie, music, fashion, cars, etc. In assignments, though, you just need to be a bit more rigorous:

- What's good about it (and why; with references to support your case)
- What's problematic about it (and why; with references...)

Critically appraising research articles in academic journals is a common assign-ment topic for students in the health and social sciences. It requires them to appraise the various parts of an article, including the title (is it clear and inform-ative?), the abstract (is it a good summary of the article, providing details about the sample, methods, results?), the methodology (was it appropriate to the aims of the study? Was it clearly explained? Was it well designed?), and so on. It's sup-posed to be a detailed critical examination of the research, but sometimes this isn't quite achieved, as the following extract from one assignment illustrates:

Critically appraising a research article (extract from student assignment)

The title is easy to read as it has big font and it's bold so it stands out ... The abstract is not as clear to read from as it has small font which makes it difficult to read because the words are so close together ... The good thing about the abstract is that it's placed in the middle so therefore it differentiates itself from the rest of the literature...

There are lots of books (and many websites) providing guidelines to help you critically appraise the quality and reliability of research studies. In the health sciences, for example, Trisha Greenhalgh's (2006) book, *How to Read a Paper*, is a classic text providing guidance on critically appraising a range of research designs (e.g. randomised controlled trials, systematic reviews, qualitative research).

Tip 46: **You think it's all about content and coverage, but tutors value argument and understanding**

Studies have highlighted a 'mismatch' between what students and tutors think is most important when writing essays (Norton, 1990; Defeyter and

McPartlin, 2007). While both students and tutors agree that the top rank goes to 'answering the question', a mismatch appears between the importance of content and argument:

- Students rank content and coverage of relevant information higher than argument
- Tutors rank argument and understanding higher than content

Another way of putting this is that tutors place greater emphasis on the importance of a deep approach – displaying *understanding* – whereas students tend to focus on a surface approach – covering lots of information. (Remember Tip 25: you should be writing 'a lot about a little, rather than a little about a lot'.)

Tip 47: **Try using the 'therefore test' to check for arguments**

If you're not totally clear about what an argument is, and whether your assignment includes any, there's a simple test you can use: see if you can insert the word 'therefore' at the end of a series of statements. Here's a simple example from Richard van de Lagemaat (2007: 10) which illustrates the difference between (1) merely listing a series of unsubstantiated statements and (2) constructing an argument:

1. Astrology is the belief that the position of the stars at the time of your birth affects your destiny. There are ten times more astrologers than astronomers in the United States. Despite its popularity, astrology cannot be classified as a science.

2. One of the hallmarks of a genuine science is that it makes testable predictions. Admittedly, astrologers do make predictions, but they are so vague that they cannot be verified or falsified. So, unlike astronomy, astrology cannot be classified as a science.

Whereas (1) lists a series of unrelated statements, (2) constructs an argument – and we could use 'therefore' to replace 'so' before the final sentence. (Other words like 'so', 'consequently', 'thus', and 'hence' may also be used to indicate the conclusion to an argument.) Out of interest, I decided to go through the excellent student assignment that I referred to in Chapter 6 to see if I could use the 'therefore' test to highlight arguments in the text, and I was pleased to find two opportunities in the opening paragraph of the introduction:

Introduction

According to the National Asthma Campaign, there are 5.4 million people in the UK currently receiving treatment for asthma and the cost to the NHS is over £996 million per year. In 2007, Killingham's Primary Care Trust had the 4th highest hospital admissions rate for asthma in the whole of the UK, which suggests [**therefore**] that the management, treatment and education of asthma is not effective in the Killingham area. [**Therefore**] New strategies to help reduce strain on emergency departments, respiratory clinics and local

GP surgeries need to be brought into play to ensure that asthma sufferers are receiving the treatment they require, when they need it.

Here we can see that the 'therefore test' makes the underlying argument in this introductory passage explicit. If we break it down into premises (statements which lead to a claim), it looks like this:

- Premise 1: Asthma affects millions of people in the UK
- Premise 2: Treatments for asthma costs millions each year
- Premise 3: Killingham Care Trust has one of the highest hospital admission rates in the UK
- Conclusion: Therefore new strategies to treat asthma might be considered: the argument provides a justification for examining the use of acupuncture as an alternative or complementary treatment for asthma

It is this logical reasoning, made explicit by the 'therefore' test, which makes this introduction so effective.

Here's one more illustration of an argument from this excellent assignment:

The review [of research studies] drew limited conclusions regarding the effectiveness of acupuncture in treating asthma. Out of all the trials, only two of them reported the participants to have an improvement in overall well-being and this could not be distinguished between needle or sham acupuncture. Patients who received the acupuncture or believed they were having acupuncture (a placebo) did improve in general health, but not specifically in their asthma symptoms. [**Therefore**] This suggests the placebo effect of acupuncture may play a part in the therapeutic role of the treatment.

If we turn the main argument here into premise and conclusion, it might look like this:

- Premise: Patients who received real acupuncture showed some improvement in general health, but so did those who received sham acupuncture
- Conclusion: This suggests [therefore] that the placebo effect plays a part in the therapeutic role of the treatment

But did you also notice another (related) argument in this passage? Sometimes the conclusion is stated prior to the premise, so if we reverse the first two sentences this reveals another premise and conclusion:

- Premise: Only two of the trials in the review of research studies reported an improvement in well-being
- Conclusion: [Therefore] There is limited evidence regarding the effectiveness of acupuncture in treating asthma

I would suggest (therefore) that this might be a useful test to apply in your assignments to see if they contain any arguments. Though it's important to note, of course, that some arguments are better than others:

There is a strong correlation between ice-cream sales and crime rates: as ice-cream sales rise, so does the crime rate. Therefore ice-cream causes crime ...

Incidentally, and perhaps unsurprisingly, since writing this book I've witnessed many assignments that are superficially peppered with the word 'therefore'. Remember that the extracts in the excellent complementary therapies assignment that I used to illustrate the presence of arguments didn't actually include the word 'therefore' – I inserted it to make the argument explicit. The point I'm making is: don't overdo it. A student who is comfortable arguing doesn't make it look like a special effort (or a cheap trick). Argument should be implicit in your discussion of the topic, not something that's superficially tagged on at the end of paragraphs with sentences beginning with 'Therefore'.

Tip 48: What do you think? Adopt a perspective – have a point of view

What tutors like

- Balanced argument but own opinion included within the arguments
- Ability to see more than one side of an argument
- The student's own conclusion
- A student not afraid to express an opinion (where relevant)
- A presence of voice – a sense that the author has a 'political' stance, or indeed conviction. The better essays are usually written by those students.

In the study by Defeyter and McPartlin (2007) referred to above, it was also noted that some students felt they shouldn't be presenting a particular view. Rather they should be presenting a balanced evaluation. Well, this is partly true – you should consider different perspectives, both sides of the argument, but as we saw in Chapter 4 (Tips 4 and 5), you should come to some position yourself before you start writing the assignment. What do you think? What will you be ultimately arguing for?

Tip 49: How to make the jump from a B to an A: act like you're a lawyer making a case

I have just spent a couple of hours comparing a batch of assignments which were awarded a B with those that were awarded an A. What was the difference?

Well, while the Bs were generally well written, structured and presented, covered all the key issues and included key references, they didn't make a clear and focused case. Most of the relevant information was there – it just wasn't organised, structured and focused like a first-class essay. This is usually apparent from the start, with a good introduction presaging a clear and focused argument – and everything in the assignment, every section, every paragraph is a building block towards a clear conclusion.

In a good essay you should take a position, take 'a line' on the subject matter, and argue for one or other position – as if you're a lawyer making a case. This will help you to structure the essay, for example, by presenting the case against your argument first, but then presenting the (better) case for your argument afterwards. So any information you are discussing is only relevant to the extent that you are using it to support your case – your argument.

A word of warning, however. I have seen students reduced to a crumbling bag of nerves because they've been told they must include more critical analysis in their assignments. Their ability to write a clear and simple descriptive account goes to pieces in their quest to embark on deep, impenetrable critical discussion. It's about finding a balance: yes, you do need to adopt a critical perspective, but this will include descriptive writing to provide essential background information so that the writing makes sense to the reader.

Tip 50: Support your argument with evidence

Now obviously you'll need to support your arguments with evidence – the best and most reliable and robust evidence – but you already knew that from Chapter 5.

What tutors like

- Statements substantiated
- Backing up of ideas
- Use of good evidence to support assertions, including research findings
- Use and critique of appropriate reference resources that demonstrate a thorough literature search
- Reading widely and using the literature to develop a critical argument
- Critical debate supported with appropriate literature

So when you're advised to say what you think, this doesn't mean, well, just saying what you think – off the top of your head, as it were. It needs to be backed up with evidence or other support.

Tip 51: **Illustrate and apply ideas to specific contexts**

The survey also highlighted the importance of 'illustrating and applying ideas to specific contexts', grounding the discussion in actual examples, rather than remaining vague about the issues under discussion. In the ranking of themes, this actually came third in the list of what most impresses tutors.

What tutors like

- Relating discussion to actual examples

- Linking theory and practice through the explicit use of examples

- Linking literature to practice

- Reflections on practice that indicate taking the assignment seriously

- Using a case study/example to illustrate their comments/analysis

- Application of the reading and student learning to the context they are discussing/analysing

For example, if you're doing an assignment on some psychological issue, let's say positive and negative reinforcement of behaviour, don't just focus on the experimental studies, relate it to real life – gambling, punishment, learning. How does it work in the real world? So if the theories say 'this' and the research says 'that', think: how does this apply to the real world?

The student assignment that I have been discussing did a very good job of illustrating and applying ideas in the 'real world', particularly in the recommendations section where the *practicalities* of introducing acupuncture as a treatment for asthma are discussed. I've extracted the key passage for illustration in Box 8.1.

box 8.1

Applying the results of research to the real world

The following extract from an example assignment critically reflects on the systematic review of research examining the use of acupuncture for asthma. It highlights the difference between research and practice, and the extent to which results are generalisable and apply in real life (actual practice).

(Continued)

(Continued)

This systematic review has several limitations. Acupuncture trials are highly complex to carry out simply due to the variation in methods. For example, the review did not specifically list the type of needle, needle depth, duration and location of needle insertion for each study, introducing potential bias. This review describes the positive outcome measures of acupuncture but does not mention any adverse effects. This does not give a fair representation of acupuncture as a whole. Another limitation is that it focuses only on mild to moderate asthma, so the findings cannot be generalised for all classifications. Finally, the accuracy of acupuncture used in the trials compared to actual acupuncture practice could be questionable. Acupuncture often comes in a complementary and alternative medicine 'package' which involves lifestyle changes and/or herbal medicines to promote physical - as well as emotional - well-being and is tailored to each person individually. This would not have been achieved in the clinical trials.

Tip 52: There are no 'right' answers – only positions you can adopt and cases you can make

It's often the case that the more you think about an issue, the more difficult it is to provide a simple, straightforward answer. So if you think you have a simple answer to an assignment question, beware. It probably means you've not looked into it deeply enough. As the saying goes: 'The more you know, the less you know.'

When William Perry (1968) studied the intellectual development of students at Harvard University, he discovered a similar progression from certainty to uncertainty. He identified three main stages or 'positions', as he referred to them:

Position 1: Student's view of knowledge is dualistic: there's 'right' and 'wrong', and 'good' and 'bad'. Knowledge consists of objective facts, and authority figures (tutors) and textbooks provide the answers. All you need to do is listen out for the right answers and reproduce them in assignments.

Position 2: Student realises that there is more than one viewpoint - there is diversity of opinion - but the right answers are out there if we can find them. From this perspective, the lecture is like a guessing game in which the student has to figure out which theory is correct but discover the answer themselves.

Position 3: Student sees all knowledge and values as contextual and relative: some solutions are better than others depending on the context - we have to assess and choose. There are no 'right' answers, only positions you can adopt and cases you can make (with supporting evidence and arguments).

Remember that we were talking about 'cue-seekers' in Chapter 3? Well, the researchers, Miller and Partlett (1974), suggest that the cue-seekers (most of whom got a first) have reached this final stage: they are aware that, for many topics, particularly in the social sciences and humanities, there are no 'right' answers – only 'positions' you can adopt and cases you can make (with pros and cons), that are supported by argument and evidence. Think about it.

This sentiment is reflected in a statement by the Higher Education Council of Australia:

> Perhaps the most important 'generic' skill that a graduate can possess is the ability to recognise that knowledge is provisional, and that no answer is final, and that there is always a potential for a better way of doing things. (Cited in Naylor, 2007: 87)

Tip 53: **Dare to know**

This is the motto of the Enlightenment, a period in the eighteenth century when philosophers questioned the received ideas derived from authorities, traditions and faith. For the philosopher Immanuel Kant (1724–1804), it was about having the courage to use your own understanding; for the philosopher Diderot (1713–1784), it was about questioning everything: 'All things must be examined, debated, investigated without exception and without regard for anyone's feelings … We must ride roughshod over all ancient puerilities, overturn the barriers that reason never erected' (Diderot, *Encyclopédie*, 1775, cited in Smith, 1998).

This is the attitude you should adopt when you're writing your assignments. The Royal Society, which is the world's oldest scientific academy (founded in 1660) bears a similar motto, *Nullius in verba* – roughly translated as 'Take nobody's word for it' (where's the evidence?).

Tip 54: **Trust no one**

This is a more contemporary take on the Enlightenment motto, which recognises the fact that, human nature being what it is, people tend to operate with their own interests at heart, and this can lead to all kinds of bias. For example, studies have shown that research funded by pharmaceutical companies is four times more likely to give results that are favourable to the companies than independent studies (Bausell, 2007; Goldacre, 2009). Box 8.2 provides another example of how bias can subtly influence the results of research, illustrating the point that you should trust no one – not even yourself.

box   8.2

Does water remember? (Or 'the devil is in the detail')

In 1988 a paper appeared in the highly prestigious journal *Nature* claiming that an allergen triggered a chemical reaction in cells even after it had been diluted to such an extent that it had long since ceased to contain a single molecule of the original ingredient (after the fifteenth

(Continued)

(Continued)

dilution it would be essentially just water, but they used 120 successive dilutions). One explanation proposed by the director of the research, Jacques Benveniste, was that the water may have retained a memory of the original ingredient. As such, the experiment would provide support for homeopathy, one of the key principles of which is that remedies (mainly herbal) become more powerful the more they are diluted.

Since this was such a remarkable finding, contradicting the laws of physics, *Nature* agreed to publish the paper (Davenas et al., 1988), but with the proviso that they could visit the laboratory to observe how the experiments were being conducted. After observing several repeated experiments, the investigators became concerned that the people recording the changes in the cells knew which ones were being treated with the highly diluted allergen: judging whether a change had occurred was quite subjective and therefore prone to interpretation and bias. So they asked them to repeat the experiment but this time they were 'blinded' to ensure there could be no bias in their observations of changes in the cells: this time there was no effect.

One of the investigators from *Nature* was very relieved: James Randi, a well-known sceptic and magician had staked $1 million on the outcome of the experiment – or any experiment which contradicts the laws of science, including the existence of psychic, supernatural, or paranormal phenomena. The money has been available since 1964 and is still there, unclaimed, to this day (despite over 1000 attempts, and a few famous refusals to accept the challenge).

This shows the importance of 'blinding' in order to avoid unconscious (or deliberate) bias in interpreting data. It also, however, raises some other issues of potential bias. The research was initiated by a young homeopathic doctor, Bernard Poitevin, and the experiments were largely conducted by Elisabeth Davenas who also believed in homeopathy. The laboratory was part funded by a French homeopathic company – the Laboratories Homéopathiques de France.

The investigation by the team from *Nature* was filmed for a BBC *Horizon* programme (26 November 2002). Further details can be found at www.bbc.co.uk/science/horizon/2002/homeopathy.shtml (accessed March 2016).

Tip 55: Ask the question, 'Whose interests are being served here?' (follow the money)

Jeremy Paxman, the presenter of BBC's *Newsnight* for over 20 years, famously said of his approach to interviewing that he starts by asking himself the question, 'Why is this lying bastard lying to me?' Perhaps it's not appropriate for every interview, but when it comes to politicians and people with a vested interest, Paxman advocates a degree of scepticism, asking yourself, 'why are they saying this?' and 'is it likely to be true?' (Wells, 2005).

Continuing on the theme of bias, then, these are important questions to pose when a particular viewpoint may be being promoted. As the example below illustrates, there may be a degree of self-interest, especially where money is involved:

> New research claims ten squares of dark chocolate a day for two weeks can cure stress ... 'The study shows that a daily consumption of 40 grams over two weeks can modify the metabolism', said Nestlé researcher Sunil Kochhar. (*Metro* newspaper, 13 November 2009)

If you want more details about how self-interest, money and the media can bias the results of research, there are a number of books and internet sources to get your critical juices flowing and develop your 'critical consciousness'. For example, Ben Goldacre has written extensively on these issues in two books (*Bad Science*, 2008, and *Bad Pharma*, 2012) and has a website at http://www.bad science.net/about-dr-ben-goldacre/. On the subject of mental health, James Davies exposes the interests of pharmaceutical companies in his book *Cracked: Why Psychiatry Is Doing More Harm Than Good* (2013). And for a more general exposé on self-interest, politicians and the media, Owen Jones's book *The Establishment: And How They Get Away With It* (2014) examines the extent to which self-interest, power and corruption may be ruling our society, and our lives.

Being critical: Strategies to detect bullshit

In this final part of the chapter I've highlighted three useful strategies for the detection of dubious claims. I've also included a few websites devoted to critical thinking and sceptical inquiry for those of you who don't like being duped.

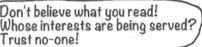

He used to be happy, but since going to university he never stops moaning...

Illustration 8.1

Tip 56: **Apply Occam's razor**

Yorkshireman wakes up from a coma speaking fluent Japanese – despite never having been to Japan!

I once overheard a conversation in which this newspaper story (or something similar) was recounted with bewildering interest: a man who'd received a bang on the head fell unconscious, and woke up speaking a different language. In the ensuing discussion it was argued that memories must have been revived from a past life or that there must have been some genes containing Japanese language, handed down from past generations, which had suddenly been released after the bang on the head. Well, that's two possible explanations, but in such circumstances we might do well to apply Occam's razor, which recommends that when two or more theories are competing to explain a phenomenon we should choose the simplest – or the one that makes the fewest assumptions.

So, returning to our proposed explanations for the mysterious case of waking up speaking a foreign language, the assumptions include:

1. We have past lives.
2. We retain memories and skills (like language) from these past lives that can suddenly spring into action.
3. Memories can be passed down through generations, through genes, which contain a whole language.
4. A bang on the head, for some reason, can ignite these memories.

Alternatively, we might opt for the slightly more prosaic and simpler explanation that it's a largely fabricated report by a newspaper based on a grain of truth (he did wake up speaking gibberish which sounded a bit like Japanese), noting the familiar newspaper motto: never let the facts get in the way of a good story.

In a more concrete example, R. Barker Bausell (2007: 109) uses Occam's razor to compare two possible explanations for why patients report reductions in knee pain after receiving acupuncture:

Explanation 1: The reduction in pain following the insertion of tiny needles in the body is due to those needles modulating the flow of a type of energy (qi) through meridians that are specifically designed for this purpose (somewhat similar to the role of arteries in blood flow) thereby reducing the subject's pain.

Explanation 2: It's the placebo effect.

In making our decision, Bausell invites us to adopt Occam's razor and count up the number of unsupported assumptions. For the first explanation we must assume:

(a) the existence of an unmeasured energy form called qi

(b) an as yet undetected system of meridians through which this qi flows

   (c) that the acupuncture needles are in fact capable of affecting this flow

   (d) that this altered flow is capable of reducing pain

The second explanation requires us to assume:

   (a) that a ceremony (of inserting tiny needles into the body accompanied by promises that such practices have reduced pain for thousands of years) can engender psychological explanations of benefit

   (b) that these psychological explanations (or suggestions) can influence our perceptions of the pain we experience (or cause us to imagine that we were experiencing less pain than we really were)

Using Occam's razor, then, combined with a large body of evidence for the analgesic placebo effect, we would be guided towards the second explanation.

Applying Occam's Razor to pretentious art descriptions

Illustration 8.2

Tip 57: **Beware of 'meaningless' statements**

In February 1968, the Beatles went to study transcendental meditation with the Indian guru Maharishi Mahesh in India. A journalist present at the time recounts:

They used to get together in a big hall in the evening and sing songs, and the Maharishi would give them a lecture which would proceed on the following lines: 'When we're delving into the meaning of the Raga you come up with those nether regions which are beyond the stellar spaces, which are so transcendental...' And the more incomprehensible he became the greater was the ecstasy and the rapture on the faces of the audience – including the Beatles.

(*Bombay's Beatle*, BBC Radio 4, 9 August 2009,
available at www.bbc.co.uk/programmes/b00hv1dt)

In the 1930s there was a movement in philosophy called 'logical positivism'. Its target was so-called metaphysical statements like those attributed to the Maharishi above. For a statement to be meaningful, the logical positivists argued, it should be possible to show that it's true or false. If we can't, then it should be dismissed as 'meaningless'. Here's an example from the philosopher Alfred Ayer (1936):

- 'To say that "God exists" is to make a metaphysical utterance which cannot be either true or false.'
    o   it is wrong to say that 'God exists' is true
    o   wrong to say that it is false
    o   wrong to say, along with the agnostic, that one does not know if it is true or false
    o   what one should say is that it is meaningless

This approach to language provides an interesting form of attack on woolly, obscure statements which often feature in the more fringe-like subjects of para-psychology and alternative medicine, as, for example, when someone offers to 'balance', 'cleanse' or 'energise' your chakras.

Tip 58: **Watch out for Barnum statements**

If you look at the palm of your hand, you'll see a line that begins between your thumb and index finger and curves down towards the centre of your wrist. It's called the 'life line' and, according to chiromancers, it can tell you lots of interesting things about your fate. For example, if you notice a break or a fork in the line this indicates a change in your life – perhaps a career break or some other change in lifestyle. You may also see a few lines that cross your lifeline, which signify obstacles in your path, perhaps an accident or an episode of ill health. Take note of where these forks and crosses occur on the lifeline, because that indicates the time in your life when these significant events will happen.

And when you get to the age of 30 or 40 or 50 – wherever the forks or crosses in the line seem to occur – and you do find yourself changing career, moving house, meeting someone (or meeting someone else), you can gaze back into the palm of your hand and it will say 'I told you so'.

Unless, that is, you are a critically aware sceptic. Then you'll say 'Hold on a minute – don't these things happen to everyone throughout their life? Don't we all change jobs, move houses, have relationship problems, go through periods of poor health during our life?' If you did say this, then you'd recognise these as 'Barnum statements', named after the circus promoter P. T. Barnum, who aimed to provide 'something for everyone'.

Imagine that I've conducted a detailed assessment of your personality, using questionnaires and other assessment techniques, such as handwriting analysis, and having analysed all the data, I can now present you with your own detailed personality profile. Here's *your* profile:

> Some of your aspirations tend to be pretty unrealistic. At times you are extroverted, affable, sociable, while at other times you are introverted, wary and reserved. You have found it unwise to be too frank in revealing yourself to others. You pride yourself on being an independent thinker and do not accept others' opinions without satisfactory proof. You prefer a certain amount of change and variety, and become dissatisfied when hemmed in by restrictions and limitations. At times you have serious doubts as to whether you have made the right decision or done the right thing. Disciplined and controlled on the outside, you tend to be worried and insecure on the inside. While you have some personality weaknesses, you are generally able to compensate for them. You have a great deal of unused capacity which you have not turned to your advantage. You have a tendency to be critical of yourself. You have a strong need for other people to like you and for them to admire you.

What do you think – pretty accurate? Most people think so. And that's the problem. This profile, which consists mainly of statements taken from an astrology book, was given to a class of students who each believed that it had been produced for them individually as a result of completing a personality assessment. When asked how accurate it was on a scale of 0 (poor) to 5 (perfect), it received an average rating of 4.26. Sixteen of the 39 students gave it a perfect rating and only five gave it a rating less than 4 (Forer, 1949). I've tried it myself with students and I'm amazed how effective it is. As the psychologist Gordon Allport puts it:

> When the analyst says, 'You have a need for other people to like and admire you,' the subject is likely to say, 'How true! How accurate you are!'. He should of course say, 'Who hasn't?' Similarly glittering and worthless are such diagnoses as, 'You like change and variety and become dissatisfied when hemmed in by restrictions'; 'Security is one of your major goals in life.' Not only do such statements catch all mortals, they are likely to be interpreted in an individual way by each subject to fit his [*sic*] unique pattern of life, and he therefore credits the diagnostician with an acumen he does not have. (Allport, 1969: 452)

The banalities of these so-called 'Barnum statements' are present in all disciplines, from politics to psychology, but they're particularly prevalent in the pseudosciences, such as astrology, palmistry and graphology, and among spiritualist mediums, especially when conveying messages from 'the dead' (Greasley, 2000a, 2000b).

Tip 59: Have a look at some websites devoted to critical thinking and sceptical inquiry

There are a number of useful websites devoted to critical thinking and sceptical inquiry. I've listed a selection below:

The James Randi Educational Foundation (www.randi.org)

James Randi is a magician famous for investigating people who claim to have psychic or paranormal abilities, e.g. Uri Geller. The Foundation offers a $1 million prize to anyone who can demonstrate psychic, supernatural or paranormal ability of any kind under mutually agreed upon scientific conditions.

The Skeptics dictionary (www.skepdic.com)

This website has lots of articles covering most supernatural, paranormal and pseudoscientific topics (from acupuncture to zombies).

Science-based Medicine (www.sciencebasedmedicine.org)

Science-based Medicine is run by a group of physicians who subject 'unscientific and pseudoscientific health care' practices to critical examination. This is an excellent resource for those studying health-related topics.

Quackwatch (www.quackwatch.com)

This is another excellent resource for students in the health sciences. It includes articles on health-related frauds, myths, fads, fallacies and misconduct. There's also a link to 'the quackometer' where you can type in the name of someone (e.g. Prince Charles) and it will provide you with a quack rating.

summary

In this chapter we've seen the importance of reaching beyond the lower levels of description that we saw in Bloom's taxonomy towards a more analytical, critical, evaluative perspective, through which an argument is developed and a particular position adopted.

There are some philosophers and psychologists who argue that we are born with a predisposition to believe what we are told, and that we wander around in a kind of hypnotic state with blind belief and uncritical obedience (Schumaker, 1990). As an influential leader once remarked: 'What good fortune for those in power that people do not think' (Adolf Hitler, cited in Macedo, 1994: 36).

One of the primary aims of a university education is to teach students to think critically about what they are told. Perhaps this is what the psychologist B. F. Skinner meant when he said: 'Education is what survives when what has been learned has been forgotten' (Skinner, 1964: 484). So when the 'facts' you learned about your subject at university have been long forgotten, you should hopefully retain the intellectual skills and abilities that encourage you to adopt a critical perspective rather than just accept what you are told. This is important because, as the Princeton philosopher Professor Harry G. Frankfurt (2005: 1 and 63) points out:

> One of the most salient features of our culture is that there is so much bullshit. Everyone knows this. Each of us contributes his share. But we tend to take the situation for granted ...

> Bullshit is unavoidable whenever circumstances require someone to talk without knowing what he is talking about. Thus the production of bullshit is stimulated whenever a person's obligations or opportunities to speak about some topic exceed his knowledge of the facts that are relevant to that topic. This discrepancy is common in public life, where people are frequently impelled – whether by their own propensities or by the demands of others – to speak extensively about matters of which they are to some degree ignorant.

PART 10

RESEARCH ETHICS

Research Ethics

Haslam, A. & McGarty, C.

Science and society

Some time ago (indeed, before the authors had even started studying psychology) a man offered $1000 to anyone who could prove that smoking causes lung cancer in humans. Of course, nobody has ever claimed the prize. Based on the principles you have already read about in this book you could help design research that would have a chance of winning that prize. But we hope that after reading this chapter on **research ethics** you will understand why nobody will ever claim the $1000. The reasons all revolve around the ethics of running the experiment that would prove that smoking causes lung cancer.

The question whether smoking causes lung cancer is really one for medical research. So, instead, let us consider an issue that is just as important, but is one that psychologists are directly concerned with – patients' attitudes to their recovery from cancer. Most people have an opinion on this issue. Some believe that positive attitudes help patients recover from cancer (or to survive longer). Others believe that if you have cancer, that's that – you will either recover or not, regardless of your attitude. Still others believe that positive attitudes do not matter all that much, but that if you have negative attitudes you will tend not to recover. There is evidence to support all of these possibilities, and substantial research into the issue has been conducted by psychologists and medical scientists.

We have chosen this issue not just because it is something you probably have an opinion about, but also because it is an important question and one to which science has not yet provided all the answers. We could have chosen a trivial issue to explain research ethics, but to do so would have risked missing the point. Research ethics relates to *serious issues*, often issues that are deeply personal for many people. Two other features of this example are important too: the facts that most people have an opinion about recovery from cancer and that science has yet to answer all their questions. Research ethics often relates to *issues that people in many different communities have opinions about.* Moreover, if you asked us 'What are the effects of attitudes to cancer on recovery?', we would have to say 'The jury is still out'. There has been much progress, but nobody can confidently say 'The effect of a person's attitude to cancer on recovery is …' . This is partly because research ethics affects *the ability of the science to answer difficult questions* about sensitive issues.

Let us consider why the question of the effects of attitudes to cancer on recovery has not yet been resolved by science. The reasons are much the same as the reasons why nobody has ever claimed the $1000 prize for proving that smoking causes lung cancer. Suppose that you believe negative attitudes to cancer reduce a patient's chance of recovery. Several simple experiments could test this idea, but they are all so obnoxious that nobody has ever carried them out. For example, researchers could randomly allocate a large sample of cancer patients to two groups and thoroughly convince one group they were not going to recover (assuming that this could be done effectively), while having no contact with the control group. A few months later they would measure the condition of the patients.

Now it is true that research even more offensive than this has been conducted – for example, by scientists in Nazi Germany. But the vast majority of people who discovered that such research was going to be carried out where they worked or studied would be shocked. Many would go to rallies, sign petitions and write to politicians. Some of the researchers' colleagues might give media interviews and call for the researchers to be thrown out of their professional associations, and all this would occur in an effort to stop the research from going ahead. It is likely that the institution in question would forbid its researchers from carrying out the research, and if the research went ahead there could be an enormous legal quagmire, possibly leading to criminal charges.

Why would all this happen? It would happen because the science of psychology, like any science, is part of the society in which the scientists work. There are three reasons why society has a right to express opinions about how scientists should carry out their research. First, society pays the bills for research (through taxes and tuition fees). Second, members of society often participate in that research. Third, the research is usually *about* society. For all these reasons, the bogus experiment that we discussed above would never be carried out because society – in the form of governments, students, other researchers, lawyers, university administrations and community action groups – would say 'Find another way to answer this important question'.

In reality there are no researchers we know of who would want to carry out the study we have described. Universities and research centres are not full of crazy psychologists who want to do research that would harm participants. Researchers are not opposed to society, they are part of society, and they generally stick to the standards and values of the society they live in. In particular, this is because researchers have ethical standards, both formal and informal. Formal codes of practice are explicitly designed to limit harm to participants. For example, participants must generally be told enough about the research to enable them to decide whether they want to participate. If researchers do not follow the principles set out in these codes, they will not receive funds from research bodies and journals will not publish their research. Moreover, their research will almost certainly be forbidden by their institutional **ethics committee**.

How, then, could the researchers address the question about the effects of attitudes to cancer in another way? Not easily. One possibility would be to change the question. The researchers could run an experiment with an experimental group comprising people whose attitudes were manipulated so that they became more positive. They could then compare this group with a control group (who could be assumed to have more negative attitudes). However, there is a major problem with this study. It would actually be testing the hypothesis that *positive* attitudes improve recovery. At the end of the day, if the research showed that attitudes did not affect cancer recovery this might be because the researchers were studying the wrong attitudes.

Another possibility would be to use a correlational or survey approach (as discussed in Chapters 5 and 9). The researchers could find a sample of cancer patients, measure their attitudes to recovery, and then follow them up six months later to see how they were doing. They could then correlate attitudes to cancer with a measure of health. Alternatively, the researchers could conduct a quasi-experiment where a group of patients with positive attitudes was matched with a group of patients with negative attitudes on variables such as the severity of cancer. Six months later the health of people in the two groups could be compared.

If you have read the previous 12 chapters of this book you will be able to see what the problems with these various research strategies are. In the case of the quasi-experiment, any number of *extraneous* variables could compromise any interpretation of the findings. For example, matching people for severity of cancer may build in other differences between groups (such as amount of treatment or age). In short, there is no way that the researchers could *prove* that negative attitudes prevent recovery from cancer.

Thus, the often quite reasonable demands that society makes on researchers mean that important questions that could in principle be answered by simple research strategies are never addressed. Although this is most obvious for serious and controversial issues such as attitudes to cancer, in fact it applies to all areas of research in psychology. Whenever psychologists design research they have to consider the effects that the research will have on participants. We have argued that to design and understand research you need to know a lot about principles such as randomization, causal inference, and so on. Ethical principles are *every bit as important* to the real business of doing psychological research as any of the other ideas that we have discussed in this book.

You may think that the example we have used seems a bit far-fetched. Would researchers really ever do something that could have very serious effects on research participants? Would people really ever care enough about psychological research to organize angry protests and write letters to politicians? The answer to both questions is 'yes'.

A striking illustration of the first point is provided by research conducted by Berkun, Bialek, Kern, and Yagi (1962) in which the participants were soldiers who thought they were being shelled by artillery while they tried to repair a broken radio. The amount of time it took to repair the radio was the dependent variable. Certainly, this study was done some time ago, and it was done by psychologists working for the US defence forces, but the fact remains that the research was done, and unless society had intervened, it is possible that psychologists would still be doing similar things.

Are there cases of strong popular reactions against psychological research? There have been many examples. One is provided by research on racial differences in intelligence. This has been controversial for a long time and continues to cause heated debate (e.g., Fraser, 1995; Gould, 1981; Herrnstein & Murray, 1994). Some prominent researchers in the area have met angry protests in universities and other forums throughout the world when they have presented their views.

The area that provokes the greatest continuing controversy, however, is research that uses animals. We will consider the rights and wrongs of animal research in a later section, but research with animals is now so controversial and produces such strong feelings in segments of the wider community that many researchers find that they can no longer perform the research they feel they need to do. All we would say for now is that the conflicts here can be quite different from those that arise in other areas of psychology.

ethics committee A body set up by a research institution such as a university to review ethical principles relating to the conduct of research at that institution. Such

Test Yourself 14.1*

Which of the following is true about the relationship between scientific research and society?

a. Science exists outside society.
b. Ethical principles are generally imposed by governments on psychologists against their will.
c. Only scientists should decide what is ethical or not about research.
d. Decisions about research ethics are always a matter of personal choice.
e. None of the above.

The correct answer is (e). This is almost a trick question. The relationship between scientific research and society is so complex that anyone who tries to reduce it to a few simple statements is always going to risk making mistakes. Statement (a) is simply wrong: science is part of society. Statement (b) is sometimes wrong, as many ethical principles have willingly been *introduced* by psychologists. If (a) is wrong, (c) must also be wrong, as by most standards members of a society have a right to say what they think is unacceptable in their society. If scientists disagree it is up to them to explain why. Statement (d) is wrong because, although people have personal views, decisions about research ethics are often made by relevant groups in society, for example funding bodies and ethics committees.

committees usually contain representatives from groups for whom research ethics is important and relevant (e.g., researchers, lawyers, medical practitioners, ministers of religion, members of the general community).

research ethics The principles by which researchers decide the best way to balance the contribution of their research to human knowledge against potential damage to human welfare. Researchers are obligated to have a knowledge of any code of ethics that applies to their research.

Ethical values

In practice, when it comes to designing and conducting research in psychology, the task of trying to specify what is and what is not ethical proves to be enormously difficult. Researchers and ethics committees can (and do) spend an extremely long time discussing and arriving at decisions about whether the methods of a given study are moral, appropriate and defensible. For this reason, although they may have clear views about what is and what is not acceptable, few ethical committees will attempt to specify in advance what constitutes ethical and unethical research. Instead, they are likely to want to examine every study on its individual merits and to identify broad ethical principles that they endorse and that they want all researchers to uphold.

Indeed, recognizing this as an important goal, the International Union of Psychological Science in 2008 ratified a *Universal Declaration of Ethical Principles for Psychologists* that aimed to provide a moral framework and generic set of principles designed to inform the conduct of psychologists around the world (see Gauthier & Pettifor, 2012). This enshrined the following four core principles that relate not only to research, but to all forms of professional activity:

1. *Respect for the dignity of persons and peoples.* The core idea here is that psychologists need to respect the value of people as both individuals and members of different communities and cultures. They need to treat every person as having value regardless of such things as social status, ethnic background, education level and gender. Moreover, they need to take account of the fact that people have different backgrounds that will determine their sensitivity to particular practices and procedures. This means that just because something is not perceived to be offensive for members of one community (e.g., middle-class men), it cannot be assumed that this will be the case for everyone else. Special care also needs to be taken to protect the dignity of individuals and groups who, for one reason or another, are vulnerable – for example, children, older adults, members of cultural minorities.

2. *Competent caring for the well-being of persons and peoples.* As with the Hippocratic oath taken by medical doctors, the overriding principle here is that psychologists should strive to ensure that their work is beneficial to others, and, most particularly, that it does not cause them harm. Apart from anything else, this commits researchers to the goal of being well trained so that they know what they are doing. It also requires them to try to correct any harm that they may commit inadvertently.

3. *Integrity.* In the course of their work psychologists need to be open, honest and truthful. They should also avoid exploiting others for their own gain, and avoid putting their own interests ahead of others. There is a strong sense of balance present in this principle. Integrity involves being open and honest about the risks involved in research when recruiting participants, but it may well involve withholding information in publications in order to maintain the confidentiality of those participants.

4. *Professional and scientific responsibilities to society.* As we have noted at several points in previous chapters, psychological research is not set apart from the 'real world', it is part of it. In this regard, research psychologists have two broad responsibilities: first, to ensure that their work contributes to understanding of that world; and second, to ensure that, as far as possible, it improves it. Among other things, this means that it is important to ensure that one's research is as well designed and well informed as possible.

Even if they do not subscribe to this particular declaration, most professional bodies that govern the research activity of psychologists around the world embrace similar principles to these. To take just one example, in Australia the National Health and Medical Research Council builds its ethical guidelines for research with human participants around four key principles that correspond closely to those in the *Universal Declaration*: respect, beneficence, justice and research merit.

RESEARCH BITE 14.1
The cultural dimensions of respect

The New Zealand researchers Natasha Tassell and Andrew Lock (2012) note that the principle of 'respect' enshrined in the *Universal Declaration of Ethical Principles for Psychologists* can have different meanings for people in different cultures. In particular, they note that while in the West respect often involves treating people as individuals, in Maori culture respect is associated with treating a person in a way befitting their place within a particular family that has particular ancestors. For research to be properly ethical, researchers thus have to be sensitive to such cultural variation and understand that, when it comes to translating values such as respect into practice, there is no 'one size fits all'.

Reference
Tassell, N. A., & Lock, A. J. (2012). Cultural considerations for professional psychology ethics: Te tirohanga ahurea hei whakatakato tika, whakapakari te aro ki te tangata: Te ahua ki Aotearoa. *Ethics and Social Welfare*, 6, 56–73.

Nevertheless, the challenge of living up to these principles is not always easy. Among other things, this is because different principles can sometimes be hard to reconcile with each other and so much depends on which one is prioritized. For example, as we will see in the next section, this occurs when researchers see the goal of understanding a given phenomenon to be more important than the goal of being totally open in one's communication with participants. At the same time, the principles themselves are open to interpretation, and it is clear that good intentions do not always translate into good outcomes.

Ethical risks associated with participation in research

Many readers of this book will have already participated in psychological research. If you are doing an introductory psychology course you may have been asked to take part in research, often in exchange for course credit. Exactly the same thing is going on right now in universities and colleges all over the world.

For this reason research ethics is not a dry, abstract concern for other people, or something you can file away until the exam comes around. Most people who read this book will participate in psychological research and many will conduct research themselves. In fact much (perhaps most) of the research that is conducted in psychology is done by students – either advanced undergraduates or postgraduates. So when you participate in research there is a good chance that you are actually helping another student. In any case you will be helping to advance the sum of psychological knowledge, as well as observing how research is done by real researchers. Some would also argue that if you are studying psychology you are consuming psychological knowledge and so it is only fair that you help to add to this knowledge. However, these arguments are not reasons to make light of ethical concerns, and if you are asked to participate in research you should be aware of your rights as a participant.

It is extremely unlikely that anyone reading this book will experience actual harm from participating in psychological experiments – not least because, as we have seen, the minimization of harm is one of the core principles by which ethical approval for research is guided. Many of you will find that research participation is interesting, engaging and informative. Even if this is not the case, research participation in psychology is probably a lot safer than attending a class or catching a bus. Indeed, the biggest risk most participants face is that they might have to spend a few less than scintillating hours watching a computer screen or filling in questionnaires.

So what exactly are the main risks to participants in research? These fall into four main categories: (a) stress; (b) breaches of confidentiality; (c) deception; and (d) invasive procedures.

Some research may cause *stress* for participants. Sometimes this cannot be avoided – especially if stress is what the researchers are actually investigating. This is quite a plausible scenario as stress is a major topic addressed by a range of psychologists (e.g., in clinical, organizational and cognitive areas). As an example of such research, take the researcher who wants to examine the hypothesis that fear or anxiety impairs intellectual performance. Clearly, there is no way for this researcher to study these issues experimentally without creating some distress in the participants. However, the researcher must strive to ensure that the stress does not persist outside the experimental session, and the research in general must minimize unintended or unnecessary stress. The research that has probably generated the most concern about stress for participants is that by Milgram (1963, 1974) on obedience. We will look at his work in more detail shortly.

Confidentiality is important because participants often give sensitive information to researchers. Participants are remarkably willing to give researchers information about their relationships, religious beliefs, sexual orientations and political attitudes – information that they would not dream of giving to even their closest friends. This is part of a general inclination on the part of research participants to be cooperative and helpful. As Orne (1969) noted, if someone walked up to people in the street and asked them to do 10 push-ups, they would ask 'Why?'. But if a psychologist made the same request in an experiment, they would ask 'Where?'.

One reason why research participants are so helpful is that many of them are committed to the research process. They want to answer researchers' questions because they want to contribute to the advancement of the science. Whatever the reasons for participation, it is essential that researchers do not abuse the trust that is placed in them, and that they maintain the confidentiality of their participants. If someone tells a researcher something, that person should be able to assume that nobody else will ever know who gave the researcher that information, and this should be especially true for any sensitive or personal information. For example, this is why participants in clinical or neuropsychological research are identified by a pseudonym or their initials (as in the case of HM, the patient with no apparent long-term memory, whom we mentioned in Chapter 3). The only exception is where participants give the researcher explicit permission to reveal their identity. This is very rarely necessary.

Deception is one feature of psychological research that contributes to more than its fair share of ethical debate – primarily because it can be seen to be inconsistent with the principle of *integrity* discussed earlier. As we discussed in Chapter 4, deception involves giving participants information that is false. You may wonder why it is necessary for researchers to deceive participants. The reason is that many experiments, especially in social psychology, involve elaborate setups where participants think that one thing is happening but actually something else is happening. This is because most social psychologists believe that people's behaviour is influenced not so much by what is actually happening as by what people *think* is happening. Deception is therefore used to control *reactivity* (Chapter 4).

Let us illustrate this point with an example. Imagine that we want to know whether people respond differently to emergency situations when they are alone rather than in a group. Latane and Darley (1970) investigated this important question by asking participants to complete a questionnaire in a small room. The experimenters then filled the room with smoke. They found that people were more likely to check on the problem if they were alone than if they were with a group of strangers who continued to fill out their questionnaires (these strangers were actually **confederates** of the experimenter). This experiment made an important contribution to our understanding of human behaviour (see Levine, 2012), but psychologists only acquired this knowledge because the researchers tricked their participants. After all, the alternatives would be starting a *real* fire (which could never be considered for all sorts of reasons) or telling the participants that the fire was *not* real before the research started. The latter simply would not work – a fire does not affect behaviour unless people believe it to be real.

Note, however, that the use of deception is not confined to the laboratory and can be used in field studies where researchers do not want their identity and purpose to be revealed. For example, this was the case when Festinger and his colleagues wanted to infiltrate a cult to see how its members would cope when their prophecy about the world's end failed to come true – a case study we referred to in Chapter 3 (Festinger et al., 1956). Similarly, researchers have examined the circumstances under which a person comes to the aid of a victim by having confederates pose as people in distress (e.g., Darley & Batson, 1973). The ethical dilemma here is clear, and is one we sometimes become aware of when exposed to similar techniques in television programmes that set out to play jokes on members of the general public by placing them in awkward situations.

The way we think about things can have a powerful effect on our behaviour. In some research psychologists use deception to *control* for these effects experimentally. Experimental control of this form occurs in **placebo** studies where participants in one condition think they receive a treatment but in fact receive no treatment. This occurs to control for any effects that might arise from the fact that when the participants think they are receiving a treatment they may get better just because they *expect* to get better. Placebo effects like this are complex and apply in many subtle ways. However, if a control were not put in place it would be impossible to know the extent to which placebo effects contributed to any treatment effects. Moreover, if participants know they are not receiving a proper treatment they might actually go looking for one and their withdrawal from the research could threaten its internal validity (this is the problem of *mortality* that we discussed in Chapter 4).

What are the arguments against deception? Understandably, some people simply feel that it is wrong for researchers to deceive participants whatever the reason. This is a moral issue, but the moral cost must be weighed against the gains to knowledge from the deceptive research. Some issues simply cannot be studied without using deception. The moral burden of deception is one that individual researchers may choose to bear or not to bear, after they have taken account of the reasons for and against the deception. Suffice it to say that most social psychologists see deception as a justifiable technique where there are appropriate safeguards.

The other major argument against deception is that being tricked by the experimenter can be stressful for the participants, not least because it can reveal to people unpleasant things about themselves. The research that illustrates this point best was conducted by Milgram (1963) on obedience. This really kicked off the major debate on ethics in psychology, largely because it was (and still is) among the most provocative and controversial research ever done.

Milgram was interested in the extent to which people were prepared to obey the unreasonable and cruel commands of authority figures. The people who participated in this research were asked to deliver electric shocks to another research participant who performed poorly on a memory task, supposedly as part of a study to investigate the effects of punishment on learning. Consistent with this cover story, the participants were instructed by the experimenter to give increasingly large electric shocks to this person (the 'Learner') every time they made a mistake. In line with the experimenter's instructions, in what as come to be seen as the standard variant of Milgram's paradigm (Reicher, Haslam, & Smith, 2012), most participants continued to administer shocks even after the Learner started to complain and scream – going all the way to a maximum shock of 450 volts (a point labelled 'DANGER: SEVERE SHOCK' – an accurate description given that an alternating current of 100–250 volts is often enough to kill someone). Indeed, most continued doing this even when the person being shocked stopped responding altogether.

It was obvious from participants' responses that when they reflected on what they had done, many participants experienced a great deal of stress. Many of them had questioned the experimenter's instructions, yet they had continued to administer what they thought were potentially lethal shocks. In fact no shocks were administered – the experimenter's cover story was an elaborate deception involving a confederate of the experimenter who only pretended to be shocked. Moreover, rather than wanting to study the effects of punishment on learning, Milgram's real goal was to see how far participants would go in carrying out the

Photo 14.1 Stanley Milgram's 'obedience to authority' studies examined the willingness of participants to administer what appeared to be lethal electric shocks to a 'Learner' when they made mistakes in a memory task. In fact this Learner was Milgram's confederate and the shocks were not real, but the participants did not find this out until they were debriefed. Milgram's study is a standard reference point for ethical debate in psychology – particularly in relation to the use of deception.

experimenter's instructions. Would they be willing to kill a man simply because they were asked to do this by a researcher in a psychology experiment?

As you can imagine, this study has raised many questions about the effect it may have had on participants. Some psychologists argue that such research is harmful for the participants as it causes stress, embarrassment and guilt. They also add that deceptive research like this can have few benefits (Baumrind, 1964, 1985). Extending this point, it has been argued that it was actually Milgram's *assistants* who, by carrying out the deception, displayed the most destructive form of obedience in the research (Harré, 1979; Russell, in press).

However, Milgram actually followed up his participants in order to find out whether they had been harmed (something only a small number of researchers do). Most participants (60%) reported that they had been 'upset' or 'somewhat nervous' at the time, but 84% were 'glad' or 'very glad' to have participated in the study as they had 'learned something of personal importance' and believed that they had made a contribution to a worthy cause – specifically, the progress of science (Haslam, Reicher, Millard, & MacDonald, in press). They arrived at these opinions largely because, after the experiment was over, Milgram provided a detailed **debriefing** that informed participants about the purpose of the experiment and explained to them why the deception was necessary.

It is worth noting, however, that Milgram's participants were healthy adults. Exactly the same study would have been far more objectionable if the participants had been people who were more susceptible to harm (e.g., children, the elderly or the mentally ill). It is also possible that reactivity (in the form of a desire to please the interviewer, as discussed in Chapters 4 and 5) may have led Milgram's participants to downplay the extent of their stress in his post-experimental enquiries. Indeed, Milgram seems to have worked hard to encourage such responses, and, at another level, one might ask – as Haslam and colleagues (in press) do – whether one would really want participants to feel quite so happy about having been prepared to kill an innocent stranger in the name of science. It is also worth pointing out, however, that awkward *political* questions of this form are rarely asked by ethics committees (an observation that touches upon points we will discuss in the next chapter).

The standard way in which such issues are addressed is to ask – in the absence of evidence of harm – whether the risk to the participants was justified given the benefit to human knowledge from the research. In his own defence Milgram pointed out that he had asked psychiatrists to estimate the percentage of people who would obey the experimenter's instructions. Because they assumed that only mentally disturbed people would administer the shocks, their estimate was 1% of the participants, this being the level of serious mental illness in the general population. In fact, none of Milgram's participants were mentally ill, and 65% of his participants were prepared to administer the maximum level of shock. Obviously, if Milgram's research had never been carried out we would never have known that such a high percentage of 'ordinary men' were willing to follow destructive instructions and we would know far less about the processes that underpin such behaviour (Reicher, Haslam, & Miller, in press).

RESEARCH BITE 14.2

Can a prison experiment be ethical?

In 2002 Steve Reicher and Alex Haslam worked with the BBC to reinvestigate issues raised by the Stanford Prison Experiment (SPE) – one of the most ethically controversial psychology studies of all time. The researchers argued that their research was scientifically justified on account of its capacity to contribute to much-needed advance in the theoretical understanding of tyranny. After a nine-month ethical review process that involved implementing multiple safeguards (including setting up an independent on-site ethics panel), the research secured approval and went ahead. Its published findings ultimately presented a range of challenges to conclusions drawn from the SPE.

Reference

Haslam, S. A., Reicher, S. D., & McDermott, M. (in press). Studying harm-doing without doing harm: The case of the BBC Prison Experiment. In R. J. Sternberg & S. E. Fiske (Eds.), *Ethical case studies and commentaries in the behavioral and brain sciences*. New York: Cambridge University Press.

So, although Milgram's research has been heavily criticized on ethical grounds (e.g., Perry, 2012), the study did provide illuminating insights into a particularly important aspect of human behaviour. These insights may, for example, help to explain why otherwise normal people are willing to commit atrocities when told to do so by their superiors. *But was it worth it?* Before you answer this question we should point out that even if this research had not already been conducted (so that the insights it provided still remained to be made), Milgram's work would not be approved by most ethics committees today. What would be the price of *not* having this knowledge?

Whatever your response to these questions, it is apparent that ethics committees are usually very sensitive to the problems caused by doing research, but are much less sensitive to the problems caused by not doing research (Pettit, 1992; Rosenthal, 1994). This is partly because if these committees were to permit harmful research to go ahead, the victims (or their representatives) would hold them responsible. In contrast, the victims of scientific ignorance hardly ever complain.

One other risk of deception is that participants may end up mistrusting all researchers (Baumrind, 1985). That is, after they have found out that the information provided in psychology experiments can be misleading, a person may come to believe that all psychological research involves tricks, even though this is not true (particularly outside social psychology). This is a problem for researchers (in so far as it is an instance of reactivity), but instilling a healthy scepticism into students who will have to read, interpret and perhaps one day conduct research may not be such a bad thing.

Photo 14.2 When conducting research with vulnerable populations, researchers need to be especially mindful of ethical risks. Ethics committees will also be very sensitive to these. In the research being conducted here, this vulnerability is associated with age, but it can arise from an array of other factors such as a person's mental and physical health, or the context in which they are being studied (e.g., during or after a traumatic event).

It is clear from these examples that research can have effects that change people. Features that produce these changes are called **invasive procedures**. Extreme examples might include giving participants drugs (under medical supervision), inserting some psychophysiological recording device into their bodies, or giving people information that they could not otherwise have obtained (e.g., their score on a personality test). Ethical research (e.g., that based on the principles of the *Universal Declaration*) always involves minimizing any long-term effects on participants to those absolutely necessary for the research, and eliminating long-term negative effects.

An interesting question that remains is whether there is actually any evidence of people being harmed by research. To address the issue in the undergraduate population Smith and Richardson (1983) surveyed 464 undergraduates in North America. One-fifth of the participants reported some harm in terms of feeling very nervous, very humiliated, very angry, excessive physical discomfort or that they were very wrongly deceived as a result of participating in research. If we exclude those who felt very nervous without other sources of harm (reasoning that this is less serious than the other types of possible harm) this leaves a total of 15 people, or 3% of the sample, who reported experiencing harm. However, as in the case of Milgram's follow-up interviews, it is possible that these results may have been contaminated by participants' reactivity – leading either to an over- or underestimation of the actual incidence of harm. Very few subsequent studies have detected negative effects of participation in psychological research.

In general, then, it seems that there is little evidence that psychology students are harmed by their participation in normal research in the main areas of psychology – for example, those that involve interaction with other people, working with computer-controlled equipment, or filling in questionnaires. Based on the available evidence, there are only two conclusions we can draw: either researchers have not looked hard enough for the harmful effects of research participation, or the harmful effects are not especially great.

The position taken on this debate depends a great deal upon how fragile research participants (and people in general) are perceived to be (West & Gunn, 1978). Those most concerned about **research risk** tend to see research participants as relatively fragile. Nevertheless, *all* psychologists would accept that the *potential* for harm does exist. This fact needs to be borne in mind at all stages of the research process.

Having considered various points, we are now in a position to summarize some of the key principles that guide ethical research with human participants in psychology. In short, the research should minimize risk to participants, and if there are any negative effects upon participants the researcher has the responsibility to correct those negative effects. Above all, participation should be based on **informed consent**, and participants should be aware of features of the research that could be expected to affect their decision to participate. It is impossible to obtain informed consent when using unobtrusive measurements (Chapter 5), so other techniques should be considered where there is a risk of harm to participants.

The principle that the participant is capable of **discontinuing participation** at any time is also extremely important. If participants feel uncomfortable or for any reason feel that they do not wish to continue taking part, then they must be free to leave at any time. They do not have to give any reason to the researcher.

The other critical feature of all research involving a researcher working with human participants is debriefing. If the research process is to be of any educational benefit for the participants – and it certainly should be – it is only fair that participants are told what the research was about and what it was trying to achieve. This debriefing should occur at the end of the research session, and certainly no later than the end of the testing programme. Above all, it is essential for the dignity of the participants that the researchers explain the nature of any deception used. As Smith and Richardson (1983) found, good debriefing seems to prevent the negative effects of deception. Researchers should try to explain deceptions in a sensitive manner – after all, nobody likes to find out that they have been tricked. They should also explain why the deception was necessary. Poor and insensitive debriefing can often turn relatively minor problems into major problems, while good debriefing can turn potentially major problems into minor ones.

For research conducted with populations that are more vulnerable to research risk (e.g., children, the mentally ill and the elderly), researchers must make extra efforts to ensure that these principles are upheld. For example, informed consent must also be provided by parents or guardians when research involves children.

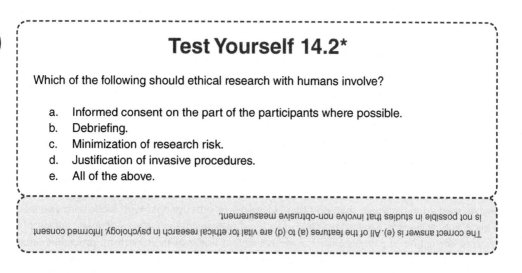

Test Yourself 14.2*

Which of the following should ethical research with humans involve?

a. Informed consent on the part of the participants where possible.
b. Debriefing.
c. Minimization of research risk.
d. Justification of invasive procedures.
e. All of the above.

The correct answer is (e). All of the features (a) to (d) are vital for ethical research in psychology. Informed consent is not possible in studies that involve non-obtrusive measurement.

confederate Someone who works for the experimenter and acts in a certain predetermined way. Normally the confederate pretends to be a genuine research participant, so the use of confederates involves deception.

confidentiality In the research process, confidentiality means ensuring that individual participants cannot be identified. This often means making sure that responses are anonymous.

debriefing Explaining the purpose and procedures of research to participants after its completion. Debriefing should include a sensitive explanation and justification of any deceptions used.

discontinuing participation An ethical principle which guarantees the right of all human participants to cease taking part in research at any time.

informed consent The ethical principle that research participants should be told enough about a piece of research to be able to make a decision about whether to participate in it.

invasive procedures Research procedures which lead to changes in participants.

placebo A device used to control for the effect of participants' expectations about the effects of research participation or the experimental treatment. An example would be giving a control group a sugar tablet rather than the real medical drug given to an experimental group. Neither group would know whether they were receiving the placebo or a real drug (i.e., the participants would be *blind* to the treatment). In other respects the groups would be treated the same.

research risk The possibility of harm to participants, usually in the form of long-term negative effects.

Research with animals

At one time a great deal of research in psychology involved animals. Indeed, in some circles the popular name for psychology was 'rats and stats'. As you have found out, the stats are still there, but there are not as many rats or other animals now. In the three-year period up to April 2013 there were 331,789 journal articles with abstracts on the PsycInfo database and of these 41,874 involved research with animals. In other words, over that period around 13% of the total amount of published research in psychology involved animals. However, animal research raises more than its fair share of debates about ethics.

We must hasten to add that the ethical debate in this area does not arise because psychologists treat animals worse than do other scientists, or other people who work with animals. This is not necessarily because psychologists are more ethical than other scientists, but simply because the nature of psychologists' work means that fewer of them perform procedures that can be distressing to animals (such as surgery). Indeed, a lot of animal research in psychology only involves the *observation* of behaviour. Moreover, most psychologists support the principles of **animal welfare**. Ethical treatment of animals involves things such as housing them in clean cages with adequate food and water, ensuring that the pain and distress they suffer is minimized, and that if it becomes necessary to kill them this is done in a humane and painless way. Ethical treatment of animals is actually in the researchers' interest. This is because if psychologists want to study the normal behaviour of animals it makes no sense to mistreat them (some people would extend this point to argue that it makes no sense to study them in laboratory cages).

Why do psychologists need to study animals? Some psychologists are simply interested in animal behaviour, and these researchers have no choice but to use animal participants. Others study animals because they are interested in questions that studies using human participants cannot address. Imagine that psychologists wanted to know whether a particular part of the brain is essential for controlling the desire to eat. There are only two ways to address this question. The researchers could attempt to find people who have had this section of their brain destroyed in accidents and see whether they still have a desire to eat. The problem is that accidents tend not to destroy isolated regions of the brain. So if it was found that the brain-injured person did not want to eat then this could be due to some other effect of the injury. As in all quasi-experiments, the interpretation of results could be contaminated by these extraneous (uncontrolled) variables.

Given that deliberately destroying parts of humans' brains would render a researcher liable for an extended prison sentence, the only alternative is to take animals with brains that are similar to our own, and conduct invasive research on these animals to see whether the animal still eats. This invasive research might involve the use of electrical probes or the destruction of specific regions of their brain. If psychologists and other scientists did not conduct these studies then important questions (e.g., concerning the biological factors that contribute to dietary disorders) would never be answered. As members of society, all of us have a right to decide whether or not we are prepared to allow animals to be harmed so that these questions can be addressed.

The fact that the work of animal psychologists has come increasingly under attack is correlated with the rise of the **animal rights movement** after the publication of Peter Singer's influential book *Animal Liberation* in 1975 (Herzog, 1995). Many members of this movement believe that animals have the same rights as humans. From this point of view the idea of keeping animals in captivity to observe their behaviour is as offensive as it would be for the researchers to take you prisoner for the same purpose. Obviously, there is a complete conflict of opinions here. The researchers believe that it is essential to study animals in ways necessary to draw the strongest scientific conclusions. Advocates of animal rights believe that the research this entails is unjustifiable. Their argument is not so much that psychologists are not obeying the ethical principles of their science, but more fundamentally that all such research is completely unethical and should be stopped.

This debate will not go away, and will remain acrimonious for the foreseeable future. The clearest conclusion we can draw is that animal research provides a good example of society at large taking an interest in what science does. Although much of the attention is unwanted by the scientists, it has had a positive effect on the welfare of research animals, and virtually all psychologists using animals are now fully committed to the cause of animal welfare (even though most reject the animal rights point of view).

However, the focus on animal research in psychology remains ironic. Much worse treatment of animals can occur in abattoirs, farms, animal refuges, restaurants, commercial research laboratories and people's own homes than in any university psychology laboratory.

Photo 14.3 Psychological research with animals is a focus for fierce and heated debate. On one side, researchers argue that such research is entirely defensible in light of its benefits for society; on the other, supporters of animal rights contend that it is entirely indefensible on moral grounds.

Animal rights advocates argue that psychologists have a much greater responsibility to act ethically and to reflect community concerns than do other people. However, it seems clear that, regardless of whether research with animals is right or wrong, the attention that university research laboratories receive from the animal rights movement reflects the fact that universities are important and relatively easy targets to influence – not necessarily the fact that university researchers are crueller to animals than most other people (indeed most researchers would contend that they are far kinder). Ultimately, the debate on this issue is as much political as ethical, and it will never be resolved purely by an appeal to ethical principles. This is because ethics are an expression and instrument of society and not everybody in society has the same principles. Instead, like science itself, ethical principles are a source of continuing argument, conflict and struggle.

animal rights movement Groups whose members believe that animals have similar or equal rights to those of human beings.

animal welfare The set of principles that guide humane organizations such as societies for the prevention of cruelty to animals and which promote consideration for the well-being of animals.

Test Yourself 14.3*

Which of the following is true about ethical research using animals?

a. It must ensure that discomfort to animals is minimized and harm only occurs where essential.
b. Ethics are not a major issue because participants are not deceived.
c. Because it is such a controversial topic, the issues it raises are only worth discussing in relation to medical research.
d. It is not really relevant to psychology.
e. None of the above.

The correct answer is (a). Answer (b) is wrong because deception is only an issue for human participants. Answer (c) is wrong because animal research in psychology and other sciences addresses issues that are just as important as those in medical research. Answer (d) is wrong because, although animal research has declined in popularity, that does not mean that it is not important – 10% of the research published in a big science like psychology is still a lot of research.

Final comment

It is obvious that this chapter has dealt a lot more with opinions than have the previous chapters in this book. Probably some of our own opinions will have become obvious, too, although we have tried our best to frame these in terms of the conflicting sets of arguments that characterize ethical debates both inside and outside psychology.

The fact that conflicts in this area are so pronounced is one reason why research ethics is such an intriguing and integral part of the research process. The science of psychology cannot be separated from society because at all times, whether they like it or not, researchers are a part of society (and quite an important part, too). As such they are guided by values that are *strong* but also *open to challenge*. It should be no surprise, then, if you react more vigorously to the issues raised here than to most of the others discussed in this book.

CHECKLIST
Revisiting the key goals for this chapter

- [ ] I understand why ethics are a central part of the research process.
- [ ] I am aware of the core ethical values that should inform psychological research.
- [ ] I am aware of the key forms of ethical risk associated with psychological research.

Further reading

Over the years, many studies have fuelled debate about ethics in society. However, because Milgram's obedience studies set the agenda for much of this debate, it is worth starting one's reading in this area by examining Baumrind's (1964) critique of this research and Milgram's (1964) own response. Blass's (2004) authoritative and highly readable biography provides fascinating insights into Milgram's work and into his life more generally. It also serves as a window onto the research process more generally, and so is relevant to a number of topics that we have discussed in earlier chapters. Reicher, Haslam, and Miller (in press) also provide a contemporary treatment of these issues in an article that introduces a special issue of the *Journal of Social Issues* published to coincide with the 50th anniversary of the publication of Milgram's initial paper.

Baumrind, D. (1964). Some thoughts on ethics of research: After reading Milgram's 'Behavioral study of obedience'. *American Psychologist, 19*, 421–423.

Blass, T. (2004). *The man who shocked the world: The life and legacy of Stanley Milgram.* New York: Basic Books.

Milgram, S. (1964). Issues in the study of obedience: A reply to Baumrind. *American Psychologist, 19*, 848–852.

Reicher, S. D., Haslam, S. A., & Miller, A. G. (in press). What makes a person a perpetrator? The intellectual, moral and methodological arguments for revisiting Milgram's research on the influence of authority. *Journal of Social Issues.*

Research ethics: A checklist for research evaluation and improvement

Table 14.1

Potential problem	Question to ask	Potential improvement
Breach of confidentiality	Is participants' contribution to research confidential?	Take steps to ensure that as far as possible the identity of individual participants and the results of their participation are kept private. This can often be achieved by referring to participants only by codenames or numbers and/or by keeping records of participants' identities separate from their data. If confidentiality and anonymity are breached this must be explicitly justified and participants need to be informed of this fact before agreeing to participate.
Breach of anonymity	Is participants' contribution to research anonymous?	
Deception	Have participants been deceived about the nature or purpose of research?	Endeavour to tell participants the truth about research and avoid making false or misleading statements or omitting important information. If any deception is deemed necessary, this must be explicitly justified and participants must be sensitively debriefed at the conclusion of the study. If deception or concealment could reasonably be expected to affect the decision to participate (and hence to compromise the principle of informed consent), then participants need to be informed of this fact before agreeing to participate.
Concealment	Has some important information about the research been kept from participants?	
Invasive procedures	Does the research change the participants in any way?	Research should be designed to ensure that, as far as possible, it has no long-term effects on participants and that there are no long-term negative effects. Where there is a risk of this, participants should be informed of this fact and monitored beyond the end of the study to ensure that harm has not occurred and that, if it has, it is corrected.
Research risk	Does the research have any long-term negative effects?	
Inadequate debriefing	At the conclusion of the research have participants been fully informed about the purpose of the research and the nature of, and reasons for, any deception?	At the end of any piece of research participants should be thanked for participating, and the nature and value of the research should be explained to them. Any questions that they have about the research should be answered, and, as far as possible, participants should feel involved and respected in the broad research process (e.g., by being made aware of the scientific benefits associated with the research). This phase of research is particularly important if a study involves invasive procedures, research risk, deception or concealment.

(Continued)

Table 14.1   (Continued)

Potential problem	Question to ask	Potential improvement
Uninformed consent	Have the participants been told enough about the research to make an informed decision about whether to participate in it?	Ensure that participants are given enough information about a piece of research to make a reasonable decision about whether they want to participate in it. If participation involves deception, or other factors that might reasonably be expected to impact on this decision (e.g., in a double-blind trial of a therapeutic technique), participants need to be made aware of this before participating. Where participants are unable to give informed consent (e.g., because they are children or impaired) special safeguards have to be set in place and consent obtained from their legal guardians.
Inability to discontinue participation	Are the participants free to withdraw from the research at any stage?	If participants do not want to continue taking part in a study they must be free to withdraw from it. They should not be placed under pressure to continue and they do not have to give reasons for withdrawing.
Harm to animals	Are animals harmed (psychologically or physically) by taking part in the study?	Animals should not be harmed in the process of conducting research. If they are, or there is a risk of harm, this must be very clearly justified and the scientific benefits of the research must also be very clear. Approval for research with animals is normally granted by a special ethics committee that has a brief to consider broad-ranging welfare issues.
Failure to weigh risks against potential benefit	Have the ethical risks associated with any research been considered in light of potential scientific gains?	Even if it contravenes the ethical guidelines outlined above, research that has clear scientific value should not be rejected out of hand. Instead, the goal of minimizing ethical concern should be weighed against the potential for scientific gain. Different groups will use different scales in this process, but all must strike a workable and moral balance between these elements.
Failure to gain ethical approval	Has the research been approved by a relevant ethical committee or body?	Researchers cannot make decisions about the above issues on their own. Instead, they must present the case for conducting their research to relevant professional bodies (e.g. a university ethics committee). In the process they must justify any procedures that raise any ethical concerns. Only after gaining approval from such a body should the research proceed.

Test Yourself 14.4**

Imagine that you are conducting a psychological experiment that has been approved by your institutional ethics committee and two participants object to answering some questions which they consider to be too personal. As a result, they decide they want to cease participating in the experiment. What are their responsibilities in this case?

a. To complete the experimental session because you would not ask personal questions unless they were really important for science.
b. To explain to you why they wish to leave so that you can conduct debriefing.
c. The participants have no responsibilities, they can leave at any time.
d. To report you to the institutional ethics committee.
e. To discuss your experiment with other students.

Test Yourself 14.5***

Informed consent means that researchers should tell participants about which of the following before they agree to participate in research?

a. The hypotheses.
b. Anything that is likely to affect the participants' decision to participate in the research.
c. Details of any deception.
d. The independent variable.
e. Whether the experiment involves a placebo.

Test Yourself 14.6**

Which of the following statements about Milgram's obedience-to-authority studies is (are) true?

a. They violated the American Psychological Association's standards at the time because they used poor debriefing procedures.
b. They led to important developments in ethical principles in psychological research.
c. They have been criticized for putting participants at risk of harm.
d. Both (b) and (c).
e. They used inadequate follow-up procedures.

The correct answer to 14.4 is (c). Participants are always free to discontinue participation at any time, even if this would be inconvenient for the researcher. If participants feel strongly about an issue then (d) and (e) are options, but they are not *required* to do anything. It is possible, for example, that questions which are deeply personal for one person are not personal for most other people and there is no way the researcher can establish this in advance. Answer (b) is a reasonable thing to do as it may be useful for participants to explain the problems they encountered with the research and to listen to the experimenter's response. However, participants are not required to do this.

(Continued)

(Continued)

The correct answer to 14.5 is (b), but this is quite a difficult question. This is mainly because the ethics of deception are complex. However, all ethical guidelines allow deception under some circumstances (so (c) and (e) are wrong), and making participants aware of the *details* of any deception is pointless as this will only ensure that the experiment does not work. There is no reason for the researcher to tell participants about the hypothesis (as (a) suggests) or about the independent variable (as (d) suggests) before the session. Any deception should be explained during debriefing.

The correct answer to 14.6 is (d). Answer (a) is wrong because, although Milgram's studies aroused a great deal of debate at the time, the debriefing was extensive and there were no guidelines on debriefing at the time. This means that (b) is true; (c) is also true (see Baumrind, 1964, 1985). Answer (e) is incorrect because Milgram actually performed very extensive follow-ups of his participants.

Discussion/essay questions

a. Do ethics committees have too little power or too much?
b. Should researchers still be able to use research procedures like those employed by Milgram in the 1960s?
c. To what extent have ethics committees influenced the way in which psychological knowledge has advanced in the last 30 years?
d. Draft some ethical guidelines that you think any research you personally conduct should meet. Justify your decisions.
e. How do you think ethical guidelines for conducting research in psychology will change in the next century? Will this change be for the better?

PART 11

RESEARCH DESIGN

How Psychologists Use the Scientific Method: Data Collection Techniques and Research Designs

McBride, D.

I magine that you work in a busy corporate office. One day your boss comes to you for advice. A report found that productivity in the office tends to decline later in the afternoon and he or she wants to find a way to increase productivity during this time period. Your boss's suggestion is that having a cappuccino machine in the office lunchroom may cause workers to drink more coffee after lunch, in turn giving them more energy and productivity in the afternoon. You are asked to use your knowledge of research methods to find out if the suggestion is a good one. How would you conduct a study to provide the advice your boss is looking for?

In this chapter, we discuss the methods psychologists use to learn about behavior. This chapter provides an overview of some of the main data collection techniques and research designs used in psychological research to illustrate how psychologists apply the scientific methods described in Chapter 1 to the study of behavior. Figure 4.1 illustrates the steps involved in the research process while designing the study. The choices of data collection technique and research design are made by the researcher. These choices depend on the type of behavior that is of interest and what kinds of questions one wants to answer about the behavior. External and internal validities also play a role in these choices. External validity is the degree to which the behavior observed in the study is realistic, would occur naturally, and can be generalized beyond the boundaries of the study to other individuals and situations. How much external validity a study has is important because the goal of research is to gain knowledge about behavior that applies to a large group of individuals in their everyday lives, not just to the individual study participants with any situational restrictions the study included. In other words, the conclusions need to generalize beyond the study itself. Some of the observation techniques and research designs that psychologists use tend to allow for higher external validity than others. However, in many cases the higher the external validity in a study, the lower the internal validity.

Internal validity is the degree to which a study provides a good test of a causal hypothesis, where alternative explanations of the data can be ruled out. A study with high internal validity

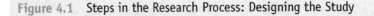

Figure 4.1   Steps in the Research Process: Designing the Study

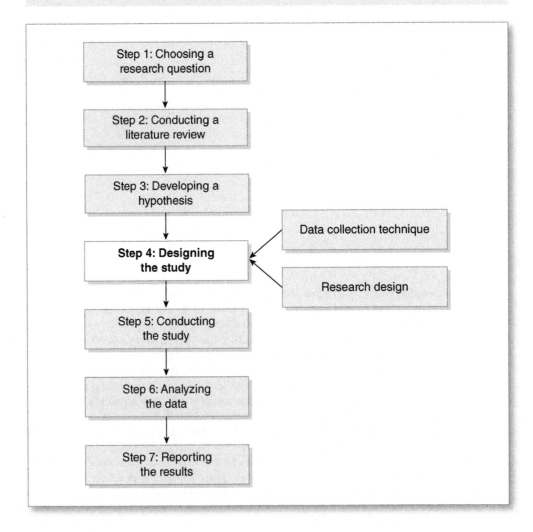

provides causal information about behavior. To increase the internal validity of a study, a researcher controls for extraneous factors that can affect the observations. With more control over the factors in a study, internal validity increases, but behavior may become more artificial and lower the external validity of that study. As we discuss the different types of studies that can be conducted by psychologists, you will see that internal and external validities are important concepts in research.

Another important issue in observing behavior is making certain that the observations are *reliable*. For some observation techniques, this means making sure that observers are categorizing behaviors the same way. For other techniques, this means making certain that different items on a survey or questionnaire designed to measure a specific behavior all provoke similar responses from the research participants. In other words, reliability in a survey means that the participants' responses are similar from item to item or from one time they complete the survey to the next. Thus, reliability is important to consider when you design a study and choose an observation technique, but how you increase reliability depends on the observation technique you are using.

External Validity: the degree to which the results of a study apply to individuals and realistic behaviors outside the study

Internal Validity: the degree to which a study provides causal information about behavior

Reliability: the degree to which the results of a study can be replicated under similar conditions

---

Stop and Think

(4.1)   For each description below, indicate if it is an issue with internal validity, external validity, or reliability:

- Subjects in a study complete a task in the lab in a different way than they would ordinarily do it.
- Subjects' scores on a mood questionnaire differ each time they complete the questionnaire.
- Different groups of subjects receive different teaching techniques to compare the effectiveness of the techniques on learning. However, the subjects in the different groups also differ in their pre-existing knowledge of the topic being taught.

DATA COLLECTION TECHNIQUES

How do psychologists observe behavior? When researchers are planning to observe a behavior, they must first decide how they are going to define that behavior. This is the operational definition of the behavior. An operational definition of an abstract concept (depression, memory ability, etc.) allows the researcher to define the concept for the purpose of measurement and data collection. Thus, an operational definition is a definition of an abstract concept that makes it concrete for the purpose of the research study. If *social behavior* is of interest, the researcher may define this as

---

Operational Definition: the definition of an abstract concept used by a researcher to measure or manipulate the concept in a research study

"the number of people who spend time in groups," "the number of times an individual approaches another individual to interact with him or her," or "the score on a questionnaire that asks about social behaviors." There are clearly many ways to define a particular behavior for data collection. Researchers choose an operational definition for behavior that they expect will provide the best (i.e., accurate and reliable) method of learning about the behavior they are interested in. In other words, they define the concept so that it can be measured by a specific behavior (or set of behaviors). See Table 4.1 for some examples of operational definitions of different concepts. The techniques described in the following sections are different ways in which psychologists collect data about behavior. As you will see, the choice of technique is linked to the operational definition the researcher uses. Table 4.2 provides an overview and comparison of these techniques in terms of their realism (i.e., external validity).

Table 4.1 Examples of Operational Definitions

Concept	Possible Operational Definitions
Depression	Score on a mood questionnaire
	Number of times someone has thought about suicide in the last month
	Measure of certain neurotransmitters in areas of the brain
Problem-Solving Ability	Amount of time it takes to complete a puzzle
	Number of problems solved correctly
	Score on a standardized test
Learning	Difference in score from pretest to posttest
	Change in time to complete a problem or test
	Change in confidence ratings to perform a skill

Table 4.2 Comparing Data Collection Techniques

Technique	Definition	Realism
Naturalistic observation	Observing individuals' behavior in their normal environments	High, but decreases if observers fail to be unobtrusive
Surveys/questionnaires	Individuals respond to items in written form or on the Internet	Moderate, but decreases with inaccurate self-reports, phrasing of the questions, and the scale used to collect responses
Systematic observation	Collection of systematic behaviors in controlled tasks	Low, due to researcher control of task situation
Archival data	Using available records to collect observations	Varies with type of record

Naturalistic Observation

A once popular show on the Animal Planet cable network called *Meerkat Manor* follows packs of meerkats as they interact with each other within the pack, with other packs of meerkats, and with the environment they live in. The show is narrated to make it more entertaining, but the animals' natural behaviors displayed on the show are observed and exhibited as they occur in their normal environment. In other words, the researchers for the show use naturalistic observation to learn about meerkat behaviors. Naturalistic observation is used when a researcher wants to learn about behavior that naturally occurs for an individual without influencing the behavior. The goal of naturalistic observation is to be unobtrusive so that the researcher does not affect the observed individuals' behavior. Naturalistic observation is often used by researchers interested in observing the behavior of animals in their natural environment or children who are in specific environments (both natural and contrived).

Naturalistic Observation: a data collection technique involving noninvasive observation of individuals in their natural environments

To understand observed behaviors using naturalistic observation, a researcher must develop a coding scheme to categorize the exhibited behaviors of the participants. This allows the researcher to quantify (i.e., count) and summarize the behaviors for the group of individuals observed. The coding scheme depends on the operational definition of the behavior the researcher is using. In other words, the behaviors the researcher indicates are part of the operational definition become categories of behaviors in the coding scheme. For example, if researchers are studying *helping* behaviors with naturalistic observations, they may define helping behavior as approaching someone who appears to need help (e.g., has dropped something, has a broken-down car, is unable to open a door, etc.) and offering help or acting to help the person. Thus, observers may sit on a university quad and count behaviors they observe that fit into categories such as "asking someone if he or she needs help," "helping someone pick something up," "giving someone directions when asked." This allows researchers to quantify the different behaviors they see. The researchers can then describe helping behaviors according to their coding scheme to indicate the frequency of helping behaviors overall for this situation and group of individuals, and which types of behaviors occur more often than others.

Developing a coding scheme generally involves defining categories of behavior that fit the type of behavior being observed. The operational definition of the behavior should guide the selection of categories of behaviors that qualify. It is important to clearly define these categories so that observers are clear about what behaviors they are looking for when they observe the individuals of interest in a study. Clear categories also help multiple observers be more consistent in how they classify the behaviors they are looking for (more on this issue below). Finally, the coding scheme can involve counting the number of certain types of behaviors and/or the amount of time individuals engage in the defined behaviors either in set time intervals or across the entire span of the observation period.

The primary advantage in using naturalistic observation to study behavior is that the behavior is likely to be more realistic compared to some of the other techniques. This can increase the external validity of a study. However, this technique has its disadvantages. It can sometimes be difficult to be unobtrusive. The presence of an observer can easily change the behavior of the individuals being observed. This is an issue that has come up for the *Meerkat Manor* show. Camera crews follow the meerkats closely all the time to record their behaviors for the show, and their presence may have affected the behaviors they observe. Thus, researchers using this

---------------- ✄ ----------------

Inter-observer/Inter-rater Reliability: a measure of the degree to which different observers observe or code behaviors in similar ways

technique must take great care to ensure that they are not influencing the behavior they are observing simply by being present in an individual's environment. Another drawback to naturalistic observation is that it can be very time-consuming. The observers must wait for the behavior they are interested in to be exhibited by the participants. Thus, this technique can be more time intensive and consume more resources than other observation techniques. A third disadvantage is that multiple observers (observing the same or different individuals) may not be recording the behaviors they observe in the same way. To deal with this problem, most studies that involve naturalistic observations include training of the observers to ensure that they are collecting the data in the same way. In fact, the similarity in coding of the data is typically measured and reported in such studies. This is known as inter-observer or inter-rater reliability (how similarly the observers are observing or coding the data). A measure of inter-observer/inter-rater reliability is usually reported based on the percentage overlap in the way the observations are classified across multiple observers. To illustrate this concept, consider the study described above that looked at helping behaviors. In this study, it is likely that more than one person would observe on the quad (either at the same time or at different times) to allow enough helping behaviors to occur and be observed. If the observers code the behaviors differently (e.g., one observer counts bending over to help as "helping someone pick something up," whereas another observer only counts this behavior if someone actually picks up something someone dropped), the internal validity of the study decreases because the observers will have different operational definitions of the behaviors.

Chiang (2008) provides an example of a study that used naturalistic observations. In this study, 32 children with autism were observed to investigate aspects of their spontaneous communication. The children were videotaped in their natural environments (classrooms at their school), while they completed normal, everyday activities (lunch, free time, academic activities, etc.). In the article reporting the study (published in the journal *Autism*), Chiang described the coding schemes developed to summarize and understand the communication behaviors that were seen in the tapes viewed by the observers coding those behaviors (speech or writing, vocalizations that were not identified as words, eye contact, common gestures such as hugging, waving, or nodding, etc.). The inter-observer/inter-rater reliability (above 80%) is also reported to provide evidence that the observers were coding the data in a similar manner. Chiang concluded that children with autism exhibit a range of communicative behaviors across the different settings and suggested a model for future studies of spontaneous communication in autistic individuals. The issue of intrusiveness can be considered for this study. How much did the presence of the video camera affect the participants' behavior? Were participants aware of the video camera? If so, were they more self-conscious or uncomfortable about their behavior because of its presence? The issue of obtrusiveness should be considered whenever naturalistic observations are used in a study.

Surveys/Questionnaires

The other data collection techniques we will discuss are more obtrusive than the naturalistic observation technique because they involve some type of interaction with the research participants. One of these techniques commonly used in psychological research is a survey in which individuals are asked about specific behaviors. (Although the terms *survey* and *questionnaire* are sometimes used in different contexts in research, in this text I will use these terms interchangeably.) Survey research is often conducted to measure mood, attitudes about a topic, or frequency of certain behaviors through self-reports from the participants. Typically, surveys contain a number of questions that ask the research participant to rate the presence or frequency of his or her own thoughts or behaviors. When surveys are used, participants are often asked to use a response scale (e.g., 1 to 5 or 1 to 7) or response category (e.g., often, sometimes, not very often, never) that matches how they feel about a behavior or how likely they are to exhibit the behavior. This means that the participants are limited in the types of responses they can make to the survey items. In other words, the survey uses a closed-ended response scale because only certain responses are valid responses to the items. The

---

Survey Research: a research study that uses the survey observational technique to measure behavior

Closed-Ended Response Scale: participants respond to survey questions according to the response options provided by the researcher

Open-Ended Response Scale: participants respond to survey questions in any manner they feel is appropriate for the question

Qualitative Data: nonnumerical participant responses

Quantitative Data: numerical data

---

scale in Table 4.3 was designed to assess how likely one is to discuss one's emotions and disclose personal problems to others. Scores on this scale have been shown to be related to higher self-esteem and general satisfaction with one's life (Kahn & Hessling, 2001). The Distress Disclosure Index provides an example of a closed-ended response scale, as a 5-point scale is given for responses.

Another way to design a survey is to ask participants to respond to questions on an open-ended response scale. In other words, they can respond in whatever way they wish to the questions you asked them. Analyzing the data from an open-ended response scale also requires the development of a coding scheme, because the responses are qualitative rather than quantitative. Such coding schemes are developed by researchers for some validated surveys used frequently in certain types of research. Using a closed-ended response scale allows the researcher to collect quantitative responses (i.e., numerical responses), so no coding scheme is needed for closed-ended scales. Surveys are often administered using pencil and paper or (as is becoming more frequent) over the Internet via website.

Researchers are often interested in testing the validity and reliability of the surveys and questionnaires they use. Checking the validity of a survey means making sure that the questions asked are really about the behavior the researcher is interested in. If a survey is designed to measure someone's level of anxiety, the questions have to be written to ask about behaviors that are related to anxiety, or the survey is not measuring what it is designed to measure. In other words, does the survey actually measure the construct it was designed to measure? Checking the reliability of a survey means making certain that the responses you get from an individual are similar either at different points in time or to similar items on the questionnaire. If an individual's responses change drastically from time to time or across similar items, even though the attitude or behavior being measured by the survey does not change, you will not get an accurate measure of that attitude or behavior. A more detailed discussion of the validity and reliability of surveys is presented in Chapter 9.

Typically, using a validated survey gives a researcher observations of behavior that are a step ahead of the other techniques discussed because the validity and reliability of a survey will already have been tested and the survey revised (if necessary) to maximize its accuracy. The primary disadvantage of using surveys to collect data is that the observations are considered self-reports, which means that they may not be correct representations of a person's behavior. Individuals do not always view their behavior accurately and may report who they think they are on a survey, not who they actually are. Participants may also want to portray themselves more positively to the researcher and intentionally respond in a way that achieves that goal (i.e., they self-monitor). This is called *social desirability* and it can bias the results of a survey or questionnaire. Thus, researchers must be careful in interpreting behaviors observed with this technique, as they may not be accurate representations of individuals' behaviors.

The Beck Depression Inventory–II (BDI–II; Beck, Steer, & Brown, 1996) and Beck Anxiety Inventory (BAI; Beck & Steer, 1993) are two commonly used surveys in psychological research on mood. These respective surveys contain items that ask individuals about the intensity of certain feelings and the intensity of specific behaviors related to depression and anxiety. For example, the BDI–II contains 21 items and asks respondents about feelings of sadness, being punished, and lack of interest in sex and behaviors such as difficulty in sleeping and changes in eating habits. Many studies use the BDI–II to measure depression or the BAI to measure anxiety, and the reliability and validity of these surveys have been frequently tested.

Interviews. Surveys can also be administered as interviews such that individuals respond to questions orally. Interviews can be done face-to-face, over the phone, or in focus groups. Like naturalistic observations, observing behaviors with interview data requires the researcher to

Interviews: a data collection technique that involves direct questioning of individuals about their behaviors and attitudes

develop a coding scheme to understand the behaviors described or exhibited in the interview. One advantage of using interviews is that you can ask about a specific behavior instead of waiting for the individual to exhibit the behavior spontaneously (as in naturalistic observations). Another advantage is that if the interview is structured to allow flexibility, different questions can be asked depending on the response that is given. For example, if a participant responds that a question particularly applies to him or her, the interviewer can follow up that response with additional questions on the topic tailored to the type of response made.

Focus groups are becoming a popular way to conduct interviews to learn about individuals' attitudes toward a societal issue, political candidate, or consumer product. Interviewing people in groups uses fewer resources and can sometimes elicit responses from individuals who may be more reluctant to voice an opinion when they are asked on their own. When reluctant individuals hear that others have an opinion similar to their own, they may be more likely to voice their opinion. However, this can also be a limitation to the use of interviews: If they are conducted in groups, individuals may go along with the group rather than voice an opinion that differs from others' (Ashe, 1955). In other words, conformity of responses occurs. Interviewees may also self-monitor during interviews, meaning that they can respond according to how they wish to appear to others instead of how they actually are (i.e., the social desirability bias can occur). Another drawback to the use of interviews is that the way a question is asked can affect the response that is given. Thus, great care must be taken in writing questions for interviews.

A study by Creasey and Ladd (2005) used interviews of individuals to investigate the relationship between parental attachment and conflict resolution behaviors in current romantic relationships. To understand attachment style to their parents, research participants were interviewed about their relationships with their parents. Responses were then coded to categorize individuals according to different types of attachments that children have with their parents. Creasey and Ladd reported that the success of conflict resolution strategies with a romantic partner depended on the type of attachment individuals had with their parents.

Systematic Observation

Systematic observations are typically used when the researchers want to exert the highest amount of control over behavior. This is typically done using a controlled task to indicate the behavior of interest (e.g., speed or accuracy for completing a task). Thus, systematic observation is often used to study behaviors that are least likely to be affected by the process of measuring them. Examples of these behaviors are often cognitive or biological in nature (e.g., memory accuracy, problem-solving speed, firing of a neuron, activity in a

Systematic Observation: data collection technique where control is exerted over the conditions under which the behavior is observed

particular brain area). However, systematic observation can be used to study behaviors in other areas of psychology as well. A method for studying automatic social attitudes called the Implicit Association Test, or IAT (Greenwald, McGhee, & Schwartz, 1998), uses systematic observation of reaction times of participant responses to sets of word or picture stimuli to measure one's unconscious prejudicial attitudes. In the IAT, the speed with which people respond to items after certain associations have been formed is recorded to determine if some judgments take longer than others. The IAT works by associating a specific response to different dimensions of a concept (e.g., press the right key when you see a female name and the left key when you see a male name; press the right key when you see items a teacher might use and the left key when you see items a firefighter might use). The concepts are then combined (e.g., press the right key when you see a female name or an item used by a firefighter and the left key when you see a male name or an item used by a teacher). The assumption is that longer responses with one combination of concepts (e.g., female names and firefighter items both requiring a right-key response) than the other combination (e.g., female names and teacher items both requiring a right-key press) may reveal unconscious social biases people may have that they either are unaware of or consciously suppress when asked explicit questions about their beliefs (e.g., Is it appropriate for a woman to become a firefighter?). Figure 4.2 illustrates the IAT procedure. You can also try out the IAT procedure for yourself at Project Implicit (http://implicit.harvard.edu).

Because a high degree of control can be exerted on the measurements of behaviors observed using systematic observations, they typically add to the internal validity of a study. The situation in which the behaviors are measured is typically controlled to eliminate influences on the behaviors that are not the focus of the study. Thus, systematic observations are often collected in a laboratory setting, where distractions of normal life are minimized and tasks are presented and completed on a computer to maximize accuracy. The drawback of this level of control is that the behaviors being studied may be artificial. In other words, external validity can be lower for systematic observations than other data collection methods, though these observations may have better internal validity.

Figure 4.2 Simplified IAT Procedures

	Gender-Key Association	Occupation-Key Association	Common Associations Provide Baseline Condition	Test of Biased Association—Slower Responses Than Baseline Indicate Bias
Response-Dimension Pairing	Male (left key) Female (right key)	Teacher (left key) Firefighter (right key)	Male/firefighter (left key) Female/teacher (right key)	Male/teacher (left key) Female/firefighter (right key)
Stimuli (With Correct Response)	John (left) Mary (right) Angela (right) Steve (left)	Ladder (right) Books (left) Hose (right) Pencil (left)	Henry (left) Desk (right) Truck (left) Heather (right)	Rick (left) Book (left) Axe (right) Judy (right)

SOURCE: Greenwald, McGhee, and Schwartz (1998).

NOTES:
1. Conditions with keys (right, left) reversed (e.g., male with right key, female with left key) are also used.
2. Longer response times for biased test trials indicate unconscious social biases.

Using Archival Data

Sometimes when researchers have questions about behavior, they find that those behaviors they are interested in have already been observed. In other words, the data they wish to analyze to answer their research question

Archival Data: a data collection technique that involves analysis of preexisting data

already exist. Someone else has collected them. For example, if researchers are interested in health-related behaviors, they may wish to use existing hospital records as their observations. An example of this type of study was done in Pueblo, Colorado, a few years ago (Bartecchi et al., 2006). Pueblo is a small town with two hospitals where residents of the town and surrounding area receive medical care. After the town passed a smoking ban, researchers decided to look at hospital records to compare the number of hospitalizations for heart attacks during the year and a half before the smoking ban began (as a way to determine the number of heart-related illnesses that occurred when people were allowed to smoke in public places) with the number of hospitalizations for heart attacks that occurred during the year and a half after the smoking ban started. They found that the number of hospitalizations for heart attacks decreased significantly during the year and a half after the smoking ban and concluded that the decrease in public smoking was related to this decrease (by comparing heart attack hospitalization rate change for comparable areas without a smoking ban over the same period of time). The use of hospital records in this study is an example of how researchers use archival data as an observation technique.

Many archival data sets are collected by agencies on a periodic basis. A quick web search will show summary results for many of these observations. For example, one can find data related to presidential approval ratings, consumer confidence, consumer spending, and opinion polls. Figure 4.3 shows approval ratings (percentage of people who approve of the job the president is doing) for President Obama over a 2-year period near the end of his presidency. A web search will yield periodic ratings for the current president because presidential approval ratings are collected and published frequently each year by many news agencies. Many of these data sets are collected by governmental agencies and are available to researchers who wish to analyze the data on their own. Corporations may also make archival data sets available to researchers who wish to study workplace behaviors such as work productivity and absenteeism.

Archival data offer researchers a means of collecting data quickly. Few resources are needed, as the data are collected by another agency or institution. However, archival data offer the researcher no control over the circumstances under which the data are collected, the sampling technique used, or the measures used to observe behavior. Researchers using archival data also have no control over how the data are coded, which can make comparisons difficult across groups or areas if data are coded differently by different organizations.

Content Analysis. Content analysis is a specific type of archival data observation technique that involves analysis of what someone has said (as in a speech or interview) or written (as in a book

Figure 4.3   **Approval Ratings for President Barack Obama**

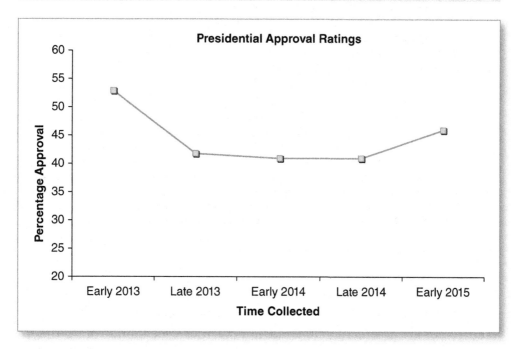

SOURCE: Gallup Poll Data retrieved February 10, 2015, from http://www.gallup.com/poll/116479/barack-obama-presidential-job-approval.aspx.

or article). This may involve analyzing the transcript of a speech someone gave, a written document, or a recorded statement. In content analysis, a researcher is analyzing a record of what someone has said or written in the past; thus, no interaction takes place between the research participant and the researcher. A coding scheme must be developed by the researcher to determine which behaviors will be considered in the analysis. This type of analysis can be resource intensive and time-consuming.

> — ❧ —
>
> **Content Analysis:** an archival data collection technique that involves analysis of the content of an individual's spoken or written record

Table 4.4 contains some examples of behaviors that psychologists might want to observe. For each behavior, consider how psychologists might use each of the observation techniques described in this chapter to measure the behavior.

The discussion of data collection techniques presented here provides examples of the primary types of observations researchers use in psychological studies. In other words, they provide a means for the researcher to focus on the measured variables (i.e., a behavior, situation, or characteristic that can differ from individual to individual) of interest. Variables can be numeric and vary continuously from person to person or can be categorical so as to group individuals into different categories that can be compared. The behavior of interest in a study is typically one variable (or more) that is of primary interest in a research study. Observations of behavior (i.e., data) in a study constitute what is called a dependent or response variable. Dependent variables are measured in every research study. For some designs, only a single dependent variable is measured and the behavior is examined descriptively or causally (if the researcher is interested in a causal relationship and uses an experiment to study this relationship). Other designs examine relationships between

> — ❧ —
>
> **Variable:** an attribute that can vary across individuals
>
> **Dependent/Response Variable:** a variable that is measured or observed from an individual

Table 4.4   Thinking About Observations

For each behavior listed below, consider how you might observe the behavior using (a) naturalistic observation, (b) surveys and questionnaires, or (c) systematic observation. Be sure to operationally define the behavior before you describe how the observations would be collected. Also consider the limitations of each observation method as you choose one for each behavior.

1. How do humans (or animals) solve a problem?

2. How do people react to bad news?

3. What types of people are most likely to disclose personal problems to others?

4. How do groups of children organize themselves to complete a task?

5. What behaviors characterize people with attention-deficit/hyperactivity disorder (ADHD)?

6. What types of brain activity result when one consumes caffeine?

multiple dependent variables. As a result, how a dependent variable is measured depends on the data collection technique used, and what is learned about a dependent variable depends on the type of research design used. The next section describes some of the common research designs that psychologists use in their studies of behavior.

Stop and Think

(4.2)   Describe a disadvantage of using closed-ended responses on a survey/questionnaire.

(4.3)   For each description below, indicate which data collection technique would be best to use:

- You want to measure someone's ability to complete a task while controlling for sources of bias and increasing internal validity as much as possible.
- You want to know about how subjects judge their own behavior.
- You want to measure the most realistic behaviors possible to increase external validity.
- You want to know how Americans' confidence in the economy has changed across 4 decades of time.

TYPES OF RESEARCH DESIGNS

Research design types differ based on the type of question the researcher wants to answer. Each of the data collection techniques described earlier can be used in any of the major research designs; however, practically speaking, some techniques are more common in certain designs than in others. As each design is discussed, examples of the most common techniques used in that design will be described. In addition, some of the more common designs are discussed in further detail in Part II of this book. Note also that you may see the term *research design* applied to many aspects of a design. Here the term applies to the major categories of research designs that are used by psychologists to answer different types of research questions. What follows is a description of the major research designs used in psychological research with some examples of these designs.

Case Studies

In 1970, a woman walked into a welfare office in Southern California with her daughter Genie. After the woman was interviewed, it became clear that although Genie appeared to be about 6 or 7 years old, she was in fact 13 years old and had no language abilities. Her parents had kept her locked in her bedroom every day since she was very young. Genie did not attend school and had not been exposed to enough language from her family to learn how to speak. After Genie's situation was discovered, psychologists became interested in her case and hoped to learn from her about the development of language and whether it can occur at such a late age in a child (Fromkin, Krashen, Curtiss, Rigler, & Rigler, 1974). Genie became the subject of intensive study by a number of individuals. From the case study of Genie, evidence was gained for a critical period of language development because Genie was raised with little language interaction with others and had difficulty learning language after she was rescued.

The goal of a case study is to gain insight into and understanding of a single individual's (or just a couple of individuals') behavior. Case studies can also be conducted for a group of

---

❦

Case Study: a research design that involves intensive study of particular individuals and their behaviors

Small-*n* Design: an experiment conducted with one or a few participants to better understand the behavior of those individuals

---

individuals, such as an agency or institution. Typically, a case study involves intensive observation of an individual's naturalistic behavior or set of behaviors. Thus, researchers often use naturalistic observations, interviews, or archival data (especially in the case of a famous individual) to learn about the individual's behavior, although some case studies have also included systematic observations and surveys to learn about an individual. Case studies are often exploratory studies, wherein a researcher can learn about a behavior when little is known about it (e.g., unusual symptoms of a new disorder). When a researcher is interested in testing theories about how behavior works or attempting to find a treatment that will help an individual or small set of individuals with a problem behavior, a small-*n* design is typically used instead of a case study. The primary difference between case studies and small-*n* designs is the goal of the researcher. In addition, small-*n* designs are often conducted as experiments (see section on Experiments later in this chapter). Small-*n* designs are further discussed in Chapter 14.

Some of the more well-known case studies conducted by psychologists have been with individuals who suffered a brain injury. Researchers study such individuals after their brain injury both while they are still alive (if possible) and after their death. Behaviors these individuals exhibit are then connected to the brain injury they suffered, which can be explored more extensively after their death. Physiological psychologists have gained a lot of important knowledge about brain functions through case studies of these individuals. A famous case is that of H.M. (typically these patients are identified by initials only or a pseudonym to keep the findings confidential for these individuals). H.M. suffered damage to a brain area known as the hippocampus during a surgery in 1953 that was done to help reduce his epileptic seizures (Hilts, 1996). As a result of the surgery, H.M. could no longer remember new experiences for longer than a few minutes. Through extensive study of this subject, psychologists learned that the hippocampus is an important structure for encoding or retrieving memories of events because H.M. lost the ability to retrieve memories of things that happened after his surgery (even though he still had access to memories of events he experienced before his surgery). From case studies of H.M. came a new set of questions about the hippocampus and exactly what function it serves in memory. In addition, researchers found that H.M. could improve on tasks over time, indicating that certain types of new memories were still available to him. For example, a study of H.M. (Bohbot & Corkin, 2007) found that his ability to learn a spatial memory task was quite good, despite having severe amnesia (his memory for things he experienced lasts only a few minutes). Case studies of H.M. are still conducted today. Although he died in 2008, H.M.'s brain will continue to be studied to further our understanding of the importance of specific brain areas in cognitive functioning.

Other case studies have used archival data or content analysis of a document to better understand an individual's behavior. For example, Lester (2006) recently examined the diaries of a man who committed suicide, in an attempt to identify specific events in his life that may have been connected to his choice to kill himself. Abramson (1984) conducted a case study of the sexual behaviors of a woman who called herself "Sarah," after receiving a letter from her. Sarah had been abused (physically and sexually) as a child and was recovering from those traumas at the time she wrote to Abramson, a psychologist at the University of California, Los Angeles. Abramson then conducted interviews with Sarah to better understand how individuals recover from such traumatic experiences. Abramson learned a good deal about psychological resilience and recovery in an individual despite traumatic childhood events.

Case studies can even be done after a person has died. When Albert Einstein died in 1955, portions of his brain were preserved to allow it to be studied. Since then scientists have examined these brain sections to look for ways in which Einstein's brain may differ from brains of other people. One difference that has been found is that Einstein's brain contains many more neuron cells in a section of his brain's cortex than in the brains of control participants that were used as a comparison (Anderson & Harvey, 1996). In addition, a section of Einstein's brain appears to have been improperly formed, allowing connections between areas of the brain that are not connected in other people's brains (Witelson, Kigar, & Harvey, 1999). These differences may account for the intellectual abilities Einstein possessed, but simply examining Einstein's brain does not allow researchers to make such strong conclusions. Instead, these studies allow researchers to start hypothesizing about which brain areas or characteristics may be important for advanced intellectual abilities, and these hypotheses can then be tested in further studies (see Figure 4.4).

Due to their exploratory nature, case studies often focus on rare or unusual cases to gain some information about a behavior that is not exhibited by all individuals. This means that the behaviors examined in case studies often cannot be generalized to all individuals. Because of the reduced generality of the behaviors, case studies do not allow for strong tests of the cause of the behavior (experiments are best for that—as explained in a later section), and researchers must be careful about drawing conclusions about the causes of the behaviors they are studying. However, case studies can give researchers a *starting place* for investigations of a behavior or a set of behaviors. Thus, they serve an important purpose in psychological research, drawing attention to new research questions that can be further explored with additional studies.

Correlational Studies

❧

Correlational Study: a type of research design that examines the relationships between multiple dependent variables, without manipulating any of the variables

Predictor Variable: the dependent variable in a correlational study that is used to predict the score on another variable

Outcome Variable: the dependent variable in a correlational study that is being predicted by the predictor variable

Is insomnia related to depression? Do students who watch more TV have lower grade point averages (GPAs)? Do children who play violent video games behave more violently? Each of these questions can be explored in a correlational study (correlation means relationship). Correlational studies allow a researcher to examine relationships between variables and, if a relationship is found, predict values for one variable from values on the other variable(s). If a predictive relationship is examined, the variable that is used to make the prediction is called the predictor variable, and the variable that is being predicted is called the outcome variable. Therefore, the goal of a correlational study is to determine if different behaviors are connected and occur together. This type of study, however, still does not allow us to determine if one variable *causes* another to occur (again, only well-designed experiments allow researchers to test causal relationships). All we can learn from a correlational study is if two variables covary (i.e., change together—up, down, or in opposite directions from each other). Then researchers may be able to predict one variable from another.

If a relationship is found in a correlational study between two variables, it can take one of two forms: a positive relationship or a negative relationship. A positive relationship means that the values on the variables change in the same direction (up or down) at the same time. A negative relationship indicates that as values on one variable increase, the values on the other

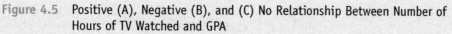

Figure 4.5   Positive (A), Negative (B), and (C) No Relationship Between Number of Hours of TV Watched and GPA

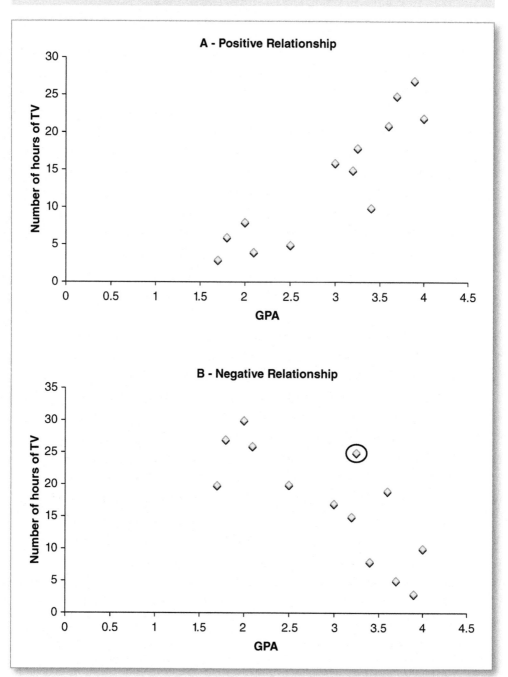

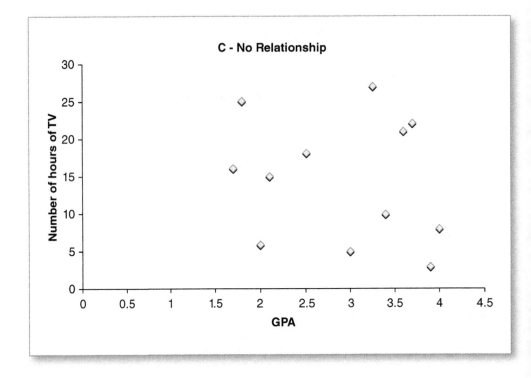

variable decrease. Figure 4.5 illustrates each type of relationship that might exist between GPA and the number of hours an individual watches TV per week. The graphs in Figure 4.5 are called scatterplots. In a scatterplot, one variable is placed on the *x*-axis, and the other variable is placed on the *y*-axis. The data points in the graph represent the scores on the two variables for each individual (horizontally for the first variable and vertically for the second variable). Thus, the data point that is circled in Panel B shows that one individual in this study reported watching 25 hours of TV per week and had a GPA of 3.25. You may also notice that there are very few data points

Positive Relationship: the variables change together in the same direction (both increasing together or decreasing together)

Negative Relationship: a relationship between variables characterized by an increase in one variable that occurs with a decrease in the other variable

Scatterplot: a graph showing the relationship between two dependent variables for a group of individuals

below 1.0 on the GPA scale in the graph. This may be because very few students in college have GPAs lower than 1.0 (if they do, they do not remain in college very long).

Remember that a relationship between these variables does not mean that watching TV will *cause* one to have a higher or lower GPA or that having a higher or lower GPA will *cause* one to watch more TV. It is quite possible that a third variable (e.g., lack of interest in academic topics, a poor academic environment while growing up, good background in academic

---

❧

Third-Variable Problem: the presence of extraneous factors in a study that affect the dependent variable and can decrease the internal validity of the study

---

topics that are covered in TV shows) is causing the number of hours of TV watched and GPA to change. This is called the third-variable problem and it is the reason that researchers cannot determine causation from correlational studies.

Experiments

Have you ever wondered why it took so long for scientists to learn that smoking causes cancer? People have been smoking for hundreds of years, and medical science has been studying the effects of smoking on health for many decades. Yet warnings on cigarette packages did not appear until 1966, and claims about smoking causing lung cancer were tentative for many years. Scientists could show that smoking and cancer were linked but could not show that smoking caused cancer in humans in a definitive way. The reason these findings were tentative for so long is that ethically it is very difficult (if not impossible) to conduct an experiment to examine whether smoking *causes* cancer in humans. An experiment involves manipulating the presumed causal variable known as the independent variable. This means that in the smoking experiment, one group of people would be assigned to smoke and a similar group of people (similar in age, weight, health, diet, etc.) would not be allowed to smoke. Obviously, researchers cannot force people to smoke (especially, if they have a hypothesis that it is harmful to them) or force

---

❧

Experiment: a type of research design that involves manipulation of an independent variable, allowing control of extraneous variables that could affect the results

Independent Variable: a variable in an experiment that is manipulated by the researcher such that the levels of the variable change across or within subjects in the experiment

Levels of the Independent Variable: different situations or conditions that participants experience in an experiment because of the manipulation of the independent variable

Experimental Group: the group of participants in an experiment that experience the treatment level of the independent variable

Control Group: the group of participants in an experiment that do not experience the treatment level of the independent variable

---

people to never smoke. Thus, it has been very difficult (and has taken many correlational studies and animal experiments) to show that smoking is a cause of lung cancer, but this example illustrates what is required to test causal hypotheses: experiments.

As mentioned above, a key aspect of experiments that allows tests of causal relationships is the manipulation of the independent variable (or independent variables—an experiment can contain more than one independent variable). The independent variable is the factor that the researcher thinks may affect the observed behavior. Thus, data are collected from the participants in an experiment under at least two different conditions. The data from these conditions are then compared with one another to see if there are differences caused by the independent variable manipulation. These different conditions created from the independent variable make up the levels of the independent variable. For example, an experiment may involve subjecting one group of participants (randomly assigned) to treatment for depression, while another group receives no treatment. In this case, the treated group is the experimental group, because they receive the treatment condition, whereas the nontreated group is the control group, because they receive no treatment. Comparison of depression scores (the dependent variable in this experiment) for the two groups would allow the researcher to determine if the treatment was helpful (scores for the treatment group are higher than the control group's), harmful (scores for the treatment group are lower than the control group's), or makes no difference (scores for the treatment and control groups are similar). Another way to conduct this experiment would be to use two different treatments (e.g., talk therapy vs. drug therapy) for the two groups. In this case, there is no control group; both groups of participants receive some type of treatment. Comparison of the scores for the two groups in this experiment would indicate which of the two therapies was more helpful or if they are

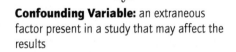

Confounding Variable: an extraneous factor present in a study that may affect the results

Random Assignment: participants are randomly assigned to levels of the independent variable in an experiment to control for individual differences as an extraneous variable

Placebo: a sugar pill given to the control group in a drug study to allow all groups to believe that they are receiving a treatment

similar. In fact, this comparison is a key feature of an experiment. The goal in an experiment is to examine the effect of the independent variable on the dependent variable. We do that by comparing the data observed in the different levels of the independent variable; this comparison tells us if the independent variable has an effect. In other words, the comparison across the levels of the independent variable provides the test of the hypothesis.

Another key feature of experiments is the control of factors that could affect the results but are not part of the manipulation of the independent variable(s). These extraneous factors are called confounding variables. If confounding variables are not controlled, the causal relationship between the independent and dependent variables will be unclear. For example, in the depression examples discussed earlier, the severity of the depression the participants have before the experiment could be a confounding variable because participants with more severe depression may show less improvement with therapy than participants with less severe depression. If the participants with more severe depression are inadvertently assigned to the therapy group in the first example or to one of the therapy groups in the second example, they may show no effect of therapy, even if an effect does exist. In other words, the severity of the depression may mask the causal relationship between therapy group and depression at the end of the study. Thus, the researcher should control for this factor in the experiment, perhaps by randomly assigning participants to groups. The control aspect of experiments is discussed further in Chapter 11.

Another example of control used in experiments with a treatment as the independent variable is the use of a placebo for the control group. A placebo is typically given as a sugar pill in a study testing a drug treatment to the control group so that the subjects do not know whether they receive a treatment or not. This controls for the effects of the belief that one is being treated that can have an influence on the results of the study. People who believe they are receiving a treatment can improve from the belief alone so a placebo is often used to give both the experimental and control groups the belief that they may be receiving the treatment.

Systematic observations and surveys are the most common observation techniques used in experiments. These observation techniques allow for more control over the measurement of behavior than the other techniques (see Table 4.2). The IAT procedure described earlier (and in Figure 4.2) provides an example of the use of systematic observation in an experiment. An independent variable in an experiment using the IAT procedure is the type of word (or image) pairing the participant is responding to. The dependent variable is often the amount of time a participant takes to respond to the word pairings.

Quasi-Experiments

In some cases, researchers want to compare the behavior of groups of individuals but are unable to manipulate the characteristic on which the groups differ. For example, suppose you wanted to compare the behavior for older and younger adults. You cannot randomly assign individuals to be of a specific age, so age cannot be a manipulated variable. This means that you lose some control over alternative explanations of the data, because participants are not randomly assigned to the groups. In this example, if younger and older adults differ on the measured behavior, age may have caused the difference or something that varies with age (e.g., experiences of different generations with technology) may have caused the difference. Thus, conclusions from quasi-experiments must be more tentative than conclusions from experiments, where a true independent variable is manipulated. However, quasi-experiments involve group comparisons just as experiments do, and data from quasi-experiments are often analyzed the same way they are analyzed in experiments (see Chapter 15 for more on data analysis). The key difference between experiments and quasi-experiments is that the random assignment of participants to groups is missing in a quasi-experiment (Shadish, Cook, & Campbell, 2002).

One type of quasi-experiment design is called an ex post facto design, because the comparison of interest is based on a grouping that already exists instead of one the researcher assigns in the study. In other words, the grouping is based on something that already happened in the past (e.g., a subject decided to be a smoker or not, a subject was in an automobile accident in the last year or not). Based on these pre-existing characteristics of the subjects, a researcher can create groups of subjects to compare on a particular behavior (e.g., anxiety level, impulsivity). However, a design can be a quasi-experiment even if the researcher assigns subjects to groups if that assignment is not done randomly. Researchers might decide to assign subjects to groups based on their availability for participation in the study (e.g., morning or afternoon session). If the assignment is not random, then there could be additional factors (other than the grouping factor) that are responsible for the results found (e.g., people who sign up for the morning session are more alert and perform better on the task because of their energy level).

Some studies also have less control over conditions under which data are collected in a repeated-measures design. For example, suppose a researcher is interested in the change in attitude regarding trust of politicians after taking a political science class. In this study, attitude is measured before and after the class in what is called a pretest-posttest design. If attitude changes from pretest to posttest (getting either better or worse), this change may be either because of the class or because of other events that occurred in the time between the tests (e.g., a political scandal may have occurred in this time). Thus,

---

Quasi-Experiment: a type of research design where a comparison is made, as in an experiment, but no random assignment of participants to groups occurs

Ex Post Facto Design: a quasi-experiment where subjects are grouped based on a characteristic they already possess (e.g., age or gender)

Pretest-Posttest Design: a type of research design (often a quasi-experiment) where behavior is measured both before and after a treatment or condition is implemented

the causal relationship between the political science class and attitude change is less clear. For this reason, pretest-posttest designs (that do not include a control group) are considered quasi-experiments. Other types of quasi-experimental designs are considered in Chapter 13.

Stop and Think

(4.4)   For each description below, indicate what research design is being used:

- To determine if there is a relationship between mood and weather, researchers measure subjects' moods and the temperature on the day that they complete the mood questionnaire.
- To examine the effect of temperature on mood, subjects are randomly assigned to a room at 86 degrees or a room at 72 degrees to complete their mood questionnaire.
- To determine if mood differs by room temperature, a researcher asks two of her classes to fill out a mood questionnaire at the end of class after adjusting the thermostat between classes. She then groups subjects by class and compares their mood scores.

(4.5)   Explain why the results from a case study might be difficult to generalize to a large population of people.

(4.6)   Imagine you wanted to learn about the factors that contribute to people quitting their jobs. Describe a study to examine this topic and identify the data collection technique and research design you would use.

CHAPTER SUMMARY

Reconsider the questions from the beginning of the chapter:

- How do psychologists observe behavior? There are some common techniques used by psychologists to observe behavior described in this chapter.
- What are some common techniques for observing and recording behavior in different situations? The common techniques used by psychologists to observe and record behavior are naturalistic observations, surveys/questionnaires, systematic observations, and archival data.
- How do psychologists use observations to learn about behavior? Each technique can be used in different research designs to allow psychologists to answer different types of questions about behavior.
- What questions about behavior do the different research methods allow psychologists to answer? Different research designs (e.g., case studies, correlational studies, experiments, and quasi-experiments) allow researchers to ask different questions about behavior. Case studies allow descriptive questions to be answered for a single individual or institution. Correlational studies allow descriptive and predictive questions to be answered about behavior. Quasi-experiments and experiments allow comparisons among groups, with experiments answering causal questions about behavior.
- Which research method is best when asking about the cause of behavior? Experiments are the best method to use when asking causal questions about behavior.

A summary of a research study in psychology is given below. As you read the summary, think about the following questions:

1. Two studies from a research article are described below. For each study, identify the data collection technique and the research design type.

2. Does Study 2 contain an independent variable? If so, what is it and what are its levels?

3. What controls did the researchers use in Study 2 to increase the internal validity of the study?

4. Would you consider Study 1 or Study 2 to have higher internal validity? Explain your answer.

5. How would you judge the external validity of this study?

Research Study. Nairne, J. S., VanArsdall, J. E., Pandeirada, J. N. S., Cogdill, M., & LeBreton, J. M. (2013). Adaptive memory: The mnemonic value of animacy. *Psychological Science, 24,* 2099–2105.

Purpose of the Study. The researchers conducted two studies to investigate whether living things have a memory advantage over nonliving things. Their research was motivated by an evolutionary perspective on the development of memory in that being able to distinguish between living and nonliving things is essential for survival. In their first study, they analyzed the relationship between the living/nonliving characteristic of words used in a past study (Rubin & Friendly, 1986) and recall of the words. They predicted a positive relationship between this living/nonliving status and recall. In their second study, they tested the hypothesis that subjects would recall more words of living objects than nonliving objects.

Method of the Study. **Study 1:** The researchers examined words from the Rubin and Friendly (1986) study. Three individuals separately coded the words according to whether they represented living or nonliving objects.

Study 2: Undergraduate students were asked to remember 24 words presented to them in random order. Twelve of the words represented living things; and 12 of the words represented nonliving things. The word sets were matched on several other characteristics (e.g., familiarity, how well an image could be brought to mind by the word, number of letters in the word, etc.). After studying the words, subjects completed a short task to categorize presented numbers as "odd" or "even." Subjects were then asked to recall the words in any order for 4 min. This entire procedure was repeated a total of three times (i.e., they studied and recalled the words three times).

Results of the Study. In Study 1, a strong positive relationship was found between the living/nonliving aspect of the words and recall of the words. In Study 2, subjects recalled more of the words for living objects than nonliving objects. Figure 4.6 presents the recall results from Study 2.

Conclusions of the Study. The researchers concluded that the living objects hold a memorial advantage, such that memory is attuned to this characteristic of objects. They suggest that this conclusion is consistent with an evolutionary perspective on the development of memory.

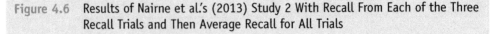

Figure 4.6   Results of Nairne et al.'s (2013) Study 2 With Recall From Each of the Three Recall Trials and Then Average Recall for All Trials

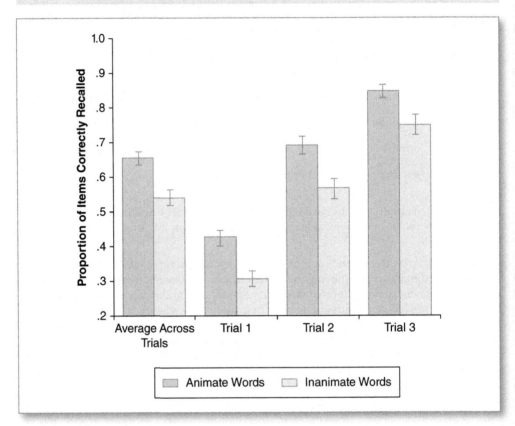

SOURCE: From Nairne et al.'s (2013) Study 2.

COMMON PITFALLS AND HOW TO AVOID THEM

Problem: Concluding cause without manipulation—nonexperimental studies are sometimes interpreted as providing causal information.

Solution: To test causal relationships, an experiment with a manipulated independent variable is needed.

Problem: External validity versus internal validity—some view external validity as more important than internal validity in all psychological research studies.

Solution: Be aware that high internal validity is required to test causal relationships but that internal and external validity typically trade off in psychological studies.

Problem: Use of control groups in experiments—students sometimes incorrectly believe that all experiments require a control group.

Solution: Remember that control groups are important in experiments if a single treatment is being evaluated or the effectiveness of multiple treatments is being tested, but control groups are not required in every type of experiment.

USING RESEARCH

In 1998, a group of British doctors published a paper suggesting that there may be a link between vaccines for measles, mumps, and rubella diseases and incidence of autism (Wakefield et al., 1998). This means the researchers were suggesting there is a positive relationship between these vaccinations and occurrence of autism in children that were tested. Their findings started a controversy over the causes of autism. Media sources in the United Kingdom (UK) reported the findings of this paper suggesting that having children vaccinated can cause them to develop autism. As a result, many parents in the UK and the United States refused to have their children vaccinated out of fear of their children becoming autistic, and the incidence of childhood diseases, such as measles, increased in the UK in the years after the paper was published. Based on the information you read in this chapter, why should parents hesitate to conclude from the findings of this paper that vaccinations can cause autism? What error did the media sources make in publicizing the study's findings? Why should the public refrain from making important decisions (such as refusing vaccinations) based on the findings of a single study? If this last question is a bit difficult to answer, consider what has happened more recently in this story: In February 2010, the journal that published the original paper describing this study retracted the paper because the study was found to have serious methodological flaws that were not entirely evident in the original report of the research. Consider what type of study would be necessary to show that vaccinations cause autism in children. How would such a study need to be done? Is this a realistic study to conduct? Why or why not?

TEST YOURSELF

Match each research design below with its appropriate description.

1. Experiment	(a) Design that focuses on observing just one or a few individuals
2. Case study	(b) Design that will allow one to look for relationships between measured variables
3. Correlational study	(c) Best design for testing a causal relationship
4. Quasi-experiment	(d) Design that allows comparison of groups but does not contain a true independent variable

5. Reread the scenario described at the beginning of the chapter about increasing work productivity. Use the concepts you read about in this chapter to design a study to test the boss's suggestion. Be sure to operationally define *work productivity* and decide what technique you will use to observe this behavior. Choose the research design that best fits the question you are trying to answer.

6. Suppose you are interested in testing the hypothesis "The herb ginkgo biloba causes one to have better memory."

(a) What is the best research design to test this hypothesis? Why?

(b) Describe the study you would conduct to test this hypothesis.

7. _____ validity indicates that a study's results can be generalized to other individuals and real-life situations. _____ validity indicates that a study's results provide causal information about the variables tested.

8. For each description below, indicate which data collection technique was used:

   (a) Medical records of patients with depression are examined to determine how often these patients attempt suicide based on what type of treatment they received

   (b) Participants are asked to perform a task on a computer where they must unscramble sentences as quickly as possible—the amount of time it takes to complete the task on each trial is recorded

   (c) A series of statements regarding their alcohol consumption behaviors is presented to participants—they are asked to rate their agreement with each statement on a scale from 1 to 5

   (d) Students in a college class are observed to record the number of times they exhibit behaviors indicating lack of attention to the lecture

9. If a study finds that as self-esteem goes up, symptoms of depression decrease, this study has found a _____ relationship.

10. _____ research designs are typically used when a researcher wants to explore the behavior of an individual or group of individuals to better understand unusual or atypical behaviors.

Answers can be found at edge.sagepub/mcbride3e.

STOP AND THINK ANSWERS

(4.1) External validity, internal validity, internal validity

(4.2) Closed-ended responses might be poorly written such that they bias subjects toward a particular response. They also don't allow for responses that do not fit the scale chosen by the researcher.

(4.3) Systematic observation, survey/questionnaire, naturalistic observation, archival data

(4.4) Correlational study, experiment, quasi-experiment

(4.5) Case studies examine just one or a small group of individuals. Thus, it may be difficult to generalize the results from a case study to others because the individual(s) tested may be unique.

(4.6) Answers will vary

$)SAGE edge™

Visit edge.sagepub.com/mcbride3e for the tools you need to sharpen your study skills:

- Web Quizzes
- eFlashcards
- Thinking About Research

- SAGE Journal Articles
- Web and Multimedia Resources

Answering the Question 'How?' The Method Section

Field, A. & Hole, G.

The idea of this section is to provide the reader with a clear idea of what you did and how you did it. The standard by which this section will be judged is: would it be possible to replicate this study, in all its important aspects, solely on the basis of the information that is provided in this section? The tricky bit is to walk the tightrope between providing too much information (including irrelevant information) and too little.

This section is sub-divided into several sections. The 'Design' section provides an overview of the overall structure of your experiment; the 'Participants' section provides the necessary information about the people who took part in your experiment; the 'Apparatus' section gives details of any equipment used (including things like questionnaires and other tests); and the 'Procedure' tells the reader how the study was carried out in practice.

12.1 Design

This section provides an overview of the formal design of the study. What were the 'independent variables' in the study? (Independent variables are the factors that you, the experimenter, manipulate: see Chapter 2).

How many conditions were there? Was it a repeated-measures design (with each participant taking part in all of the conditions of the study), an independent-measures design (in which participants performed in one and only one condition), or a more complex, 'mixed design' (using a combination of repeated-measures and independent-measures variables)? (See Chapter 3). What was measured – in other words, what were the dependent variables?

The 'Design' section summarizes the formal structure of your study.

This may all seem rather arcane, so here's a concrete example that will hopefully clarify what's required. Suppose you are interested in factors affecting how well factory workers can spot black cornflakes on the cornflake production-line. You might devise an experiment in which you examine the effects of age and time of day on workers' ability to detect the dodgy cornflakes. You obtain groups of young, medium and old workers. For each of these age-groups, you have a group of morning-shift workers, and a group of evening-shift workers. You measure the number of black cornflakes that each worker detects during a four-hour shift. (You cunningly arrange it so that, unknown to the workers, the same number of black cornflakes is presented during each worker's shift).

The formal design section for this experiment would look something like this:

'There were two independent variables: age of worker (with three levels: young (21–30 years), medium (31–40 years) and old (41–50 years)) and time of shift (with two levels: morning or evening). The experiment used a wholly between-groups design, with each worker assigned to only one of the permutations of age and shift. The dependent variable was the number of black cornflakes detected within a shift (out of a maximum of 20).'

12.2   Participants

These used to be called 'subjects', but psychology is as vulnerable to political correctness as anything else! Give details of how many participants you used, and how many took part in each condition (if a between-groups design was used). Include information on demographic variables such as age and gender, and provide brief details of how you obtained the participants – for example, did they volunteer, and were they paid for taking part? Were they naive about the purpose of the experiment? Participants in psychology experiments are often 'blind' to the purposes of the study. However, you need to be careful about how you express this – reading some practical reports, with phrases such as 'blind participants were used' or 'all participants were blind', you could be forgiven for thinking that many participants in psychology experiments have profound eyesight difficulties!

Give the relevant characteristics of the poor gullible fools who took part in your study.

Sometimes, you might use a special population of participants, such as colour-blind individuals, learning-disabled people, hyperactive children or spider-phobics. If so, further relevant details should be provided about them. For example, in the case of the spider phobics, give brief details of the criteria by which they are defined as 'phobic', such as their mean scores on some recognised phobia test.

As mentioned earlier, you need to think about what information is relevant and what's not relevant. This may depend on the circumstances. Thus, if you are measuring people's ability to estimate distances, the issue of ethnic grouping is irrelevant and need not be mentioned, but details of whether the individuals concerned had normal stereoscopic vision should be given. Conversely, if you are conducting a study on attitudes to racial prejudice, ethnic grouping might be highly relevant and hence details should be provided in this section.

12.3	**Apparatus**

This section is reasonably straightforward. You have to provide enough details of the apparatus that was used, for someone to be able to replicate the experiment. Avoid writing 'shopping lists' of apparatus – write in full English sentences. Instead of writing 'Stopwatch. Questionnaire. Tape recorder', write 'The apparatus consisted of a stopwatch, a questionnaire, and a tape-recorder'.

In the case of questionnaires and other pencil-and-paper tests, if it's widely used (such as Eysenck's Personality Inventory and Witkin's Embedded Figures Test, tests which are in common use amongst psychologists) give its name, a reference to where a full account of it can be obtained, and some justification for why you used that particular test. Briefly provide evidence that it's a good measure. This might include reference to studies which have shown that the measure is reliable, valid and is appropriate for participants similar to the ones you are testing. (Many widely-used questionnaires and pencil and paper tests have been standardized on different sub-groups of people, so that there are sub-group norms for performance which differ according to the group under consideration).

If you are using a novel or home-brewed test (e.g. a questionnaire that you have devised yourself) then put the test or questionnaire in an appendix at the end of the report, and state in the apparatus section that it can be found there.

If the experiment involves presenting stimuli and/or recording responses on a computer, it is normally sufficient to give the generic type of computer used, plus a brief mention of what software was used. For example, 'The stimuli were presented on the screen of an Apple Macintosh Quadra, using a program written in Supercard'. If the equipment is a little more out of the ordinary, give the name of the manufacturer and of the product. For example, 'Electric shocks were administered using a 'Sizzler Mk. II' shock-generator (manufactured by Megajolt Ltd., Ohio)'.

Once again, consider the issue of relevance. If the experiment consists of completing a questionnaire, you probably need only mention the questionnaire itself: you can reasonably assume the reader realises that a pen or a pencil was required to fill in the questionnaire, and you might even be bold enough to let them assume that doing the questionnaire involved using a table, a seat and a floor. You certainly wouldn't need to mention how the room was lit, unless it was something out of the ordinary. Details of the typeface and font size in which the questionnaire was written would also be superfluous. However, if you were doing a study of eye-movements during reading, the ambient lighting and typeface might well be influential factors, so they should be clearly specified. In short, only mention things that could reasonably be expected to have a bearing on the outcome of the study.

Sometimes you may see this section divided into two, 'Apparatus' and 'Materials'. If so, 'Apparatus' is the place in which to describe things like computers and other hardware, whereas details of questionnaires, visual stimuli and the like should go in the 'Materials' section.

12.4 Procedure

This section gives details of how you carried out the experiment in practice. Suppose your experiment involves examining the effects of cerebral blood-flow on memory. Participants are given a memory test twice, once after being held upside down on a rope, and once after being allowed to stand upright. How were these two conditions administered? Were all participants exposed to them in the same order, or was order of presentation randomized? Were participants tested one at a time, or in groups? How long did they dangle upside-down on the rope? How long did they stand? How long was the interval between these two experiences? How long was the memory test, in terms of time and number of items? What instructions were given to the participants? If there were long and detailed instructions, consider putting them in an appendix and referring the reader to that. However, if the instructions were short and fairly simple, this may not be necessary: it

Give relevant details –
the rope's colour appears to
be irrelevant to this experiment!

may suffice to mention them briefly only in this section of the report. Here's an example from a face-recognition experiment in which measurements are taken of the speed with which participants can make judgements about whether or not a face is familiar to them.

'Participants were asked to press the letter 'S' on the keyboard if the face was familiar to them, and the letter 'L' if it was not. They were asked to respond as quickly but as accurately as possible'.

As with the 'Apparatus' section, provide details only if they are needed for replication purposes, and if they are potentially relevant to the outcome of the experiment.

12.5 Summary

The 'Method' section sub-divides into the 'Design', 'Participants', 'Apparatus' and 'Procedure' sections. Together, they give the reader enough details for them to replicate the study should they wish to do so. The 'Design' section outlines the formal structure of the study: it identifies the experiment's independent and dependent variables (i.e. the things that you, as experimenter, manipulate and measure, respectively). It also tells the reader whether you used an independent-measures, repeated-measures or 'mixed' design. The 'Participants' section gives relevant details of the people who took part in your experiment. The 'Apparatus' section provides information on what equipment you used to run your experiment. Depending on the nature of your research, 'equipment' may include questionnaires and pencil and paper tests, as well as computers and the like. Provide enough details for replication purposes, but don't include irrelevant and unimportant details. The 'Procedure' section describes how you actually carried out the study in practice: again, include only details that would be required for replication purposes.

12.6 Practical Tasks

Identify the problems with the following procedure section:

Subjects were tested one at a time. Each subject arrived at the time that their appointment had been set for, and was asked to sit down at the table and to fill in the first questionnaire, which measured their mood before the experimental manipulations were administered. The questionnaire was administered via an

EverKrash™ 1 GHz PC, with a 17 inch Trashiba™ monitor screen. This was placed by the window of the test room. The room measured approximately 10 ft by 15 ft. After they had completed the first questionnaire, which took about 10 minutes, half of the subjects listened to a tape of sad music, while the other half listened to a tape of dance music. The mood of all subjects was then re-tested with a second questionnaire, administered under the same conditions as the first. Subjects were then debriefed and thanked for their participation in the study. The results were then analysed on the same computer by the experimenter, using Excel.

Answers:

1. The writer should refer to 'participants' rather than 'subjects'.
2. It's not really necessary to know that the participants had made an appointment to take part in the experiment and had arrived on time.
3. You need to use your judgement about whether or not to give precise details of equipment used. In this particular case, we probably don't need to know the make and model of the PC and its screen because the computer is merely a vehicle for administering the questionnaire: presumably using a different computer – or even pencil and paper – would have made little difference to this particular study.
4. The computer's location in the room is irrelevant detail that can be dispensed with.
5. We do not need to know the room's dimensions in this case: and if we did, they should be presented in metric units, rather than imperial.
6. We are told how long participants took to complete the first questionnaire, but other – more important – information is missing: for how long did the participants listen to the mood-inducing music? How long afterwards did they complete the second questionnaire?
7. More details of the music should be given, such as the name of the composer and the title of the piece of music, so that the reader could use the same music in their own study if they so wished. Otherwise the study is potentially unreplicable – what constitutes 'sad' music? Does 'dance' music refer to modern popular music with no tune and an irritatingly monotonous beat or to the exquisite creations of someone like Johann Strauss?

8. We probably don't need to know that 'subjects were then debriefed and thanked for their participation in the study': this should occur as a matter of course.

9. We do not need to know the mechanics of how the experimenter analysed the results, such as which computer was used and which software.

Here's a better version of the same procedure section:

Participants were tested one at a time. Each participant completed the first questionnaire, which was administered by computer. After they had completed the first questionnaire, which took about 10 minutes, half of the participants listened to a tape of sad music (Samuel Barber's 'Adagio') for ten minutes, while the other half listened for the same amount of time to a tape of dance music (J. Strauss' 'The Blue Danube' waltz). The mood of all participants was then re-tested with a second questionnaire, administered under the same conditions as the first.

PART 12

WRITING A RESEARCH PROPOSAL

Crafting a Research Proposal

O'Leary, Z.

ROLE OF THE PROPOSAL

Let us read with method, and propose to ourselves an end to which our studies may point.

Edward Gibbon

When it comes to research, very few projects get off the ground without some sort of approval. It may be as straightforward as verbal approval from your lecturer, but it is equally likely to involve a formal approval process gained through an admissions board, an ethics committee or a funding body. And of course you may need approval from more than one of these.

This means you will need to develop a research proposal. Now many see the proposal as an opportunity to clarify thinking, bed down ideas and articulate thoughts in a way that will provide a study's outline as well as a blueprint for future action. And yes, a research proposal is all these things. *But* – and this is important – a proposal is not something you write for yourself. It is, without a doubt, a sales pitch. Your proposal is your opportunity, and sometimes your only opportunity, to sell your project and get your study off the ground.

So whether you are after admission to a university research programme, seeking ethics approval or looking for funding, the role of the proposal is to convince the powers that be that what you are proposing meets their requirements. Namely, that the research question, the proposed methods and the researcher all have merit. In other words, a committee will assess not only whether a project is useful and practicable, but also whether or not it thinks you as the proposer have the ability to carry the project out.

Now keep in mind that the weight given to various aspects of a proposal varies according to the type of committee you are addressing and the type of approval you are seeking.

For example, a proposal written to get into a PhD programme really needs to sell your potential as a researcher. A proposal written for an ethics committee needs to focus on the relationship between methods and participants. A proposal to a funding body, however, would need to have a strong emphasis on practicalities of method and the benefits of potential outcomes.

Demonstrating Merits of the Research Question

Essential to any successful proposal is your ability to sell the merits of your research question. Demonstrating merits will rely on two things. The first is that you are able to clearly and succinctly share your research topic and question (generally the work of the title, summary/abstract, aims/objectives, research question/hypothesis). The second thing is that you can demonstrate that your research question is worth answering; that is, your question is significant enough to warrant support either at the level of admission to a programme or via funding (generally the work of the introduction/background/rationale).

When it comes to a committee's assessment there are several possible scenarios:

1   The worth of the research question is self-evident (e.g. 'What are the most effective strategies for curbing binge drinking in under-18s?'), and you are able to argue the importance and significance of your question to the satisfaction of the assessors. So far so good.
2   The worth of the research question is, as above, self-evident, but you do a lousy job arguing the case and do not convince the assessors that you are capable of mounting what should be a straightforward argument. Major problem.
3   The worth of the research question is not self-evident (e.g. 'Do residents of the UK enjoy watching *Big Brother* more than US residents?'), but you are able to convincingly argue the case by citing evidence that attests to a real issue and what benefits there might be in conducting research into this area. If you can do this (particularly for this question), that's impressive!
4   The worth of the research question is, as above, not self-evident, and you do little to help your case. Your arguments are weak so assessors are left scratching their heads and quickly put your proposal into the reject pile.

The point here is that while the significance of the research question is important, what is actually being assessed is your ability to argue the significance. It is therefore crucial that your writing be tight, well structured and well referenced.

Demonstrating Merits of the Proposed Methods

Once your assessors are convinced that your research question has merit, their focus will turn to methods. Here they are looking for several things:

1   Are the proposed methods clearly articulated? If your assessors cannot make sense of what you are proposing, your proposal has little chance of getting off the ground.
2   Are the proposed methods logical? In other words, do they make sense and do the assessors believe your approach can lead to credible data (generally the work of the methods section)?
3   Has the candidate considered the study's boundaries as well as any potential hurdles to effective data collection and analysis? Established assessors know that all research is constrained; your job here is

to acknowledge this and show the credibility of your methods in spite of any limitations (generally the work of the methods and limitations/delimitations sections).

4   Are the proposed methods ethical? As discussed in Chapter 3, ethics are central to all research processes (and of course the main focus of an ethics proposal). Your proposal needs to show that the dignity and well-being of respondents, both mentally and physically, are fully protected (the work of the methods and ethical considerations sections).

5   Are the proposed methods practical/doable? It doesn't matter how logical and well considered your methods are if your assessors do not believe they can be implemented. You need to show that you have or can develop the necessary expertise; that you can gain access to required data; that your timeline is realistic; and that you will come within budget (the work of the methods section as well as, if required, the timeline and budget).

Basically, your methods section needs to convince readers that your approach is an efficient, effective and ethical way to get credible answers to your questions and that you are capable of pulling this off.

Demonstrating Merits of the Researcher

Let's assume the assessors are happy with both your questions and your methods. The final issue is whether they think you are the right person for the job. Do they trust that you can pull this off? Do they believe you have the necessary background knowledge, at least some familiarity with the literature and writing skills commensurate to the task?

Now that's a lot of questions, and it would be great if your assessors could get to know you and get a real feel for what you are capable of. But that's not likely to happen. In fact, there is a good chance your proposal will be reviewed by people you have never met. So what do they use to assess your potential? Simply your proposal. Assessors will judge your ability to engage with the literature through your proposal's short literature review. They will assess your ability to carry out methods, based on the knowledge you show and how well you argue your methodological case. And they will assess your potential to write by the quality of writing in your proposal. It therefore pays to give close attention to detail and make your proposal one of the tightest pieces of writing you have ever attempted.

ELEMENTS OF THE PROPOSAL

Proposal requirements vary according to the role of the proposal and by institution. But generally you will be required to include some combination of the following:

- *Title* – Go for clear, concise and unambiguous. Your title should indicate the specific content and context of the problem you wish to explore in as succinct a way as possible.
- *Summary/abstract* – Proposals often require a project summary, usually with a very tight word count. The trick here is to briefly state the what, why and how of your project in a way that sells it in just a few sentences – and trust me, this can take quite a few drafts to get right.
- *Aims/objectives* – Most proposals have one overarching aim that captures what you hope to achieve through your project. A set of objectives, which are more specific goals, supports that aim.

Aims and objectives are often articulated in bullet points and are generally 'to' statements: for example, to develop ...; to identify ...; to explore ...; to measure ...; to explain ...; to describe ...; to compare ...; to determine .... In management literature you are likely to come across 'SMART' objectives – SMART being an acronym for *s*pecific, *m*easurable, *a*chievable, *r*elevant/*r*esults-focused/*r*ealistic and *t*ime-bound. The goal is to keep objectives from being airy-fairy or waffly; clearly articulating what you want to achieve aids your ability to work towards your goal.

- *Research question/hypothesis* – As discussed in Chapter 4, a well-articulated research question (or hypothesis) should define your investigation, set boundaries, provide direction and act as a frame of reference for assessing your work. Any committee reviewing your proposal will turn to your question in order to get an overall sense of your project. Take time to make sure your question/hypothesis is as well defined and as clearly articulated as possible.
- *Introduction/background/rationale* – The main job of this section is to introduce your topic and convince readers that the problem you want to address is significant and worth exploring and even funding. It should give some context to the problem and lead your readers to the conclusion that, yes, research into this area is absolutely essential if we really want to work towards situation improvement or problem resolution.
- *Literature review* – A formal 'literature review' (discussed in more depth in Chapter 6) is a specific piece of argumentative writing that engages with relevant scientific and academic research in order to create a space for your project. The role of the literature review is to inform readers of developments in the field while establishing your own credibility as a 'player' capable of adding to this body of knowledge. This is a tough piece of writing with a very tight word count, so be prepared to run through a few drafts.
- *Theoretical perspectives* – This section asks you to situate your study in a conceptual or theoretical framework. The idea here is to articulate the theoretical perspective(s) that underpin and inform your ideas, and, in particular, to discuss how 'theory' relates to and/or directs your study.
- *Methods* – Some form of 'methods' will be required in all proposals. The goal here is to articulate your plan with enough clarity and detail to convince readers that your approach is practical and will lead to credible answers to the questions posed (see Chapter 7). Under the heading of methods you would generally articulate:

  - the approach/methodology – for example, if you are doing ethnography, action research or maybe a randomized controlled trial (see Chapters 8, 9 and 10);
  - how you will find respondents – this includes articulation of population and sample/sampling procedures (see Chapter 11);
  - data collection method(s) – for example, surveying, interviewing and document analysis (see Chapters 12 and 13);
  - methods of analysis – whether you will be doing statistical or thematic analysis and perhaps variants thereof (see Chapters 14 and 15).

- *Limitations/delimitations* – Limitations refer to conditions or design characteristics that may impact the generalizability and utility of findings, such as small sample size or restricted access to records. Keep in mind that most projects are limited by constraints such as time, resources, access or organizational issues. So it is much better to be open about 'flaws' than leave it to assessors who might be much more critical. Delimitations refer to a study's boundaries or how your study was deliberately narrowed by conscious exclusions and inclusions, e.g. limiting your study to children of a certain age only, or schools from one particular region. Now remember that your overarching goal here is to convince readers that your findings will be credible in spite of any limitations or delimitations. So the trick is to be open about your study's parameters without sounding defensive or apologetic. It is also worth articulating any strategies you will be using to ensure credibility despite limitations.

- *Ethical considerations* – Whenever you are working with human participants there will be ethical issues you need to consider (see Chapter 3). Now if this were an application for an ethics committee you would need to focus much of your proposal on ethical issues. But even if this were a proposal for admission, your readers would still need to be convinced that you have considered issues related to integrity in the production of knowledge and responsibility for the emotional, physical and intellectual well-being of your study participants.
- *Timeline* – This is simply superimposing a timeline on your methods, and is often done in a tabular or chart form. The committee reading your proposal will be looking to see that your plan is realistic and can conform to any overarching timeframes or deadlines.
- *Budget/funding* – This is a full account of costs and who will bear them. While not always a required section for ethics proposals or proposals for academic student research, it will certainly be a requirement for a funding body. Now it is definitely worth being realistic – it's easy to underestimate costs. Wages, software, hardware, equipment, travel, transcription, administrative support, etc. can add up quite quickly, and running short of money mid-project is not a good option. But also keep in mind that if you are tendering for a commissioned project, it's a good idea to get a ballpark figure of the funding body's budget. This will put you in a position to design your methods accordingly and hopefully make you competitive.
- *References* – This can refer to two things. The first is citing references in the same way as you would in any other type of academic/professional writing. Believe it or not, it's often missed. The second is that some committees want a list of, say, 10 or 15 primary references that will inform your work. This information can help a committee assess your knowledge and give its members a clearer indication of the direction your study may take.

 **I have a question!**

So should I put in all the elements you talk about, or should I just stick with the template they have given me?

The template, definitely the template. The list above will give you some idea of what you *might* expect, and it will give you some guidance about what goes into each of these sections, but it should not override what you are directly asked to provide. Stick with the template, and its word counts. As discussed below, when it comes to proposals, being pedantic is a good thing.

WRITING A WINNING PROPOSAL

In my experience, when a person or a committee has the power to make major decisions about someone else's work/future, they like to wield that power, and they often wield it in very defined ways. When it comes to assessing research proposals, this translates into committees wanting what they want, the way they want it, when they want it. If you are the person writing the proposal, this means you need to be just as pedantic and make sure you follow all guidelines, write purposively and be prepared to work through several drafts. Box 5.1, below, takes you through a real-world example.

Following Guidelines

So how many words can you get away with when the application says the title needs to be no more than 20 words or that the abstract must be less than 150 words? Well, it is certainly not uncommon for applicants to try to stretch these limits – but I would advise against it. Some assessors can judge harshly when they think applicants cannot follow simple directions. Are they being too harsh? Maybe. But you need to realize that assessors often see the application as a test of whether you will be able to meet requirements when you actually start working on your project. It may seem a bit parochial, but if you cannot follow guidelines in a short application, your assessors might just ask what that says about your potential to complete.

The best advice here is to follow guidelines as close to the letter as possible. This means:

- constructing your proposal according to, or as close as possible to, the recommended sections/headings;
- keeping to all word limits;
- being absolutely meticulous about spelling and grammar;
- strictly adhering to deadlines.

Writing Purposively

It is important to recognize that a proposal should never be sloppy, rushed or thrown together at the last minute. It needs to be a highly polished and well-constructed piece of writing. Remember: the clarity of your thoughts, the veracity of your arguments and the quality of your writing will be used to judge your potential as a researcher.

The following tips should help you craft a winning proposal:

- *See if you can get access to a few successful proposals* – If possible, seek out proposals that have gone through the committee you are applying to, or to as similar a committee as possible. The institution assessing your application may have proposals online. If they don't, then I would google 'research proposal example'. You can combine that with the level of study (PhD, undergraduate) and/or your broad area of study (business, sociology, policy). But keep in mind that not all proposals up on the Internet are good ones! You can also refer to the examples in the books cited at the end of the chapter.
- *Find a voice* – The convention here is third person; however, using 'I' to state what you will do is now more commonly accepted. Also remember to write in the future tense. A proposal is about what you will do, not what you are doing now, or have done in the past.
- *'Write tight'* – Your writing needs to be concise and succinct, direct and straightforward. Avoid rambling and/or trying to show off by using unnecessary jargon.
- *Write enough* – Somewhat paradoxical to the above, you also need to make sure you write a sufficient amount for assessors to make judgements.
- *Write for the 'non-expert'* – Your proposal needs to be 'stand-alone' and be comprehensible to someone potentially outside your field.
- *Do your homework* – The last thing you want in a short formal proposal is 'mistakes'. Get your facts right, make sure you don't have gaping holes in your literature, and make sure any references to theory and/or methods are accurate.
- *Don't over-quote* – Generally the writing expected is so tight that you probably won't have enough room for too many direct quotes. Keep the words and ideas yours, supported by the literature.

- *Don't let the deadline sneak up on you* – Plan on finishing early so that you have time to review and redraft. Remember: deadlines are often inflexible, and this is a case where you do not want to have to rush and let quality suffer.
- *As discussed below, be prepared to draft and redraft.*

Drafting and Redrafting

The best advice here is to leave yourself enough time to get feedback and redraft, if possible, more than once. Remember: even if your reader does not understand the details, the over-arching arguments should make sense to the non-expert – so don't hesitate to ask a peer, parent, friend, etc. if they can follow the proposal and if it makes sense. But if you have access, I certainly recommend seeking the advice of someone who has experience in research and research proposals.

Chapter 16 offers detailed checklists for working towards final drafts, but to summarize here, your final draft should: follow set criteria; be logical; make your point with convincing arguments; contain sufficient information; use a consistent voice; avoid being repetitious; be clear and fluent; avoid waffling; avoid paragraph-long sentences; limit acronyms and jargon; strictly adhere to word counts; have exemplary spelling and grammar; avoid all typos; and be well formatted.

BOX 5.1

Proposal Example

Here are a few sections from a longer funding proposal a colleague and I submitted some time back. My goal was to make sure my proposal met the funding body's specifications quite directly. Surprisingly, they did not ask for any background literature, so none was provided.

Project title: Great Speech: De-mystifying Powerful Presentations in the Public Sector

Project overview (150–250 words): We all know outstanding presentations and inspirational speakers when we hear them. We know because we are moved. We know because we want to tell others about it. We know because we feel inspired. Yet inspiring can be a difficult objective to reach. In spite of the abundance of advice, dry, tedious, uninspired presentations are often the norm – public sector presentations included. Change within the public sector, however, is generally reliant on cycles of advocacy; and such cycles often culminate in presentations. Reform is often reliant on influence, so the need to drive an idea and inspire an audience is undeniable. Knowing the best means for influencing an audience through an effective presentation is often challenging, particularly in an information age, where Google and Wikipedia now hold knowledge once the domain of experts.

The goal of this project is to offer recommendations for improved teaching and learning in the space of public sector presentations. Through an analysis of 70 of the best, most inspired presentations of the past decade, with particular reference to the public sector, this project will deconstruct the core elements that underlie truly inspirational presentations. The project will then analyse a cross-section of Trans-Tasman public sector presentations in a bid to identify gaps in best practice and thus training needs.

Project objectives (100–200 words): The overarching aim of this research project is to offer clear recommendations for improved teaching and learning in the space of public sector presentations.

The objectives of this project are:

- to identify the core elements that make for highly effective, highly motivational presentations;
- to identify core elements and contextual issues of particular relevance to the public sector;
- to create a qualitative matrix for easy identification of core elements;
- to assess the effectiveness of presentations in the Australia/New Zealand public sector and identify gaps in effective Australia/New Zealand public sector presentations in order to develop and enhance teaching and learning development within this space.

Project benefits (100–200 words): Within the public sector, rarely is there an initiative, project, programme or policy reform that does not need to be championed. Advocacy is essential and presentations that fail to motivate can end the run of a potentially good reform. This project, with its goal of improving teaching and learning in the arena of public sector presentation, offers benefits to three stakeholder groups.

The Trans-Tasman public sector will benefit via increased ability to influence the policy cycle. Improved presentations can lead to more engaged debate on key public administration issues, and contribute to continuing reform in the public sector.

The funding institution will benefit through the development of resources for future teaching and applied learning/knowledge activities. The aim is to enhance leadership in public sector communication training, while supporting the development of best practice in government.

Students will benefit from increased skills, confidence and levels of influence.

Methodology – What research method(s) will your project use (50–150 words)? The methodology will rely on a two-phase qualitative approach reliant on both online and 'face-to-face' data.

Phase One – Analysis of 70 highly motivational presentations of the past decade. *Population:* Online presentations (in English) deemed highly motivational by media/speaking experts. *Sampling Strategy:* Targeted sampling designed to include a wide range of speaker demographics – with a minimum of 35 public sector presentations. *Analysis:* Development of a best practice matrix through the use of narrative analysis, content analysis and semiotics.

Phase Two – Analysis of 30 public sector presentations in the Trans-Tasman region. *Population:* Presentations at ANZSOG's annual conference as well as online presentations. *Sampling Strategy:* Random, cross-sectional. *Analysis:* Gap analysis via assessment of presentations against the matrix developed in Phase One. All presentations used in this phase will be de-identified and aggregated without identifying data. The aim is to identify common gaps in practice rather than critique individual presentations.

What is the rationale for using this method/these methods for this project (100–150 words)? The methodology for this project does not neatly fall within one particular approach, or even one particular paradigm, but rather represents a question-driven approach that utilizes both traditional social science methods as well as project management tools. Specifically, this project relies on: sampling

(Continued)

(Continued)

strategies developed within the quantitative paradigm; data analysis methods such as content analysis, narrative analysis and semiotics drawn from the qualitative school; and a gap analysis more traditionally found in project management. Such mixed methodologies are often advocated for applied research not tied to paradigmatic traditions. The ability to draw from varied schools of thought as well as the ability to leverage the power of the Internet gives veracity to methods and allows for the development of context-driven methods. The particular methods to be employed in this project are those considered most likely to give credible results within the desired timeframe.

(Check the companion website ⚲ for more examples.)

OBSTACLES AND CHALLENGES

So if you do all of the above, surely you are bound to impress? It should all be smooth sailing, shouldn't it? Well, hopefully that will be the case. But there are a couple of sticky situations you may need to negotiate.

When Your Design Does Not Fit Proposal Requirements

If you have read this far, you know how important I think it is to give a committee what it asks for. But what if your research design simply does not fit in with the committee's requirements? Now this is likely to be the case in 'qualitative' research where terms like hypothesis, variables, validity and reliability may not be appropriate to your study, but may nonetheless be required 'sections' in your proposal.

Unfortunately, there can still be a bias towards the quantitative paradigm, the legacy of which can be reflected in proposal proformas and even committee expectations. If this is the case, I would suggest seeking the advice of someone who has worked with the committee to see how it tends to handle such dilemmas – each committee will have a different approach. If, however, you cannot get this insider information, or are told 'Just do the best you can', I would suggest remembering the bigger agenda of the proposal: that is, to demonstrate the merits of the research question, the merits of the proposed methods and the merits of the researcher. So, regardless of paradigm, you will need to show you are confident with the theoretical, conceptual and methodological landscape you are proposing to enter. To that end, write confidently, not aggressively nor apologetically. If the committee wants a hypothesis, yet it is not appropriate, you have the option of writing 'N/A' and giving justification for inappropriateness (see Chapter 4). If the committee wants you to list variables but your study is more exploratory, say so. If validity, reliability or generalizability is inappropriate, confidently talk about credibility indicators that are more appropriate (see Chapter 3). Any committee worth its weight will be able to spot a researcher who knows what he or she is talking about, even when it doesn't fit with the committee's expectations/jargon.

⚲ https://study.sagepub.com/oleary3e

When Your Design Is Emergent

Another major dilemma is when you are proposing a study that will have evolving methods that cannot be fully articulated at the time proposal applications are required. This is particularly problematic for ethics proposals, which are used to protect the dignity and welfare of the 'researched' as well as protect the researcher and home institution from legal liability. These proposals often demand a full account of methods, which often includes appending things like surveys and interview schedules.

Once again 'qualitative' researchers who wish to use conversational/unstructured data-gathering techniques that are not fully predetermined will face a dilemma. Those undertaking action research can also struggle as their methodological protocols are based on stakeholder collaboration in multiple cycles (see Chapter 9). In fact, there are many research projects (including quantitative studies) in which methods are conducted in multiple phases, with each phase determined by what has happened previously. For example, key informant interviews may be used to inform survey design, or survey results may determine the questions used in in-depth interviewing.

The best strategy here is to be open and knowledgeable about your approach. Show that your design is not haphazard or ill considered. Show that even if you cannot articulate all the specifics, your required flexibility is planned and you have a defined framework. Show the committee forethought. Offer, if possible, indicative questions. And finally, show that you can link your approach back to accepted methodological literature. If you can manage to make such arguments your chances of success will be greatly enhanced.

Of course, even if you are able to make such arguments there is the possibility that the committee will require further information. If this is the case, you can attempt to add more definition to your methodological plan. But if your overarching design makes this impossible and your committee is immovable, you will need (1) to see if it is possible to put in a supplementary application as your methods evolve; or (2) to talk to your supervisor about required methodological modifications.

When You Want to or Need to Change Direction/Method

Suppose you are all set to interview 15 CEOs, but, try as you might, you just can't get more than three to participate. Or suppose you plan on surveying 1,000 homeless people, but after much effort you only have 36 surveys returned. Or imagine that you have undertaken a much more comprehensive literature review than included in your proposal and you realize that the survey questions you originally proposed are way off target.

What do you do? Well, from a methodological standpoint, you improvise. You think about your question, talk to your supervisor and determine the most 'doable' way to get some credible data. But disappointingly, most students in this situation simply charge ahead and change their study protocols without further committee consultation. And while this may be the path of least resistance, it is not recommended. If your application represents a 'contract' to do a job for a funding body, for example, you need to inform it of shifts in your approach. Updating ethics applications is equally important. Not only do you want an outside committee to see that you will not threaten the dignity and well-being of the researched, but you also want to ensure that you have protected yourself and your institution from potential lawsuits.

I have a question!

What do I do if my proposal is knocked back?

That is a very difficult situation. One that often leads to an emotional response: anger, disappointment, feeling disheartened, etc. A knock back is never easy, but it is particularly difficult when it is one that sees you having to 'reassess' where you are going. I think the best advice here is to take a deep breath and regroup. Once you have worked through the emotional side, it will be time to get information; to figure out where you went wrong, and what you need to do now. Read the feedback carefully, seek clarification, talk to others. The more you know, the better position you will be in to avoid pitfalls in the future.

Chapter summary

- A research proposal offers an opportunity to clarify your thinking, bed down ideas and articulate thoughts in a way that will provide a blueprint for future action. It is also a means for 'selling' your project by articulating the merits of the research question and proposed methods.
- Proposals differ in requirements, but most will ask you to articulate some combination of the following: title; summary/abstract; aims/objectives; research question/hypothesis; introduction/ background/rationale; literature review; theoretical perspectives; methods; limitations/delimitations; ethical considerations; timelines; budget/funding; and references.
- Writing a winning proposal requires you to closely follow your institution's guidelines and to write purposively. This involves good planning, knowing your subject, finding a voice, writing tightly yet sufficiently, writing for the non-expert and being prepared to redraft.
- Obstacles you may face include proposals that do not fit a committee's requirements and proposals with emergent designs. In both cases, being knowledgeable, confident and open will enhance your chances of success.
- Even though it may seem painful, if you want or need to change direction/method it is a good idea to keep your approval body informed.

FURTHER READING

There are quite a few books that can help you navigate your way through proposal development, most of which give good examples. Have a look at:

Krathwohl, D. R. and Smith, N. L. (2005) *How to Prepare a Dissertation Proposal: Suggestions for Students in Education and the Social and Behavioral Sciences*. Syracuse, NY: Syracuse University Press.

A good step-by-step guide that covers qualitative, quantitative and mixed methodology. I like the way they have used student examples to ground recommendations.

Locke, L. F., Spirduso, W. W. and Silverman, S. J. (2013) *Proposals That Work: A Guide for Planning Dissertations and Grant Proposals*. London: Sage.
A comprehensive guide for students undertaking a thesis or applying for a grant – easy to follow and offers a range of relevant examples.

Ogden, T. E. and Goldberg, I. A. (eds) (2002) *Research Proposals: A Guide to Success*, 3rd Edition. New York: Academic Press.
While making reference to the National Institutes of Health proposal process, this book offers clear examples and several tips for enhancing proposals. It also covers the role of the Internet in the proposal process.

Punch, K. (2013) *Developing Effective Research Proposals*, 3rd Edition. London: Sage.
Terrific guide that covers both qualitative and quantitative research. It takes you through the basics of a proposal, how to go about writing one and what it should look like when complete.

Companion website materials available at
https://study.sagepub.com/oleary3e

PART
13

AVOIDING PLAGIARISM

How to Reference and Avoid Plagiarism

Burns, T. & Sinfield, S.

'Many students I met did not understand referencing straight away. They wanted to write something that showed what *they* thought, not what someone else had said. We didn't understand that using someone else's argument is a tool to support our own. Students are very keen for you to "see" them, to hear their voice. In many ways we are puppies wanting to please. We need to know why referencing does not detract from our own voice being heard.'

Introduction

> To my mind there is a solution. We need to chill out. First year students should be given time and freedom to learn. During this time plagiarism should not result in punishment for the student, but should be seen as a weakness of the teaching. Students should be free to make mistakes, and every university should be teaching referencing positively with the same rigour you would expect for any subject. After all, if it is that important, then we should be willing to give students time to learn how to reference correctly.

The English university system is based on research and independent learning: you are not *taught* your degree, but are expected *to read for it*: in the process you are acquiring ideas, arguments and evidence from other people. This may feel frustrating – you want to tell us what you think; but it is the academic way – you are expected to learn from and use the ideas of others. The reading that you do to prepare for your assignments helps you to engage with the thinkers in your subject – and it provides you with more ideas, knowledge-claims, arguments and evidence to develop your thinking and your writing. Yes, you are not 'empty', you do already have ideas and thoughts of your own, but you are supposed to do this reading to deepen your understanding and engage with the key people, ideas, concepts and theories that make up the subject you are studying.

Much is made in university of plagiarism and plagiarism offences – even first year students may be punished for not correctly showing their sources even if they stumble into plagiarism by accident. The aim of this chapter is to briefly discuss the what, why and how of referencing – and to explore some common reasons for accidental plagiarism – and how to avoid them. Meanwhile, keep this image in your mind: if studying is exploration, your *references are your maps* – recording your footsteps through the subject as it already exists.

TIP

When you read, record your sources immediately. Use online apps or index cards to keep a record of everything that you read – as you read it. Read Chapter 4 on how to survive academic reading.

Should I reference?

> Soon after the end of my first semester at university I heard about a course friend who had been accused of plagiarising. I never saw him again as he left soon after,

his confidence having been taken away by the experience. His 'crime' was simply that he had been educated in a different country that looks upon these things in a different way, and he had not fully understood the consequences of not properly referencing. To me though, the real crime was that education had lost a bright and inquisitive mind.

When you write, when you deliver a presentation, you must reference every time you 'refer to' or quote other people. This includes when you paraphrase their ideas – it even includes when you agree with them. For example, if you believe that we learn best when we learn actively, you might write:

Burns and Sinfield (2012) argue that we learn best when we learn actively and interactively.

Acknowledging a source does not weaken your own opinion – it demonstrates that you have ideas – and that you are prepared to do the reading to support your ideas. Your references show what a good student you are. Check out the flow chart in Figure 11.4.1.

TIPS

- Use Manchester University's Academic Phrasebank for examples of *how to write about your sources*. This link takes you straight to that section: www.phrase bank.manchester.ac.uk/referring-to-sources/.
- This easy to use resource from Nottingham shows how to reference: www.notting ham.ac.uk/nmp/sonet/rlos/studyskills/harvard/.
- If you want to follow this further, feel free to use both our Preventing Plagiarism and our Heroes & Villains websites:
  - http://learning.londonmet.ac.uk/TLTC/learnhigher/Plagiarism/ – if the link breaks, search online for LearnHigher + preventing plagiarism.
  - http://learning.londonmet.ac.uk/epacks/heroes-&-villains/ – if the link breaks, do an online search for Londonmet + Heroes and Villains.

Some reasons for plagiarising

Here are some reasons other students have given for plagiarising. As you read, think about how you could avoid making the mistakes that they made:

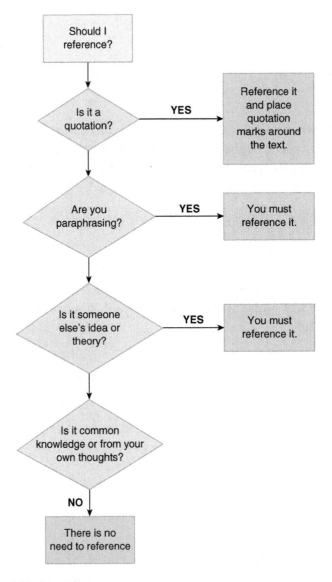

FIGURE 11.4.1   Should I reference?

> We were working on the assignment together. It was a group project – but we were supposed to write individual reports. Somehow, I couldn't write a different report to my mate – so I copied her version and handed it in as my own. I was punished for plagiarism and got zero for that module.

I had done the reading for that assignment ages ago. When I finally wrote it up, I couldn't remember what was my work and what I'd read. I really didn't know that this was plagiarism …

I found an essay on the web that was exactly on my topic. I did write my own introduction and conclusion – but it was still plagiarism. I'm lucky I didn't get suspended.

Well I did read that stuff – but it was what I was thinking anyway – so I didn't think
I had to give any sources. Turns out I was wrong …

I just thought I had to write a bibliography at the end. No! You have to mention
your reading as you write. You have to give the name and date of the source *where*
you refer to it – and you have to give the page number as well if you actually
quote it. Then you have to give the full author, date, title, town, publisher in the
bibliography as well.

I thought I was doing well. I put all the good quotes down on the page – and just
wrote little bits of essay around them. But that didn't work. You have to put it in
your own words – still giving a reference – and discuss it. The tutor said I'd just
handed in my notes rather than an essay. She said I was lucky not to be accused of
plagiarism – and to digest my reading first next time. It's quite hard getting this bit
right – harder than I thought it would be.

What advice would you have given these people? What advice would you give
yourself if you find yourself doing these things? One big piece of advice would be
to give yourself *time* to read, write and understand.

Further, these students did the reading but obviously did not record enough
source information. Develop the habit of recording your sources every time you
make notes. You save time – and you have your index cards to use again in future
assignments. Remember to record the page numbers too in case you want to quote.
Read Chapter 4 on how to survive academic reading.

A third issue seems to be about not understanding the referencing tradition in
academic life. You are supposed to note where ideas come from. Even when you
agree with what you are reading – or where the author agrees with you – you still
have to acknowledge that those ideas also emerged from somebody in your subject.
Your subject has not just been born – the ideas are out there – they exist in the history and practice of your subject. You are showing off what a good student you are
when you reference these ideas – when you acknowledge those debates – especially
when you do so correctly.

Summary

So, what do I think? Well, I feel all this stuff on plagiarism comes from the wrong
angle and I would turn this topic on its head. It isn't about plagiarism and in many

ways it isn't about referencing, it's about being honest and having integrity. It is also about community. I reference every single day through sharing on Facebook, re-blogging and re-tweeting on Twitter. I want to acknowledge (and associate myself) when someone has said something I agree with or with something that supports my argument or beliefs. It is positive – and in social media it is inclusive and empowering for the person you're sharing.

We hope that you can see that giving references reveals that you are an engaged, thinking, focused student – yes, you have opinions of your own – but you have also done the reading. When you write with reference to your reading, you are showing that you have understood your subject, you can use sources well and you are joining your academic community – you are joining the conversation.

In our experience, many students plagiarise because they do not understand the convention of referencing – or because they agree with what they are reading … Do not plagiarise by mistake! Give yourself time to read and digest information. Keep good records of your sources and make sure you understand how to reference correctly – both in your writing and in your bibliographies. Plagiarism is treated as a serious academic offence – even when you do it in ignorance or by mistake. If in doubt, explore our Heroes & Villains website – or use the Preventing Plagiarism tutorial (search online). In the learning resources section of that resource, there are small animations that show you how to reference correctly – from a range of sources. Look at these animations and make sure you see and understand what is going on.

Activity

Use your index cards

Every time you read, keep a record – author (date) *title*, place of publication: publisher:

Author(s):

Date:

Title:

Place published:

Publisher:

Key quotes (and page numbers):

Always note these essential details so you can cite them correctly in assignments – and in your bibliographies:

- Record details of your reading on your index cards. Note the information above on one side of the card.
- Experiment: you could note what essay you used the book for; you could note the chapter or paragraph headings – so that you have an outline of the book; you can note a couple of good quotes … The trick is to make this process as useful to you as possible.
- There is software, extensions to browsers and apps for phones, tablets and computers which can also be used.

PART 14

PREPARATION FOR RESEARCH METHODS

Editors' Note

Wheeler-Mundy, R. & Bedwell, S.

You've come to the end of your journey on Psychology and Research Skills. We hope you've enjoyed the module and have mastered the techniques needed to aid your success as a researcher.

By now you should have understanding of core academic abilities as varied as *critical litera-ture reviewing*, *writing in an appropriate academic style regardless of assignment type*, *ethical research design* and *APA style referencing*.

This isn't the end of your research journey. The information you've covered so far will provide the foundation for understanding and implementing statistical analysis. This will help you as you are introduced to research methods and statistics in the second half of level 4 and beyond – right up to your dissertation project.

The skills you've developed will also help you in your future careers, even if you don't go into research directly. You've been reflecting on how the knowledge and experience you have gained could contribute to your academic success and employability. Look back over the top-ics you've covered in this text: you now have expertise in *working effectively in groups*, *giving engaging presentations*, *critically analysing a variety of literature* and *constructing a persuasive argument*.

We wish you luck as you take your next steps as a developing researcher! The next chapter will help you prepare for level 4 *Introduction to Research Methods and Statistics*.

Your module leaders,

Rebecca Wheeler-Mundy and Stacey Bedwell

Why is my Evil Lecturer Forcing me to Learn Statistics?

Field, A.

1.1 What will this chapter tell me?

I was born on 21 June 1973. Like most people, I don't remember anything about the first few years of life and, like most children, I went through a phase of driving my dad mad by asking 'Why?' every five seconds. With every question, the word 'dad' got longer and whinier: 'Dad, why is the sky blue?', 'Daaad, why don't worms have legs?', 'Daaaaaaaaad, where do babies come from?' Eventually, my dad could take no more and whacked me around the face with a golf club.[1]

My torrent of questions reflected the natural curiosity that children have: we all begin our voyage through life as inquisitive little scientists. At the age of 3, I was at my friend Obe's party (just before he left England to return to Nigeria, much to my distress). It was a hot day, and there was an electric fan blowing cold air around the room. My 'curious little scientist' brain was working through what seemed like a particularly pressing question: 'What happens when you stick your finger in a fan?' The answer, as it turned out, was that it hurts – a lot.[2] At the age of 3, we intuitively know that to answer questions you need to collect data, even if it causes us pain.

My curiosity to explain the world never went away, which is why I'm a scientist. The fact that you're reading this book means that the inquisitive 3-year-old in you is alive and well and wants to answer new and exciting questions, too. To answer these questions you need 'science' and science has a **pilot fish** called 'statistics' that hides under its belly eating ectoparasites. That's why your evil lecturer is forcing you to learn statistics. Statistics is a bit like sticking your finger into a revolving fan blade: sometimes it's very painful, but it does give you answers to interesting questions. I'm going to try to convince you in this chapter that statistics are an important part of doing research. We will overview the whole research process, from why we conduct research in the first place, through how theories are generated, to why we need data to test these theories. If that doesn't convince you to read on then maybe the fact that we discover whether Coca-Cola kills sperm will. Or perhaps not.

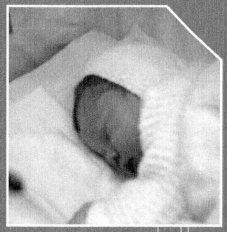

Figure 1.1 When I grow up, please don't let me be a statistics lecturer

1   He was practising in the garden when I unexpectedly wandered behind him at the exact moment he took a back swing. It's rare that a parent enjoys the sound of their child crying, but, on this day, it filled my dad with joy because my wailing was tangible evidence that he hadn't killed me, which he thought he might have done. Had he hit me with the club end rather than the shaft he probably would have. Fortunately (for me, but not for you), I survived, although some might argue that this incident explains the way my brain functions.

2   In the 1970s, fans didn't have helpful protective cages around them to prevent idiotic 3-year-olds sticking their fingers into the blades.

1.2 What the hell am I doing here? I don't belong here ▌▌▌▌

You're probably wondering why you have bought this book. Maybe you liked the pictures, maybe you fancied doing some weight training (it *is* heavy), or perhaps you needed to reach something in a high place (it *is* thick). The chances are, though, that given the choice of spending your hard-earned cash on a statistics book or something more entertaining (a nice novel, a trip to the cinema, etc.), you'd choose the latter. So, why have you bought the book (or downloaded an illegal PDF of it from someone who has way too much time on their hands if they're scanning 900 pages for fun)? It's likely that you obtained it because you're doing a course on statistics, or you're doing some research, and you need to know how to analyse data. It's possible that you didn't realize when you started your course or research that you'd have to know about statistics but now find yourself inexplicably wading, neck high, through the Victorian sewer that is data analysis. The reason why you're in the mess that you find yourself in is that you have a curious mind. You might have asked yourself questions like why people behave the way they do (psychology) or why behaviours differ across cultures (anthropology), how businesses maximize their profit (business), how the dinosaurs died (palaeontology), whether eating tomatoes protects you against cancer (medicine, biology), whether it is possible to build a quantum computer (physics, chemistry), whether the planet is hotter than it used to be and in what regions (geography, environmental studies). Whatever it is you're studying or researching, the reason why you're studying it is probably that you're interested in answering questions. Scientists are curious people, and you probably are too. However, it might not have occurred to you that to answer interesting questions, you need data and explanations for those data.

The answer to 'What the hell are you doing here?' is simple: to answer interesting questions you need data. One of the reasons why your evil statistics lecturer is forcing you to learn about numbers is that they are a form of data and are vital to the research process. Of course, there are forms of data other than numbers that can be used to test and generate theories. When numbers are involved, the research involves quantitative methods, but you can also generate and test theories by analysing language (such as conversations, magazine articles and media broadcasts). This involves qualitative methods and it is a topic for another book not written by me. People can get quite passionate about which of these methods is *best*, which is a bit silly because they are complementary, not competing, approaches and there are much more important issues in the world to get upset about. Having said that, all qualitative research is rubbish.[3]

1.3 The research process ▌▌▌▌

How do you go about answering an interesting question? The research process is broadly summarized in Figure 1.2. You begin with an observation that you want to understand, and this observation could be anecdotal (you've noticed that your cat watches birds when they're on TV but not when jellyfish are on)[4] or could be based on some data (you've got several cat owners to keep diaries of their cat's TV habits and noticed that lots of them watch birds). From your initial observation you consult relevant theories and generate explanations (hypotheses) for those observations, from which you can make predictions. To

How do I do research?

---

3 This is a joke. Like many of my jokes, there are people who won't find it remotely funny. Passions run high between qualitative and quantitative researchers, so its inclusion will likely result in me being hunted down, locked in a room and forced to do discourse analysis by a horde of rabid qualitative researchers.

4 In his younger days my cat actually did climb up and stare at the TV when birds were being shown.

Misconception Mutt 1.1
Hypotheses and predictions

One day the Misconception Mutt was returning from his class at Fetchington University. He'd been learning all about how to do research and it all made perfect sense. He was thinking about how much fun it would be to chase some balls later on, but decided that first he should go over what he'd learnt. He was muttering under his breath (as I like to imagine that dogs tend to do).

'A hypothesis is a prediction about what will happen,' he whispered to himself in his deep, wheezy, jowly dog voice. Before he could finish, the ground before him became viscous, as though the earth had transformed into liquid. A slightly irritated-looking ginger cat rose slowly from the puddle.

'Don't even think about chasing me,' he said in his whiny cat voice.

The mutt twitched as he inhibited the urge to chase the cat. 'Who are you?' he asked.

'I am the Correcting Cat,' said the cat wearily. 'I travel the ether trying to correct people's statistical misconceptions. It's very hard work, there are a lot of misconceptions about.'

The dog raised an eyebrow.

'For example,' continued the cat, 'you just said that a hypothesis is a prediction, but it is not.' The dog looked puzzled. 'A hypothesis is an explanatory statement about something, it is not itself observable. The prediction is not the hypothesis, it is something derived from the hypothesis that operationalizes it so that you can observe things that help you to determine the plausibility of the hypothesis.' With that, the cat descended back into the ground.

'What a smart-arse,' the dog thought to himself. 'I hope I never see him again.'

---

about 1%, so we'd be able to see whether the ratio of narcissistic personality disorder to not is higher at the audition than in the general population. If it is higher then our prediction is correct: a disproportionate number of people with narcissistic personality disorder turned up at the audition. Our prediction, in turn, tells us something about the hypothesis from which it derived.

This is tricky stuff, so let's look at another example. Imagine that, based on a different theory, we generated a different hypothesis. I mentioned earlier that people with narcissistic personality disorder tend to engage in conflict, so a different hypothesis is that producers of reality TV shows select people who have narcissistic personality disorder to be contestants because they believe that conflict makes good TV. As before, to test this hypothesis we need to bring it into the observable domain by generating a prediction from it. The prediction would be that (assuming no bias in the number of people with narcissistic personality disorder applying for the show) a disproportionate number of people with narcissistic personality disorder will be selected by producers to go on the show.

Jane Superbrain 1.1
When is a prediction not a prediction? ▯▮▮▮

A good theory should allow us to make statements about the state of the world. Statements about the world are good things: they allow us to make sense of our world, and to make decisions that affect our future. One current example is global warming. Being able to make a definitive statement that global warming is happening, and that it is caused by certain practices in society, allows us to change these practices and, hopefully, avert catastrophe. However, not all statements can be tested using science. Scientific statements are ones that can be verified with reference to empirical evidence, whereas non-scientific statements are ones that cannot be empirically tested. So, statements such as 'The Led Zeppelin reunion concert in London in 2007 was the best gig ever,'[6] 'Lindt chocolate is the best food' and 'This is the worst statistics book in the world' are all non-scientific; they cannot be proved or disproved. Scientific statements can be confirmed or disconfirmed empirically. 'Watching *Curb Your Enthusiasm* makes you happy,' 'Having sex increases levels of the neurotransmitter dopamine' and 'Velociraptors ate meat' are all things that can be tested empirically (provided you can quantify and measure the variables concerned). Non-scientific statements can sometimes be altered to become scientific statements, so 'The Beatles were the most influential band ever' is non-scientific (because it is probably impossible to quantify 'influence' in any meaningful way) but by changing the statement to 'The Beatles were the best-selling band ever,' it becomes testable (we can collect data about worldwide album sales and establish whether the Beatles have, in fact, sold more records than any other music artist). Karl Popper, the famous philosopher of science, believed that non-scientific statements were nonsense and had no place in science. Good theories and hypotheses should, therefore, produce predictions that are scientific statements.

Imagine we collected the data in Table 1.1, which shows how many people auditioning to be on a reality TV show had narcissistic personality disorder or not. In total, 7662 people turned up for the audition. Our first prediction (derived from our first hypothesis) was that the percentage of people with narcissistic personality disorder will be higher at the audition than the general level in the population. We can see in the table that of the 7662 people at the audition, 854 were diagnosed with the disorder; this is about 11% (854/7662 × 100), which is much higher than the 1% we'd expect in the general

Table 1.1 The number of people at the TV audition split by whether they had narcissistic personality disorder and whether they were selected as contestants by the producers

	No Disorder	Disorder	Total
Selected	3	9	12
Rejected	6805	845	7650
Total	6808	854	7662

6 It was pretty awesome actually.

population. Therefore, prediction 1 is correct, which in turn supports hypothesis 1. The second prediction was that the producers of reality TV have a bias towards choosing people with narcissistic personality disorder. If we look at the 12 contestants that they selected, 9 of them had the disorder (a massive 75%). If the producers did not have a bias we would have expected only 11% of the contestants to have the disorder (the same rate as was found when we considered everyone who turned up for the audition). The data are in line with prediction 2 which supports our second hypothesis. Therefore, my initial observation that contestants have personality disorders was verified by data, and then using theory I generated specific hypotheses that were operationalized by generating predictions that could be tested using data. Data are *very* important.

I would now be smugly sitting in my office with a contented grin on my face because my hypotheses were well supported by the data. Perhaps I would quit while I was ahead and retire. It's more likely, though, that having solved one great mystery, my excited mind would turn to another. I would lock myself in a room to watch more reality TV. I might wonder at why contestants with narcissistic personality disorder, despite their obvious character flaws, enter a situation that will put them under intense public scrutiny.[7] Days later, the door would open, and a stale odour would waft out like steam rising from the New York subway. Through this green cloud, my bearded face would emerge, my eyes squinting at the shards of light that cut into my pupils. Stumbling forwards, I would open my mouth to lay waste to my scientific rivals with my latest profound hypothesis: 'Contestants with narcissistic personality disorder believe that they will win'. I would croak before collapsing on the floor. The prediction from this hypothesis is that if I ask the contestants if they think that they will win, the people with a personality disorder will say 'yes'.

Let's imagine I tested my hypothesis by measuring contestants' expectations of success in the show, by asking them, 'Do you think you will win?' Let's say that 7 of 9 contestants with narcissistic personality disorder said that they thought that they would win, which confirms my hypothesis. At this point I might start to try to bring my hypotheses together into a theory of reality TV contestants that revolves around the idea that people with narcissistic personalities are drawn towards this kind of show because it fulfils their need for approval and they have unrealistic expectations about their likely success because they don't realize how unpleasant their personalities are to other people. In parallel, producers tend to select contestants with narcissistic tendencies because they tend to generate interpersonal conflict.

One part of my theory is untested, which is the bit about contestants with narcissistic personalities not realizing how others perceive their personality. I could operationalize this hypothesis through a prediction that if I ask these contestants whether their personalities were different from those of other people they would say 'no'. As before, I would collect more data and ask the contestants with narcissistic personality disorder whether they believed that their personalities were different from the norm. Imagine that all 9 of them said that they thought their personalities *were* different from the norm. These data contradict my hypothesis. This is known as **falsification**, which is the act of disproving a hypothesis or theory.

It's unlikely that we would be the only people interested in why individuals who go on reality TV have extreme personalities. Imagine that these other researchers discovered that: (1) people with narcissistic personality disorder think that they are more interesting than others; (2) they also think that they deserve success more than others; and (3) they also think that others like them because they have 'special' personalities.

This additional research is even worse news for my theory: if contestants didn't realize that they had a personality different from the norm, then you wouldn't expect them to think that they were more interesting than others, and you certainly wouldn't expect them to think that others will *like* their unusual personalities. In general, this means that this part of my theory sucks: it cannot explain all of the data,

---

7   One of the things I like about many reality TV shows in the UK is that the winners are very often nice people, and the odious people tend to get voted out quickly, which gives me faith that humanity favours the nice.

predictions from the theory are not supported by subsequent data, and it cannot explain other research findings. At this point I would start to feel intellectually inadequate and people would find me curled up on my desk in floods of tears, wailing and moaning about my failing career (no change there then).

At this point, a rival scientist, Fester Ingpant-Stain, appears on the scene adapting my theory to suggest that the problem is not that personality-disordered contestants don't realize that they have a personality disorder (or at least a personality that is unusual), but that they falsely believe that this special personality is perceived positively by other people. One prediction from this model is that if personality-disordered contestants are asked to evaluate what other people think of them, then they will overestimate other people's positive perceptions. You guessed it, Fester Ingpant-Stain collected yet more data. He asked each contestant to fill out a questionnaire evaluating all of the other contestants' personalities, and also to complete the questionnaire about themselves but answering from the perspective of each of their housemates. (So, for every contestant there is a measure of what they thought of every other contestant, and also a measure of what they believed every other contestant thought of them.) He found out that the contestants with personality disorders did overestimate their housemates' opinions of them; conversely, the contestants without personality disorders had relatively accurate impressions of what others thought of them. These data, irritating as it would be for me, support Fester Ingpant-Stain's theory more than mine: contestants with personality disorders do realize that they have unusual personalities but believe that these characteristics are ones that others would feel positive about. Fester Ingpant-Stain's theory is quite good: it explains the initial observations and brings together a range of research findings. The end result of this whole process (and my career) is that we should be able to make a general statement about the state of the world. In this case we could state 'Reality TV contestants who have personality disorders overestimate how much other people like their personality characteristics'.

SELF TEST
Based on what you have read in this section,
what qualities do you think a scientific theory should have?

1.6 Collecting data: measurement ▮▮▮▮

In looking at the process of generating theories and hypotheses, we have seen the importance of data in testing those hypotheses or deciding between competing theories. This section looks at data collection in more detail. First we'll look at measurement.

1.6.1 Independent and dependent variables ▮▮▮▮

To test hypotheses we need to measure variables. Variables are things that can change (or vary); they might vary between people (e.g., IQ, behaviour) or locations (e.g., unemployment) or even time (e.g., mood, profit, number of cancerous cells). Most hypotheses can be expressed in terms of two variables: a proposed cause and a proposed outcome. For example, if we take the scientific statement, 'Coca-Cola is an effective spermicide'[8] then the proposed cause is 'Coca-Cola' and the proposed effect is dead

---

8 Actually, there is a long-standing urban myth that a post-coital douche with the contents of a bottle of Coke is an effective contraceptive. Unbelievably, this hypothesis has been tested and Coke does affect sperm motility (movement), and some types of Coke are more effective than others – Diet Coke is best, apparently (Umpierre, Hill & Anderson, 1985). In case you decide to try this method out, I feel it worth mentioning that despite the effects on sperm motility a Coke douche is ineffective at preventing pregnancy.

Cramming Sam's Tips
Variables

When doing and reading research you're likely to encounter these terms:

- *Independent variable*: A variable thought to be the cause of some effect. This term is usually used in experimental research to describe a variable that the experimenter has manipulated.
- *Dependent variable*: A variable thought to be affected by changes in an independent variable. You can think of this variable as an outcome.
- *Predictor variable*: A variable thought to predict an outcome variable. This term is basically another way of saying 'independent variable'. (Although some people won't like me saying that; I think life would be easier if we talked only about predictors and outcomes.)
- *Outcome variable*: A variable thought to change as a function of changes in a predictor variable. For the sake of an easy life this term could be synonymous with 'dependent variable'.

sperm. Both the cause and the outcome are variables: for the cause we could vary the type of drink, and for the outcome, these drinks will kill different amounts of sperm. The key to testing scientific statements is to measure these two variables.

A variable that we think is a cause is known as an independent variable (because its value does not depend on any other variables). A variable that we think is an effect is called a dependent variable because the value of this variable depends on the cause (independent variable). These terms are very closely tied to experimental methods in which the cause is manipulated by the experimenter (as we will see in Section 1.7.2). However, researchers can't always manipulate variables (for example, if you wanted see whether smoking causes lung cancer you wouldn't lock a bunch of people in a room for 30 years and force them to smoke). Instead, they sometimes use correlational methods (Section 1.7), for which it doesn't make sense to talk of dependent and independent variables because all variables are essentially dependent variables. I prefer to use the terms predictor variable and outcome variable in place of dependent and independent variable. This is not a personal whimsy: in experimental work the cause (independent variable) is a predictor, and the effect (dependent variable) is an outcome, and in correlational work we can talk of one or more (predictor) variables predicting (statistically at least) one or more outcome variables.

1.6.2   Levels of measurement ▮▮▮▮

Variables can take on many different forms and levels of sophistication. The relationship between what is being measured and the numbers that represent what is being measured is known as the level of measurement. Broadly speaking, variables can be categorical or continuous, and can have different levels of measurement.

A categorical variable is made up of categories. A categorical variable that you should be familiar with already is your species (e.g., human, domestic cat, fruit bat, etc.). You are a human or a cat or a fruit bat: you cannot be a bit of a cat and a bit of a bat, and neither a batman nor (despite many fantasies to the contrary) a catwoman exist (not even one in a PVC suit). A categorical variable is one that names distinct entities. In its simplest form it names just two distinct types of things, for example male or female. This is known as a binary variable. Other examples of binary variables are being alive or dead, pregnant or not, and responding 'yes' or 'no' to a question. In all cases there are just two categories and an entity can be placed into only one of the two categories. When two things that are equivalent in some sense are given the same name (or number), but there are more than two possibilities, the variable is said to be a nominal variable.

It should be obvious that if the variable is made up of names it is pointless to do arithmetic on them (if you multiply a human by a cat, you do not get a hat). However, sometimes numbers are used to denote categories. For example, the numbers worn by players in a sports team. In rugby, the numbers on shirts denote specific field positions, so the number 10 is always worn by the fly-half[9] and the number 2 is always the hooker (the ugly-looking player at the front of the scrum). These numbers do not tell us anything other than what position the player plays. We could equally have shirts with FH and H instead of 10 and 2. A number 10 player is not necessarily better than a number 2 (most managers would not want their fly-half stuck in the front of the scrum!). It is equally daft to try to do arithmetic with nominal scales where the categories are denoted by numbers: the number 10 takes penalty kicks, and if the coach found that his number 10 was injured, he would not get his number 4 to give number 6

Jane Superbrain 1.2
Self-report data ▌▌▌▌

A lot of self-report data are ordinal. Imagine two judges on *The X Factor* were asked to rate Billie's singing on a 10-point scale. We might be confident that a judge who gives a rating of 10 found Billie more talented than one who gave a rating of 2, but can we be certain that the first judge found her five times more talented than the second? What if both judges gave a rating of 8; could we be sure that they found her equally talented? Probably not: their ratings will depend on their subjective feelings about what constitutes talent (the quality of singing? showmanship? dancing?). For these reasons, in any situation in which we ask people to rate something subjective (e.g., their preference for a product, their confidence about an answer, how much they have understood some medical instructions) we should probably regard these data as ordinal, although many scientists do not.

---

9 Unlike, for example, NFL football where a quarterback could wear any number from 1 to 19.

a piggy-back and then take the kick. The only way that nominal data can be used is to consider frequencies. For example, we could look at how frequently number 10s score compared to number 4s.

So far, the categorical variables we have considered have been unordered (e.g., different brands of Coke with which you're trying to kill sperm), but they can be ordered too (e.g., increasing concentrations of Coke with which you're trying to skill sperm). When categories are ordered, the variable is known as an ordinal variable. Ordinal data tell us not only that things have occurred, but also the order in which they occurred. However, these data tell us nothing about the differences between values. In TV shows like *The X Factor, American Idol*, and *The Voice*, hopeful singers compete to win a recording contract. They are hugely popular shows, which could (if you take a depressing view) reflect the fact that Western society values 'luck' more than hard work.[10] Imagine that the three winners of a particular *X Factor* series were Billie, Freema and Elizabeth. The names of the winners don't provide any information about where they came in the contest; however, labelling them according to their performance does – first, second and third. These categories are ordered. In using ordered categories we now know that the woman who won was better than the women who came second and third. We still know nothing about the differences between categories, though. We don't, for example, know how much better the winner was than the runners-up: Billie might have been an easy victor, getting many more votes than Freema and Elizabeth, or it might have been a very close contest that she won by only a single vote. Ordinal data, therefore, tell us more than nominal data (they tell us the order in which things happened) but they still do not tell us about the differences between points on a scale.

The next level of measurement moves us away from categorical variables and into continuous variables. A continuous variable is one that gives us a score for each person and can take on any value on the measurement scale that we are using. The first type of continuous variable that you might encounter is an interval variable. Interval data are considerably more useful than ordinal data, and most of the statistical tests in this book rely on having data measured at this level at least. To say that data are interval, we must be certain that equal intervals on the scale represent equal differences in the property being measured. For example, on www.ratemyprofessors.com, students are encouraged to rate their lecturers on several dimensions (some of the lecturers' rebuttals of their negative evaluations are worth a look). Each dimension (helpfulness, clarity, etc.) is evaluated using a 5-point scale. For this scale to be interval it must be the case that the difference between helpfulness ratings of 1 and 2 is the same as the difference between (say) 3 and 4, or 4 and 5. Similarly, the difference in helpfulness between ratings of 1 and 3 should be identical to the difference between ratings of 3 and 5. Variables like this that look interval (and are treated as interval) are often ordinal – see Jane Superbrain Box 1.2.

Ratio variables go a step further than interval data by requiring that in addition to the measurement scale meeting the requirements of an interval variable, the ratios of values along the scale should be meaningful. For this to be true, the scale must have a true and meaningful zero point. In our lecturer ratings this would mean that a lecturer rated as 4 would be twice as helpful as a lecturer rated with a 2 (who would, in turn, be twice as helpful as a lecturer rated as 1). The time to respond to something is a good example of a ratio variable. When we measure a reaction time, not only is it true that, say, the difference between 300 and 350 ms (a difference of 50 ms) is the same as the difference between 210 and 260 ms or between 422 and 472 ms, but it is also true that distances along the scale are divisible: a reaction time of 200 ms is twice as long as a reaction time of 100 ms and half as long as a reaction time of 400 ms. Time also has a meaningful zero point: 0 ms does mean a complete absence of time.

Continuous variables can be, well, continuous (obviously) but also discrete. This is quite a tricky distinction (Jane Superbrain Box 1.3). A truly continuous variable can be measured to any level of

---

10 I am in no way bitter about spending years learning musical instruments and trying to create original music, only to be beaten to musical fame and fortune by 15-year-olds who can sing, sort of.

precision, whereas a discrete variable can take on only certain values (usually whole numbers) on the scale. What does this actually mean? Well, our example of rating lecturers on a 5-point scale is an example of a discrete variable. The range of the scale is 1–5, but you can enter only values of 1, 2, 3, 4 or 5; you cannot enter a value of 4.32 or 2.18. Although a continuum exists underneath the scale (i.e., a rating of 3.24 makes sense), the actual values that the variable takes on are limited. A continuous variable would be something like age, which can be measured at an infinite level of precision (you could be 34 years, 7 months, 21 days, 10 hours, 55 minutes, 10 seconds, 100 milliseconds, 63 microseconds, 1 nanosecond old).

1.6.3 Measurement error ▌▐▐▐

It's one thing to measure variables, but it's another thing to measure them accurately. Ideally we want our measure to be calibrated such that values have the same meaning over time and across situations. Weight is one example: we would expect to weigh the same amount regardless of who weighs us, or where we take the measurement (assuming it's on Earth and not in an anti-gravity chamber). Sometimes, variables can be measured directly (profit, weight, height) but in other cases we are forced to use indirect measures such as self-report, questionnaires, and computerized tasks (to name a few).

It's been a while since I mentioned sperm, so let's go back to our Coke as a spermicide example. Imagine we took some Coke and some water and added them to two test tubes of sperm. After several minutes, we measured the motility (movement) of the sperm in the two samples and discovered no difference. A few years passed, as you might expect given that Coke and sperm rarely top scientists' research lists, before another scientist, Dr Jack Q. Late, replicated the study. Dr Late found that sperm motility

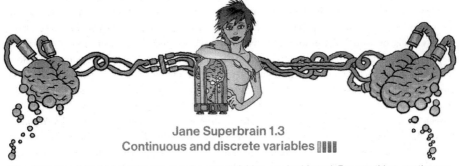

Jane Superbrain 1.3
Continuous and discrete variables ▌▐▐▐

The distinction between continuous and discrete variables can be blurred. For one thing, continuous variables can be measured in discrete terms; for example, when we measure age we rarely use nanoseconds but use years (or possibly years and months). In doing so we turn a continuous variable into a discrete one (the only acceptable values are years). Also, we often treat discrete variables as if they were continuous. For example, the number of boyfriends/girlfriends that you have had is a discrete variable (it will be, in all but the very weirdest cases, a whole number). However, you might read a magazine that says 'The average number of boyfriends that women in their 20s have has increased from 4.6 to 8.9'. This assumes that the variable is continuous, and of course these averages are meaningless: no one in their sample actually had 8.9 boyfriends.

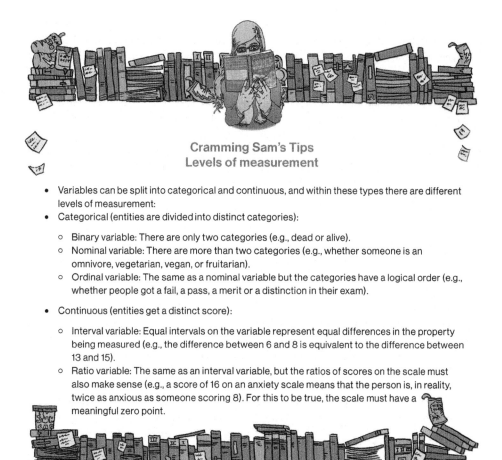

Cramming Sam's Tips
Levels of measurement

- Variables can be split into categorical and continuous, and within these types there are different levels of measurement:
- Categorical (entities are divided into distinct categories):

  ○ Binary variable: There are only two categories (e.g., dead or alive).
  ○ Nominal variable: There are more than two categories (e.g., whether someone is an omnivore, vegetarian, vegan, or fruitarian).
  ○ Ordinal variable: The same as a nominal variable but the categories have a logical order (e.g., whether people got a fail, a pass, a merit or a distinction in their exam).

- Continuous (entities get a distinct score):

  ○ Interval variable: Equal intervals on the variable represent equal differences in the property being measured (e.g., the difference between 6 and 8 is equivalent to the difference between 13 and 15).
  ○ Ratio variable: The same as an interval variable, but the ratios of scores on the scale must also make sense (e.g., a score of 16 on an anxiety scale means that the person is, in reality, twice as anxious as someone scoring 8). For this to be true, the scale must have a meaningful zero point.

was worse in the Coke sample. There are two measurement-related issues that could explain his success and our failure: (1) Dr Late might have used more Coke in the test tubes (sperm might need a critical mass of Coke before they are affected); (2) Dr Late measured the outcome (motility) differently than us.

The former point explains why chemists and physicists have devoted many hours to developing standard units of measurement. If you had reported that you'd used 100ml of Coke and 5ml of sperm, then Dr Late could have ensured that he had used the same amount – because millilitres are a standard unit of measurement – we would know that Dr Late used exactly the same amount of Coke that we used. Direct measurements such as the millilitre provide an objective standard: 100ml of a liquid is known to be twice as much as only 50ml.

The second reason for the difference in results between the studies could have been to do with how sperm motility was measured. Perhaps in our original study we measured motility using absorption spectrophotometry, whereas Dr Late used laser light-scattering techniques.[11] Perhaps his measure is more sensitive than ours.

---

11 In the course of writing this chapter I have discovered more than I think is healthy about the measurement of sperm motility.

There will often be a discrepancy between the numbers we use to represent the thing we're measuring and the actual value of the thing we're measuring (i.e., the value we would get if we could measure it directly). This discrepancy is known as measurement error. For example, imagine that you know as an absolute truth that you weigh 83kg. One day you step on the bathroom scales and they read 80kg. There is a difference of 3kg between your actual weight and the weight given by your measurement tool (the scales): this is a measurement error of 3kg. Although properly calibrated bathroom scales should produce only very small measurement errors (despite what we might want to believe when it says we have gained 3kg), self-report measures will produce larger measurement error because factors other than the one you're trying to measure will influence how people respond to our measures. For example, if you were completing a questionnaire that asked you whether you had stolen from a shop, would you admit it, or might you be tempted to conceal this fact?

1.6.4 Validity and reliability ▮▮▮

One way to try to ensure that measurement error is kept to a minimum is to determine properties of the measure that give us confidence that it is doing its job properly. The first property is validity, which is whether an instrument measures what it sets out to measure. The second is reliability, which is whether an instrument can be interpreted consistently across different situations.

Validity refers to whether an instrument measures what it was designed to measure (e.g., does your lecturer helpfulness rating scale actually measure lecturers' helpfulness?); a device for measuring sperm *motility* that actually measures sperm *count* is not valid. Things like reaction times and physiological measures are valid in the sense that a reaction time does, in fact, measure the time taken to react and skin conductance does measure the conductivity of your skin. However, if we're using these things to infer other things (e.g., using skin conductance to measure anxiety), then they will be valid only if there are no other factors other than the one we're interested in that can influence them.

Criterion validity is whether you can establish that an instrument measures what it claims to measure through comparison to objective criteria. In an ideal world, you assess this by relating scores on your measure to real-world observations. For example, we could take an objective measure of how helpful lecturers were and compare these observations to students' ratings of helpfulness on ratemyprofessor.com. When data are recorded simultaneously using the new instrument and existing criteria, then this is said to assess concurrent validity; when data from the new instrument are used to predict observations at a later point in time, this is said to assess predictive validity.

Assessing criterion validity (whether concurrently or predictively) is often impractical because objective criteria that can be measured easily may not exist. Also, with measuring attitudes, you might be interested in the person's perception of reality and not reality itself (you might not care whether a person *is* a psychopath but whether they *think* they are a psychopath). With self-report measures/questionnaires we can also assess the degree to which individual items represent the construct being measured, and cover the full range of the construct (content validity).

Validity is a necessary but not sufficient condition of a measure. A second consideration is reliability, which is the ability of the measure to produce the same results under the same conditions. To be valid the instrument must first be reliable. The easiest way to assess reliability is to test the same group of people twice: a reliable instrument will produce similar scores at both points in time (test–retest reliability). Sometimes, however, you will want to measure something that does vary over time (e.g., moods, blood-sugar levels, productivity). Statistical methods can also be used to determine reliability (we will discover these in Chapter 18).

SELF ✂ TEST

What is the difference between reliability and validity?

1.7 Collecting data: research design ▌▌▌

We've looked at the question of *what* to measure and discovered that to answer scientific questions we measure variables (which can be collections of numbers or words). We also saw that to get accurate answers we need accurate measures. We move on now to look at research design: *how* data are collected. If we simplify things quite a lot then there are two ways to test a hypothesis: either by observing what naturally happens, or by manipulating some aspect of the environment and observing the effect it has on the variable that interests us. In **correlational** or **cross-sectional research** we observe what naturally goes on in the world without directly interfering with it, whereas in **experimental research** we manipulate one variable to see its effect on another.

1.7.1 Correlational research methods ▌▌▌

In correlational research we observe natural events; we can do this by either taking a snapshot of many variables at a single point in time, or by measuring variables repeatedly at different time points (known as **longitudinal research**). For example, we might measure pollution levels in a stream and the numbers of certain types of fish living there; lifestyle variables (smoking, exercise, food intake) and disease (cancer, diabetes); workers' job satisfaction under different managers; or children's school performance across regions with different demographics. Correlational research provides a very natural view of the question we're researching because we're not influencing what happens and the measures of the variables should not be biased by the researcher being there (this is an important aspect of **ecological validity**).

What's the difference between experimental and correlational research?

At the risk of sounding like I'm absolutely obsessed with using Coke as a contraceptive (I'm not, but my discovery that people in the 1950s and 1960s actually tried this has, I admit, intrigued me), let's return to that example. If we wanted to answer the question, 'Is Coke an effective contraceptive?' we could administer questionnaires about sexual practices (quantity of sexual activity, use of contraceptives, use of fizzy drinks as contraceptives, pregnancy, etc.). By looking at these variables, we could see which variables correlate with pregnancy and, in particular, whether those reliant on Coca-Cola as a form of contraceptive were more likely to end up pregnant than those using other contraceptives, and less likely than those using no contraceptives at all. This is the only way to answer a question like this because we cannot manipulate any of these variables particularly easily. Even if we could, it would be totally unethical to insist on some people using Coke as a contraceptive (or indeed to do anything that would make a person likely to produce a child that they didn't intend to produce). However, there is a price to pay, which relates to causality: correlational research tells us nothing about the causal influence of variables.

1.7.2 Experimental research methods ▌▌▌

Most scientific questions imply a causal link between variables; we have seen already that dependent and independent variables are named such that a causal connection is implied (the dependent variable *depends* on the independent variable). Sometimes the causal link is very obvious in the research question, 'Does low self-esteem cause dating anxiety?' Sometimes the implication might be subtler; for example, in 'Is dating anxiety all in the mind?' the implication is that a person's mental outlook causes them to be anxious when dating. Even when the cause–effect relationship is not explicitly stated, most research questions can be broken down into a proposed cause (in this case, mental outlook) and a proposed outcome (dating anxiety). Both the cause and the outcome are variables: for the cause, some people will perceive themselves in a negative way (so it is something that varies); and, for the outcome, some people will get more anxious on dates than others (again, this is something that varies). The key to answering the research question is to uncover how the proposed cause and the proposed outcome relate to each other; are the people who have a low opinion of themselves the same people who are more anxious on dates?

David Hume, an influential philosopher, defined a cause as 'An object precedent and contiguous to another, and where all the objects resembling the former are placed in like relations of precedency and contiguity to those objects that resemble the latter' (1739–40/1965).[12] This definition implies that (1) the cause needs to precede the effect, and (2) causality is equated to high degrees of correlation between contiguous events. In our dating example, to infer that low self-esteem caused dating anxiety, it would be sufficient to find that low self-esteem and feeling anxious when on a date co-occur, and that the low self-esteem emerged before the dating anxiety did.

In correlational research variables are often measured simultaneously. The first problem with doing this is that it provides no information about the contiguity between different variables: we might find from a questionnaire study that people with low self-esteem also have dating anxiety but we wouldn't know whether it was the low self-esteem or the dating anxiety that came first. Longitudinal research addresses this issue to some extent, but there is still a problem with Hume's idea that causality can be inferred from corroborating evidence, which is that it doesn't distinguish between what you might call an 'accidental' conjunction and a causal one. For example, it could be that both low self-esteem and dating anxiety are caused by a third variable (e.g., poor social skills which might make you feel generally worthless but also puts pressure on you in dating situations). Therefore, low self-esteem and dating anxiety do always co-occur (meeting Hume's definition of cause) but only because poor social skills causes them both.

This example illustrates an important limitation of correlational research: the tertium quid ('A third person or thing of indeterminate character'). For example, a correlation has been found between having breast implants and suicide (Koot, Peeters, Granath, Grobbee, & Nyren, 2003). However, it is unlikely that having breast implants causes you to commit suicide – presumably, there is an external factor (or factors) that causes both; for example, low self-esteem might lead you to have breast implants and also attempt suicide. These extraneous factors are sometimes called confounding variables, or confounds for short.

The shortcomings of Hume's definition led John Stuart Mill (1865) to suggest that, in addition to a correlation between events, all other explanations of the cause–effect relationship must be ruled out. To rule out confounding variables, Mill proposed that an effect should be present when the cause is present and that when the cause is absent, the effect should be absent also. In other words, the only way to infer causality is through comparing two controlled situations: one in which the cause is present and one in which the cause is absent. This is what *experimental methods* strive to do: to provide a comparison of situations (usually called *treatments* or *conditions*) in which the proposed cause is present or absent.

---

12 As you might imagine, his view was a lot more complicated than this definition alone, but let's not get sucked down that particular wormhole.

As a simple case, we might want to look at the effect of feedback style on learning about statistics. I might, therefore, randomly split[13] some students into three different groups, in which I change my style of feedback in the seminars on my course:

- Group 1 (supportive feedback): During seminars I congratulate all students in this group on their hard work and success. Even when they get things wrong, I am supportive and say things like 'that was very nearly the right answer, you're coming along really well' and then give them a nice piece of chocolate.
- Group 2 (harsh feedback): This group receives seminars in which I give relentless verbal abuse to all of the students even when they give the correct answer. I demean their contributions and am patronizing and dismissive of everything they say. I tell students that they are stupid, worthless, and shouldn't be doing the course at all. In other words, this group receives normal university-style seminars.☺
- Group 3 (no feedback): Students are not praised or punished, instead I give them no feedback at all.

The thing that I have manipulated is the feedback style (supportive, harsh or none). As we have seen, this variable is known as the independent variable and, in this situation, it is said to have three levels, because it has been manipulated in three ways (i.e., the feedback style has been split into three types: supportive, harsh and none). The outcome in which I am interested is statistical ability, and I could measure this variable using a statistics exam after the last seminar. As we have seen, this outcome variable is the dependent variable because we assume that these scores will depend upon the type of teaching method used (the independent variable). The critical thing here is the inclusion of the 'no feedback' group because this is a group in which our proposed cause (feedback) is absent, and we can compare the outcome in this group against the two situations in which the proposed cause is present. If the statistics scores are different in each of the feedback groups (cause is present) compared to the group for which no feedback was given (cause is absent), then this difference can be attributed to the type of feedback used. In other words, the style of feedback used caused a difference in statistics scores (Jane Superbrain Box 1.4).

1.7.3 Two methods of data collection ▮▮▮

When we use an experiment to collect data, there are two ways to manipulate the independent variable. The first is to test different entities. This method is the one described above, in which different groups of entities take part in each experimental condition (a between-groups, between-subjects, or independent design). An alternative is to manipulate the independent variable using the same entities. In our motivation example, this means that we give a group of students supportive feedback for a few weeks and test their statistical abilities and then give this same group harsh feedback for a few weeks before testing them again and, then, finally, give them no feedback and test them for a third time (a within-subject or repeated-measures design). As you will discover, the way in which the data are collected determines the type of test that is used to analyse the data.

1.7.4 Two types of variation ▮▮▮

Imagine we were trying to see whether you could train chimpanzees to run the economy. In one training phase they are sat in front of a chimp-friendly computer and press buttons that change various parameters of the economy; once these parameters have been changed a figure appears on the screen

---

13 This random assignment of students is important, but we'll get to that later.

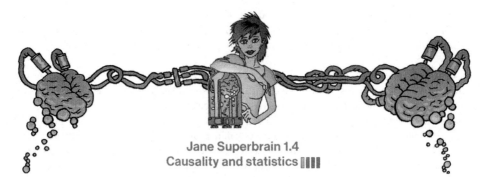

Jane Superbrain 1.4
Causality and statistics ▌▌▌▌

People sometimes get confused and think that certain statistical procedures allow causal inferences and others don't. This isn't true, it's the fact that in experiments we manipulate the causal variable systematically to see its effect on an outcome (the effect). In correlational research we observe the co-occurrence of variables; we do not manipulate the causal variable first and then measure the effect, therefore we cannot compare the effect when the causal variable is present against when it is absent. In short, we cannot say which variable causes a change in the other; we can merely say that the variables co-occur in a certain way. The reason why some people think that certain statistical tests allow causal inferences is that, historically, certain tests (e.g., ANOVA, *t*-tests, etc.) have been used to analyse experimental research, whereas others (e.g., regression, correlation) have been used to analyse correlational research (Cronbach, 1957). As you'll discover, these statistical procedures are, in fact, mathematically identical.

indicating the economic growth resulting from those parameters. Now, chimps can't read (I don't think) so this feedback is meaningless. A second training phase is the same, except that if the economic growth is good, they get a banana (if growth is bad they do not) – this feedback is valuable to the average chimp. This is a repeated-measures design with two conditions: the same chimps participate in condition 1 *and* in condition 2.

Let's take a step back and think what would happen if we did *not* introduce an experimental manipulation (i.e., there were no bananas in the second training phase, so condition 1 and condition 2 were identical). If there is no experimental manipulation then we expect a chimp's behaviour to be similar in both conditions. We expect this because external factors such as age, sex, IQ, motivation and arousal will be the same for both conditions (a chimp's biological sex, etc. will not change from when they are tested in condition 1 to when they are tested in condition 2). If the performance measure (i.e., our test of how well they run the economy) is reliable, and the variable or characteristic that we are measuring (in this case ability to run an economy) remains stable over time, then a participant's performance in condition 1 should be very highly related to their performance in condition 2. So, chimps who score highly in condition 1 will also score highly in condition 2, and those who have low scores for condition 1 will have low scores in condition 2. However, performance won't be *identical*, there will be small differences in performance created by unknown factors. This variation in performance is known as **unsystematic variation**.

If we introduce an experimental manipulation (i.e., provide bananas as feedback in one of the training sessions), then we do something different to participants in condition 1 than in condition 2. So, the *only* difference between conditions 1 and 2 is the manipulation that the experimenter has made (in this case that the chimps get bananas as a positive reward in one condition but not in the other).[14] Therefore, any differences between the means of the two conditions are probably due to the experimental manipulation. So, if the chimps perform better in one training phase than in the other, this *has* to be due to the fact that bananas were used to provide feedback in one training phase but not in the other. Differences in performance created by a specific experimental manipulation are known as systematic variation.

Now let's think about what happens when we use different participants – an independent design. In this design we still have two conditions, but this time different participants participate in each condition. Going back to our example, one group of chimps receives training without feedback, whereas a second group of different chimps does receive feedback on their performance via bananas.[15] Imagine again that we didn't have an experimental manipulation. If we did nothing to the groups, then we would still find some variation in behaviour between the groups because they contain different chimps who will vary in their ability, motivation, propensity to get distracted from running the economy by throwing their own faeces, and other factors. In short, the factors that were held constant in the repeated-measures design are free to vary in the independent design. So, the unsystematic variation will be bigger than for a repeated-measures design. As before, if we introduce a manipulation (i.e., bananas), then we will see additional variation created by this manipulation. As such, in both the repeated-measures design and the independent design there are always two sources of variation:

- Systematic variation: This variation is due to the experimenter doing something in one condition but not in the other condition.
- Unsystematic variation: This variation results from random factors that exist between the experimental conditions (such as natural differences in ability, the time of day, etc.).

Statistical tests are often based on the idea of estimating how much variation there is in performance, and comparing how much of this is systematic to how much is unsystematic.

In a repeated-measures design, differences between two conditions can be caused by only two things: (1) the manipulation that was carried out on the participants, or (2) any other factor that might affect the way in which an entity performs from one time to the next. The latter factor is likely to be fairly minor compared to the influence of the experimental manipulation. In an independent design, differences between the two conditions can also be caused by one of two things: (1) the manipulation that was carried out on the participants, or (2) differences between the characteristics of the entities allocated to each of the groups. The latter factor, in this instance, is likely to create considerable random variation both within each condition and between them. When we look at the effect of our experimental manipulation, it is always against a background of 'noise' created by random, uncontrollable differences between our conditions. In a repeated-measures design this 'noise' is kept to a minimum and so the effect of the experiment is more likely to show up. This means that, other things being equal, repeated-measures designs are more sensitive to detect effects than independent designs.

1.7.5 Randomization ▌▌▌▌

In both repeated-measures and independent designs it is important to try to keep the unsystematic variation to a minimum. By keeping the unsystematic variation as small as possible we get a more

---

14 Actually, this isn't the only difference because, by condition 2, they have had some practice (in condition 1) at running the economy; however, we will see shortly that these practice effects are easily eradicated.

15 Obviously I mean that they receive a banana as a reward for their correct response and not that the bananas develop little banana mouths that sing them a little congratulatory song.

sensitive measure of the experimental manipulation. Generally, scientists use the randomization of entities to treatment conditions to achieve this goal. Many statistical tests work by identifying the systematic and unsystematic sources of variation and then comparing them. This comparison allows us to see whether the experiment has generated considerably more variation than we would have got had we just tested participants without the experimental manipulation. Randomization is important because it eliminates most other sources of systematic variation, which allows us to be sure that any systematic variation between experimental conditions is due to the manipulation of the independent variable. We can use randomization in two different ways depending on whether we have an independent or repeated-measures design.

Let's look at a repeated-measures design first. I mentioned earlier (in a footnote) that when the same entities participate in more than one experimental condition they are naive during the first experimental condition but they come to the second experimental condition with prior experience of what is expected of them. At the very least they will be familiar with the dependent measure (e.g., the task they're performing). The two most important sources of systematic variation in this type of design are:

- Practice effects: Participants may perform differently in the second condition because of familiarity with the experimental situation and/or the measures being used.
- Boredom effects: Participants may perform differently in the second condition because they are tired or bored from having completed the first condition.

Although these effects are impossible to eliminate completely, we can ensure that they produce no systematic variation between our conditions by counterbalancing the order in which a person participates in a condition.

We can use randomization to determine in which order the conditions are completed. That is, we randomly determine whether a participant completes condition 1 before condition 2, or condition 2 before condition 1. Let's look at the teaching method example and imagine that there were just two conditions: no feedback and harsh feedback. If the same participants were used in all conditions, then we might find that statistical ability was higher after the harsh feedback. However, if every student experienced the harsh feedback after the no feedback seminars then they would enter the harsh condition already having a better knowledge of statistics than when they began the no feedback condition. So, the apparent improvement after harsh feedback would not be due to the experimental manipulation (i.e., it's not because harsh feedback works), but because participants had attended more statistics seminars by the end of the harsh feedback condition compared to the no feedback one. We can use randomization to ensure that the number of statistics seminars does not introduce a systematic bias by randomly assigning students to have the harsh feedback seminars first or the no feedback seminars first.

If we turn our attention to independent designs, a similar argument can be applied. We know that participants in different experimental conditions will differ in many respects (their IQ, attention span, etc.). Although we know that these confounding variables contribute to the variation between conditions, we need to make sure that these variables contribute to the unsystematic variation and *not* to the systematic variation. A good example is the effects of alcohol on behaviour. You might give one group of people 5 pints of beer, and keep a second group sober, and then count how many times you can persuade them to do a fish impersonation. The effect that alcohol has varies because people differ in their tolerance: teetotal people can become drunk on a small amount, while alcoholics need to consume vast quantities before the alcohol affects them. If you allocated a bunch of hardened drinkers to the condition that consumed alcohol, and teetotal people to the no alcohol condition, then you might find that alcohol doesn't increase the number of fish impersonations you get. However, this finding could be because (1) alcohol does not make people engage in frivolous activities, or (2) the hardened drinkers were unaffected by the dose of alcohol. You have no way to dissociate these explanations because the groups varied not just on dose of alcohol but also on their tolerance of alcohol (the systematic variation created by their past experience with alcohol cannot be separated from the effect of the experimental manipulation). The best way to reduce this eventuality is to randomly allocate participants to conditions: by doing so you minimize the risk that groups differ on variables other than the one you want to manipulate.

SELF TEST

Why is randomization important?

1.8 Analysing data ‖‖

The final stage of the research process is to analyse the data you have collected. When the data are quantitative this involves both looking at your data graphically (Chapter 5) to see what the general trends in the data are, and also fitting statistical models to the data (all other chapters). Given that the rest of the book is dedicated to this process, we'll begin here by looking at a few fairly basic ways to look at and summarize the data you have collected.

1.8.1 Frequency distributions ‖‖

Once you've collected some data a very useful thing to do is to plot a graph of how many times each score occurs. This is known as a **frequency distribution**, or **histogram**, which is a graph plotting values of observations on the horizontal axis, with a bar showing how many times each value occurred in the data set. Frequency distributions can be very useful for assessing properties of the distribution of scores. We will find out how to create these types of charts in Chapter 5.

What is frequency distribution and when is it normal?

Frequency distributions come in many different shapes and sizes. It is quite important, therefore, to have some general descriptions for common types of distributions. In an ideal world our data would be distributed symmetrically around the centre of all scores. As such, if we drew a vertical line through the centre of the distribution then it should look the same on both sides. This is known as a **normal distribution** and is characterized by the bell-shaped curve with which you might already be familiar. This shape implies that the majority of scores lie around the centre of the distribution (so the largest bars on the histogram are around the central value). Also, as we get further away from the centre, the bars get smaller, implying that as scores start to deviate from the centre their frequency is decreasing. As we move still further away from the centre our scores become very infrequent (the bars are very short). Many naturally occurring things have this shape of distribution. For example, most men in the UK are around 175 cm tall;[16] some are a bit taller or shorter, but most cluster around this value. There will be very few men who are really tall (i.e., above 205 cm) or really short (i.e., under 145 cm). An example of a normal distribution is shown in Figure 1.3.

---

16 I am exactly 180 cm tall. In my home country this makes me smugly above average. However, I often visit the Netherlands, where the average male height is 185 cm (a little over 6ft, and a massive 10 cm higher than the UK), and where I feel like a bit of a dwarf.

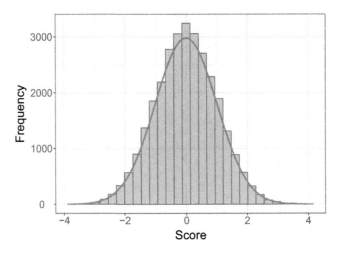

Figure 1.3   A 'normal' distribution (the curve shows the idealized shape)

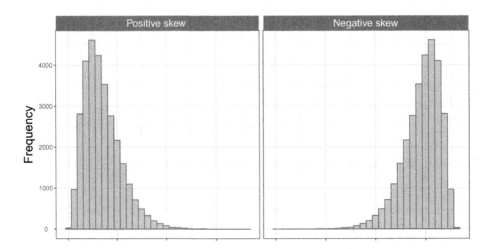

Figure 1.4   A positively (left) and negatively (right) skewed distribution

There are two main ways in which a distribution can deviate from normal: (1) lack of symmetry (called skew) and (2) pointyness (called kurtosis). Skewed distributions are not symmetrical and instead the most frequent scores (the tall bars on the graph) are clustered at one end of the scale. So, the typical pattern is a cluster of frequent scores at one end of the scale and the frequency of scores tailing off towards the other end of the scale. A skewed distribution can be either *positively skewed* (the frequent scores are clustered at the lower end and the tail points towards the higher or more positive scores) or *negatively skewed* (the frequent scores are clustered at the higher end and the tail points towards the lower or more negative scores). Figure 1.4 shows examples of these distributions.

Distributions also vary in their kurtosis. Kurtosis, despite sounding like some kind of exotic disease, refers to the degree to which scores cluster at the ends of the distribution (known as the *tails*)

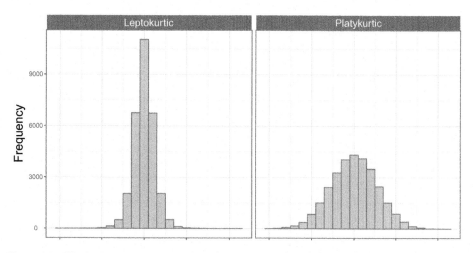

Figure 1.5 Distributions with positive kurtosis (leptokurtic, left) and negative kurtosis (platykurtic, right)

and this tends to express itself in how pointy a distribution is (but there are other factors that can affect how pointy the distribution looks – see Jane Superbrain Box 1.5). A distribution with *positive kurtosis* has many scores in the tails (a so-called heavy-tailed distribution) and is pointy. This is known as a leptokurtic distribution. In contrast, a distribution with *negative kurtosis* is relatively thin in the tails (has light tails) and tends to be flatter than normal. This distribution is called platykurtic. Ideally, we want our data to be normally distributed (i.e., not too skewed, and not too many or too few scores at the extremes). For everything there is to know about kurtosis, read DeCarlo (1997).

In a normal distribution the values of skew and kurtosis are 0 (i.e., the tails of the distribution are as they should be).[17] If a distribution has values of skew or kurtosis above or below 0 then this indicates a deviation from normal: Figure 1.5 shows distributions with kurtosis values of +2.6 (left panel) and −0.09 (right panel).

1.8.2 The mode ▌▐▐▐

We can calculate where the centre of a frequency distribution lies (known as the central tendency) using three measures commonly used: the mean, the mode and the median. Other methods exist, but these three are the ones you're most likely to come across.

The mode is the score that occurs most frequently in the data set. This is easy to spot in a frequency distribution because it will be the tallest bar. To calculate the mode, place the data in ascending order (to make life easier), count how many times each score occurs, and the score that occurs the most is the mode. One problem with the mode is that it can take on several values. For example, Figure 1.6 shows an example of a distribution with two modes (there are two bars that are the highest), which is said to be bimodal, and three modes (data sets with more than two modes are multimodal). Also, if the frequencies of certain scores are very similar, then the mode can be influenced by only a small number of cases.

---

17 Sometimes no kurtosis is expressed as 3 rather than 0, but SPSS uses 0 to denote no excess kurtosis.

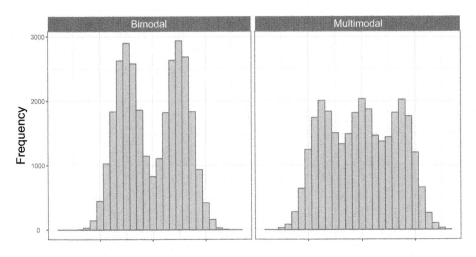

Figure 1.6   Examples of bimodal (left) and multimodal (right) distributions

1.8.3   The median ▌▌▌

Another way to quantify the centre of a distribution is to look for the middle
score when scores are ranked in order of magnitude. This is called the median.
Imagine we looked at the number of friends that 11 users of the social networking website Facebook had. Figure 1.7 shows the number of friends for
each of the 11 users: 57, 40, 103, 234, 93, 53, 116, 98, 108, 121, 22.

To calculate the median, we first arrange these scores into ascending order:
22, 40, 53, 57, 93, 98, 103, 108, 116, 121, 234.

Next, we find the position of the middle score by counting the number of
scores we have collected (n), adding 1 to this value, and then dividing by 2. With 11 scores, this gives
us $(n + 1)/2 = (11 + 1)/2 = 12/2 = 6$. Then, we find the score that is positioned at the location we have
just calculated. So, in this example, we find the sixth score (see Figure 1.7).

This process works very nicely when we have an odd number of scores (as in this example), but
when we have an even number of scores there won't be a middle value. Let's imagine that we decided
that because the highest score was so big (almost twice as large as the next biggest number), we would

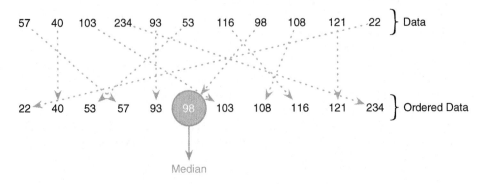

Figure 1.7   The median is simply the middle score when you order the data

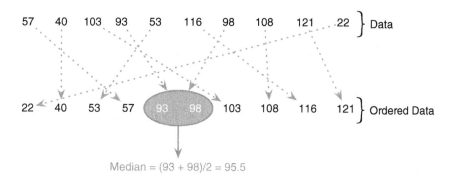

Figure 1.8 When the data contain an even number of scores, the median is the average of the middle two values

ignore it. (For one thing, this person is far too popular and we hate them.) We have only 10 scores now. Figure 1.8 shows this situation. As before, we rank-order these scores: 22, 40, 53, 57, 93, 98, 103, 108, 116, 121. We then calculate the position of the middle score, but this time it is $(n + 1)/2 = 11/2 = 5.5$, which means that the median is halfway between the fifth and sixth scores. To get the median we add these two scores and divide by 2. In this example, the fifth score in the ordered list was 93 and the sixth score was 98. We add these together ($93 + 98 = 191$) and then divide this value by 2 ($191/2 = 95.5$). The median number of friends was, therefore, 95.5.

The median is relatively unaffected by extreme scores at either end of the distribution: the median changed only from 98 to 95.5 when we removed the extreme score of 234. The median is also relatively unaffected by skewed distributions and can be used with ordinal, interval and ratio data (it cannot, however, be used with nominal data because these data have no numerical order).

1.8.4 The mean ▌▌▌▌

The **mean** is the measure of central tendency that you are most likely to have heard of because it is the average score, and the media love an average score.[18] To calculate the mean we add up all of the scores and then divide by the total number of scores we have. We can write this in equation form as:

$$\overline{X} = \frac{\sum_{i=1}^{n} x_i}{n} \qquad (1.1)$$

This equation may look complicated, but the top half simply means 'add up all of the scores' (the x_i means 'the score of a particular person'; we could replace the letter i with each person's name instead), and the bottom bit means, 'divide this total by the number of scores you have got (n)'. Let's calculate the mean for the Facebook data. First, we add up all the scores:

$$\sum_{i=1}^{n} x_i = 22 + 40 + 53 + 57 + 93 + 98 + 103 + 108 + 116 + 121 + 234 = 1045 \qquad (1.2)$$

---

18 I wrote this on 15 February, and to prove my point, the BBC website ran a headline today about how PayPal estimates that Britons will spend an average of £71.25 each on Valentine's Day gifts. However, uSwitch.com said that the average spend would be only £22.69. Always remember that the media is full of lies and contradictions.

We then divide by the number of scores (in this case 11) as in equation (1.3):

$$\overline{X} = \frac{\sum_{i=1}^{n} x_i}{n} = \frac{1045}{11} = 95 \qquad\qquad (1.3)$$

The mean is 95 friends, which is not a value we observed in our actual data. In this sense the mean is a statistical model – more on this in the next chapter.

Compute the mean but excluding the score of 234.

If you calculate the mean without our most popular person (i.e., excluding the value 234), the mean drops to 81.1 friends. This reduction illustrates one disadvantage of the mean: it can be influenced by extreme scores. In this case, the person with 234 friends on Facebook increased the mean by about 14 friends; compare this difference with that of the median. Remember that the median changed very little – from 98 to 95.5 – when we excluded the score of 234, which illustrates how the median is typically less affected by extreme scores than the mean. While we're being negative about the mean, it is also affected by skewed distributions and can be used only with interval or ratio data.

If the mean is so lousy then why do we use it so often? One very important reason is that it uses every score (the mode and median ignore most of the scores in a data set). Also, the mean tends to be stable in different samples (more on that later too).

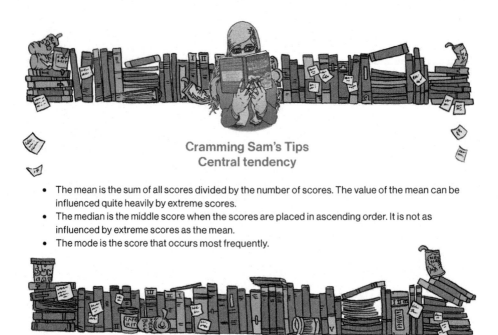

Cramming Sam's Tips
Central tendency

- The mean is the sum of all scores divided by the number of scores. The value of the mean can be influenced quite heavily by extreme scores.
- The median is the middle score when the scores are placed in ascending order. It is not as influenced by extreme scores as the mean.
- The mode is the score that occurs most frequently.

1.8.5 The dispersion in a distribution ▊▊▊

It can also be interesting to quantify the spread, or dispersion, of scores. The easiest way to look at dispersion is to take the largest score and subtract from it the smallest score. This is known as the range of scores. For our Facebook data we saw that if we order the scores we get 22, 40, 53, 57, 93, 98, 103, 108, 116, 121, 234. The highest score is 234 and the lowest is 22; therefore, the range is 234–22 = 212. One problem with the range is that because it uses only the highest and lowest score, it is affected dramatically by extreme scores.

SELF TEST

Compute the range but excluding the score of 234.

If you have done the self-test task you'll see that without the extreme score the range drops from 212 to 99 – less than half the size.

One way around this problem is to calculate the range but excluding values at the extremes of the distribution. One convention is to cut off the top and bottom 25% of scores and calculate the range of the middle 50% of scores – known as the interquartile range. Let's do this with the Facebook data. First, we need to calculate what are called quartiles. Quartiles are the three values that split the sorted data into four equal parts. First we calculate the median, which is also called the *second quartile*, which splits our data into two equal parts. We already know that the median for these data is 98. The lower quartile is the median of the lower half of the data and the upper quartile is the median of the upper half of the data. As a rule of thumb the median is not included in the two halves when they are split (this is convenient if you have an odd number of values), but you can include it (although which half you put it in is another question). Figure 1.9 shows how we would calculate these values for the Facebook data. Like the median, if each half of the data had an even number of values in it, then the upper and lower quartiles would be the average of two values in the data set (therefore, the upper and lower quartile need not be values that actually appear in the data). Once we have worked out the values of the quartiles, we can calculate the interquartile range, which is the difference between the upper and lower quartile. For the Facebook data this value would be 116–53 = 63. The advantage of the interquartile range is that it isn't affected by extreme scores at either end of the distribution. However, the problem with it is that you lose a lot of data (half of it, in fact).

It's worth noting here that quartiles are special cases of things called quantiles. Quantiles are values that split a data set into equal portions. Quartiles are quantiles that split the data into four

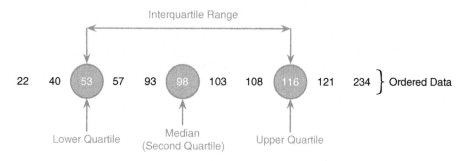

Figure 1.9 Calculating quartiles and the interquartile range

equal parts, but there are other quantiles such as percentiles (points that split the data into 100 equal parts), noniles (points that split the data into nine equal parts) and so on.

Twenty-one heavy smokers were put on a treadmill at the fastest setting. The time in seconds was measured until they fell off from exhaustion:

18, 16, 18, 24, 23, 22, 22, 23, 26, 29, 32, 34, 34, 36, 36, 43, 42, 49, 46, 46, 57

Compute the mode, median, mean, upper and lower quartiles, range and interquartile range.

If we want to use all the data rather than half of it, we can calculate the spread of scores by looking at how different each score is from the centre of the distribution. If we use the mean as a measure of the centre of a distribution, then we can calculate the difference between each score and the mean, which is known as the deviance (Eq. 1.4):

$$\text{deviance} = x_i - \bar{x} \tag{1.4}$$

If we want to know the total deviance then we could add up the deviances for each data point. In equation form, this would be:

$$\text{total deviance} = \sum_{i=1}^{n} (x_i - \bar{x}) \tag{1.5}$$

The sigma symbol (Σ) means 'add up all of what comes after', and the 'what comes after' in this case is the deviances. So, this equation simply means 'add up all of the deviances'.

Let's try this with the Facebook data. Table 1.2 shows the number of friends for each person in the Facebook data, the mean, and the difference between the two. Note that because the mean is at the centre of the distribution, some of the deviations are positive (scores greater than the mean) and some are negative (scores smaller than the mean). Consequently, when we add the scores up, the total is zero. Therefore, the 'total spread' is nothing. This conclusion is as silly as a tapeworm thinking they can have a coffee with the Queen of England if they don a bowler hat and pretend to be human. Everyone knows that the Queen drinks tea.

To overcome this problem, we could ignore the minus signs when we add the deviations up. There's nothing wrong with doing this, but people tend to square the deviations, which has a similar effect (because a negative number multiplied by another negative number becomes positive). The final column of Table 1.2 shows these squared deviances. We can add these squared deviances up to get the sum of squared errors, SS (often just called the *sum of squares*); unless your scores are all exactly the same, the resulting value will be bigger than zero, indicating that there is some deviance from the mean. As an equation, we would write: equation (1.6), in which the sigma symbol means 'add up all of the things that follow' and what follows is the squared deviances (or *squared errors* as they're more commonly known):

$$\text{sum of squared errors (SS)} = \sum_{i=1}^{n} (x_i - \bar{x})^2 \tag{1.6}$$

We can use the sum of squares as an indicator of the total dispersion, or total deviance of scores from the mean. The problem with using the total is that its size will depend on how many scores we have in

Table 1.2   Table showing the deviations of each score from the mean

Number of Friends (x_i)	Mean ($\bar{x}$)	Deviance ($x_i - \bar{x}$)	Deviance squared ($x_i - \bar{x}$)²
22	95	−73	5329
40	95	−55	3025
53	95	−42	1764
57	95	−38	1444
93	95	−2	4
98	95	3	9
103	95	8	64
108	95	13	169
116	95	21	441
121	95	26	676
234	95	139	19321
		$\sum_{i=1}^{n} x_i - \bar{x} = 0$	$\sum_{i=1}^{n}(x_i - \bar{x})^2 = 32246$

the data. The sum of squares for the Facebook data is 32,246, but if we added another 11 scores that value would increase (other things being equal, it will more or less double in size). The total dispersion is a bit of a nuisance then because we can't compare it across samples that differ in size. Therefore, it can be useful to work not with the *total* dispersion, but the *average* dispersion, which is also known as the variance. We have seen that an average is the total of scores divided by the number of scores, therefore, the variance is simply the sum of squares divided by the number of observations (N). Actually, we normally divide the SS by the number of observations minus 1 as in equation (1.7) (the reason why is explained in the next chapter and Jane Superbrain Box 2.2):

$$\text{variance}\left(s^2\right) = \frac{\text{SS}}{N-1} = \frac{\sum_{i=1}^{n}(x_i - \bar{x})^2}{N-1} = \frac{32,246}{10} = 3224.6 \tag{1.7}$$

As we have seen, the variance is the average error between the mean and the observations made. There is one problem with the variance as a measure: it gives us a measure in units squared (because we squared each error in the calculation). In our example we would have to say that the average error in our data was 3224.6 friends squared. It makes very little sense to talk about friends squared, so we often take the square root of the variance (which ensures that the measure of average error is in the same units as the original measure). This measure is known as the standard deviation and is the square root of the variance (Eq. 1.8).

$$s = \sqrt{\frac{\sum_{i=1}^{n}(x_i - \bar{x})^2}{N-1}}$$
$$= \sqrt{3224.6} \tag{1.8}$$
$$= 56.79$$

The sum of squares, variance and standard deviation are all measures of the dispersion or spread of data around the mean. A small standard deviation (relative to the value of the mean itself)

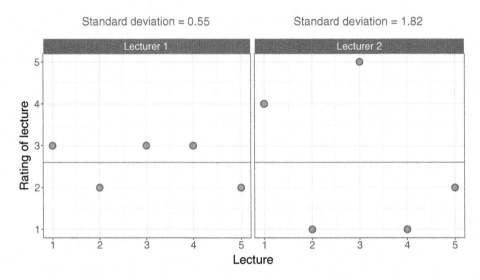

Figure 1.10 Graphs illustrating data that have the same mean but different standard deviations

indicates that the data points are close to the mean. A large standard deviation (relative to the mean) indicates that the data points are distant from the mean. A standard deviation of 0 would mean that all the scores were the same. Figure 1.10 shows the overall ratings (on a 5-point scale) of two lecturers after each of five different lectures. Both lecturers had an average rating of 2.6 out of 5 across the lectures. However, the first lecturer had a standard deviation of 0.55 (relatively small compared to the mean). It should be clear from the left-hand graph that ratings for this lecturer were consistently close to the mean rating. There was a small fluctuation, but generally her lectures did not vary in popularity. Put another way, the scores are not spread too widely around the mean. The second lecturer, however, had a standard deviation of 1.82 (relatively high compared to the mean). The ratings for this second lecturer are more spread from the mean than the first: for some lectures she received very high ratings, and for others her ratings were appalling.

1.8.6 Using a frequency distribution to go beyond the data ▌▌▌▌

Another way to think about frequency distributions is not in terms of how often scores actually occurred, but how likely it is that a score would occur (i.e., probability). The word 'probability' causes most people's brains to overheat (myself included) so it seems fitting that we use an example about throwing buckets of ice over our heads. Internet memes tend to follow the shape of a normal distribution, which we discussed a while back. A good example of this is the ice bucket challenge from 2014. You can check Wikipedia for the full story, but it all started (arguably) with golfer Chris Kennedy tipping a bucket of iced water on his head to raise awareness of the disease amyotrophic lateral sclerosis (ALS, also known as Lou Gehrig's disease).[19] The idea is that you are challenged and have 24 hours to post a video of you having a bucket of iced water poured over your head; in

19 Chris Kennedy did not invent the challenge, but he's believed to be the first to link it to ALS. There are earlier reports of people doing things with ice-cold water in the name of charity, but I'm focusing on the ALS challenge because it is the one that spread as a meme.

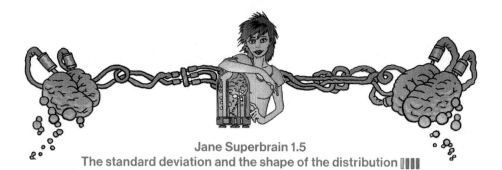

Jane Superbrain 1.5
The standard deviation and the shape of the distribution ▮▮▮

The variance and standard deviation tell us about the shape of the distribution of scores. If the mean represents the data well then most of the scores will cluster close to the mean and the resulting standard deviation is small relative to the mean. When the mean is a worse representation of the data, the scores cluster more widely around the mean and the standard deviation is larger. Figure 1.11 shows two distributions that have the same mean (50) but different standard deviations. One has a large standard deviation relative to the mean ($SD = 25$) and this results in a flatter distribution that is more spread out, whereas the other has a small standard deviation relative to the mean ($SD = 15$) resulting in a pointier distribution in which scores close to the mean are very frequent but scores further from the mean become increasingly infrequent. The message is that as the standard deviation gets larger, the distribution gets fatter. This can make distributions look platykurtic or leptokurtic when, in fact, they are not.

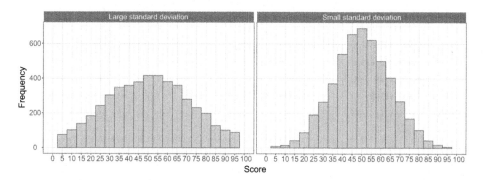

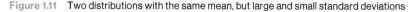

Figure 1.11 Two distributions with the same mean, but large and small standard deviations

this video you also challenge at least three other people. If you fail to complete the challenge your forfeit is to donate to charity (in this case, ALS). In reality many people completed the challenge *and* made donations.

The ice bucket challenge is a good example of a meme: it ended up generating something like 2.4 million videos on Facebook and 2.3 million on YouTube. I mentioned that memes often follow a normal distribution, and Figure 1.12 shows this: the insert shows the 'interest' score from Google Trends

Labcoat Leni's Real Research 1.1

Is Friday 13th unlucky? ▌▌▌▌

Scanlon, T. J., et al. (1993). *British Medical Journal, 307,* 1584–1586.

Many of us are superstitious, and a common superstition is that Friday the 13th is unlucky. Most of us don't literally think that someone in a hockey mask is going to kill us, but some people are wary. Scanlon and colleagues, in a tongue-in-cheek study (Scanlon, Luben, Scanlon, & Singleton, 1993), looked at accident statistics at hospitals in the south-west Thames region of the UK. They took statistics both for Friday the 13th and Friday the 6th (the week before) in different months in 1989, 1990, 1991 and 1992. They looked at both emergency admissions of accidents and poisoning, and also transport accidents.

Date	Accidents and Poisoning		Traffic Accidents	
	Friday 6th	Friday 13th	Friday 6th	Friday 13th
October 1989	4	7	9	13
July 1990	6	6	6	12
September 1991	1	5	11	14
December 1991	9	5	11	10
March 1992	9	7	3	4
November 1992	1	6	5	12

Calculate the mean, median, standard deviation and interquartile range for each type of accident and on each date. Answers are on the companion website.

for the phrase 'ice bucket challenge' from August to September 2014.[20] The 'interest' score that Google calculates is a bit hard to unpick but essentially reflects the relative number of times that the term 'ice bucket challenge' was searched for on Google. It's not the total number of searches, but the relative number. In a sense it shows the trend of the popularity of searching for 'ice bucket challenge'. Compare the line with the perfect normal distribution in Figure 1.3 – they look fairly similar, don't

---

20 You can generate the insert graph for yourself by going to Google Trends, entering the search term 'ice bucket challenge' and restricting the dates shown to August 2014 to September 2014.

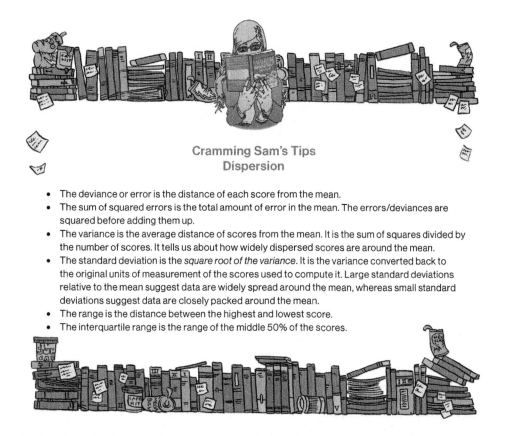

Cramming Sam's Tips
Dispersion

- The deviance or error is the distance of each score from the mean.
- The sum of squared errors is the total amount of error in the mean. The errors/deviances are squared before adding them up.
- The variance is the average distance of scores from the mean. It is the sum of squares divided by the number of scores. It tells us about how widely dispersed scores are around the mean.
- The standard deviation is the *square root of the variance*. It is the variance converted back to the original units of measurement of the scores used to compute it. Large standard deviations relative to the mean suggest data are widely spread around the mean, whereas small standard deviations suggest data are closely packed around the mean.
- The range is the distance between the highest and lowest score.
- The interquartile range is the range of the middle 50% of the scores.

they? Once it got going (about 2–3 weeks after the first video) it went viral, and popularity increased rapidly, reaching a peak at around 21 August (about 36 days after Chris Kennedy got the ball rolling). After this peak, popularity rapidly declines as people tire of the meme.

The main histogram in Figure 1.12 shows the same pattern but reflects something a bit more tangible than 'interest scores'. It shows the number of videos posted on YouTube relating to the ice bucket challenge on each day after Chris Kennedy's initial challenge. There were 2323 thousand in total (2.32 million) during the period shown. In a sense it shows approximately how many people took up the challenge each day.[21] You can see that nothing much happened for 20 days, and early on relatively few people took up the challenge. By about 30 days after the initial challenge things are hotting up (well, cooling down, really) as the number of videos rapidly accelerated from 29,000 on day 30 to 196,000 on day 35. At day 36, the challenge hits its peak (204,000 videos posted) after which the decline sets in as it becomes 'yesterday's news'. By day 50 it's only the type of people like me, and statistics lectures more generally, who don't check Facebook for 50 days, who suddenly become aware of the meme and want to get in on the action to prove how down with the kids we are. It's too late, though: people at that end of the curve are uncool, and the trendsetters who posted videos on day 25 call us lame and look at us dismissively. It's OK though, because we can plot sick histograms like the one in Figure 1.12; take that, hipster scum!

---

21 Very very approximately indeed. I have converted the Google interest data into videos posted on YouTube by using the fact that I know that 2.33 million videos were posted during this period and by making the (not unreasonable) assumption that behaviour on YouTube will have followed the same pattern over time as the Google interest score for the challenge.

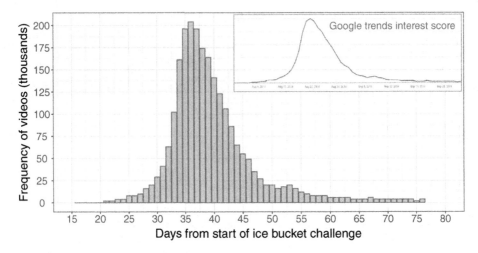

Figure 1.12   Frequency distribution showing the number of ice bucket challenge videos on YouTube by day since the first video (the insert shows the actual Google Trends data on which this example is based)

I digress. We can think of frequency distributions in terms of probability. To explain this, imagine that someone asked you 'How likely is it that a person posted an ice bucket video after 60 days?' What would your answer be? Remember that the height of the bars on the histogram reflects how many videos were posted. Therefore, if you looked at the frequency distribution before answering the question you might respond 'not very likely' because the bars are very short after 60 days (i.e., relatively few videos were posted). What if someone asked you 'How likely is it that a video was posted 35 days after the challenge started?' Using the histogram, you might say 'It's relatively likely' because the bar is very high on day 35 (so quite a few videos were posted). Your inquisitive friend is on a roll and asks 'How likely is it that someone posted a video 35 to 40 days after the challenge started?' The bars representing these days are shaded orange in Figure 1.12. The question about the likelihood of a video being posted 35–40 days into the challenge is really asking 'How big is the orange area of Figure 1.12 compared to the total size of all bars?' We can find out the size of the dark blue region by adding the values of the bars (196 + 204 + 196 + 174 + 164 + 141 = 1075); therefore, the orange area represents 1075 thousand videos. The total size of all bars is the total number of videos posted (i.e., 2323 thousand). If the orange area represents 1075 thousand videos, and the total area represents 2323 thousand videos, then if we compare the orange area to the total area we get 1075/2323 = 0.46. This proportion can be converted to a percentage by multiplying by 100, which gives us 46%. Therefore, our answer might be 'It's quite likely that someone posted a video 35–40 days into the challenge because 46% of all videos were posted during those 6 days'. A very important point here is that the size of the bars relates directly to the probability of an event occurring.

Hopefully these illustrations show that we can use the frequencies of different scores, and the area of a frequency distribution, to estimate the probability that a particular score will occur. A probability value can range from 0 (there's no chance whatsoever of the event happening) to 1 (the event will definitely happen). So, for example, when I talk to my publishers I tell them there's a probability of 1 that I will have completed the revisions to this book by July. However, when I talk to anyone else, I might, more realistically, tell them that there's a 0.10 probability of me finishing the revisions on time (or put another way, a 10% chance, or 1 in 10 chance that I'll complete the book in time). In reality, the

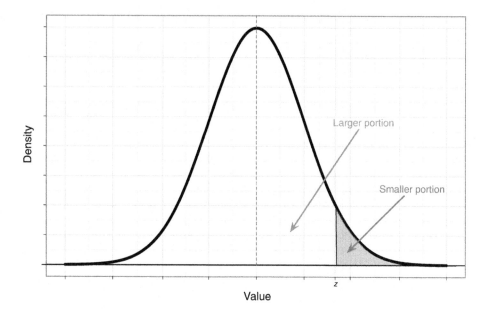

Figure 1.13   The normal probability distribution

probability of my meeting the deadline is 0 (not a chance in hell). If probabilities don't make sense to you then you're not alone; just ignore the decimal point and think of them as percentages instead (i.e., a 0.10 probability that something will happen is a 10% chance that something will happen) or read the chapter on probability in my other excellent textbook (Field, 2016).

I've talked in vague terms about how frequency distributions can be used to get a rough idea of the probability of a score occurring. However, we can be precise. For any distribution of scores we could, in theory, calculate the probability of obtaining a score of a certain size – it would be incredibly tedious and complex to do it, but we could. To spare our sanity, statisticians have identified several common distributions. For each one they have worked out mathematical formulae (known as **probability density functions, PDF**) that specify idealized versions of these distributions. We could draw such a function by plotting the value of the variable (x) against the probability of it occurring (y).[22] The resulting curve is known as a **probability distribution**; for a normal distribution (Section 1.8.1) it would look like Figure 1.13, which has the characteristic bell shape that we saw already in Figure 1.3.

A probability distribution is just like a histogram except that the lumps and bumps have been smoothed out so that we see a nice smooth curve. However, like a frequency distribution, the area under this curve tells us something about the probability of a value occurring. Just like we did in our ice bucket example, we could use the area under the curve between two values to tell us how likely it is that a score fell within a particular range. For example, the blue shaded region in Figure 1.13 corresponds to the probability of a score being z or greater. The normal distribution is not the only distribution that has been precisely specified by people with enormous brains. There are many distributions that have characteristic shapes and have been specified with a probability density function. We'll encounter some of these other distributions throughout the book, for example the t-distribution, chi-square (χ^2) distribution, and F-distribution. For now, the important thing to remember is that all of

---

22 Actually we usually plot something called the *density*, which is closely related to the probability.

these distributions have something in common: they are all defined by an equation that enables us to calculate precisely the probability of obtaining a given score.

As we have seen, distributions can have different means and standard deviations. This isn't a problem for the probability density function – it will still give us the probability of a given value occurring – but it is a problem for us because probability density functions are difficult enough to spell, let alone use to compute probabilities. Therefore, to avoid a brain meltdown we often use a normal distribution with a mean of 0 and a standard deviation of 1 as a standard. This has the advantage that we can pretend that the probability density  function doesn't exist and use tabulated probabilities (as in the Appendix) instead. The obvious problem is that not all of the data we collect will have a mean of 0 and a standard deviation of 1. For example, for the ice bucket data the mean is 39.68 and the standard deviation is 7.74. However, any data set can be converted into a data set that has a mean of 0 and a standard deviation of 1. First, to centre the data around zero, we take each score (X) and subtract from it the mean of all scores ($\bar{X}$). To ensure the data have a standard deviation of 1, we divide the resulting score by the standard deviation (s), which we recently encountered. The resulting scores are denoted by the letter z and are known as z-scores. In equation form, the conversion that I've just described is:

$$z = \frac{X - \bar{X}}{s} \tag{1.9}$$

The table of probability values that have been calculated for the standard normal distribution is shown in the Appendix. Why is this table important? Well, if we look at our ice bucket data, we can answer the question 'What's the probability that someone posted a video on day 60 or later?' First, we convert 60 into a z-score. We saw that the mean was 39.68 and the standard deviation was 7.74, so our score of 60 expressed as a z-score is 2.63 (Eq. 1.10):

$$z = \frac{60 - 39.68}{7.74} = 2.63 \tag{1.10}$$

We can now use this value, rather than the original value of 60, to compute an answer to our question.

Figure 1.14 shows (an edited version of) the tabulated values of the standard normal distribution from the Appendix of this book. This table gives us a list of values of z, and the density (y) for each value of z, but, most important, it splits the distribution at the value of z and tells us the size of the two areas under the curve that this division creates. For example, when z is 0, we are at the mean or centre of the distribution so it splits the area under the curve exactly in half. Consequently, both areas have a size of 0.5 (or 50%). However, any value of z that is not zero will create different sized areas, and the table tells us the size of the larger and smaller portions. For example, if we look up our z-score of 2.63, we find that the smaller portion (i.e., the area above this value, or the blue area in Figure 1.14) is 0.0043, or only 0.43%. I explained before that these areas relate to probabilities, so in this case we could say that there is only a 0.43% chance that a video was posted 60 days or more after the challenge started. By looking at the larger portion (the area below 2.63) we get 0.9957, or put another way, there's a 99.57% chance that an ice bucket video was posted on YouTube within 60 days of the challenge starting. Note that these two proportions add up to 1 (or 100%), so the total area under the curve is 1.

Another useful thing we can do (you'll find out just how useful in due course) is to work out limits within which a certain percentage of scores fall. With our ice bucket example, we looked at how likely it was that a video was posted between 35 and 40 days after the challenge started; we could ask a similar question such as 'What is the range of days between which the middle 95% of videos were posted?' To answer this question we need to use the table the opposite way around. We know that the

A.1. Table of the standard normal distribution

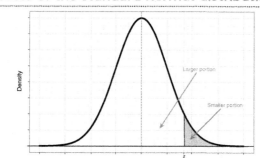

z	Larger Portion	Smaller Portion	y		z	Larger Portion	Smaller Portion	y
.00	.50000	.50000	.3989		.12	.54776	.45224	.3961
.01	.50399	.49601	.3989		.13	.55172	.44828	.3956
.02	.50798	.49202	.3989		.14	.55567	.44433	.3951
.03	.51197	.48803	.3988		.15	.55962	.44038	.3945
.04	.51595	.48405	.3986		.16	.56356	.43644	.3939
1.56	.94062	.05938	.1182		1.86	.96856	.03144	.0707
1.57	.94179	.05821	.1163		1.87	.96926	.03074	.0694
1.58	.94295	.05705	.1145		1.88	.96995	.03005	.0681
1.59	.94408	.05592	.1127		1.89	.97062	.02938	.0669
1.60	.94520	.05480	.1109		1.90	.97128	.02872	.0656
1.61	.94630	.05370	.1092		1.91	.97193	.02807	.0644
1.62	.94738	.05262	.1074		1.92	.97257	.02743	.0632
1.63	.94845	.05155	.1057		1.93	.97320	.02680	.0620
1.64	.94950	.05050	.1040		1.94	.97381	.02619	.0608
1.65	.95053	.04947	.1023		1.95	.97441	.02559	.0596
1.66	.95154	.04846	.1006		1.96	.97500	.02500	.0584
1.67	.95254	.04746	.0989		1.97	.97558	.02442	.0573
1.68	.95352	.04648	.0973		1.98	.97615	.02385	.0562
2.27	.98840	.01160	.0303		2.57	.99492	.00508	.0147
2.28	.98870	.01130	.0297		2.58	.99506	.00494	.0143
2.29	.98899	.01101	.0290		2.59	.99520	.00480	.0139
2.30	.98928	.01072	.0283		2.60	.99534	.00466	.0136
2.31	.98956	.01044	.0277		2.61	.99547	.00453	.0132
2.32	.98983	.01017	.0270		2.62	.99560	.00440	.0129
2.33	.99010	.00990	.0264		2.63	.99573	.00427	.0126

Figure 1.14   Using tabulated values of the standard normal distribution

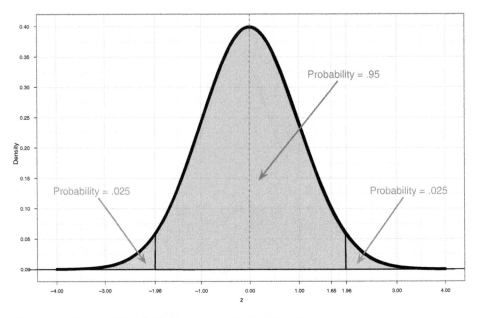

Figure 1.15   The probability density function of a normal distribution

total area under the curve is 1 (or 100%), so to discover the limits within which 95% of scores fall we're asking 'What is the value of z that cuts off 5% of the scores?' It's not quite as simple as that because if we want the *middle* 95%, then we want to cut off scores from both ends. Given the distribution is symmetrical, if we want to cut off 5% of scores overall but we want to take some from both extremes of scores, then the percentage of scores we want to cut from each end will be 5%/2 = 2.5% (or 0.025 as a proportion). If we cut off 2.5% of scores from each end then in total we'll have cut off 5% scores, leaving us with the middle 95% (or 0.95 as a proportion) – see Figure 1.15. To find out what value of z cuts off the top area of 0.025, we look down the column 'smaller portion' until we reach 0.025, we then read off the corresponding value of z. This value is 1.96 (see Figure 1.14) and because the distribution is symmetrical around zero, the value that cuts off the bottom 0.025 will be the same but a minus value (–1.96). Therefore, the middle 95% of z-scores fall between –1.96 and 1.96. If we wanted to know the limits between which the middle 99% of scores would fall, we could do the same: now we would want to cut off 1% of scores, or 0.5% from each end. This equates to a proportion of 0.005. We look up 0.005 in the *smaller portion* part of the table and the nearest value we find is 0.00494, which equates to a z-score of 2.58 (see Figure 1.14). This tells us that 99% of z-scores lie between –2.58 and 2.58. Similarly (have a go), you can show that 99.9% of them lie between –3.29 and 3.29. Remember these values (1.96, 2.58 and 3.29) because they'll crop up time and time again.

SELF TEST

Assuming the same mean and standard deviation for the ice bucket example above, what's the probability that someone posted a video within the first 30 days of the challenge?

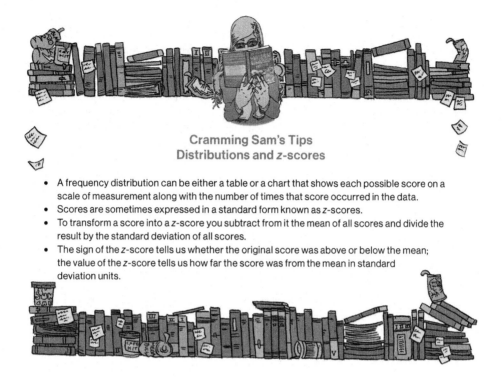

Cramming Sam's Tips
Distributions and z-scores

- A frequency distribution can be either a table or a chart that shows each possible score on a scale of measurement along with the number of times that score occurred in the data.
- Scores are sometimes expressed in a standard form known as z-scores.
- To transform a score into a z-score you subtract from it the mean of all scores and divide the result by the standard deviation of all scores.
- The sign of the z-score tells us whether the original score was above or below the mean; the value of the z-score tells us how far the score was from the mean in standard deviation units.

1.8.7 Fitting statistical models to the data ▌▌▌▌

Having looked at your data (and there is a lot more information on different ways to do this in Chapter 5), the next step of the research process is to fit a statistical model to the data. That is to go where eagles dare, and no one should fly where eagles dare; but to become scientists we have to, so the rest of this book attempts to guide you through the various models that you can fit to the data.

1.9 Reporting data ▌▌▌▌

1.9.1 Dissemination of research ▌▌▌▌

Having established a theory and collected and started to summarize data, you might want to tell other people what you have found. This sharing of information is a fundamental part of being a scientist. As discoverers of knowledge, we have a duty of care to the world to present what we find in a clear and unambiguous way, and with enough information that others can challenge our conclusions. It is good practice, for example, to make your data available to others and to be open with the resources you used. Initiatives such as the Open Science Framework (https://osf.io) make this easy to do. Tempting as it may be to cover up the more unsavoury aspects of our results, science is about truth, openness and willingness to debate your work.

Scientists tell the world about our findings by presenting them at conferences and in articles published in scientific journals. A scientific journal is a collection of articles written by scientists on a vaguely similar topic. A bit like a magazine, but more tedious. These articles can describe new research, review existing research, or might put forward a new theory. Just like you have magazines such as *Modern Drummer*, which is about drumming, or *Vogue*, which is about fashion (or Madonna, I can never remember which), you get journals such as *Journal of Anxiety Disorders*, which publishes articles about anxiety disorders, and *British Medical Journal*, which publishes articles about medicine (not specifically British medicine, I hasten to add). As a scientist, you submit your work to one of these journals and they will consider publishing it. Not everything a scientist writes will be published. Typically, your manuscript will be given to an 'editor' who will be a fairly eminent scientist working in that research area who has agreed, in return for their soul, to make decisions about whether or not to publish articles. This editor will send your manuscript out to review, which means they send it to other experts in your research area and ask those experts to assess the quality of the work. Often (but not always) the reviewer is blind to who wrote the manuscript. The reviewers' role is to provide a constructive and even-handed overview of the strengths and weaknesses of your article and the research contained within it. Once these reviews are complete the editor reads them and then assimilates the comments with his or her own views on the manuscript and decides whether to publish it (in reality, you'll be asked to make revisions at least once before a final acceptance).

The review process is an excellent way to get useful feedback on what you have done, and very often throws up things that you hadn't considered. The flip side is that when people scrutinize your work, they don't always say nice things. Early on in my career I found this process quite difficult: often you have put months of work into the article and it's only natural that you want your peers to receive it well. When you do get negative feedback, and even the most respected scientists do, it can be easy to feel like you're not good enough. At those times, it's worth remembering that if you're not affected by criticism, then you're probably not human; every scientist I know has moments when they doubt themselves.

1.9.2 Knowing how to report data ▌▌▌▌

An important part of publishing your research is how you present and report your data. You will typically do this through a combination of graphs (see Chapter 5) and written descriptions of the data. Throughout this book I will give you guidance about how to present data and write up results. The difficulty is that different disciplines have different conventions. In my area of science (psychology), we typically follow the publication guidelines of the American Psychological Association or APA (American Pyschological Association, 2010), but even within psychology different journals have their own idiosyncratic rules about how to report data. Therefore, my advice will be broadly based on the APA guidelines, with a bit of my own personal opinion thrown in when there isn't a specific APA 'rule'. However, when reporting data for assignments or for publication, it is always advisable to check the specific guidelines of your tutor or the journal.

Despite the fact that some people would have you believe that if you deviate from any of the 'rules' in even the most subtle of ways then you will unleash the four horsemen of the apocalypse onto the world to obliterate humankind, the 'rules' are no substitute for common sense. Although some people treat the APA style guide like a holy sacrament, its job is not to lay down intractable laws, but to offer a guide so that everyone is consistent in what they do. It does not tell you what to do in every situation, but does offer sensible guiding principles that you can extrapolate to most situations you'll encounter.

1.9.3 Some initial guiding principles ▌▌▌▌

When reporting data, your first decision is whether to use text, a graph or a table. You want to be succinct, so you shouldn't present the same values in multiple ways: if you have a graph showing some results then don't also produce a table of the same results: it's a waste of space. The APA gives the following guidelines:

* Choose a mode of presentation that optimizes the understanding of the data.
* If you present three or fewer numbers then try using a sentence.
* If you need to present between 4 and 20 numbers consider a table.
* If you need to present more than 20 numbers then a graph is often more useful than a table.

Of these, I think the first is most important: I can think of countless situations where I would want to use a graph rather than a table to present 4–20 values because a graph will show up the pattern of data most clearly. Similarly, I can imagine some graphs presenting more than 20 numbers being an absolute mess. This takes me back to my point about rules being no substitute for common sense, and the most important thing is to present the data in a way that makes it easy for the reader to digest. We'll look at how to present graphs in Chapter 5 and we'll look at tabulating data in various chapters when we discuss how best to report the results of particular analyses.

A second general issue is how many decimal places to use when reporting numbers. The guiding principle from the APA (which I think is sensible) is that the fewer decimal places the better, which means that you should round as much as possible but bear in mind the precision of the measure you're reporting. This principle again reflects making it easy for the reader to understand the data. Let's look at an example. Sometimes when a person doesn't respond to someone, they will ask 'What's wrong, has the cat got your tongue?' Actually, my cat had a large collection of carefully preserved human tongues that he kept in a box under the stairs. Periodically, he'd get one out, pop it in his mouth and wander around the neighbourhood scaring people with his big tongue. If I measured the difference in length between his actual tongue and his fake human tongue, I might report this difference as 0.0425 metres, 4.25 centimetres, or 42.5 millimetres. This example illustrates three points: (1) I needed a different number of decimal places (4, 2 and 1, respectively) to convey the same information in each case; (2) 4.25 cm is probably easier for someone to digest than 0.0425 m because it uses fewer decimal places; and (3) my cat was odd. The first point demonstrates that it's not the case that you should always use, say, two decimal places; you should use however many you need in a particular situation. The second point implies that if you have a very small measure it's worth considering whether you can use a different scale to make the numbers more palatable.

Finally, every set of guidelines will include advice on how to report specific analyses and statistics. For example, when describing data with a measure of central tendency, the APA suggests you use M (capital M in italics) to represent the mean but is fine with you using the mathematical notation ($\bar{X}$) too. However, you should be consistent: if you use M to represent the mean you should do so throughout your article. There is also a sensible principle that if you report a summary of the data such as the mean, you should also report the appropriate measure of the spread of scores. Then people know not just the central location of the data, but also how spread out they were. Therefore, whenever we report the mean, we typically report the standard deviation also. The standard deviation is usually denoted by SD, but it is also common to simply place it in parentheses as long as you indicate that you're doing so in the text. Here are some examples from this chapter:

✓ Andy has 2 friends on Facebook. On average, a sample of other users (N = 11), had considerably more, M = 95, SD = 56.79.
✓ The average number of days it took someone to post a video of the ice bucket challenge was $\bar{X}$ = 39.68, SD = 7.74.

✓ By reading this chapter we discovered that (*SD* in parentheses), on average, people have 95 (56.79) friends on Facebook and on average it took people 39.68 (7.74) days to post a video of them throwing a bucket of iced water over themselves.

Note that in the first example, I used *N* to denote the size of the sample. This is a common abbreviation: a capital *N* represents the entire sample and a lower-case *n* represents a subsample (e.g., the number of cases within a particular group).

Similarly, when we report medians, there is a specific notation (the APA suggests *Mdn*) and we should report the range or interquartile range as well (the APA does not have an abbreviation for either of these terms, but IQR is commonly used for the interquartile range). Therefore, we could report:

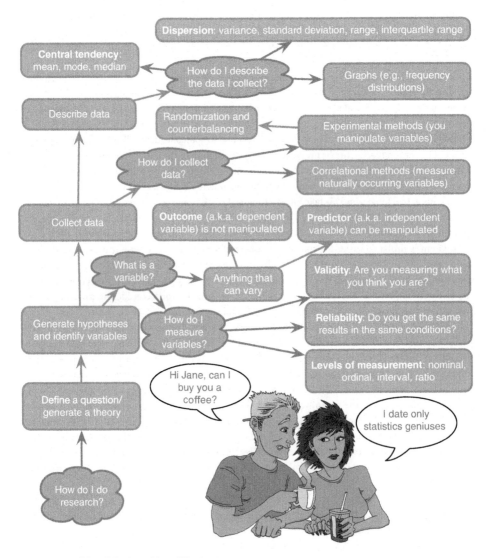

Figure 1.16   What Brian learnt from this chapter

✓ Andy has 2 friends on Facebook. A sample of other users ($N = 11$) typically had more, *Mdn* = 98, *IQR* = 63.

✓ Andy has 2 friends on Facebook. A sample of other users ($N = 11$) typically had more, *Mdn* = 98, *range* = 212.

1.10 Brian's attempt to woo Jane ▌▌▌▌

Brian had a crush on Jane. He'd seen her around campus a lot, always rushing with a big bag and looking sheepish. People called her a weirdo, but her reputation for genius was well earned. She was mysterious, no one had ever spoken to her or knew why she scuttled around the campus with such purpose. Brian found her quirkiness sexy. He probably needed to reflect on that someday.

As she passed him on the library stairs, Brian caught her shoulder. She looked horrified.

'Sup,' he said with a smile.

Jane looked sheepishly at the bag she was carrying.

'Fancy a brew?' Brian asked.

Jane looked Brian up and down. He was handsome, but he looked like he might be an idiot ... and Jane didn't trust people, especially guys. To her surprise, Brian tried to woo her with what he'd learnt in his statistics lecture that morning. Maybe she was wrong about his idiocy, maybe he was a statistics guy ... that would make him more appealing, after all stats guys always told the best jokes.

Jane took his hand and led him to the Statistics section of the library. She pulled out a book called *An Adventure in Statistics* and handed it to him. Brian liked the cover. Jane turned and strolled away enigmatically.

1.11 What next? ▌▌▌▌

It is all very well discovering that if you stick your finger into a fan or get hit around the face with a golf club it hurts, but what if these are isolated incidents? It's better if we can somehow extrapolate from our data and draw more general conclusions. Even better, perhaps we can start to make predictions about the world: if we can predict when a golf club is going to appear out of nowhere then we can better move our faces. The next chapter looks at fitting models to the data and using these models to draw conclusions that go beyond the data we collected.

My early childhood wasn't all full of pain, on the contrary it was filled with a lot of fun: the nightly 'from how far away can I jump into bed' competition (which sometimes involved a bit of pain) and being carried by my brother and dad to bed as they hummed Chopin's *Marche Funèbre* before lowering me between two beds as though being buried in a grave. It was more fun than it sounds.

1.12 Key terms that I've discovered

Between-groups design	Central tendency	Counterbalancing
Between-subjects design	Concurrent validity	Criterion validity
Bimodal	Confounding variable	Cross-sectional research
Binary variable	Content validity	Dependent variable
Boredom effect	Continuous variable	Deviance
Categorical variable	Correlational research	Discrete variable

Ecological validity	Multimodal	Range
Experimental research	Negative skew	Ratio variable
Falsification	Nominal variable	Reliability
Frequency distribution	Nonile	Repeated-measures design
Histogram	Normal distribution	Second quartile
Hypothesis	Ordinal variable	Skew
Independent design	Outcome variable	Standard deviation
Independent variable	Percentile	Sum of squared errors
Interquartile range	Platykurtic	Systematic variation
Interval variable	Positive skew	*Tertium quid*
Journal	Practice effect	Test–retest reliability
Kurtosis	Predictive validity	Theory
Leptokurtic	Predictor variable	Unsystematic variance
Level of measurement	Probability density function (PDF)	Upper quartile
Longitudinal research	Probability distribution	Validity
Lower quartile	Qualitative methods	Variables
Mean	Quantile	Variance
Measurement error	Quantitative methods	Within-subject design
Median	Quartile	z-scores
Mode	Randomization	

Smart Alex's tasks

Smart Alex knows everything there is to know about statistics and IBM SPSS Statistics. She also likes nothing more than to ask people stats questions just so that she can be smug about how much she knows. So, why not really annoy her and get all of the answers right!

- **Task 1**: What are (broadly speaking) the five stages of the research process? ▌▌▌
- **Task 2**: What is the fundamental difference between experimental and correlational research? ▌▌▌
- **Task 3**: What is the level of measurement of the following variables? ▌▌▌

  o   The number of downloads of different bands' songs on iTunes
  o   The names of the bands that were downloaded
  o   Their positions in the download chart
  o   The money earned by the bands from the downloads
  o   The weight of drugs bought by the bands with their royalties
  o   The type of drugs bought by the bands with their royalties
  o   The phone numbers that the bands obtained because of their fame

I'm trying to measure. There's one variable in this example: the personality of the contestant. I could measure this variable by giving them one of the many well-established questionnaires that measure personality characteristics. Let's say that I did this and I found that 75% of contestants did have narcissistic personality disorder. These data support my observation: a lot of reality TV contestants have extreme personalities.

1.5 Generating and testing theories and hypotheses ▮▮▮

The next logical thing to do is to explain these data (Figure 1.2). The first step is to look for relevant theories. A **theory** is an explanation or set of principles that is well substantiated by repeated testing and explains a broad phenomenon. We might begin by looking at theories of narcissistic personality disorder, of which there are currently very few. One theory of personality disorders in general links them to early attachment (put simplistically, the bond formed between a child and their main caregiver). Broadly speaking, a child can form a secure (a good thing) or an insecure (not so good) attachment to their caregiver, and the theory goes that insecure attachment explains later personality disorders (Levy, Johnson, Clouthier, Scala, & Temes, 2015). This is a theory because it is a set of principles (early problems in forming interpersonal bonds) that explains a general broad phenomenon (disorders characterized by dysfunctional interpersonal relations). There is also a critical mass of evidence to support the idea. Theory also tells us that those with narcissistic personality disorder tend to engage in conflict with others despite craving their attention, which perhaps explains their difficulty in forming close bonds.

Given this theory, we might generate a **hypothesis** about our earlier observation (see Jane Superbrain Box 1.1). A hypothesis is a proposed explanation for a fairly narrow phenomenon or set of observations. It is not a guess, but an informed, theory-driven attempt to explain what has been observed. Both theories and hypotheses seek to explain the world, but a theory explains a wide set of phenomena with a small set of well-established principles, whereas a hypothesis typically seeks to explain a narrower phenomenon and is, as yet, untested. Both theories and hypotheses exist in the conceptual domain, and you cannot observe them directly.

To continue the example, having studied the attachment theory of personality disorders, we might decide that this theory implies that people with personality disorders seek out the attention that a TV appearance provides because they lack close interpersonal relationships. From this we can generate a hypothesis: people with narcissistic personality disorder use reality TV to satisfy their craving for attention from others. This is a conceptual statement that explains our original observation (that rates of narcissistic personality disorder are high on reality TV shows).

To test this hypothesis, we need to move from the conceptual domain into the observable domain. That is, we need to operationalize our hypothesis in a way that enables us to collect and analyse data that have a bearing on the hypothesis (Figure 1.2). We do this using predictions. Predictions emerge from a hypothesis (Misconception Mutt 1.1), and transform it from something unobservable into something that is. If our hypothesis is that people with narcissistic personality disorder use reality TV to satisfy their craving for attention from others, then a prediction we could make based on this hypothesis is that people with narcissistic personality disorder are more likely to audition for reality TV than those without. In making this prediction we can move from the conceptual domain into the observable domain, where we can collect evidence.

In this example, our prediction is that people with narcissistic personality disorder are more likely to audition for reality TV than those without. We can measure this prediction by getting a team of clinical psychologists to interview each person at a reality TV audition and diagnose them as having narcissistic personality disorder or not. The population rates of narcissistic personality disorder are

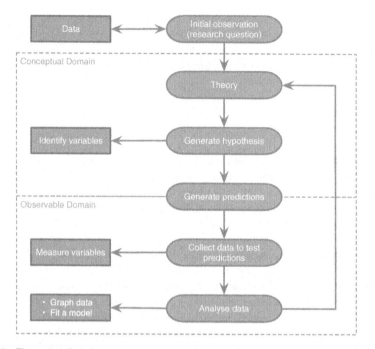

Figure 1.2   The research process

test your predictions you need data. First you collect some relevant data (and to do that you need to identify things that can be measured) and then you analyse those data. The analysis of the data may support your hypothesis, or generate a new one, which, in turn, might lead you to revise the theory. As such, the processes of data collection and analysis and generating theories are intrinsically linked: theories lead to data collection/analysis and data collection/analysis informs theories. This chapter explains this research process in more detail.

1.4 Initial observation: finding something that needs explaining ▌▌▌▌

The first step in Figure 1.2 was to come up with a question that needs an answer. I spend rather more time than I should watching reality TV. Over many years, I used to swear that I wouldn't get hooked on reality TV, and yet year upon year I would find myself glued to the TV screen waiting for the next contestant's meltdown (I am a psychologist, so really this is just research). I used to wonder why there is so much arguing in these shows, and why so many contestants have really unpleasant personalities (my money is on narcissistic personality disorder).[5] A lot of scientific endeavour starts this way: not by watching reality TV, but by observing something in the world and wondering why it happens.

Having made a casual observation about the world (reality TV contestants on the whole have extreme personalities and argue a lot), I need to collect some data to see whether this observation is true (and not a biased observation). To do this, I need to define one or more variables to measure that quantify the thing

---

5 This disorder is characterized by (among other things) a grandiose sense of self-importance, arrogance, lack of empathy for others, envy of others and belief that others envy them, excessive fantasies of brilliance or beauty, the need for excessive admiration, and exploitation of others.

- o   The gender of the people giving the bands their phone numbers
- o   The instruments played by the band members
- o   The time they had spent learning to play their instruments

- **Task 4**: Say I own 857 CDs. My friend has written a computer program that uses a webcam to scan the shelves in my house where I keep my CDs and measure how many I have. His program says that I have 863 CDs. Define measurement error. What is the measurement error in my friend's CD-counting device? ▐▐▐

- **Task 5**: Sketch the shape of a normal distribution, a positively skewed distribution and a negatively skewed distribution. ▐▐▐

- **Task 6**: In 2011 I got married and we went to Disney World in Florida for our honeymoon. We bought some bride and groom Mickey Mouse hats and wore them around the parks. The staff at Disney are really nice and, upon seeing our hats, would say 'Congratulations' to us. We counted how many times people said congratulations over 7 days of the honeymoon: 5, 13, 7, 14, 11, 9, 17. Calculate the mean, median, sum of squares, variance, and standard deviation of these data. ▐▐▐

- **Task 7**: In this chapter we used an example of the time taken for 21 heavy smokers to fall off a treadmill at the fastest setting (18, 16, 18, 24, 23, 22, 22, 23, 26, 29, 32, 34, 34, 36, 36, 43, 42, 49, 46, 46, 57). Calculate the sum of squares, variance and standard deviation of these data. ▐▐▐

- **Task 8**: Sports scientists sometimes talk of a 'red zone', which is a period during which players in a team are more likely to pick up injuries because they are fatigued. When a player hits the red zone it is a good idea to rest them for a game or two. At a prominent London football club that I support, they measured how many consecutive games the 11 first-team players could manage before hitting the red zone: 10, 16, 8, 9, 6, 8, 9, 11, 12, 19, 5. Calculate the mean, standard deviation, median, range and interquartile range. ▐▐▐

- **Task 9**: Celebrities always seem to be getting divorced. The (approximate) lengths of some celebrity marriages in days are: 240 (J-Lo and Cris Judd), 144 (Charlie Sheen and Donna Peele), 143 (Pamela Anderson and Kid Rock), 72 (Kim Kardashian, if you can call her a celebrity), 30 (Drew Barrymore and Jeremy Thomas), 26 (W. Axl Rose and Erin Everly), 2 (Britney Spears and Jason Alexander), 150 (Drew Barrymore again, but this time with Tom Green), 14 (Eddie Murphy and Tracy Edmonds), 150 (Renée Zellweger and Kenny Chesney), 1657 (Jennifer Aniston and Brad Pitt). Compute the mean, median, standard deviation, range and interquartile range for these lengths of celebrity marriages. ▐▐▐

- **Task 10**: Repeat Task 9 but excluding Jennifer Anniston and Brad Pitt's marriage. How does this affect the mean, median, range, interquartile range, and standard deviation? What do the differences in values between Tasks 9 and 10 tell us about the influence of unusual scores on these measures? ▐▐▐

Answers & additional resources are available on the book's website at
https://edge.sagepub.com/field5e